MARK F. FISCHER

PASTORAL COUNCILS
in **Today's**
CATHOLIC PARISH

TWENTY-THIRD PUBLICATIONS
A Division of Bayard MYSTIC, CT 06355

Twenty-Third Publications
A Division of Bayard
185 Willow Street
P.O. Box 180
Mystic, CT 06355
(860) 536-2611
(800) 321-0411
www.twentythirdpublications.com

ISBN:1-58595-168-4
Printed in the U.S.A.

Table of Contents

Acknowledgments

Of the many people who contributed to this book, the first I want to acknowledge are my former colleagues at the Diocese of Oakland. Bishop John S. Cummins introduced me to church consultation through Father Joseph Carroll, SJ, Sister Marcia Frideger, SNJM, and above all, Father George E. Crespin.

In 1995, the Conference for Pastoral Planning and Council Development began to develop a monograph entitled *Parish, Laity and Ministry*, to which my contribution eventually became Chapters One to Two of the present book. Many thanks to CPPCD members Robert J. Burke, Rev. Eugene Costa, Ruth N. Doyle, John P. Flaherty, Jeff Rexhausen, and Rev. Francis Kelly Scheets, OSC, for their criticism and advice. Thanks are due as well to the 98 members of the CPPCD who completed my questionnaire about the numbers of and support for pastoral councils.

Also in 1995 I completed an essay comparing the pastoral council guidelines published by thirteen different dioceses. This became the basis for Chapters Three to Seven, and prompted written reflections from Mary E. Gindhart of Philadelphia, Sr. Joanne Graham, OSB, JCL of Bismarck, and Rev. Kenneth P. Lohrmeyer of Salina. The late Father James H. Provost also commented on this empirical survey and on Chapter Twelve in letters from 1995, 1996, and 1997.

Chapter Eight's history of the earliest parish councils benefited from the correspondence I had in 1996, 1997, and 1998 with Charles A. Fecher of Baltimore, Rev. Robert G. Howes of Worcester, and William J. Rademacher of Las Cruces. James F. Walsh, Jr. helped me to understand Chapter Nine's history of the National Council of Catholic Laity. Rev. John A. Coleman, SJ, who introduced me to Catholic social theory when I was a student at Berkeley's Graduate Theological Union, and Rev. Robert J. Ahlin of Pittsburgh, clarified Chapter Ten's treatment of the Circular Letter on Pastoral Councils by the Congregation for the Clergy. Rev. James

A. Coriden contributed insights to Chapters Nine, Ten, and Twelve.

The growth in pastoral council in the 1970s is linked to the creation of the National Pastoral Planning Conference and the Parish and Diocesan Council Network, described in Chapter Eleven. In 1991 I corresponded with many of the founders of the NPPC and PADICON. Written memories of these years were sent by Father Howes and other early leaders: Gerald Blake, Rev. Msgr. Frank E. Bognanno, Rev. Richard Conboy, Rev. Canice Connors, OFM Conv, Rev. John Dreher, Rev. Charles J. Giglio, Rev. Roger E. McGrath, Mary Ann Pobicki, Rev. Bernard Quinn, Rev. Richard M. Reis, Sr. Judy Shanahan, SP, Cynthia S. Thero, and Joseph Vancio.

The effort to re-write the history of parish councils after the publication of the Code of Canon Law is the topic of Chapter Twelve. Rev. Peter Kim Se-Mang, SJ (whom I knew in the Diocese of Oakland) provided an early impetus, and Rev. Msgr. Helmut Hefner (now Rector of St. John's Seminary, Camarillo) commented on a draft in 1998. Rev. Roch Pagé and Prof. Michel Thériault of the University of St. Paul in Ottawa arranged in 1999 for a version to be published in *Studia Canonica*.

The popular development of the parish "pastoral" council (Chapter Thirteen) coincided with the origin of the Conference for Pastoral Planning and Council Development, many of whose leaders in 1999 offered written comments: Rev. Msgr. William C. Harms, Richard Krivanka, Rev. Msgr. John F. Murphy, Dennis J. O'Leary, Rev. Msgr. James Picton, Marliss A. Rogers, Eileen Tabert, and especially Arthur X. Deegan, II and Sr. Rosalie Murphy, SND.

St. John's Seminary granted me a sabbatical in the fall semester of 2000. I am grateful to Rev. Msgr. Jeremiah J. McCarthy (recently retired as Rector), and to Rev. Richard Benson, CM, the Academic Dean, for their support. I was able to complete Chapters Fourteen through Twenty in the peaceful home of Maria Isabel Rodriguez in Salamanca. Siobhan Marie Verbeek of the National Conference of Catholic Bishops offered valuable criticisms of the way that I have expressed (in Chapter Eighteen) the purpose of councils.

Daniel Connors has edited this book with intelligence and good sense. He has advised me well over the ten years in which I have contributed to *Today's Parish* magazine. I thank my oldest son, Carl, for creating the index, and my other sons, David and Paul, for their help in proofreading. Finally, I dedicate this book to my wife, Bridget Lynch Fischer.

Pastoral Councils in Today's Catholic Parish

Introduction

On March 14, 1992, I visited the University of Dallas to participate in a diocesan-sponsored workshop on parish councils and pastoral planning. At the end of my presentation a man from a rural parish spoke to me. He said it bothered him to hear me speak about "parish" councils. His parish had a better council, a "pastoral" council. He asked whether I knew the difference.

My answer was that a "pastoral" council is a "parish" council doing what it is supposed to be doing—namely, studying pastoral problems, considering them, and proposing practical recommendations. But this answer did not satisfy him. He told me that his "pastoral" council differed from a mere "parish" council. It was more focused on the future, more discerning in style, and more spiritual in orientation than what I had said. It was, in a word, more respectful of its members. He would participate in a pastoral council, he concluded, not in a parish council.

His comments disturbed me. I thought I knew a lot about councils,

1

"pastoral" councils included. But he had spoken to me with the kind of assurance and conviction usually reserved for speaking to the uninformed who ought to know better. I had answered with a textbook answer that was couched in the language of the church's documents. But his question was based on experience. He had had an experience in his local parish, an experience to which my answer did not correspond. Parish experience does not always accord with the church's official teaching. Which is more correct?

This book provides an answer. It examines, first of all, the current state of parish pastoral councils in the U.S., showing the wide variety of practices recommended for councils. Second, it sketches their history, narrating the development of U.S. councils in the thirty-five years since the Second Vatican Council. Finally, it presents a theory of councils. It argues for a particular understanding of representation, purpose, and consultation. It synthesizes empirical experience and church doctrine, distinguishing between the official and popular senses of the word pastoral.

This book takes issue with a number of writers, many of whom have made sweeping generalizations based on insufficient evidence. For example, some advocate a particular style of council without knowing that there are different and competing styles. Others make pronouncements about the church's intentions, pronouncements ignorant of the Vatican II teaching about councils and its evolution in later documents. Still others define the purpose of the council so broadly that it resembles the proverbial jack of all trades, master of none. This book aims to sharpen the focus of discussions about councils. It broadens the base of evidence on which we can judge the council movement.

Theory and Reality

Parish pastoral councils in the United States are one of the great success stories of Vatican II. Thirty-five years after the ecumenical council, they exist in the vast majority of U.S. Catholic parishes. Bishops support them to an extraordinary degree, mandating their existence, publishing guidelines, hiring support personnel, and establishing diocesan pastoral councils. There is an extensive literature about councils. One would imagine that they are among the best-understood features of the American Catholic Church. One would expect the church's teaching about councils to be scientific and consistent.

But a survey of guidelines for councils published by U.S. dioceses suggests that our understanding of councils is haphazard and contradictory. Most councils, for example, meet on a monthly basis. Prudence dictates that they have a clearly expressed goal for the few hours they meet. Such a clear goal is necessary for councils to render good service. In reality, however, diocesan guidelines and the publications of experts show that councils often lack a clear focus. One publication gives them fourteen purposes, seven characteristics, and ten functions. With such a broad scope, it is no wonder that councils often flounder, jerking from topic to topic, wasting their energy on projects of unequal value.

Inconsistent is the word that best describes the teaching about councils in guidelines. Some emphasize that the pastor consults the council, but is not bound by its advice. Others insist that the council makes policy and implements it through the council's own committees. Some make the finance council subordinate to the pastoral council; others make it independent. Some say that the pastor presides at council meetings; others describe him as a member who has a vote, just like the other members. Vatican II recommended that laypeople and pastors examine and solve pastoral problems by the kind of general discussion that takes place in councils. But if no one agrees on how this general discussion should take place, how can it solve problems?

Reviewing various diocesan guidelines shows us what diocesan officials recommend for councils. It illuminates the variety in their purpose, their committees, their understanding of consultation and leadership, and their methods of councillor selection. To be sure, a survey of guidelines does not describe what actual councils *do*. It is hard to generalize about thousands of U.S. councils. Nor does it say what councils ought to do. But by exposing the enormous variety in what officials recommend, the empirical portrait offers us a first step toward a better synthesis of actual practice and church teaching.

The Historical Development of Councils
The most significant development in the relatively brief history of the church's teaching about parish councils was the publication in 1983 of the revised Code of Canon Law. There, in six canons, the church promulgated as law many of the teachings of Vatican II regarding councils. The Code affirmed post-Vatican II recommendations about pastoral councils at the parish level and mandated the existence in every parish of a finance council. For the first time the church legislated about consulta-

tion with faithful Catholics who reflect the entire people of God. The second part of this book examines the history of the council movement and how the new Code affected it.

In light of the Code, a number of authors sought to reinterpret parish councils. They noted discrepancies between what councils actually did and what the new Code said they should do. These authors presented two basic arguments. One was that the Code was homogeneous with Vatican II and simply wrote its intentions into law. The other was that the Code corrected mistakes in the council movement. Among these seeming mistakes was the belief that councils can coordinate parish committees and can treat parish administration. In the light of the new Code, said the authors, coordination and administration do not belong to councils—even though most councils do in fact coordinate and administrate.

Such assertions about the new Code were momentous. The authors were attempting to rewrite, in effect, the history of the council movement.

This rewriting implied that council pioneers had misinterpreted Vatican II and wrongly believed that the Vatican II Decree on the Apostolate of Lay People was the source for parish councils, and not the Decree on the Pastoral Office of Bishops. Pastoral councils should not take upon themselves the task of coordinating parish committees, said the critics, and parish administration belongs not to parish councils but to finance councils. These authors implied that the earliest parish councils were not faithful to the ecumenical council. A new interpretation of Vatican II, an interpretation in the light of the 1983 Code, seemed to turn the assumptions of council pioneers on their heads.

Was this new interpretation correct? Were council pioneers wrong about the intentions of Vatican II regarding councils? If the pioneers had made such an enormous mistake, one would think that someone would have noticed before 1983. The fact that no one did is a telling point. A study of the history of the council movement puts the new interpretation in doubt. To be sure, council advocates have taken a number of missteps. But to say that they all misread the documents of Vatican II, or that early councils were preoccupied with temporal affairs, self-aggrandizing, or unspiritual, is a caricature. The second part of this book suggests that the intentions of Vatican II regarding councils, and the relationship between the ecumenical council and the Code, are topics far more complicated than anyone suspected in the years immediately after 1983. The Code, we will see, did not merely legislate what Vatican II intended regarding councils. It innovated and made selective use of the Vatican II documents.

Proposing a Theory of Councils

Councils are supposed to be representative, purposeful, and consultative. But the meaning of these words is far from clear. Are councils representative in the same way that elected public officials are? What is their main purpose, of the fourteen or more purposes assigned to them? And does consultative mean simply that pastors do not have to take their advice? The third part of this book answers these questions.

Vatican documents state that pastoral councils are to reflect the people of God. Almost every diocesan guideline affirms that they should be representative. But no one can agree about what representation means. Should council membership mirror the demographic profile of the parish, with so many people of this or that ethnic group, age cohort, and level of education? Should council membership be drawn from parish ministerial groups? Experts disagree about these questions. The disagreement stems from a faulty understanding of representation. The third part of this book clarifies the term. To be sure, the popular election of councillors is the most common method of selection, and this book affirms the importance of informed popular participation in the choice of councillors. But it also argues that representation has more to do with practical wisdom than with parish demographics or ministerial membership.

What is the main purpose of councils? If the church could answer this, it could resolve a host of other problems. Pastors could clearly state their expectations. Parishioners could choose potential councillors specifically for their ability to achieve the council's goal. Council leaders could streamline overloaded meeting agendas and avoid distractions. But with an undifferentiated profusion of council purposes, no one can say what councils should do first. This is where Vatican documents prove their efficacy. An analysis of them helps define the main purpose of councils. Although Vatican references to councils in the past thirty-five years are not wholly of one mind—the Code of Canon Law, as we have said, revealing a selective and innovative use of Vatican II documents—nevertheless they indicate a clear priority. The threefold task of investigating, pondering, and concluding (what we in the U.S. call pastoral planning) comes first. It is more important than coordinating parish committees or commissions.

The church is unambiguous, however, about the consultative-only vote of councils. Councils do not legislate, and pastors are not obligated to take their advice. This disqualifies councils, in the eyes of many people, from being worthwhile. In a secular age, they ask, why should Catholics participate in an institution that apparently insists that pastors have a divine right to govern capriciously, as they alone see fit? Why should parishioners advise pastors who are free to disregard their advice? Pastoral councils, they say, belong to an outmoded type of church governance and should be replaced by other types of governance, such as that of the Orthodox patriarchate, boards of elders, or rule by councils.

But these critics are wrong. The term "consultative" has many shades of meaning. The good pastor has a wide repertoire of consultative styles, and consultation cannot be reduced to a pastor's right to refuse the council's advice. Indeed, the church teaches that a pastor is obliged to seek the advice of parishioners in order to serve them better. Intelligent parishioners walk away from dysfunctional pastors. Without a context of faith, consultation is not properly ecclesial. Pastors and councillors form one people of God and desire the same thing, practical wisdom. Consultation does not mean that pastors have a right to ignore parishioners. It means rather that they and their people have the same motive. By seeking the best action for the parish, pastors and councillors strive to preserve the credibility of the gospel.

The Church's Intention

After reflecting on the critique of old-fashioned "parish" councils by the gentleman from Fort Worth, I could only rejoice. His participation in a pastoral council was a worthwhile experience. His pastor asked important questions. The council did serious planning. Discernment marked the style of meetings in which a Christian spirituality was apparent. One can only be happy when parishioners find council work satisfying, whether they call the council "parish" or "pastoral."

The gentleman from Fort Worth was using the word "pastoral" in a distinctly popular sense. For him, the word meant that his council was not occupied with parish administration but rather with visioning and planning. The word referred to a style of procedure. It suggested spiritual concerns. He identified the word pastoral with a good experience at his local parish.

But the gentleman had done more than offer a popular definition. He had also raised a scientific question and implicitly proposed a hypothesis. He suggested, in effect, that the terminology of "pastoral" councils, which began to gain popularity after the 1983 publication of the Code of Canon Law, intended something radically new. He implied that the church's use of the phrase "pastoral council" meant that existing "parish" councils should stop what they were doing and start doing something different. They should start being "pastoral." This book argues that he was wrong. In the church's general sense of the word, councils were already pastoral. The new terminology was not meant to signal a radical change.

How were early parish councils pastoral? To be sure, they did not compare themselves to the "pastoral councils" that Vatican II called for at the diocesan level. They were not pastoral councils in the technical sense. But every parish council deserves to be called "pastoral" when it shares responsibility with the pastor as the head of the parish. Early "parish" councils sought to do that as much as today's "parish pastoral" councils do. In order to prove this point in Chapter Eight, we have to describe the current reality of councils. That is the task of this book's first part, "A Look at Councils Today: An Empirical Portrait."

Part 1

A Look at Councils Today
An Empirical Portrait

W hen I began working with councils in the Diocese of Oakland in 1984, I started to hear about councils that were different from the ones with which I was familiar.

- Some councils, I discovered, make ministerial policy for the parish. But I only knew about pastoral planning councils.
- Some councils coordinate a system of standing committees, of which the finance council is one. This was also new to me.
- Some parishes select councillors by a process of discernment. I was used to elections.

These encounters raised questions about the reality of councils. How many are there? What do councils actually do? What are they supposed to do?

This last question was about the church's intention for councils.

Councils are meant to help the church. Do bishops and pastors want this help? Do they support councils to a measurable extent? My diocese did. It supported them by hiring staff members to assist councils, by creating a diocesan pastoral council, by encouraging pastors to establish councils, and by publishing guidelines for parish councils. I wanted to find out if other dioceses did the same.

In 1990 I moved from the Diocese of Oakland to St. John's Seminary in the Archdiocese of Los Angeles. There I was able to develop a method to answer these questions. The method had two parts. First, I sent out a questionnaire, to which I received replies from 98 dioceses. They told me about the number of councils and the ways in which bishops support them. Second, I made a comparative analysis of guidelines for councils published by dioceses. The guidelines reveal a variety of council types and recommendations for councils. This two-part method, plus a review of published literature, laid the foundation for a portrait of councils.

This empirical portrait stands or falls on the strength of its method. The questionnaire sample was limited, and not every diocese responded to my queries. Moreover, a survey of guidelines does not show what councils actually *do*. It shows rather what the guideline authors *recommend* that councils do. Hence the portrait does not generalize on the basis of actual council practices. Rather, it sketches a variety of actual types. It aims to present the range of council styles recommended by diocesan practitioners.

Councils receive less publicity today than they did in the 1970s. This may lead some to the conclusion that councils are declining in number or that they are less important today than they were a quarter century ago. Some may think that councils express the laity's desire to share responsibility more than they express the pastors' desire to consult. Is this true? The 98 replies to the questionnaire, as we shall see in Chapters One and Two, test the validity of this hypothesis.

Chapters Three to Seven, based on an analysis of diocesan guidelines, show the diversity of council types. The purpose of councils, their use of committees, the meaning of consultation, their leadership, and the selection of members, are all described in different ways. There is no one way of being a pastoral council. Some types of council, however, are more faithful to the church's intentions than others. In order to pass this judgment, we must first see what the types are.

Chapter One

The Number of Councils

Not long ago I received a telephone call from Laurie Nieb, coordinator for stewardship in the Archdiocese of Denver. Laurie is an energetic laywoman who first joined the archdiocesan staff in order to promote parish councils. Like so many Americans in the council ministry, she had begun as a member of her own parish council, and there gained a solid working knowledge of church consultation. In time she found herself assisting councils in neighboring parishes. After she joined the archdiocesan staff Archbishop J. Francis Stafford tapped her to coordinate Denver's stewardship program.

Laurie had received a call from a veteran pastor whom the archbishop had recently assigned to a new parish. The pastor was thinking of revitalizing his parish council and asked Laurie for help. He wanted to know how many parishes still had councils, and what were the latest council resources. Laurie described him as a leader. "This pastor has always fancied himself among the avant-garde," Laurie said. "He likes to be the first with the latest."

I had to smile at Laurie's image of the avant-garde pastor. Although there are many recent publications about parish councils, one no longer thinks of councils as trend-setting, innovative, or revolutionary. Catholic parishes around the world established them after the Second Vatican Council, and today councils are a commonplace of parish life in the United States. Moreover, the fundamental idea behind such councils is ancient. Consulting the community about pastoral matters is as old as the search for wisdom and prudence. The juxtaposition of "parish council" and "avant-garde" seemed a little incongruous.

There was more to my conversation with Laurie, however, than how avant-garde parish councils might be. As I reflected on the question about how many parishes still had councils, I detected an assumption that disturbed me. It was the assumption that, if the number of councils is not large and growing, then something is amiss with councils themselves. Someone could well argue that parish councils were merely an experiment of the Second Vatican Council, an experiment that failed. Could this be true? Judging solely from the number of references to parish and diocesan councils in *Origins*, the documentary periodical of the Catholic News Service, interest in councils peaked in the late 1970s. The number of articles has declined since then. One might be tempted to infer that the number of councils has also declined. Has what seemed like a good idea after Vatican II been played out? Are parish councils, now in decline?

Are Councils in Decline?

In order to answer these questions, I sent a questionnaire in 1994 and 1995 to a number of diocesan officials. These were people, such as Laurie, whom I had met at the annual conventions of the Conference for Pastoral Planning and Council Development. The CPPCD is an organization of people who serve the council and planning ministries, mainly in the U.S. In 1994, there were 174 U.S. dioceses, and officials from 98 of them responded to my questionnaire. Their responses gave me some basic facts about parish councils in the United States.[1] Thanks to them, we can now say how many parish councils there are, where they are, how bishops support them, and whether or not these councils are in decline.

There have been efforts in the past to estimate the number of parish councils. As early as 1970 Charles A. Fecher, writing on behalf of the National Council of Catholic Men, estimated that there were already 10,000 councils in the U.S., or roughly a council in every other parish. By

1976 some were even suggesting that three-fourths of American parishes had such councils.[2] Ten years later a reliable sociological survey confirmed this figure. The Notre Dame Study of Catholic Parish Life, based on a survey of 1,099 parishes, stated that three-fourths of all parishes have a parish council "or its equivalent."[3] If this is true, then the number of parish councils is very large indeed.

When I first read the estimate of the Notre Dame Study, however, I was skeptical. My own experience of councils in California did not confirm its projections. In the Archdiocese of Los Angeles, where I reside and work, pastoral councils exist in less than half the parishes. More to the point, the Notre Dame Study speaks of the parish council "or its equivalent." The study does not explain what the "equivalent" of a parish council might be. I suspected that the study counted many groups as parish councils that did not deserve to be counted as such. I anticipated that the results of my questionnaire would yield a lower number.

Questionnaire Results

My questionnaire invited respondents to state how many pastoral councils there are in their diocese's parishes and missions. The 98 responses enabled me to calculate percentages. I counted the overall number of parishes and missions from the *Official Catholic Directory* published by P.J. Kenedy and Sons.[4] Then I compared this to the number of councils reported by my respondents.

The results surprised me. The sum of reported councils, when divided by the sum of parishes and missions in the respondent dioceses, yields a quotient of 78.62. In other words, almost 79 percent of the parishes and missions in 98 respondent dioceses reportedly have pastoral councils. This was nearly four percentage points higher than the Notre Dame Study reported!

In 1994 there were 18,764 parishes in the United States, according to the Kenedy Directory. In addition, there were 2,866 missions or quasi-parishes. Missions are generally equivalent to a parish, according to canon 516, but, lacking one or more qualifications, they have not yet been formally erected as such. If we multiply the number of parishes and missions by 78.62 percent, we come to a figure of 17,006 councils. Granted, this is not an actual count. It is merely an application of a percentage drawn from a survey of only 98 dioceses. There may not be in fact that many councils. But even if we exclude the missions and apply the figure of 78.62 percent to parishes alone, we come to the figure of 14,752 councils. This is a large number, but a sound one.[5] If the average number of council members is ten, then some 150,000 Americans sit on councils.[6]

Now, with the results of my questionnaire before me, I believe that the Notre Dame Study estimate is indeed reliable. In fact, my questionnaire results suggest that more than three-fourths of all parishes have a parish council. Discussion about councils, judged by the number of articles published about them, may have peaked in the 1970s, but council numbers have continued to grow. The Notre Dame Study provides a conservative benchmark.

Regional Differences

The number does not correspond, however, to the experience of California Catholics. In the Far West, the number of parish councils seems somewhat lower. The results of my questionnaire confirm this. When we separate the 98 dioceses of my survey into the 13 episcopal regions of the National Conference of Catholic Bishops, we note where councils are more and less common (see Table One). Overall, Midwestern dioceses

Table One: Number of Councils by Episcopal Regions

Episcopal Region	States in the Region	Dioceses Reporting	Councils Reported	Parishes and Missions in Reporting Dioceses	% of Parishes and Missions with Councils
1	New England States	6/11	819	1102	74.3
2	New York State	5/8	887	1127	78.7
3	New Jersey, Pennsylvania	8/13	957	1380	69.3
4	DE, DC, FL, GA, MD, SC, NC, VA, WV	12/18	1051	1200	87.6
5	AL, KY, LA, MS, TN	11/18	669	881	75.9
6	Michigan, Ohio	8/13	945	1031	91.7
7	Illinois, Indiana, Wisconsin	8/16	1150	1319	87.2
8	Minnesota, North & South Dakota	4/10	510	542	94.1
9	Kansas, Missouri, Nebraska, Iowa	9/15	1097	1226	89.5
10	Arkansas, Oklahoma, Texas	6/16	372	430	86.5
11	California, Hawaii, Nevada	8/14	520	898	57.9
12	AK, ID, MT, OR, WA	6/11	410	605	67.8
13	AZ, CO, NM, UT, WY, El Paso	7/11	344	636	54.1
Totals		98/174	9731	12377	78.6

(Regions 7, 8, and 9) and dioceses in the Southeast (Region 4) have the highest percentage of parishes and missions with pastoral councils. Western dioceses (Regions 11, 12, and 13) have the lowest percentage. Dioceses whose percentage of parishes and missions with pastoral councils is closest to the national average are in New England (Region 1), New York (Region 2), and the South (Region 5). In general, the Midwest has the highest percentage of parishes and missions with pastoral councils, followed by the East, with the West trailing considerably.

That explains the discrepancy between my personal experience and the questionnaire results. Councils are indeed less prevalent in California. But three-fourths of parishes do have parish councils in the East and in the South, and that is the national average. Close to ninety percent of parishes in the Midwest have councils. One cannot judge the number of parish councils nationwide by looking at a single region.

Does a Decline in Priests Mean a Decline in Councils?
What effect will fewer Catholic priests in the U.S. have on the number of pastoral councils? In order to answer this question, we have to say a few words about the extent of the priest shortage. Most parishes have not yet felt it deeply. Approximately 83% of U.S. parishes still have their own resident pastor. This widespread state of affairs is also the norm according to canon law. But the number of Catholics per priest continues to climb. With fewer priests, will there be fewer councils?

The U.S. bishops recently stated that more than half of U.S. dioceses employ the strategy of having a single pastor care for two or more neighboring parishes. Non-resident pastors administer approximately 15% of all U.S. parishes. In addition, almost one-quarter of U.S. dioceses employ the strategy of entrusting the care of a parish to a deacon or to a lay member of the Christian faithful, such as a religious sister. Deacons or laypersons have oversight for approximately 2% of all U.S. parishes.[7] As the number of priests declines, we can expect that more and more dioceses will use a single priest to pastor more than one parish, and use deacons and laity to care for parishes as well.

It is a defining feature of pastoral councils that pastors preside at their meetings. A parish without a resident pastor can still have a parish pastoral council, if the pastor attends its meetings as presider. But what about those parishes entrusted to the care of a deacon or a member of the lay faithful? In terms of canon law, these "parish coordinators" are not pastors. And if they are not pastors, they cannot preside (in the canonical sense) at meetings of the parish pastoral council. To be sure, one can expect that the supervisor of the parish coordinators, the "priest moderator," will receive the advice of the pastoral council.[8] He can preside in terms of canon law. For this reason we can say that, even in those situations where the parish is entrusted to someone who is not a priest, there may well be a pastoral council. Strictly speaking, it advises the priest moderator. Thus the fact of fewer priests does not necessarily mean fewer parish pastoral councils.

Can parish coordinators, that is, the deacons or laypersons to whom the care of a parish may be entrusted, have a pastoral council? Coordinators certainly can profit from the advantages that a pastoral council offers. Like priests, they too need help in fostering pastoral activity. Like priests, they can benefit from the study, reflection, and recommendations offered by a council. But in terms of canon law, the coordinators' councils are not "pastoral" councils. If we want to preserve this canonical distinction, let us call them committees, advisory groups, or boards—not pastoral councils. These groups do, however, offer parish coordinators the same benefits that pastoral councils offer pastors. They help the coordinators foster pastoral activity by studying, reflecting, and drawing sound conclusions. Without being called pastoral councils, their function is similar to them.

Conclusion: An All-time High

Questions about the number of councils, questions such as those of Laurie Nieb's pastor, can put council advocates on the defensive. Perhaps we fear that, because one does not read much about councils in the religious press, the number is dropping. These fears are unfounded. It is a mistake to conclude from the relatively low profile of councils that councils are in decline. My survey revealed a high number of parish pastoral councils. More than 78 percent of parishes and missions have them. This figure is even higher than the Notre Dame Study's projection of 75 percent. There may well be 15,000 pastoral councils in parishes in the United States, with 150,000 Americans sitting on councils at any one time.

Laurie Nieb's "avant-garde" pastor wanted to know how many parishes still had councils. He may have thought they were dying out. The opposite is true. The number of councils is at an all-time high, and it continues to grow.

Chapter Two

Support by the Bishops

In 1984, the bishops of Canada published a slim pamphlet entitled "The Parish Pastoral Council."[1] In a brief nineteen pages, the pamphlet laid out the nature of the council, its membership, how to select members, and how long they are to serve. It also described the roles of presider and chairperson, council procedures and responsibilities, and the council's authority. The document was remarkable as a sign of encouragement and support for councils by the entire Canadian hierarchy.

The bishops of the United States have never published a document about councils at the parish level. To be sure, they have written at some length about diocesan and national councils, but there is no episcopal document about parish councils alone. This is surprising, given the enormous number of parish councils in the U.S.

Why have the U.S. bishops not published a document akin to the one published by the Canadian bishops? Could it be that the U.S. bishops do not support parish councils to the same degree as their counterparts to the north?

To this question I would give a firm "no." Episcopal support is a major reason for the large number of U.S. councils. My conviction about this springs from personal experience. During the years 1984 to 1990 I

17

worked in the Diocese of Oakland under Bishop John S. Cummins. I recall his own enthusiasm for consultation, and how he encouraged the establishment of councils, first through the senate of priests and later through the diocesan pastoral council. The relatively high number of councils in the Oakland diocese is due in large part to the support of Bishop Cummins, and I suspect that other U.S. bishops support parish councils in a similar fashion.

My questionnaire was designed to test that hypothesis.[2] It provided four ways to measure the support of bishops for pastoral councils. These are (1) the number of diocesan employees engaged in the council ministry, (2) the presence of a diocesan pastoral council, (3) the existence of a diocesan mandate for councils, and (4) the publication of diocesan guidelines (see Table Two, below). My hypothesis was as follows: if a bishop employs council support personnel, convenes a DPC, mandates councils, and publishes guidelines, then it is fair to say that he supports councils. And when the results of the questionnaire were collated, widespread episcopal support was very much in evidence.

Table Two: Episcopal Support for Pastoral Councils

	Number of Dioceses (Out of 98)	Percent of 98 Dioceses
The Number of Bishops who:		
Employ Support Staff for Councils:	64	65.3 percent
Consult an APC or DPC:	61	62.2 percent
Mandate the Existence of Parish Councils	81	82.7 percent
Publish Guidelines for Parish Councils:	88	89.8 percent

Employees

My first measure of a bishop's support for parish councils is the employment of diocesan officials to promote and serve them. I knew that bishops do employ such people—after all, I myself worked in that capacity at the Diocese of Oakland. And during my time in Oakland I met many people throughout the United States who spend at least a part of their time in the council ministry. But when I began my study, I had no idea how many of us there were.

How do diocesan officials support councils? Some, like Philadelphia's Mary Gindhart, prepare councils for participation in pastoral planning.

Mary is the archdiocese's full-time coordinator for pastoral councils. In 1996, Philadelphia Archbishop Anthony Bevilacqua embarked on an ambitious archdiocesan-wide consultation designed to spur greater cooperation among parishes, especially in light of a diminishing number of priests. Mary's task has been to encourage the development of councils, which will then play a role in the consultation.

Others, like Chuck Siebenand of Oakland, respond to requests from councils for education and problem solving. Chuck is diocesan director of strategic planning. His main work is to monitor the implementation of Oakland's strategic plan, the result of six years of diocesan consultation, and to cultivate small Christian communities. But in the course of his work, he has surveyed councils in the diocese. He knows their number, composition, and methods of selecting members. Individual councils call upon him for advice and resource materials. They even invite him to give retreats.

Some officials promote parish councils in conjunction with diocesan pastoral councils. In Omaha, for example, the council of Archbishop Elden F. Curtiss draws members largely from parish councils. Responsibility for the archdiocesan pastoral council belongs to Mary Jo Husten, pastoral council coordinator. Mary Jo helps parish councils prepare for and select delegates to the APC, which in Omaha takes the unusual form of an archdiocesan assembly that meets every two years.

These anecdotes suggest the range of activities by which diocesan officials support parish councils. They also suggest that this support is usually a part-time occupation, one part of planning, consultation, or diocesan pastoral council duties. My questionnaire confirmed this. I found that the chancery staffs in 64 out of 98 respondent dioceses include one or more persons who devote at least a part of their time to the establishment and aid of councils. In these dioceses, one can calculate the percent of time an official spends on pastoral councils. Those bishops who employ support staff for councils dedicate about 38 percent of an official's time to the council ministry.[3] This is a relatively small figure, but it shows that bishops offer councils more than moral support.

Diocesan Pastoral Councils

In Oakland, Bishop Cummins held diocesan conventions in 1985 and 1988 to select a twenty-member diocesan pastoral council (DPC). The creation of a DPC signified his support for parish councils. In 1985, he asked the first council to study the goals of the diocese and recommend how to achieve them. In 1988, he asked the second DPC to consider ways to strengthen the essential features of parish life. The councils served as research and development groups, and Bishop Cummins implemented many of their recommendations.

Establishing a DPC is a common way for bishops to show their support for parish councils. DPCs, which were recommended at Vatican II and in canons 511-514 of the Code of Canon Law, help bishops consider pastoral problems and their solutions at the diocesan level, just as parish councils do at the neighborhood level. The manner in which a bishop consults his diocesan council can provide a model for pastors and parish councils.

How many DPCs are there in the United States? This question is hard to answer, because the number changes from year to year. In 1984, the National Conference of Catholic Bishops published a study of DPCs. It counted 89 DPCs out of (at that time) 170 dioceses, or 52 percent.[4] My own research based on my survey of 98 dioceses, found that that a majority of U.S. bishops have councils.[5] In 1996, the bishops began another study of DPCs. It found that that the number of DPCs had risen slightly.[6]

Mandating Councils

Canon 536 states that bishops, after consulting their councils of priests, may judge it "opportune" to establish pastoral councils in every parish. This judgment then becomes a diocesan mandate. Pastors are obligated, in effect, to establish parish councils. My survey showed that bishops in 81 out of 98 dioceses have "mandated" councils.[7] That represents 82.7 percent of the total. The insistence by bishops that pastors create councils, even against occasional resistance, signifies the bishops' conviction that pastoral councils benefit parishes.

Mandates, however, can create ill will between bishops and pastors. A good example from an earlier period was the 1972 pastoral letter from Bishop Christopher Weldon of Springfield in Massachusetts. His mandate for parish councils was met by the disapproval of some pastors, and their disapproval angered him. In his pastoral letter, he remarked sarcastically that recalcitrant pastors "feel that the work of Christ can only be effectively carried out by the clergy."[8] For Bishop Weldon, mandating councils expressed a desire to involve parishioners more fully in the apostolate of the parish.

A few bishops promote councils but do not require them. They believe that pastors know their people best, and do not mandate councils out of respect for the pastor's freedom to consult as he sees fit. This is true in the Archdiocese of Los Angeles, where Archbishop Roger Mahony has established an office to promote councils, but does not mandate their existence. He has encouraged parishes to "consider" the establishment of a council, but states that it "is still young in the history of our church . . . and its full impact as a consultative body . . . has not yet been fully realized."[9] In Los Angeles, only 47 percent of parishes have councils. Bishops are reluctant to insist upon them when many pastors and people cannot use them properly.

Mandating councils undoubtedly has a regional dimension. Among the seven California dioceses that responded to my questionnaire, only four mandated the establishment of parish councils. But eight dioceses from Illinois, Indiana, and Wisconsin responded, and all eight mandated councils. This helps explain why only 58 percent of California parishes have councils, as compared to 87 percent in the midwestern episcopal region seven. Councils are more prevalent where bishops mandate them.

And most bishops do mandate them. They do so, after consulting with their presbyteral councils, because most priests accept councils as a fixture of parish life. They are the norm in the United States.

Council Guidelines

When I first began working with pastoral councils, Jesuit Father Joseph Carroll—at that time Oakland's director of pastoral research—placed a heavy carton on my desk. The carton was full of diocesan publications about parish councils. There were council guidelines, pastoral letters, synod statements, sample constitutions, outlines for group processes, and plans for council days of retreat. Joe suggested that I read them. He said they would teach me a lot about councils.

For several years, the carton lay on a shelf, relatively untouched. Often I tried to read some of the publications, but usually gave up. The sheer profusion of materials, my unfamiliarity with councils, and the diverse ways in which the publications approached their subject matter—all this overwhelmed me. I did not know where to begin.

Finally in 1990, anticipating my departure from the Oakland chancery, I catalogued the materials. I organized the publications geographically by diocese, grouping diocesan materials according to the thirteen regions of the National Conference of Catholic Bishops. This taught me not only from where the materials came, but indicated in what regions councils are aggressively promoted. Father Carroll had provided me with both materials and a method for studying them.

Since that time, I have been collecting diocesan guidelines for councils. My bibliography now contains more than 100 items, from four to more than 100 pages in length. Some are old, and have gone through numerous revisions. A good example is the 60-page guideline for parish pastoral councils published by the Archdiocese of Newark's Department of Shared Responsibility. Department director Regina Suplick, a Sister of Charity who recently celebrated her golden jubilee, worked on the first guideline in 1976. She saw it through major revisions in 1986 and 1996. Other dioceses have published their first guidelines more recently. The Diocese of Greensburg published its first in 1996 as "New Wine, New Wineskins." This 59-page guideline emerged from a consultation involving over 300 people from 30 parishes, led by Mary Ann Gubish, director of the Office of Parish life and Ministry. New and old, long and short, guidelines show the dioceses' interest in councils.

My survey found that 88 out of 98 dioceses publish guidelines for pastoral councils. The fact that 90 percent of U.S. dioceses have published their own guidelines suggests that bishops want to support a relatively new and imperfectly understood parish structure. Undoubtedly, not all parish councils follow the diocesan guidelines. But guidelines enable a bishop to both encourage councils and to have a say about how they conduct themselves.

Numerous and Supported

The U.S. bishops have never issued a document specifically about the role and importance of parish councils. One might wrongly conclude that they are uncommitted to them. My survey suggests otherwise. Parish councils in the United States are not only numerous, but solidly supported. Bishops in 64 out of 98 dioceses employ officials whose duties in part include the support and assistance of councils. Sixty-one of these bishops have diocesan or archdiocesan pastoral councils, 81 mandate the establishment of parish councils, and 88 publish guidelines.

The diocesan guidelines for parish councils, however, are more than a sign of the bishops' support for councils. They also indicate what diocesan officials believe councils ought to do, and reflect the actual practice of parish councils. Guidelines are the single most important basis for an empirical study of councils. No one without an enormous team of researchers can hope to analyze and interview even a tenth of the 15,000 parish councils in the U.S. This limits our ability to answer the question, "What are parish councils really like?" But diocesan guidelines for councils give us a clue. A comparison of them suggests both the common features and the variety of councils. Thanks to the guidelines, we can state with confidence the purpose of councils—a topic that the next chapter will treat.

Chapter Three

The Purpose
of Councils

The parish council of Father Ken Palacci at Blessed Sacrament
Church in central California coordinates the parish's various volunteer ministries. It is a good example of the "coordinating" type
of council, one of the two most common types in the U.S. Composed of
representatives of the parish's various ministerial commissions—the
worship commission, the education commission, and so forth—the
Blessed Sacrament council ensures their cooperation.

This style of council is a common one. It illustrates one purpose of
councils, namely, the coordination of parish commissions. But this is not
the only style of council. This chapter will show that there is another
main purpose for councils, that of pastoral planning. The two are not
mutually exclusive. But the council that focuses on coordinating may
find that it has little time for planning, and vice versa.

The Coordinating Council
The coordinating style council helped Father Palacci (not his real name)
recently when he faced a serious problem. He had just met with his
finance council and realized that the parish's income would be many

thousands of dollars less than he had estimated. How could Father Palacci reduce budgeted expenses? He did not want to bluntly decree an across-the-board cut of a certain percentage of every expense account. He felt that that would be unfair to those on the parish payroll. Moreover, there were many fixed expenses, such as taxes, insurance, and repayment of a diocesan loan, that he could not reduce. An across-the-board cut, achieved by the pastor's *fiat*, would not do.

He discussed the problem with the finance council chairman, an M.B.A. who had also been elected to chair the pastoral council. Then the two of them presented the matter at the next pastoral council meeting. They told the members about the shortfall in projected income. Then they invited the council to discuss the problem for the next 45 minutes and brainstorm solutions. The pastor and the chairman listened to the discussion, answering questions of fact, but not trying to suggest an answer.

At the end of 45 minutes, the chairman (not Father Palacci) proposed the idea of an across-the-board cut in the percentages of each of the five commission budgets. After some further discussion, the council members agreed that such a cut would be fair. The meeting ended with the members promising to consult the ministerial commissions. And, at the next month's council meeting, the commission representatives reported that their constituencies had accepted the proposed cut. The reduction compensated exactly for the shortage in projected income. Father Palacci was overjoyed.

When he told me the story, I could see why he was so happy. His budget problem was solved in the way he had hoped. And it was solved, not by some Draconian decision made by him alone, but by him at the council's recommendation. He was assisted by a superbly gifted chairperson who was a proven leader. Since each council member had been chosen by a given ministerial commission, and represented the commission, each felt confident about consulting it. After the consultation, each council member could speak for his or her commission, saying that it would accept the proposed cuts. A financial crisis was averted and peace was maintained.

Father Palacci's council provides a good example of the coordinating "council of ministries."[1] Blessed Sacrament Church's extensive program of volunteers, divided into ministerial commissions, invites large numbers of parishioners to participate. Each ministry has a representative who sits on the pastoral council. The council members thus represent the ministerial

groups, and the council serves to coordinate the parish's volunteer program. It enables Father Palacci to involve the ministers in shaping parish
policy through their representatives. The council of ministries shares
responsibility as appropriate with the parish's ministerial commissions.

The Planning Council
The coordinating council of ministries, however, is not the only style of
parish council. A second style is the planning council, which the following fictionalized story illustrates.

In a suburb of Los Angeles, Father Juan Calzo presides over the council of San Ysidro Church. He had established the council when he
became the pastor, and it was the parish's first ever. In its inaugural year,
the council faithfully carried out the work recommended in the Los
Angeles archdiocesan guidelines for councils: the members worked
together on a mission statement and discussed ways to achieve the mission. But Father Calzo was not content.

He was painfully aware that San Ysidro was undergoing a change.
Newer and poorer families were moving in. Many of these were immigrant Asians and Pacific Islanders. The new families had problems that
the older and more established parishioners did not face. Above all, they
faced the problem of Asian youth gangs in their neighborhoods. Father
Calzo wanted to bring the new parishioners to the council's attention.
He wanted to see how the parish could serve them better.

Father Calzo explained his concern about the gangs to the council. He
invited the members to pray and share their reflections about the problem. He then asked the council to help him plan a series of parish meetings to educate parishioners about the gangs.

Together they held three parish assemblies about the youth gang problem. The topics for the three meetings were as follows:

- Youth Gangs: The Experience in Our Neighborhood
- The Roots of the Youth Gang Problem
- What Can We Do About Youth Gangs?

More than 300 parishioners attended the meetings. They learned about
the gang problem, shared their experience, and brainstormed solutions
to it. The parish council facilitated the meetings. The members listened
and kept extensive notes about what they heard.

Over the following two years, the San Ysidro council studied the problem, invited experts to present city and state efforts to halt the spread of gangs, considered a number of parish responses to the problem, and created a plan for establishing a youth group and youth ministry. By focusing on the youth gang project, the councillors grew in knowledge, confidence, and insight. Their creativity and shared wisdom made a profound contribution to the parish. The creation of the parish youth group is already having an impact on the safety of San Ysidro neighborhoods and the well being of the parish's young people. Father Calzo had the satisfaction of seeing the council identify a problem, study it, and develop concrete solutions to it.

Father Calzo's council fits the profile of the pastoral "planning" council.[2] The main work of this kind of council is studying pastoral issues, reflecting on them, and recommending conclusions. Unlike the coordinating council, which monitors and directs the standing committees of the parish, San Ysidro's planning council is an agency of research and design. It analyzes pastoral issues and suggests responses. And unlike the coordinating council, it does not implement its recommendations through a system of standing committees. No, it leaves implementation to the pastor and his staff, who establish committees as they see fit. Lastly, the San Ysidro council, unlike the coordinating council, has little to do with the day-to-day administration of the parish. It studies, reflects, designs, and recommends, without participating in daily operations.

The Two Purposes

Coordinating and planning are not the only tasks assigned to parish councils. Indeed, there are so many opinions about the purpose of councils that a concise statement of purpose may seem unattainable. One handbook states that councils are to promote the good, seek unity, accept responsibility, achieve dialogue, coordinate ministries, utilize parish talent, participate in diocesan life, and witness to Jesus Christ. The list of purposes is so long that council members can despair of accomplishing even a part of it. Yet this impossibly long list is typical.[3] Publications assign councils so many purposes that councils often lack a clear identity.

It is possible, however, to make sense of this diversity and to see that planning and coordinating—the purposes of the Blessed Sacrament and San Ysidro councils—are the most common purposes. How do we know that these two are the most common? The best evidence comes from the guidelines for councils published by various dioceses in the United States. My first study of thirteen such guidelines found that the purposes of the pastoral council can be described in terms of a spectrum. Coordinating councils are at one end of the spectrum, planning at the other, with a mixed purpose of planning and coordinating in the middle.[4]

In 1995, I duplicated my earlier study. I used thirteen other guidelines for councils published by dioceses—one diocese from each of the thirteen episcopal regions of the United States. The guidelines showed a similar difference between coordinating and planning. In them, the task most often assigned to parish councils is pastoral planning.[5] But at the same time, most of these guidelines recommend a specific structure of standing committees, all coordinated by the parish council.[6] The survey shows that planning and coordinating are the tasks most often assigned to councils.

Published guidelines for parish councils give them more to do than just coordinating and planning. Some speak of the spiritual purpose of councils as if it were primary. In these guidelines, spirituality takes two forms. Councils are, first, to develop themselves as Christian communities; and second, to be instruments of discernment, registers of the movement of God's Holy Spirit.[7] Apart from these spiritual purposes, some guidelines describe councils in terms of communication. Councils listen to parishioners, they say, and share with them the council's work.[8] But I would argue that spirituality and communication do not qualify as major purposes of parish pastoral councils. The spiritual purposes of councils are no different from those of every Christian group. And the communicative purposes can as well be served by a standing committee on public relations. Coordinating and planning are the purposes that belong especially to councils.

Two Distinctive Understandings

These two purposes express distinctly different understandings of the parish pastoral council (see Table Three, next page). The coordinating council, for example, understands itself as an agent of participation. The council coordinates the participation of parish volunteer ministers. It makes sure that parishioners exercise their various ministries or apostolates in a concerted manner.

Composed of representatives from the ministries, the council receives

Table Three: The Difference between "Coordinating" and "Planning" Councils		
	The Coordinating Council	The Planning Council
Fundamental Value	Promotes and directs the participation of volunteers.	Does pastoral research and design.
Task	Ensures cooperation among ministries.	Studies problems, recommends solutions.
Administrative Role	Develops policy for the various ministries.	Advises pastor about pastoral matters.
Membership Criterion	Is composed of ministry representatives.	Selects members for their ability to reflect and synthesize.

their reports and discusses the issues they raise. Council members then recommend a particular judgment, policy, or disposition. In this way, the council facilitates the participation of volunteers in ministry.

The planning council, for its part, has a different and more studious goal. It aims at aiding pastoral matters by investigation and reflection. This was what the San Ysidro council did. Such a planning council achieves its goal not by coordinating committees, but by designing and recommending solutions. As a research group, the planning council has a broader scope of study than the coordinating council. Its effect, however, is less tangible and immediate. For that reason, councils of the planning type tends to draw their members not from ministerial groups whom the members are to represent, but rather on the basis of their ability to analyze, deliberate, and reach a common understanding. Study enables these councils to make wise recommendations about pastoral issues.

Parish Clusters: Recommendations to Whom? About What?
Whether the parish pastoral council is of the coordinating or the planning type, it makes its recommendations to a pastor. He is the one who consults the council, asking it to help foster pastoral activity or to undertake pastoral planning. Without a pastor, canonically speaking, there is no pastoral council. But what happens to the purpose of councils as the number of pastors declines? About one thing we can be certain. Pastoral

councils were never intended to take the place of a pastor or govern in his stead. They do not signal rule by the congregation in the absence of a pastor. Fewer priests in the U.S. may mean that a single pastor has to care for two or more neighboring parishes, as we saw in Chapter One. But fewer priests does not mean that the church will embrace a strategy of governance by councils.

The Archdiocese of Dubuque has faced the problem of fewer priests forthrightly. In Dubuque, 68 parishes (more than 31% of the total) are without a resident pastor.[9] In response, Archbishop Jerome Hanus has formed parish "clusters." Clusters are "the grouping of two or more parishes served by one or more priests," we read in *Vision 2000*, the title of the archdiocese's vision and plan. The parishes "retain their separate identities, but collaborate in sharing ministries and resources."[10] The separate identity of each parish includes the parish's pastoral and finance councils. They do not disband when faced with the prospect of clustering. Instead, pastoral councils have a specific task. They become planning agents that share responsibility with the pastor for implementing the clustering plan.

Dubuque's pastoral councils offer the clustering process what has sometimes been called "pre-planning."[11] This is the effort to invite the participation of parishioners in making a transition (e.g., from being a parish with a resident pastor to being a parish without one.) Consultation with the pastoral council takes place before the actual decision to form a cluster. Once Archbishop Hanus and his staff identify a group of parishes that might form a cluster, they share the chosen goals and strategies with the parish councils for "feedback." The word feedback indicates the planning role of the council.

In addition to planning for the cluster, Dubuque councils also help implement the plan. When parishioners lose a resident pastor, for example, they may feel that their parish is no longer important to the archdiocese. *Vision 2000* anticipates that parish pastoral councils can help parishioners deal "with the emotions involved in the clustering process." This is one way in which councils can "assist the pastor in the implementation of the plan."[12] In other words, Dubuque councils facing the prospect of clustering not only help plan, but also share responsibility for implementation.

Once a cluster is formed, each parish pastoral council contributes one or more members to a "cluster council." The task of the cluster council has been defined by Dominican Sister Mary Montgomery, Dubuque's Director of Pastoral Planning. Cluster councils "assist the pastor by consulting on all that pertains to the mission of the parishes and . . . streamline the administration of a multi-parish cluster."[13] The eight responsibilities of Dubuque's cluster councils closely resemble the job descriptions of parish pastoral councils throughout the U.S. They include providing leadership, formulating policies, assessing needs, and implementing the cluster's mission statement.

This raises a technical question: is a "cluster council" (a council made up of representatives of several pastoral councils) a "pastoral" council in the canonical sense? This question is a tricky one. A cluster council certainly meets two of the criteria of the pastoral council. First, the cluster council's pastor presides over council meetings. Second, such cluster councils are governed by archdiocesan norms, and Archbishop Hanus has judged the formation of such councils as "opportune." But a cluster council is not, by definition, a parish pastoral council. Can there be such a thing as a pastoral council for clusters?

My answer is yes. When in 1973 the Vatican first allowed pastoral councils other than the diocesan pastoral council, it stated that they could exist at the "regional" level. The Vatican explained the word "region" with references to "various deaneries or social bodies."[14] This suggests to me that the concept of the "pastoral" council is applicable to a council representing the cluster of neighboring parishes. They constitute a region of the diocese. Although the Archdiocese of Dubuque does not use the adjective "pastoral" to describe its cluster councils, the adjective does fit. The cluster council is a pastoral council insofar as a pastor consults it about pastoral matters according to norms established by his bishop. Dubuque cluster councils appear to do the two kinds of work that parish pastoral councils do throughout the U.S. They *coordinate* the work of the parish cluster and they *plan* by assessing needs and developing policies.

Conclusion: Two Ideal types

These two types of councils, coordinating and planning, represent different understandings of the parish pastoral council. The differences between the two can be explained in terms of their Vatican II origins and of the experience of the U.S. Church. We will examine these more closely in Chapters Eleven and Twelve. For the present, it is enough to say that the coordinating council hearkens back to the Vatican II Decree on the Apostolate of Lay People. There, in no. 26, the decree called for "apostolic" councils that "can take care of the mutual coordinating of the various lay associations and undertakings." The roots of the planning council, on the other hand, lie in the Vatican II Decree on the Pastoral Office of Bishops. Section no. 27 of that decree called for "pastoral" councils to "investigate and consider" matters relating to pastoral activity and to draw conclusions. After Vatican II, these and other official texts were applied by parishes throughout the United States. The result was two types of parish councils, the coordinating and the planning type, each differing in its task and fundamental purpose.

These ideal types, the coordinating and planning councils, are not as clearly distinguished in guidelines as I have distinguished them here. In fact, published guidelines often assign both coordination and planning to one and the same parish pastoral council. Rarely do we find a coordinating council, such as Father Palacci's, that does not also do some planning. Planning councils, such as Father Calzo's, often coordinate committees.

Councils with a mixed purpose, the guidelines suggest, create pastoral plans and coordinate a system of committees. Such guidelines can create problems, as we shall see. They can lead to impossibly high expectations, expectations that no council can meet. In most guidelines (and, I suspect, in most U.S. councils), the tension between the two types is not even acknowledged. Councils are expected to perform both a coordinating and planning role. The tension becomes visible, however, as soon as we ask about the relation between the parish council and the parish's committees. That is the topic of the next chapter.

Chapter Four

Committees and the Council

S ome time ago my parish held the first meeting of a search committee to find a "Director of Music Ministries." I was pleased at the invitation to serve on it, for I was eager to prevent another debacle like the one that occurred with our previous director. He was an amateur musician, chosen without a concerted search process, who demoralized the choir and eventually resigned. After that music director resigned, the pastor was urged to conduct a thorough search. And so he established the new committee.

Even at the first meeting the committee was eagerly debating the shape of the parish music program. Two distinctive positions emerged. Some committee members (including the pastor) advocated a heavy reliance on trained cantors to promote congregational singing. They wanted a scaled-back role for the choir. The choir should be prominent only at major feasts, they argued, because choirs turn congregants into passive listeners, not active participants. Other committee members wanted a bigger role for the choir. I was a choir member and belonged to this faction. We saw the choir as the primary leader of the assembly's song and disliked the heavy amplification used to project the cantor's voice—amplification that drowned us out. The search committee had to find a compromise between these views. Only then could it finalize a job description and begin to interview applicants.

I found the work exhilarating. It was a task on which I could make a well-informed contribution. Our pastor had asked the committee to update the music director job description, advertise the position, interview and audition applicants, and recommend a final roster of applicants for his interview and selection. In the screening of applicants, the pastor urged the committee to consider how the parish music program might develop in the years to come. This gratified me, because I am as strongly committed to good music as I am to good committee work. And since the parish council was working on a five-year-plan for the parish—a plan that included a vision for the parish's liturgy—the pastor urged us to acquaint ourselves with the plan and keep the council abreast of our progress.

The charge given by the pastor to our committee was a representative example of one kind of relationship between councils and committees. First of all, our committee was a consultative one. We had not been asked to hire a music director ourselves, but rather to advise the pastor. He would do the actual hiring. Second, the search committee was to cooperate with the parish council. It was to keep the council abreast of the committee's work and to take into account the council's development of a five-year plan for the parish. The search committee was not, however, a committee "of" the council. Not to the council were we to make our recommendations, but rather to the pastor. And finally, the search committee hoped to complete its work in three months' time. It was not a standing committee, as the parish liturgy committee was. No, it was an ad hoc committee, convened for one purpose only, after which it disbanded. Consultative, cooperating, ad hoc—these were the features of our parish search committee.

These features of the search committee are not, however, the most common features belonging to committees of parish councils throughout the U.S. The most common structure is that of the standing committee or commission. These are officially established parish ministerial groups that the parish council coordinates. In my 1990 study, ten out of thirteen dioceses specified a structure of standing committees.[1]

In other words, most guidelines provide councils with a number of committees, committees so important that they are permanent parish fixtures. When in 1995 I duplicated my study with a different set of guidelines, I found that the average number of standing committees is five.[2] Most dioceses seem to recommend a system of standing committees, and I believe that most councils have them.

The distinction between standing and ad hoc committees is the first important difference in council-committee relationships. There is a tension between the two types that is worth exploring. No one disputes that committees should have an explicit purpose, prepare themselves suitably, and be well facilitated. About that, all of the literature on church committee work agrees.[3] But not everyone agrees that parish councils ought to coordinate a system of standing committees. Some diocesan guidelines for councils do not even mention such a system. Moreover, some of the literature about councils questions whether the coordination of standing committees is the task of the parish council.[4]

But this is a minority opinion. Most guidelines emphasize standing committees rather than ad hoc committees. They thereby suggest that this is the most common kind of council-committee relation.[5]

The Nature of Standing Committees

What are these standing committees? Different ones appear from guideline to guideline. Their names reveal the ministries considered more important than others by diocesan guideline authors. Education, social justice, and liturgy are the most common types of standing committees, and they are recommended in diocesan guidelines more than any other types. The next most common standing committees are spiritual life, administration or stewardship, and evangelization or outreach. Altogether these six ministries are the ones for which standing committees are most often specified. They perform a wide variety of parish tasks: inviting speakers, running programs, planning liturgies, maintaining the parish plant, raising money, doing publicity, and promoting the gospel.[6] Such tasks are considered so important that guidelines establish permanent committees to accomplish them.

Do parish councils with such standing committees spend most of their time on education, social justice, the liturgy, and so on? One cannot answer this question by reading the guidelines. They prescribe a structure, and the application of it varies from parish to parish. But the frequency with which guidelines call for these standing committees implies the guideline-writers' conviction that the ministries named by these committees are fundamental council concerns. The committees do not undertake the ministries on their own, but as standing committees of the parish council. Most guidelines that recommend standing committees require that the parish council consist in part of standing committee members. Representatives of the ministries are chosen for council membership. Council members often "represent" ministries.

It is worth noting, however, that the guideline authors do not all agree that a council should have standing committees. Nor do all agree about which standing committees a council ought to have. Although most councils with standing committees have a standing committee on Christian education, for example, not all have standing committees on social justice, administration, or evangelization. One can conclude that the standing committee structure is embraced by many councils, and perhaps by most. It is the most commonly recommended council structure in the U.S. But the structure varies from diocese to diocese, and probably from parish to parish.[7]

Consultative and Executive Functions

A second important difference between my parish's ad hoc search committee for a music director and the standing committee structure has to do with the task of committees. In my parish's committee, the task was a consultative one. We committee members advised our pastor about the music director, and did not make the decision ourselves. But in eight of the thirteen guidelines examined in 1995, the task of the council's committees is executive, and not merely advisory. The committees implement the work of the council. The Green Bay guidelines make the point explicit: "The function of the *council* is policy *making*," they state; "The function of a *committee* is policy *implementation*."[8]

The committees are described as the "working arms," "working bodies," or "working groups" of the council.[9] In many cases, the pastor's supervision of committee work is completely unspecified. Committees implement policy, but not necessarily under the pastor's direct supervision. When a council coordinates a system of standing committees, the committees often enjoy a certain independence from the pastor.

To be sure, several guidelines back away from a view of committees as independent groups that implement parish council policy.[10] Some say that "parish" committees (not council committees) implement "parish" policies (not council policies). The guidelines imply that the pastor accepts the recommendations of the council, and then asks standing committees to implement the recommendations, presumably under his own direction.[11] But these refinements are either presupposed or neglected in most guidelines. They suggest that councils have an executive role, directing the "working arms" of committees, implementing through them the policies that the council itself makes. The executive role differs from the advisory role of my parish search committee.

Coordination: To Direct or to Facilitate?

The coordination of committees is the third and final difference between ad hoc and standing committees. Ad hoc committees may or may not be committees of the council. If they are not, the council does not coordinate them. They are "parish" committees, not "council" committees. But in most parishes, there are standing committees of the parish council, and the council coordinates them. This is the language of the Vatican II Decree on the Apostolate of the Laity, which in no. 26 called for apostolic councils, councils that may coordinate autonomous lay initiatives. Nine out of thirteen guidelines state that the council "coordinates" its committees.

What does coordination mean? This is not always clear, but in many cases coordination means that committees are directed by the council. Councils make policy, which committees implement. Some guidelines even state that the committees are "accountable" to the council.[12] But softer language is ordinarily used to describe the ways in which councils coordinate their committees. The council coordinates committees, one reads, by "ensuring" that policies are implemented.[13] Sometimes the committees coordinate activities themselves, and sometimes they defer to the council.[14]

When councils are said to "coordinate" committees, most guidelines imply that they facilitate the work of the committees. In this case, the committees are co-responsible. They do not merely carry out the council's directives. But even here the council enjoys a superior status. It facilitates, or directs, or ensures compliance. Although the council may comprise committee representatives, the committees do not run the council. The council coordinates them.

This is markedly different from the experience of my parish's ad hoc committee. Its relation to the council was one of cooperation. Our committee was to inform the parish council of our progress and to keep ourselves abreast of the council's development of a five-year plan. But we were not merely implementers of the council's plans. We were a committee of the parish, not of the council. Some of the diocesan guidelines recognize and affirm this difference. Their standing committees work with councils but are not directed by them. They either state that the council "cooperates with" its committees (rather than coordinating them) or they ignore the relation between councils and committees altogether. Here it is clearly the pastor, not the council, who retains the executive function.[15]

Most guidelines, however, do not make this distinction. We can conclude that many councils do not make it either. Councils usually "coordinate" standing committees by making decisions on their behalf. The committees implement these decisions. This is the most common assumption in the "council of ministries" type, that is, the "coordinating" parish council. Parish councils without a system of standing committees, councils that regard themselves as "planning" bodies (rather than as coordinators of a system of committees), have different assumptions. They assume that the parish council is mainly to advise rather than to foster lay participation, and that committees assist the council but do not execute its policies. Like my own parish's search committee, these councils recommend conclusions but do not carry them out on their own authority. Implementation of the conclusions is the pastor's responsibility.

The Popularity of Standing Committees

It is easy to understand, however, the popularity of the coordinating council of ministerial standing committees. Most guidelines recommend such a committee structure because it has two advantages. First, it enables dioceses to have a say in the topics that councils address. By stipulating the parish council's standing committees—education, social justice, liturgy, and so on—the diocesan officials ensure that these topics receive council attention. Second, a large standing committee structure offers wide opportunities for lay involvement. The more parish committees, the more parishioners can participate. In sum, establishing a committee structure ensures that there will be parish conversation in specific areas, orderly lay participation, and the hoped-for emergence of parish-wide consensus.

Despite the popularity of the standing committee structure, there seem to be genuine reservations about it. A number of dioceses, such as Philadelphia, Sacramento, and Denver, do not recommend a system of standing committees. Some allow committees, as does the Bismarck diocese, but not as the executive arms of a policy-making council. Still others, such as Ogdensburg and Salina, give to council committees a "planning" but not an "implementing" role. This suggests a certain ambivalence toward the typical standing committee structure. The ambivalence has to do with the consultative nature of councils, the topic of the next chapter.

Chapter Five

Five Types of Consultation

O n September 6, 1986, Oakland's diocesan pastoral council gathered for its eleventh meeting. John S. Cummins, the Bishop of
Oakland, was present for it as usual. It was a gathering of some
significance, for the twenty-month-old DPC was scheduled to receive a
proposal from its social justice committee. The committee was one of five
established in 1985 to study the goals of the diocese, and the first to complete a draft report. The draft had been in the hands of the nineteen DPC
members for over a week. In order to understand its significance, a word
about the DPC is necessary.

When we say that pastoral councils have a consultative vote only, we
may think that consultation is a simple matter: pastors consult;
Councillors recommend. But the reality is far more complex. Oakland's
DPC illustrates five distinct meanings or "types" of consultation. This
chapter's examination of the five types will show that ecclesial consultation is anything but simplistic.

Oakland's DPC was chosen by and from 350 delegates at a diocesan-
wide convention that was held over two weekends in late 1984 and early
1985. The convention defined "goals" for the diocese, goals that were
statements of need and concern. The job of the DPC was to study these

goal statements and recommend how to implement them. The social justice committee—the first to complete its report—had a proposal for strengthening the diocese's awareness of and commitment to social justice. The committee wanted to persuade the DPC, and ultimately the bishop, to accept its proposal. The September 6 meeting was a test of the process of consultation on which the diocese had embarked.

It also exemplifies consultation in the church today. The social justice committee had taken twelve meetings to develop its draft report. The starting point was the language of the 1984-85 Oakland diocesan convention:

> The diocese shall establish mechanisms (e.g., social justice committees) on both parish and diocesan levels to prophetically challenge the personal and structural injustices which dehumanize us.

The committee then wrestled with the meaning of the words "injustice" and "challenge," and of parish and diocesan "mechanisms." After a year of work, it had developed some basic convictions. Injustice is not merely the breaking of laws, said the committee, but any violation of people's dignity and community. Christians should challenge injustice by comparing the signs of the times—the just or unjust ways in which people live today—with the vision implicit in the gospels. The committee proposed that the diocese hire people to promote this kind of reflection at the parish level by helping people to compare the signs of the times with the gospel. The committee's idea was a deceptively simple one. It took the form of a mere four-page draft report, but it had not come quickly or easily.

After the ten members of the social justice committee had made their oral presentation to the diocesan pastoral council, the councillors began to discuss it. The DPC was friendly, but had a number of questions. One member said the "prophetic" dimension was missing. He wanted to see the diocesan church take a stand against various social ills. Another said the proposal was too vague. How would gathering people to discuss social justice promote greater fidelity to the gospel? A third wanted to know more about the implementation of the proposal. Who would continue discussions in the parish about social justice after the initial visit of a diocesan official? In general, the DPC members liked the proposal, but had more questions than the social justice committee was prepared to answer at that time.

The Bishop Speaks

Then it was Bishop Cummins's turn to speak. All the council members were deeply interested in what he had to say. The bishop had set the consultative machinery in operation by holding the diocesan convention, by establishing the DPC, and by presiding over the council's creation of a social justice committee. All wanted to know how he would respond to this, the "first fruits" of the consultation. Would he accept it enthusiastically, even uncritically? Or would he dismiss it out of hand, sending the committee back to the drawing board?

As it turned out, the bishop took a middle road. He began with effusive praise for the work of the committee. He was grateful for the generosity of the members, he said, who had given many hours to develop the proposal. And he appreciated their skill in navigating the Scylla of activism and the Charybdis of individualism. The committee might have recommended that the bishop become an activist for various causes, using the authority of his office to promote them throughout the diocese. The committee rightly rejected this approach, said the bishop, because it showed scant regard for the delicacy of his role in character formation and moral development. The bishop wanted to work with his people, he said, not dictate to them. At the same time, the committee avoided the kind of individualism that would have reduced social justice to a merely personal initiative. Justice is not solely a matter of private conscience, the committee said, but a communal discernment. Cummins saw the committee's intention, and approved of it.

He was not, however, without criticism. The bishop reechoed the earlier comment that the report was vague. He wanted some concrete examples of social justice. Indeed, he was not shy about asking the committee to illustrate the meaning of justice with examples taken from the current efforts of the diocesan staff. In addition, he wanted to know what the duties of a new diocesan social justice officer might be. Further, he cautioned against a certain preachiness in the report's tone. "There is no all-knowing 'we,'" he said, "who can educate an ignorant 'they.'" And finally, the bishop cocked a critical eye at the notion of prophetism. The prophetic denunciation of injustice is important, he insisted, but no more than maintaining the communion of Christians, however imperfect that communion may be. In short, Cummins wanted the social justice committee to keep working. He requested a second draft more concrete, less condescending, and more sensitive to pastoral realities.

The bishop's response to the committee illustrates the meaning of consultation. Consultation means more than soliciting the opinions of others. In addition, it implies a dialogue. The committee expressed its opinion, yes, but the bishop also prodded the committee to reconsider what it might have overlooked or taken for granted. He not only wanted to receive the committee's opinions, he wanted to shape them. Moreover, the bishop's response showed how pastors can negotiate, in actual practice, the twists and turns of consultation theory. Various theories about consultation compete today for the attention of council members and pastors. They may even appear mutually incompatible. Good pastoral practice, however, dissolves the apparent contradictions.

The Forms of Consultation
When we compare the way Bishop Cummins consulted his DPC with theoretical models of consultation, two things become apparent. First, his repertoire of consultative styles was large. He "consulted" by spending time with the council, by reflecting aloud and by listening, by asking for further information, by praising and criticizing. And second, his actual practices illuminate theories that otherwise may seem abstract or inadequate. It is one thing to generalize about how consultation ought to happen. It is quite another to illustrate a theory from experience. In the guidelines for pastoral councils published by dioceses throughout the United States, there are five general "models" of consultation, but many of them are vague, inexplicit, or overly general. Let us review them in light of Oakland's DPC.

1. The Legal Approach
Some pastoral council guidelines start with an analysis of canon law and emphasize that councils are only consultative. This truly describes councils, but it says what they are *not* rather than what they *are*. The guidelines published by Sacramento and Denver exemplify this legal approach. They state that the council "advises" the pastor, and they add—in identical language—that the council "is not a policy-making, decree-issuing, statute-formulating body."[1] The pastor consults his council, but is not bound by its recommendations. Unlike deliberative bodies, which can legislate or whose consent is required by an executive, pastoral councils have no ruling power.[2]

The language of Sacramento and Denver is taken from a pastoral letter written by the late Bishop John Keating of Arlington, Virginia. He stated that "the single greatest weakness" of some councils was their conviction that they needed "real power" to dictate parish policy and programs. This statement suggests a context for Bishop Keating's legal approach. Overweening parish councils worried him. When parish councils are power hungry, beleaguered pastors need a defensive weapon. Canon law provides one: the "consultative only" clause. The fact that the Sacramento and Denver guidelines emphasize the limits of council power suggests that this approach is occasionally necessary and may well be used in numerous councils.

But pastors under fire are not the norm. A siege mentality is not the most appropriate for understanding consultation. Guidelines emphasizing that councils "have only a consultative vote" are correct but not always illuminating. They minimize the richness of consultation by focusing on what it is not.

2. The Authoritative Council

Many guidelines soften the consultative-only clause by emphasizing the "authority" or "leadership" of the council. They imply that being *truly* consultative differs from being *merely* consultative. The guidelines for the Hartford archdiocese take this tack. They state that councils "give direction" to parishes. The Bismarck guidelines are similar. Bismarck councils, the guidelines say, have "consultative authority." Fort Worth councils, to give a third example, are said to have a "leadership role."[3] These guidelines do not explain how the council becomes authoritative. But they get at a basic truth: councils may not have the final say, but in many parishes throughout the U.S. they exercise power and influence.[4]

The concept of power sheds light on the meaning of consultation. Whenever parish councils effectively do what canon law says they should do—namely, investigate pastoral matters, give them due consideration, and make solid recommendations—they wield power. But power is linked in the popular imagination with being power hungry. Council guidelines usually do not discuss power, probably for fear of misleading readers. The Hartford, Bismarck, and Fort Worth guidelines do not explain how councils give direction, exercise authority, or provide leadership. But we can assume many councils throughout the U.S. exercise power in those ways.

3. The Consensus Approach

In the 1980s many councils began to emphasize the development of consensus as the goal of consultation. If pastor and council members could reach one mind about an issue, many believed, then the tension would dissolve between the consultor and those consulted. A pastor who seeks consensus would never merely consult his council only to turn and make a decision on his own. To the contrary, he would studiously avoid making decisions until he and the council had reached accord.

In order to promote the search for consensus, many diocesan guidelines recommend deliberate group processes. These are specific techniques and procedures designed to ensure amicable discussions. The guidelines published by the Diocese of Ogdensburg are a good example. They call for prayer as an explicit part of making every council decision. For Ogdensburg councils, making a decision is subordinate to praying, that is, to maintaining the communion that exists among members. Other guidelines endorse specific techniques for reaching group consensus. The Baltimore and Seattle guidelines, for example, reject the parliamentary process of *Robert's Rules of Order*. Instead, they affirm a model of spiritual discernment.[5] In these consensus-seeking councils, consultation does not mean that pastors consult and councillors are consulted. It means that all are engaged in a search for a decision that will express and confirm their unity.

Not everyone, however, rejects *Robert's Rules of Order*. Many follow parliamentary procedure as a tried-and-true method for reaching decisions.[6] But the search for consensus has grown in recent years as an effort to strengthen council unity. However slow, inefficient, or even at times inappropriate, consensus maintains the Christian communion of members. That is what many diocesan guidelines imply. Many councils throughout the U.S. (no one can say how many) seek consensus to ensure that all members will support a decision. Consensus prevents councils from putting task before relationship or from allowing the majority faction to ride roughshod over the minority. It ensures that communion is not subordinated to mission.

4. The Pastor as Ratifier

In order to cement the relation between pastor and council members, some dioceses describe the pastor as a ratifier. They mean that he does more than consult. In addition, he promotes consensus and ratifies the achievement of it. Unlike those versions of consultation that emphasize that the pastor is independent of and unbound by those whom he consults (the legal approach), this version sees the pastor as deeply committed to the council's deliberations. And unlike those versions of consultation that regard the pastor as one member of the group, linked to them in a common search for the truth of a pastoral matter (the consensus approach), this version sees the pastor as an authoritative presider. His job is to detect the arrival of consensus. When he senses its approach, he ratifies it as the official policy of the parish.

The ratification approach gives pastors a preeminently pastoral role. They are the ones to detect consensus or the lack of it. If a council remains divided, and if consensus is not possible, the pastor must acknowledge that he cannot accept the majority's recommendations. The Detroit guidelines, for example, speak of the pastor in these terms. He is the one who, for the sake of consensus, grants or withholds ratification. The Salina guidelines also link ratification and consensus.[7] Without consensus, they imply, no ratification is possible. When these guidelines describe the pastor as a ratifier, they mean that he ought to accept the council's good advice as his own work and that of the local church. It is fair to assume that many pastors see themselves precisely that way in relation to their councils.

Ratification combines the best insights of canon law and consensus. The pastor remains the one to whom the parish is entrusted, just as canon law says, and he has the final say. But his authoritative word is uttered when the council members have reached agreement. They submit their search for agreement to him. He ratifies what the council has unanimously recommended.

5. Consultation as Policy-Making

Where consensus exists, the council and the pastor can be extraordinarily fruitful. They work so well together that we can say that they jointly make parish policy. That is why some council guidelines make consensus a goal and speak as if all councils share that goal. For example, the Green Bay and Nashville guidelines presume that there is a consensus among council members and the pastor. Indeed, both guidelines treat the subject of consensus at some length. Nashville defines it as "intellectual agreement." Green Bay defines it as "group acceptance based on at least general agreement." When such consensus exists, when pastor and councillors take the same view of a matter, one can well say that the council makes policy and plays an executive role.[8]

The guidelines of Nashville and Green Bay, for example, explicitly state that the pastoral council "makes" policy. They assume that, among pastors and council members, a consensus exists. A council can be said to "make policy" when it is of one mind with the pastor. The Nashville guidelines emphasize the unity of pastor and council to such a degree that they speak of pastors "delegating authority" to councillors "with the same trust that the bishop shows" to the pastors.[9] This is an authority that undoubtedly belongs to a number of councils in the U.S. It is the authority that stems from the trust of the pastor who habitually consults.

To be sure, perfect consensus does not always exist. And when consensus falls apart, especially when the pastor does not share in the consensus of the council members, then problems arise. Guidelines that speak of consensus treat it as something that must be constantly tested. Even a consensus that falls apart can be rebuilt. When trust exists, when pastors and council members agree, the council becomes a policy maker, pastor and council acting as one.

The Oakland Example

Consultation can take many forms, as our survey of pastoral council guidelines suggests. At one extreme is the legal approach, which insists that consultation is not the same as deliberation. At the other extreme, consultation means that a council, in union with the pastor, actually makes policy. In the middle are three forms: consultation as leadership by the council being consulted, consultation as the search for consensus, and consultation as the ratification by pastors of the consensus they have recognized. Although a survey of guidelines cannot tell us which forms of consultation are more or less popular, we can assume that each form has its adherents and practitioners in U.S. councils. Taken together, the guidelines suggest the many forms of consultation.

Bishop Cummins consulted Oakland's pastoral council in each of the five ways sketched above. His council eventually accepted a much-revised version of the social justice committee's proposal for a "social justice resource center" in 1987, and recommended it to him. In 1989, the bishop established the center under the aegis of Catholic Charities and hired a director. By asking the director to promote the council's vision of social justice education, the bishop showed his commitment to the DPC recommendations.

Bishop Cummins' repertoire of consultative practices was large, and he tactfully used each in the necessary measure. The one he emphasized least, however, was the legal aspect of consultation. From the start of Oakland's 1984-85 diocesan convention, every participant knew that it was consultative, not deliberative. The same was true for the pastoral council. So at no point did the bishop himself have to say, "Your vote is consultative only—

I am not bound by your advice." He recognized that such a statement, however true, was unnecessary. It would have been a breach of tact.

Those who served on the council readily acknowledged that their service gave them a certain power. Although the bishop was the final decision maker, council members shaped his decisions. They created ideas, collected data, planned the implementation of projects, and evaluated them. By cultivating the council, Bishop Cummins made it an "authority" and a "leader." Many guidelines do not adequately explain how this happens, and guideline descriptions can seem like wishful thinking. The Oakland experience showed that they are not.

At every step in the three-year tenure of the DPC, the bishop sought consensus. He did not always use a specific consensus-building technique, but he made it abundantly clear that council recommendations would not persuade him unless he was confident of the council's unanimity. Consensus was the means by which he tested the soundness of the council's thinking. If any members had serious reservations, so did the bishop. If there was general agreement, the bishop accepted the DPC's recommendations, ratifying them in a formal way.

How can a pastoral council be a decision maker when it possesses only a consultative vote? And how can a pastor "share" responsibility for parish decisions if the council cannot actually "assume" responsibility for those decisions? The apparent contradiction between the "consultative only" council and the "shared decision-making" council is hard to unravel.

In the actual practice of Bishop Cummins, however, the apparent contradiction resolved itself. Without a doubt, he was explicitly "consulting" the council. He fully recognized that he was not bound by the DPC's recommendations. But the bishop had initiated the consultation. He had invested his time and diocesan resources to make it work. He had formed the council so that it could advise him soundly, and had labored to build the members' trust in him. He himself dissolved the apparent contradiction between an unbinding consultation and a genuine sharing of responsibility—a contradiction that we begin to see is no contradiction at all.

Chapter Six

Leadership in the Council

In pastoral councils, the pastor is the primary leader. Canon 536 speaks of him as the presider, because to him the bishop has entrusted the parish. The pastor consults the council and accepts or rejects its advice. He may share responsibility with the council for the parish's mission, and he may invite the council's advice about parish governance. But when he does so, the council serves at his invitation. Indeed, only a pastor may convoke the pastoral council.[1] The council's very identity is dependent on the pastor. In that sense the pastor is the council's primary leader.

The pastor, however, is not the only one who exercises leadership in the council. On this, most pastoral council guidelines agree. Pastoral councils themselves "lead" the parish, say the guidelines. Councils exemplify Christian leadership in general, and parish leadership in particular, by sharing leadership with the pastor. Moreover, particular members take a lead in the council. This is especially true of the lay chairperson who, in many councils, facilitates meetings. Leadership in the council apparently belongs to more than the pastor. But this poses a logical problem. How can both the pastor and the councillors be said to "lead"?

In order to answer this question, we will describe the leadership of parish pastoral councils in empirical terms. They represent a synthesis of what thirteen guidelines for pastoral councils, surveyed in 1995, say about leadership. Guidelines use the word "leadership" to describe the role of the pastor, of the chairperson, and of the council in general. But they do not usually explain how the leadership of pastor, chairperson, and council differ. That is the task of this chapter.

We shall begin by looking at the way guidelines explain the leadership of the pastor. Some guidelines describe this leadership as directing, and others as facilitating. There is a tension between these styles, and we shall try to both explain the tension and to suggest how it might be resolved. Next, our goal is to look at other kinds of council leadership: leadership by the council itself and leadership by council members. Guidelines are vague about these kinds of non-pastor leaders. But experience suggests that the guidelines' vague generalizations are an attempt to describe a complex and distinctly Pauline reality, namely, the diversity of spiritual gifts at the service of Christian unity.

Leadership by the Pastor

Pastors are described as the "presider" over the council in eleven out of thirteen guidelines surveyed.[2] The guidelines typically do not define "presider" or "president," except to say that canon 536 gives the pastor this presiding role (and even the Code of Canon Law does not define it).[3] Instead of explaining what "presider" means, guidelines give the pastor a variety of roles that we normally associate with leadership. And so the curious reader of guidelines who wants to know what it means for the pastor to "preside" at the pastoral council, remains somewhat in the dark.

Presiding over the council, however, is not utterly mysterious. The guidelines suggest that it means both decisive direction setting for the council and support for the council's own initiatives. As an illustration, consider the following cases of Fathers John Sweeney and Thaddeus Colman, fictional pastors of nearby churches.

Father Sweeney and St. Bridget Parish

When Father Sweeney came to St. Bridget's, the parish council could be called "conventional." The council gathered in the same place on a regular basis, the parish hall, and observed the familiar rituals: call to order, opening prayer, reading of the minutes, old business, new business, and so on. This was what the council had always done. After he had been pastor for a

year, Father Sweeney said that he wanted to steer the council into uncharted waters. The parish was changing, he said, and the number of Hispanic
parishioners was growing. He wanted to lay the basis for a renewal of the
parish, and he invited the council to plan it with him.

Father Sweeney proposed a year-long process to reflect on the parish's
changing members. As chairman of the council, he felt that he had a right
to do so. In his direction to the council, he was very explicit. He formed
sub-committees to document the number and neighborhoods of
Hispanic parishioners, to explore how other parishes had become more
hospitable to Hispanics, and to research how to invite more participation
by Hispanics in the liturgy. Not every council member liked Father
Sweeney's proposals, but there was no doubt about what he wanted. Their
task was one of study and reflection.

Fr. Colman and St. Emerich

At St. Emerich Church, Father Colman faced a different situation. As soon
as he became pastor, Father Colman wanted to let the parish council exercise its own initiative. He started with a hospitality survey. Father Colman
wanted to discover how hospitable St. Emerich Church is. Instead of simply asking the council to help him administer a survey that he had
designed, he asked members to collaborate on the survey instrument.
They did, and it was a success. Parishioners gave valuable feedback about
the ushers, and the parish started to serve coffee and donuts after Mass.

From that point on Father Colman gave the council more and more
responsibility. He asked them to develop a policy about renting the parish
hall, and they consulted every parish organization about it. He requested
an assessment of the effectiveness of the Sunday bulletin, and council
members compared it with the bulletins of every other church in the city.
He wanted to survey what other parishes were doing about adult education, and the council developed a column in the bulletin listing adult education events in parishes throughout the diocese. The council rose to
Father Colman's challenges.

Eventually, members no longer waited for Father Colman's direction,
but began to exercise their own initiative. It was the council that first proposed an assessment of the parish youth ministry, that first studied and
suggested a children's liturgy of the word, and that first recommended the
establishment of a food pantry. Father Colman encouraged the council.
He believed that his role was to help the council achieve its goals.

The Guidelines on Presiding

The examples of Fathers Sweeney and Colman illustrate the two main tendencies in pastoral leadership suggested by guidelines for councils. Some guidelines bluntly direct the pastor to take the helm in seeking advice. They state that he sets the agenda, consults, receives proposals, and decides.[4]

This is the kind of leadership that Father Sweeney exercised. He clearly defined tasks for his council: a demographic survey, consulting with other parishes about hospitality, and research on liturgical participation by Hispanics. His clear direction is a leadership style suggested by many guidelines. The Ogdensburg and Philadelphia guidelines even make the pastor the chairman of the council.[5]

In these guidelines, the pastor has a clear and directive role. Other guidelines, however, suggest that the pastor's role is to help the council achieve its task. They say that the pastor "presides" by ratifying the council's decisions, by participating, and by listening. He may chair the meeting or he may not. He may help determine the agenda with the executive committee, but he does not set it by himself.[6]

This is the kind of leadership exercised by Father Colman. When his councillors proposed an assessment of youth ministry, or a children's liturgy, or a food pantry, he participated in their discussions and ratified their proposals. His was the leadership style recommended in many guidelines in which the pastor is less directive than he is supportive.

Diocesan guidelines overall are ambiguous about the strength with which the pastor ought to lead the council in accomplishing its task. Some give the pastor a strongly directive role. Others do not, preferring to cast him as a servant leader, one who serves the council by helping it achieve its own tasks.[7] Council guidelines suggest that all pastors promote the task of councils, but they do so in different ways.

So much for task-centered behavior. What about the pastor's leadership in fostering good relations with the council?[8]

Here the guidelines are less ambiguous. In most guidelines, the pastor is typically the consensus-builder, the spiritual leader, and the creator of trust. He fosters a sense of community in the council by serving, that is, by helping the council achieve its ends in regular meetings.[9]

A pastor reading these descriptions of his role may not be certain how to build consensus or community. But no one is telling him not to try. "Presiding" means behaving as a servant, a trusted friend, and a spiritual leader. In these ways the pastor shows concern for council relationships.

Leadership by Non-Pastors

When we consider leadership in the council we mean more than what the *pastor* does. Many pastoral council guidelines give the council itself a leadership role in the parish. The Ogdensburg guidelines, for example, state that the parish council "provides leadership and direction." The Detroit guidelines speak of the parish council as "the leadership body of the parish," and the Bismarck guidelines make substantially the same point.[10] These guidelines assign a guiding role to councils. It is a role by which the council can be said to guide the parish in a direction that the council itself sets.

Some might suppose that the council leads in only a metaphorical way. They might think that council recommendations bear merely a distant likeness to the decisions of the actual leader. But evidence from the Notre Dame Study of Catholic Parish Life suggests otherwise. In 1986 it emphasized the leadership that councils provide. It spoke of "governance" by the council, described a council whose committees actually "run" the parish, and praised the council's ability to make "hard decisions."[11] The means by which councils lead remain somewhat obscure in the Notre Dame Study. Leading, however, is what many councils apparently do.

Leadership fittingly describes not only the council in general, but also the role of gifted lay individuals in it. Guidelines suggest that the lay chairperson, for example, actually conducts the meetings in many councils. Other leaders, apart from the pastor, may facilitate discussions and contribute to the council's organization and task. As an illustration, consider the situation of St. Monica Church, a fictional suburban parish with a large number of retirees.

St. Monica Church

At St. Monica's, the chairman is John O'Connor, an executive retired after many years with a public utility company. In his profession, John was an acknowledged leader, and the same is true in the parish council. He chairs meetings with a sure hand, moving the items briskly, and making certain that the pastor, Father Jean Duval, is satisfied with the council's discussions. As chairman, John knows how to develop an agenda with the executive committee beforehand and follow the agenda when the council is convened. He is skilled at inviting members to take on various responsibilities pertaining to the council.

One of the council members, Heidi Frieden, is an organizational development consultant. She helps businesses reorganize as they grow or as they respond to product or market changes. When the council faces an especially difficult issue, one that requires an extensive discernment, John O'Connor calls upon Heidi to create and facilitate a group process. This happened recently when Father Duval asked the council's help in deciding a major allocation of parish funds.

The council was divided over the establishment of a new parish ministry. Some council members had, at Father Duval's request, studied youth ministry with the aim of establishing such a ministry at St. Monica. They had done copious research, developed a plan, and had created a job description for the youth minister they hoped the parish would eventually recruit. Other council members were not certain, however, that St. Monica's needed to hire a youth minister. Far more important to the well-being of the parish, in their opinion, was the development of an outreach to retired parishioners. They felt that an eldercare coordinator, not a youth minister, should be the parish's priority. Resentment soon developed between the two factions.

Father Duval was aware of the tension and discussed with John O'Connor how it might be resolved. John invited Heidi Frieden, who was not associated with either faction, into the discussion. She recommended that the council give each side a chance to thoroughly air its point of view. She developed a group process and prayers to encourage a climate of discernment. She even offered to facilitate the meeting.

Father Duval took her advice. After the meeting, the two factions realized that they did not know as much about eldercare as they did about youth ministry. They postponed making any decision until they could more thoroughly study the need for and the costs of a ministry to retired parishioners. John asked the leader of the "eldercare faction" to head an ad hoc committee to study how the parish might accomplish a more effective outreach to the elderly. Father Duval was delighted at the resolution of the meeting. The leadership exercised by Heidi as facilitator, and by John as chairman, had lowered tensions at St. Monica's.

Lay Leadership in the Guidelines

The story of St. Monica's illustrates the roles that diocesan guidelines for pastoral councils assign to lay leaders. Most guidelines speak of such a chairperson and assign to that officer specific leadership tasks. The lay chairperson is usually not the "presider," the technical term that canon 536 reserves to the pastor.[12] But the lay chairperson does exercise many leadership functions that build up relationships in the council and help it accomplish its tasks. Chairpersons are most commonly described as "facilitators." They communicate, organize, coordinate, and help the council evaluate itself. In two guidelines the council chairperson is even directed to appoint the chairpersons of parish standing committees.[13] John O'Connor and Heidi Frieden shared some of these duties at St. Monica's. They were council leaders: they helped the council achieve its task.

What about developing good relations in the council? Every council guideline describes the pastor's role in terms of spiritual leadership, community building, and the development of trust—all of which foster good relationships. Do guidelines describe the lay chairperson's role in the same way? No. Many guidelines say little about the chairperson's role in supporting good relations in the council. Five out of thirteen guidelines do not even mention that the chairperson has relationship-building duties. One might conclude that the pastor fosters good relationships and helps the council achieve its tasks, but the lay chairperson does not. The chairperson assists mainly in achieving the council's tasks, one might think, and has little to do with developing good relationships.

This inference is not supported, however, by the majority of council guidelines that do assign relationship-building roles to the lay chairperson. Those guidelines describe the lay chairperson as one who does show a concern for relationships. The chairperson creates a climate of prayer, motivates council members, develops consensus, and resolves conflict.[14]

We saw these behaviors in the fictional illustration from St. Monica's. John O'Connor and Heidi Frieden developed a group process to enable parish councillors to reflect prayerfully. They motivated the factions to express themselves, to study the eldercare option more fully, and to seek a peaceful resolution. It is unfair to conclude that the lay chairperson assumes no relationship-building roles simply because some guidelines do not mention them.

But relationship-building duties are assigned to the chairperson less frequently than to the pastor. The guidelines give him, not the chairperson, the task of spiritual leadership. The chairperson is more commonly described as the facilitator of the council task than the builder of council relationships.

In Cases of Conflict
Based on these descriptions of leadership we can assume that lay chairpeople often duplicate the work of pastors. Guidelines describe both as facilitators, communicators, agenda-shapers, collaborators, and consensus-

builders. This creates opportunities for conflict. The Denver and Sacramento guidelines hint at such conflict by insisting that the pastoral council is consultative—consultative, that is, as opposed to decision-making. Moreover, the Sacramento guidelines state that pastors are dissatisfied because councils misunderstand their limited authority.[15] When conflict occurs in the pastoral council, according to the Notre Dame Study, "pastors are about twice as likely as staff and volunteers to say that it originates with the parish council and that it pits the pastor against the council."[16] When both pastor and council assume leadership duties, conflict is inevitable.

The guidelines recommend a number of strategies to minimize the conflict. One is to stress consensus decision making and discourage a formal parliamentary procedure. "Conflicts between the pastor and the Parish Pastoral Council will rarely arise," state the Nashville guidelines, "if the pastor actively participates in the process of consensus decision-making."[17] Another response, found in three guidelines, is the institution of formal conciliation or appeal procedures in the case of pastor-council conflict. A third is to emphasize a climate of prayer and the establishment of trust.[18] In short, some guidelines recognize that conflict is inescapable. They attempt to reduce it by means of consensus, conciliation, and prayer.

In general, however, the guidelines assume that the pastor, as the canonical presider of the parish, is the primary leader. Many guidelines do not even mention conflict. They naively assume that, because the pastor is not obligated to accept the council's advice, no one should be offended when he rejects it.

Conclusion: The Pastor and the Lay Leader

In summary, we can say that leadership in the pastoral council belongs primarily to the pastor. It also belongs to the council as a whole, and especially to the lay chairperson. The three exercise leadership to varying degrees. Guidelines focus more attention on leadership *in* the council—the leadership of pastor and chairperson—than they focus on the council's leadership *of* the parish. The council leads the parish, one can say, only to the extent that its advice is accepted and implemented by the pastor. It leads when it and the pastor are of one mind. The chairperson helps the council develop recommendations that persuade the pastor. He or she is even more clearly a leader, the one who enables councillors to agree. The pastor is a leader in the strongest sense. He leads by convoking the council, asking its advice, and drawing conclusions based on that advice.

Ultimately his goal is to employ good advice so that he might lead the parish better.

Leadership by pastors and chairpersons differs in the way each shows concern for the council's task and for council relationships. The guidelines suggest that task leadership by the pastor is ambiguous. Some guidelines have him driving the task forcefully; others have him step back so that the chairperson can drive the task. By contrast, the pastor's leadership in developing relations of prayer and trust among council members is unambiguous. He is to be a "spiritual" leader. On this, the guidelines agree. Pastors may be strong or weak leaders of the task, but their lead in developing relationships must be consistent.

The chairperson, by contrast, is given less to do in the way of developing relationships among council members. Chairpersons, the guidelines suggest, are more task-oriented than they are focused on relations. This raises but begs the question: who is really in charge of helping the council achieve its task? The fact that the same verbs are used to describe what the pastor and the chairperson do—namely, communicate, collaborate, facilitate, shape the agenda, and develop consensus—suggests that there is a considerable overlapping of roles. Although most guidelines discuss these two forms of leadership separately, they do not always clarify where the chairperson's job ends and the pastor's begins. When the line between consultor and the consulted becomes indistinct, problems arise.

Overlapping roles may confuse the question of leadership in the pastoral council. The answer does not lie with theories of management. It lies in the Pauline doctrine of gifts. "There is a diversity of gifts," wrote St. Paul (1 Cor. 12:12), "but one Spirit." We will return to this doctrine of gifts in Chapter Twenty. Our next step is to define the kinds of gifts that pastors seek in councillors.

Chapter Seven

The Selection of Council Members

On November 19-20, 1983, parishioners at St. Joseph Church in Berkeley, California, cast 441 ballots and elected three new members to the parish council. I was one of the new members. A friend had submitted my name to the council's nominations committee, and the chairman had telephoned to ask if I would accept the nomination. When I said yes, he asked me to write a 100-word statement about myself, which was ultimately published in a flyer and distributed with the parish bulletin. At each of the Masses on that weekend, parishioners were asked to vote. Council members collected and counted the ballots. On that basis, we new members were elected to a three-year term.

Our election was typical of parish councils throughout the United States. The basic features—open nominations, a formal decision whether to run, the making of informative statements about oneself, and a secret ballot—are well known from civic life. The goal is to have a representative council, that is, a council that represents the parishioners who voted for its members. In most parishes, that seemed to suffice.

In the late 1970s and 1980s, however, a number of writers began to criticize the normal way of selecting parish council members. They argued that elections might be inadequate for a thorough discernment of council members. Elections stem from a secular model of decision making, the critics said, and may be inappropriate for the church.[1] As the wisdom of their critique was seen, a number of dioceses began to recommend other ways of selecting councillors, ways that promised to incorporate an extended discernment of potential council members. Judging from a survey of guidelines the numbers of these dioceses are still small but significant.

Let us begin by looking at the norm, which remains the election of council members (supplemented by appointed and *ex officio* members). Then we will look at council selection methods incorporating a more thorough discernment. Finally, we shall see what criteria, if any, are applied to potential councillors. Our goal is to describe what is the case in pastoral councils, insofar as we can judge by surveying guidelines. We will presume that, if a large number of guidelines recommend a certain practice, the practice is a common one.

The Norm of Election

Most of the pastoral council guidelines I surveyed in 1990 and 1995 recommend the election of council members. The 1990 survey found that ten out of thirteen guidelines recommend that the majority of councillors be elected either at-large or from parish organizations and standing committees.[2] The 1995 survey found that nine out of thirteen guidelines call for elections as the primary means of choosing councillors.[3]

Three other guidelines studied in 1995 make the election of council members an option. For these three, the alternative to straightforward elections is a process of more thorough discernment, which we shall examine below. Only one guideline, that of the Denver archdiocese, says nothing about elections. It leaves the process for councillor selection entirely in the pastor's hands. So election seems to be the norm in most pastoral council guidelines, and a process of discernment is the exception. The same is true, I daresay, in most U.S. councils.

When I served on my parish council, virtually all lay members were either elected at large or elected to represent a parish committee. The aim, our council constitution said, was to make the council representative of the whole community. Elections were meant to guarantee representation. But councillor selection in my parish, I later discovered, was eccentric in one respect. Our constitution made no provision for the appointment of council members by the pastor.

Appointed Members

Ten out of thirteen guidelines I surveyed in 1995 make provisions for appointed members, as a supplement to elected members. Of these ten, five call for appointment by the pastor of council members to achieve a specific purpose. The purpose, they say, is to make the council representative, diverse, or balanced.[4] Pastors may add to the elected number of parish council members in order to be advised by people who might not otherwise be elected.

The guidelines imply that an elected council may well "represent" the majority of parishioners, as we usually understand the word in American political parlance, but that such representation is not necessarily adequate. They imply further that an elected council, representative of the majority of parishioners, may lack diversity or balance. A still further implication of the appointment provision is that a good pastor wants minority opinions, and that "balance" (understood as the presence in the council of disparate viewpoints) will not be achieved by democratic elections alone. In short, the apparently widespread practice of appointment is a tacit critique of political representation. We shall treat the meanings of "representation" below in conjunction with the criteria for council membership. But for now, this much can be said: guidelines that call for elected councillors, and which also make provision for appointed councillors to achieve "representation," mean by that word something unusual. Pastoral councils, the guidelines suggest, seek a different kind of representation than what we usually find in U.S.-style political elections.

The fact remains, however, that most guidelines call for the election of pastoral council members. They allow for the appointment of some members as a supplement to elections. This is the practice, we can infer, of most pastoral councils in the U.S. Elections are the norm because they guarantee a representative council, but the guarantee is not foolproof, and so some council members are appointed by the pastor.

Ex Officio Members

In addition to the election and appointment of council members, people serve on the pastoral council as a part of their function as parish officers.

When I was on the St. Joseph parish council, the associate pastors and the council's immediate past president (yes, in 1984 we called the lay chairperson the "president") were *ex officio* members. Ten out of thirteen guidelines surveyed in 1995 specify *ex officio* membership. This includes parish clergy apart from the pastor (in eight dioceses), trustees where state law requires them (in four dioceses), and a representative of the finance council (in three dioceses).[5] The goal of having *ex officio* members is to include in the council those who are particularly knowledgeable.

At St. Joseph's parish council, there was no provision for the parish staff to serve as *ex officio* council members. But the constitution did allow for "representatives" of the parish elementary and high school to serve as council members, and the representatives were usually the principals of the schools—in effect, parish staff members. This seems to be common throughout the U.S. Members of the parish staff are required or permitted to be *ex officio* councillors in the guidelines of eight dioceses.[6]

Three guidelines, however, qualify the membership on the council of the parish staff.[7] They state that some staff members serve on the council as merely "a resource" (rather than as a full member) or as a "non-voting" member. This qualification is meant to serve two purposes: first, that the council might include members with an intimate knowledge of the parish's administration, and, second, that these staff members' greater expertise might not dominate council meetings. It would seem that staff members are welcome in most U.S. councils provided that they do not stifle the representative voice of the elected members.

The Process of Discernment
In 1989, I received a phone call from the pastor of Our Lady of Lourdes Church in Oakland, a handsome Irishman with the improbable name of Seamus Genovese. By that time I had had more experience with pastoral councils, having worked with them at the diocesan level. He wanted to start a parish pastoral council, but did not want to elect the members. He had read criticisms of the straightforward election method, and was afraid that the election of councillors might create factions in his parish. He also feared that only the well-known older parishioners might run for election, and that younger parishioners might have no chance.

After our conversation, Father Genovese decided to employ a method recommended by Mary Benet McKinney in her book *Sharing Wisdom*.[8] It allows interested parishioners to discern, over a period of time, those from among their number who are able and ready to serve as councillors. A series of four open meetings on successive Wednesday evenings was announced at Our Lady of Lourdes. The aim of the meetings was to hear from parishioners about their hopes for the parish and to select members for a new parish council. The first two meetings had higher attendance than the last two. Parishioners spoke out about the parish and the ways in which it could grow. Father Genovese explained that he wanted a council that would study how to develop the parish—in particular, how to reach out to young adults who had fallen away from the practice of faith or who were unchurched—and make practical recommendations to strengthen the parish's effectiveness.

Only the most committed parishioners attended the last two meetings. They had a special interest in the subject or desired to serve on the council. At the third meeting Father Genovese (following the recommendations of McKinney) asked for nominations. He invited participants to reflect on what they had heard about the parish's mission and the plan for the council, and to identify those (including themselves) who would be able to serve the parish as councillors. At the last meeting, the nominees spoke about their dreams for the council and about how they hoped to contribute to it. The others affirmed them, noting their gifts and the parish's need for them. Father Genovese led the group in prayer. Finally, there was a ballot, and ten were selected (out of thirteen nominees) for the council.

This kind of discernment is not as common as holding elections. My 1995 survey found that only three out of thirteen guidelines recommended discernment as an alternative or an adjunct to parish-wide elections.[9] For that reason we can suppose that it occurs in less than one in four parish councils. In Fort Worth, where discernment is presented as a necessary adjunct to elections, the guidelines call for either a face-to-face interview between individual nominees and a member of the parish staff, or a group discernment (comparable to the one at Our Lady of Lourdes). These encounters serve to educate nominees about council membership, to help them discover the extent of their gifts and their willingness to serve, and to encourage nominees to decline council membership if others are better qualified. That is the essence of discernment: to unlock the depth of a nominee's ability and desire, based on real knowledge of the nominee and of the council ministry.

After the discernment, guidelines usually recommend a ballot by those who participated in it. The number of people voting is less than those who vote in a traditional parish-wide election, but advocates of discernment say that the smaller number is more knowledgeable. Remarkably, the guidelines of Detroit and Green Bay offer an alternative to elections as the final step in a discernment. Instead of a ballot, they say, final selection of parish council members may be made by drawing lots. They assume that, after a thorough discernment, all of the remaining nominees are qualified. A drawing by lots is a method of leaving the final selection to chance, a method for which advocates claim biblical precedent.

The Criteria for Membership

When I was elected to the parish council at St. Joseph's, no one interviewed me or invited me to discern whether I was suited for council membership. The nominating committee chairman merely telephoned me to ask if I accepted the nomination and asked me to write a statement about myself for the parish bulletin. Nothing more was requested. I occasionally wondered if every nominee was screened in the same way.

We cannot judge from a survey of pastoral council guidelines whether such minimal screening is the norm. But I suspect it is. The grounds for my suspicion are (1) the paucity of stated criteria for pastoral council membership, (2) the vagueness of the criteria, and (3) the wide disparity among them. Guidelines do not say much about the kind of person wanted for council membership. When they do say something, they are often unclear, and they frequently disagree. My hunch is that parishioners do in fact apply criteria in the selection of council members. For the most part, however, the criteria are inexplicitly stated and informally applied.

The one criterion that most guidelines agree on is that council members should be "representative." Twelve out of thirteen guidelines state that council members should represent the parish. But as we saw above, representation can mean many things. In nine cases, the guidelines refer to demographic representation.[10] The composition of the parish council, they say, should mirror the demographic profile of the parish: sex, race, ethnicity, culture, and age. When guidelines speak of representation, that is what they most often mean.

Demographic representation, however, is not the only kind. In some guidelines, representation means something other than the reflection of a demographic profile. The Baltimore guidelines, for example, call for appointment of members to achieve a balance of "knowledge and competence" as well as of sex, race, and age. The Detroit guidelines want the council to reflect not just ethnicity, culture, and race, but also "the concerns and needs of significant groups." The Salina guidelines speak of representation in terms of "attitude" as well as demographic "structure."[11] Appointments and discernment processes seek to achieve a more representative council than straightforward elections allow. But there is no agreement about whether a council represents a demographic profile, the wisdom of the parish, or specific constituencies.

Apart from wanting representation, guidelines show little agreement about the criteria that councillors should meet. Nine guidelines state that council members should have certain moral qualities, dispositions, or talents.[12] The most common moral quality is church membership. Seven guidelines want councillors to be Catholics "in good standing," that is, baptized, confirmed, and registered. Other guidelines speak of certain dispositions. They state that council members should be involved, willing, active, and open-minded. These guidelines indicate the desired moral fiber of council members, but not necessarily their skill or expertise. It is more important for a council member to be morally upright and well intentioned, the guidelines suggest, than to have specific talents.

Some few guidelines do call for skill and expertise in council members. Four guidelines state that council members should be informed, knowledgeable, skillful, experienced, and understanding. These are skills, but only in a general sense, and the guidelines fail to define them in any detail. Two other guidelines speak of "pastoral expertise" or "competence," but are no more precise than that.[13]

Council membership is apparently for generalists. One might expect higher qualifications in councils whose potential members enter into a process of discernment. But even where discernment is recommended, the emphasis is more on the "process" skills of listening, cooperation, creativity, and spirituality than on the "product" skills of technical knowledge or ability. There is no unanimity in the guidelines about the skills that councillors ought to have. Moreover, apart from discernment processes and appointment by the pastor, the guidelines offer no certain way of selecting councillors with the desired skills.

Conclusion: What Kind of Councillors?

Most parish pastoral councils, we conclude, are formed by means of parish-wide elections. But elections are not the sole means of recruitment. *Ex officio* members supplement elected members in most councils, and appointed members complete the council roster. Americans apparently prefer to elect council members, but also allow appointed and *ex officio* members to achieve a representative, balanced, and competent council.

In a minority of dioceses, guidelines recommend methods of selecting councillors that incorporate an extended discernment. This discernment is endorsed as an adjunct to or as a substitute for straightforward elections. The aim of discernment is to inform parishioners about the council ministry and to prompt a thorough reflection about whether a nominee is gifted and called to the ministry. We suppose that this discernment is practiced in less than a quarter of parish pastoral councils.

Most guidelines for councils recommend some criteria for councillor selection, but the criteria differ and are vaguely expressed. The most common criterion is that a potential council member be representative, but the concept of representation remains unclear. Certain moral qualities are recommended, most commonly that councillors be members of the Catholic Church. Apart from these moral criteria, the guidelines say little about other requirements for council membership. We can presume that parishioners seek councillors who are morally upright and skillful (e.g., who are informed, experienced, and understanding), but these parishioners are reluctant to state the criteria precisely or apply them formally.

Why are guidelines so vague about the kind of parishioners sought for the pastoral council? My hunch is that we fear to prescribe specialized criteria for council membership. If we precisely defined the gifts we require in councillors, it might seem that we were requiring specialists. And when council members become specialists, they cease to be representatives. The church states that pastoral council members represent the Christian community, although not in a juridical sense. This will be the theme of Chapter Fifteen. For now, we have to consider a different question. How has the U.S. church emphasized the representative nature of council members? The answer is central to our next part, "Where We Came From: A History of Parish Pastoral Councils."

Part II

Where We Came From: *A History of Parish Pastoral Councils*

T he first part of this book showed a great diversity in types of councils. Some coordinate committees, others develop pastoral plans. Some have a standing committee structure, others do not. In some, the pastor seeks consensus; in others, he does not make a final decision with his councillors present. Some councils emphasize the leadership of the pastor, others the leadership of the laity. Most elect councillors, but some employ a process of discernment. In short, diocesan guidelines suggest that there are many ways of being a pastoral council.

In this section we will see how these differences arose. Chapter Eight describes early councils, with the help of documents from the period 1967-68. It suggests that early councils were anything but myopically secular, power-hungry, and unspiritual. Their story provides more than a narrative. It shows how early councils sought to plant a recommendation of the Second Vatican Council in American soil. The bishops of Vatican II had endorsed councils but provided only the briefest of guides for them. Council pioneers had to establish a Roman recommendation in an American way. The history of U.S. councils is the story of an experiment, a method of trial and error, a journey into uncharted lands.

Inevitably there were missteps. Chapter Nine describes two of them, the efforts to create a national pastoral council (NPC) and a national council of Catholic laity (NCCL). Neither one reached fruition. The national pastoral council wanted to legislate for the U.S. church, an idea out of harmony with episcopal governance. The Vatican's 1973 Circular Letter on Pastoral Councils, analyzed in Chapter Ten, put a stop to it. Advocates of the NPC had to settle for the National Advisory Council to the U.S. bishops, which exists to this day. The other misstep, the national council of catholic laity, wanted to be a House of Commons, separate from the bishops. It recruited its advocates from the National Councils of Catholic Men (NCCM) and of Catholic Women (NCCW). But it gradually lost the support of the NCCW, and the NCCM eventually died. The word "missteps" describes the proposed national pastoral council and the national council of Catholic laity because they wandered into regions inhospitable to a Catholic ecclesial sensibility.

Despite these missteps, councils flourished, and their numbers grew. Hundreds of books and articles about councils appeared. A national organization for council practitioners emerged. A second national organization, focused on pastoral planning, began to appreciate the contribution to planning that councils could make. Many of the same people joined both organizations. Americans developed a considerable body of theory about councils, as we shall see in Chapter Eleven, and had an enormous enthusiasm for them.

The appearance in 1983 of the Code of Canon Law, with its unambiguous statement that councils have only a consultative vote, dampened the enthusiasm. Many council advocates regretted that the new code had expressed the consultative-only vote so bluntly. They felt that it had brought a fruitful period of experimentation to an end. Council critics, however, welcomed the straightforward assertions of canon 536. Chapter Twelve examines their argument, namely, that the new Code was a corrective to parish councils. It used the term "pastoral" to describe a particular kind of council, the kind recommended in the Vatican II Decree on the Office of Bishops. The critics interpreted this text to mean that parish councils may no longer coordinate lay initiatives or treat parish administration. They claimed that the warrant for such activities, hitherto found in the Vatican II Decree on the Apostolate of Lay People, was no longer valid. The new code publicly canonized one kind of council, said the critics, and silently outlawed another. This argument proved unpersuasive, as we shall see in Part III, but many accepted it. They believed that pastoral councils had supplanted parish councils.

While the critics were advancing one (supposedly official) interpretation of the word "pastoral," many council advocates were advancing a different and more popular (but less precise) meaning. They did not define the pastoral council mainly in terms of canon law and other church documents. They defined it rather in terms of their experience. Experience convinced them that the pastoral council, as we will see in Chapter Thirteen, should discern carefully, emphasize spirituality, and, above all, focus on pastoral planning. To be sure, this was not how the church's official documents defined pastoral councils. It was a popular definition, and its advocates often and unfairly contrasted their pastoral council with the reputedly outdated parish council. But at least this definition did not contradict Vatican documents. It has led to the growing conviction that pastoral planning is the best way to describe the church's intention for councils.

Chapter Eight

The Earliest Parish Councils

For years popular writers have contrasted the old-fashioned "parish" councils of the 1960s and 1970s with the more recent "parish pastoral" councils of the 1980s, 1990s, and today. Old fashioned parish councils, it is commonly said, focused exclusively on finance and administration, viewed themselves as superior to the pastor, and lacked spirituality. More recent parish pastoral councils, by contrast, repudiate the older council model. Today's parish pastoral councils, one hears, envision the future, reach decisions by consensus, and focus on the parish's spiritual well-being. The newer pastoral council is precisely what the older parish council was not.[1]

Is this a fair characterization of early parish councils? Or is it an exaggeration designed to highlight the improvements of "parish pastoral" councils at the expense of "parish" councils? In order to answer, let us examine some recent critiques of parish councils. Then we can compare what recent authors have said with the way authors from the late 1960s described parish councils. The early descriptions illuminate the dim view of parish councils taken by later writers without firsthand or accurate knowledge of them.

The Critique of "Parish" Councils

Most criticisms of early parish councils have been made by people who are themselves council advocates. They have had experience of councils, and they do not want to see early mistakes repeated. The most common critique of early councils is that they were preoccupied with finances and building maintenance. A good example of this kind of critique comes from Dennis O'Leary, director of the chancery for the Archdiocese of Seattle. He begins with a memory from boyhood:

> My first recollection of a parish council was my father coming home from helping count the collection after mass on Sunday and announcing that Father had asked the group of counters to be his council.[2]

The recollection is illustrative but secondhand. The experience was not O'Leary's own, but his father's. O'Leary junior uses the anecdote to introduce a twofold complaint. He says, first, that the role of councils in finance, organization, and administration grew because early members, like his father, felt at ease with affairs of the temporal order. His second complaint is related to the first. O'Leary says that "the laity in general still [in the unspecified early years of parish councils] did not see any responsibility for themselves in shaping the pastoral mission of the parish."[3] So early councils, according to this critique, were limited by the horizons of early council members. They were more comfortable with the temporal order than with the pastoral or spiritual. They gravitated to what they knew best.

If the first shortcoming of early parish councils was their limited scope, then the second shortcoming was their ambition to make parish decisions. This was pointed out by Robert R. Newsome, one of the first and most thorough critics of early parish councils. Although he did not document actual cases, Newsome criticized parish councils in general from a structural point of view. He said that, wherever councils envisioned themselves in the role of "a corporate board of directors," with executive authority for parish decisions, they inevitably experienced burnout. The pressures of making daily administrative decisions overwhelmed and exhausted conscientious members. But woe to the pastor who tried to lower his council's expectations. If a pastor did not grant his council executive authority, Newsome said, members felt disillusioned and disappointed. They inevitably found their pastor mean-spirited and dictatorial.

This problematic (either too much responsibility leading to burnout or too little responsibility leading to frustration) was predictable, Newsome said. It "emerged in almost every parish council across the country, virtually without exception."[4] Newsome offered no evidence to support this generalization. But his book was an important salvo of criticism by an advocate of councils who saw them mired in contention.[5]

So it is commonly said that early parish councils (1) focused on money and the parish plant, and (2) burned themselves out when they tried to take from pastors the executive responsibility for the parish. A third critique is that parish councils lacked spirituality. One finds this critique implied, rather than systematically developed, in writings on the spirituality of parish councils. In 1977, Redemptorist Father Earnest Larsen described the enemy of such councils as "do-ism," namely, the preoccupation with fixing superficial problems rather than with the mystery of the church. He was criticizing an absence of spirit.[6] Father Larsen did not aim at a historical or sociological description of early parish councils, but he implied that their insight into the church's spiritual nature was severely limited. A similar critique was made in 1987 by Benedictine Sister Mary Benet McKinney. When she lamented that, "Monthly meetings for many [parish councils] have become battlegrounds," she was not just stating the need for her own more peaceful approach to sharing wisdom. She was implying that the widespread combativeness of councils sprang from their unspiritual deliberations and decision making.[7] Early councils lacked spirituality, these authors said, because they misunderstood the church and its own ways of reaching the truth.

Most critics of early parish councils were friendly to councils. Writers such as O'Leary, Newsome, Larsen, and McKinney are knowledgeable council advocates and want councils to succeed. But they sketched a portrait of early councils that is anything but flattering. Is their portrait of early councils accurate? Published documents about parish councils from the late 1960s can help us answer this question. The documents reveal how contemporaries of the earliest councils understood them. To be sure, these documents from the 1960s did not offer a historical or sociological description. But they tell us two things: first, what the early experts recommended for councils; and second, how they viewed their purpose.

Early Councils in Documents from the Period

The image of early councils presented by popular authors from 1967-68 differs from that presented by their later critics. Early councils were quasi-democratic bodies that aimed at involving people in parish life more than at accomplishing any other single purpose. Influenced by U.S.-style electoral politics, they strove to be "representative" in American terms, usually conducting their affairs by means of parliamentary procedure. Respectful of pastors and marked by a spirituality that saw councils as sharing responsibility with pastors for the church's mission, they did not incorporate any deliberate spiritual practices in their meetings other than opening and closing prayers. Early councils emphasized participation, procedure, and practical matters.

So much, at any rate, can be gathered from five books published in 1967 and 1968 by Robert C. Broderick, Bernard Lyons, David P. O'Neill, the National Council of Catholic Men, and Edward E. Ryan.[8] They were among the earliest writers about councils in the United States. They emphasized the participation of the laity in the church, and each said council meetings should be open to all parishioners. They wanted councils to be representative of the parish and composed mainly of laypeople. They saw the spiritual focus of councils as the church apostolate. Participation, representation, spirituality—let us treat each of these in turn.

Participation
The five early authors believed that greater participation by the laity in the parish was the principal aim of Vatican II's teaching on councils. No longer must American Catholics accept a passive relationship to their parishes and pastors, said these authors, for parishioners now share responsibility for the church. The ideal of adults jointly undertaking the mission of a church in which all are partners was a common theme of parish council writers in 1967 and 1968,[9] and gave parishioners a wide

field of play. Almost every early author affirmed, for example, that the scope of the council included the parish's full pastoral life, and not just "temporal" concerns.[10] Early efforts to limit the scope of the parish council were few and far between.[11]

The virtually unlimited scope of parish councils in 1967-68 can be seen in the vociferous reaction that met those who tried to curtail that scope in any way. An early article by T. Whelan stands out because it recommended a highly restricted role for the parish council. Father Whelan said that a council "must not, at any time, feel free to comment on or advise the Parish Priest on matters which are exclusively pastoral matters."[12] It is unusual in the literature to find the word "pastoral" applied to matters off-limits for parish councils. Father Whelan was criticized, the next year, by Joseph C. Buckley. Father Buckley, referring to the language of the earlier article, rejected the view that councils should be concerned only with temporal matters.[13] He urged that councils develop plans for Christian action and worship, which were precisely matters of "pastoral" concern. His view ultimately proved more persuasive.

The scope of councils, then, was practically unlimited. But because councils could do so much, at least in theory, no one could agree about how they should begin. Robert C. Broderick's book promised that councils would "bring the power of renewal to your parish," and Bernard Lyons saw councils as "renewing the Christian community." Renewal is a praiseworthy goal. But how were councils to achieve it? The five authors from 1967-68 described the task of the council in different terms:

- to "advise the pastor" and "initiate programs";
- to "create, inspire, and demonstrate leadership";
- to foster "cooperation and apostolic work";
- to engage in "dialogue, mutual listening . . . shared responsibility and care";
- to "participate in parish administration."[14]

One might justifiably criticize these early authors for their vagueness. To accuse them all of narrowness or a purely administrative interest, however, is patently unjust.

Many early authors promoted a system of standing committees as a means to foster involvement. In doing so, they believed they were responding explicitly to a phrase in the Vatican II Decree on the Apostolate of Lay People, no. 26. The decree states that apostolic councils on the parish and other levels "can take care of the mutual coordinating of the various lay associations and undertakings, the autonomy and particular nature of each remaining untouched."[15]

Most of our writers from 1967-68 interpreted this phrase as granting to councils a right to coordinate parish committees that would carry out parish council directives.

What committee system did they want? Broderick, Lyons, and Ryan envisioned a system of six or seven standing committees.[16] These committees, they believed, would carry out the work of the council. Less enthusiastic about standing committees, at least in 1968, was the National Council of Catholic Men (NCCM). It preferred ad hoc committees. Such ad hoc committees, with a limited task and timetable, expressed a laudable desire to assume responsibility. The NCCM allowed permanent standing committees, but warned that they might be a temptation to those who were merely interested in permanent titles.[17] The only one of the early authors truly skeptical about standing committees was David O'Neill. He feared, not without reason, a bureaucratic structure that would prove unwieldy.[18] But all of these authors endorsed the ideal of participation, and most regarded committees, at least ad hoc committees, as a way to increase it.

Early parish councils neither emphasized daily administration in an exclusive way nor even gave councils a focused task. The testimony of our authors from 1967-68 makes that much clear. Far from giving the council a narrow focus on finance, building maintenance, or daily administration, the early authors were virtually unwilling to limit the council's scope in any way. They gave to the parish council tasks that were as various as they were vague. This helps explain the lack of unanimity about council committees. If the task of the council was unclear, so too was the task of committees. Both were seen as agencies of involvement and participation, which the early authors believed would renew parishes—but no one knew quite how. For this reason, generalizations about the scope, task, and committee structure of early parish councils should be treated circumspectly.

Democratic Representation

We said earlier that the parish councils of 1967-68 strove to be representative of the parish in American terms and usually conducted their business by means of parliamentary procedure. Most of our five early authors agreed that elected council members should be more numerous than *ex officio* members, and that council meetings should be open to all parishioners.[19] The parish council, David O'Neill said, is not a "cosy group of 'in people.'"[20] Representation was understood in popular terms. The council, these authors believed, should speak for all the people.

Was representation understood in the contentious terms of U.S. politics? Were council members elected as a house of representatives, a "legislative" branch of government, distinct from (and possibly opposed to) the "executive" branch of the pastor? Some later writers have suggested this. But apart from a few telling anecdotes, there is little systematic evidence. To the contrary, there are indicators that early councils were very much concerned about amicable relations and fair play.

Consider, for instance, the use of parliamentary procedure. Later authors criticized the early parish councils for an undue reliance upon such procedure and for an insensitive application of it. But in 1967 and 1968, most authors saw parliamentary procedure as a way to encourage equality in the council, rule by the majority, and teamwork.[21] Not everyone agreed about the process by which councils should conduct their business. But without a clear alternative, parliamentary procedure was the usual practice advocated for councils as a means to ensure fairness.

Another unsettled area was the authority of the council. Some have suggested that authority was a focus of constant tension, but it might be better to speak of ambiguity. Robert Broderick struck the note of ambiguity characteristic of the early years when he stated that "The Parish Council shall be at least advisory, preferably decision-making, in all matters of the parish."[22] Broderick and other early writers preferred the decision-making council to one that merely advised pastors, but they acknowledged that this is only a preference. They saw that, in practical terms, the decision-making authority of the council hinges upon the will of the pastor. Indeed, many authors conceded this by granting pastors a veto over council decisions.[23] There are good reasons to give a council decision-making authority, the early writers said. But the power to grant such authority, they acknowledged, was out of their hands.[24]

To be sure, most of the early authors advocated an appeals process for use when the pastor rejected a council proposal.[25] But this recommendation was not always accepted by pastors.[26] There is little evidence of appeals being made, either successfully or not. It simply was not clear to the popular mind in 1967-68 what authority councils had.

Linked to this ambivalence about the authority of the council was the question of whether the pastor ought to vote. For the advocates of a decision-making council, a voting pastor was problematic. Some feared that a pastor, by casting his vote, would unduly sway lay members. He already possesses the veto, according to this viewpoint, so why does he need to vote? Others feared that a decision not to grant the pastor a vote would improperly set him apart and undermine the democratic nature of a council, where laity and pastors ought to sit as equals. A third (minority) group viewed the council not in legal terms but as a "sharing community." For them the question of a pastor's vote was irrelevant. His task was not to take sides but to promote dialogue.

These three conflicting viewpoints show us that the issue of the enfranchisement of pastors was as difficult as the issue of council authority. Neither matter was settled in the 1960s.[27]

To summarize, the authors from 1967-68 were wholly enthusiastic about "representative" councils elected by the parish at large in a democratic process. But they were undecided in their reception of other "democratic" elements connected with councils. We see this in the less-than-unanimous way in which they treated parliamentary procedure, the decision-making authority of councils, and the pastor's right to vote. There was simply no consensus about these matters in 1967-68. And because consensus was lacking, we cannot accept the view that most councils were adversaries of the pastor and eager to seize power from him. Although all of the five early authors stated that they would prefer a decision-making council to a merely advisory one, nevertheless they recognized that they did not have the power to grant that authority to councils.

Spirituality

Some writers have said that the later parish "pastoral" councils are prayerful, pastoral, and discerning, in contrast to the early "parish" councils, which were not. There is some justification for the criticism. The writers from 1967-68 did not refer to prayer in the council meetings,[28] made no provision for annual council retreats, and did not advocate discernment as a decision-making style. Early authors usually did not see the connection between council leadership and liturgical leadership, and tended to view the council's administrative role in contrast to the pastor's sacerdotal role. Prayer, retreats, and discernment, the spiritual hallmarks of the later "pastoral" council are simply absent in the early literature. But it would be manifestly unjust to conclude from this that early councils were not prayerful, pastoral, or discerning. It does not do justice to the spirituality of early councils. The writers of 1967-68 articulated a spirituality that can be called participative, apostolic, and communal. They suggest that the portrait of early councils as having no spiritual life is a caricature.[29]

Let us see how the distinctive spirituality of early councils expressed itself. Each of our five authors from 1967 and 1968 emphasized that the genius of the parish council lies in the participative role it gives the laity. By means of councils, laypeople play a role in church governance, involving themselves more deeply in pastoral life, and sharing responsibility for the parish.[30] Doubtless, some of the expressions from this period now sound quaint. Broderick spoke of "gaining leverage for the multi-purposes of the message of Christ," and Lyons, in a book from 1971, referred to the council as part of "Christ's Master Plan for World Conquest."[31] Despite these naive formulations, the mission-centered spirituality of early councils is apparent. These early authors believed that parish councils would give people a role in the church's apostolate.

The goal of such participation was the upbuilding of Christian community, and that too is a consistent (if somewhat indefinable) theme in the early authors. "Community" was part of the very title of the books by Lyons and O'Neill. Both authors made a positive and explicit link between community and liturgy. Celebration of the liturgy builds community, they suggested, and community expresses itself in liturgical celebration. O'Neill stated that the pastor presides at council meetings just as he does at the liturgy, and Lyons spoke of the council as a skeleton for his ideal parish, the parish as a "liturgical community."[32] The ideal of community was at the heart of the spirituality of the early parish councils.

Why were apostolate and community the hallmarks of council spirituality in the early literature? The answer lies in the two problems that the early authors believed councils would solve: apathy and alienation. Early authors regarded the Catholic laity as generally apathetic. Habits of docile submissiveness had for so long been inculcated, they said, that the laity had atrophied.[33] Councils, according to the early literature, would reinvigorate the laity by giving them voice and vote in parish governance.

Furthermore, councils would also solve the problem of lay Catholic alienation from their pastors. This alienation was described as lay "estrangement" from priests who had become busy, distant, and coolly professional administrators. Even O'Neill, himself a priest, could speak of the veto in the parish council as "a sop to the vanity of pastors" who wrongly believe that they have ultimate authority in their parishes.[34] These early authors were convinced that parish councils, by involving parishioners, would overcome the people's alienation from pastors. Councils would free pastors to serve their people better.[35] To be sure, much of the new lay involvement was in the temporal order. This has given rise to the caricature of early councils as focused myopically on finance and maintenance. But that was only a part of what councils did, and they did it in cooperation with pastors. Instead of fostering pastor-parishioner tension, literature from 1967-68 suggested that councils would make the two allies.

In summary, the early councils had a distinctive spirituality. They were implicitly prayerful, in the sense that their deliberations were marked by concern for the church's apostolate and the well being of the parish as a community of prayer. Furthermore, one could argue that parish councils in the 1960s had a thorough "pastoral" orientation that embraced more than the temporal order and included every dimension of the parish. And the early councils could be called "discerning" in that their goal was to study the signs of the times. The attention the authors of 1967-68 paid to overcoming lay apathy and alienation from pastors surely suggests an attempt to discern problems and create solutions. That was the spirituality of councils in the late 1960s.

Conclusion: Council Life in the Late 1960s

An analysis of the five authors from 1967-68 does not suffice as a definitive portrait of early parish councils in the United States. The authors were advocating a philosophy of councils, based on limited experience, and a method for establishing them. They did not pretend to offer a systematic picture of actual councils. Prescription, not description, was their goal.

Despite that concession, however, the five authors concur to a remarkable degree. Their general approach to councils, advocacy of their representative nature, and expression of council spirituality all suggest a common direction. For that reason, I believe that from a synthesis of the five authors we can induce a fairly reliable portrait of council life in the late 1960s.

This synthetic portrait corrects the relatively dim view that later advocates of the "pastoral" council movement took of early councils. By promoting widespread participation rather than any particular task, the early advocates of parish councils gave the lie to later writers who claimed that councils in the 1960s were narrowly focused on temporal matters. It would be truer to say that there was no clear focus whatsoever—that is, no clear and distinct task that every parish council undertook.

Everyone agreed, however, that a parish council should be representative. By emphasizing this representative nature, the early advocates underlined their belief that councils should be a popular movement. But it is an unfounded generalization to say, as some later writers did, that early councils were mainly about wresting political power from pastors. The concern was not mainly to wrest power, but to share responsibility. This was a spiritual as well as a political concern. The earliest councils were a means to promote participation in the church's mission and to build community. This was their spiritual focus. To be sure, early writers did not advocate any particular discipline of formal prayer or pious practice. But participation and shared responsibility marked the parish council spirituality.

In short, the critique of early parish councils was exaggerated. Some councils undoubtedly focused on temporal matters. Some quite likely tried to lord it over their pastors. Some may have disconnected their work and spirituality. But the literature of 1967-68 is optimistic. It suggests that the real scope, relation to pastors, and spirituality of early councils was far brighter than later critics said it was. It was so bright, in fact, that leaders at the national level contemplated a national pastoral council for the United States.

Chapter Nine

American Missteps

From August 28-30, 1970, Monsignor J. Paul O'Connor assembled an "interdisciplinary convocation" in Chicago, sponsored by the United States Catholic Conference, to study the establishment of a national pastoral council. Attended by representatives of 97 dioceses and 45 national Catholic organizations, it included pastors, theologians, historians, management consultants, and canon lawyers. Five years after the publication of Vatican II's Decree on the Apostolate of Lay People, the members were responding to the decree's recommendation of councils at every level of the church, from the parish to the national and international plane.[1]

The Dutch had had a national pastoral council since 1966, and the U.S. bishops had had a "National Advisory Council," originally proposed by Cardinal John Dearden of Detroit, since 1969.[2] Was it time to establish a pastoral council for the U.S. church?

In 1971, the U.S. bishops published the consultation's proceedings. The optimistic conclusion, presumably written by O'Connor, was that the creation of a national pastoral council "is necessary and inevitable if the Church of America is to bear its greatest fruit."[3] It seemed as if the national pastoral council was well on its way to being established.

Two years later, the proposal for a national pastoral council was dead. On October 1, 1973, Bishop James S. Rausch of Phoenix, who was General Secretary of the National Conference of Catholic Bishops, issued a press release. It stated that the NCCB had decided to "suspend" efforts to create a national pastoral council. In the press release Rausch gave three reasons for the bishops' decision: lack of public support, lack of Vatican support, and lack of support by other national conferences of bishops. Most interesting is the comment that the U.S. bishops' existing consultative structure, namely, the "National Advisory Council," already sufficed. The NAC itself had established the steering committee under Monsignor O'Connor to study the feasibility of a national pastoral council. "The advisory council itself is now doing many of the things which a national pastoral council might be expected to do," said Bishop Rausch.[4]

The Death of the National Pastoral Council

Why did the proposal for the national pastoral council, considered "necessary and inevitable" in 1970, die in 1973? In order to answer this question, we must explore the reasons given by Bishop Rausch. The widespread enthusiasm at the 1970 convocation and its optimistic conclusion make the bishop's statement puzzling. Something diminished the popular, episcopal, and Vatican support for a national pastoral council that was felt in 1970. The lack of Vatican support can be explained by the 1973 "Circular Letter on 'Pastoral Councils'" to the world's bishops from the Congregation for the Clergy, the topic of the next chapter. About the lack of support from U.S. Catholics or from other national episcopal conferences, Bishop Rausch offered no details.

The U.S. bishops never rejected a specific national pastoral council plan because there was no single plan. There were rather a variety of plans, each competing with the other, none proving ultimately persuasive. The "proceedings" of the 1970 interdisciplinary convocation in Chicago did not include, for example, a sample NPC constitution. Rather, they offered an opening essay by Avery Dulles and four research papers (plus responses). The papers were by Thomas F. O'Meara, James Hennesey, William LaDue, and Arthur X. Deegan II on the ecclesiology, history, competence, and organization of a possible NPC. From a perusal of these "proceedings," one cannot say in any detail what the final shape of an NPC would be. We cannot know with certainty to what aspect of the imagined NPC the bishops objected.

But we may form a conjecture. The basis for the conjecture is what I call

American "missteps" in the evolution of councils. Two major missteps were the relatively unsuccessful efforts in the early 1970s to create councils with an authority independent of the bishops. One proposal was to establish a national council of catholic laity as the voice of lay Catholics. It would implement its policies through a network of diocesan and parish laity councils. This council actually came into existence in 1971. Although it ultimately fell apart, it may have raised fears of a similarly independent NPC that would split the laity and the hierarchy. To this the bishops would almost certainly have objected.

Another proposal was for a national pastoral council that would elect bishops and enact legislation for the American church. U.S. canonists and theologians actually made this proposal at Fordham University in 1970. If enacted, it would have established the NPC as a governance structure parallel to that of the U.S. bishops. We may conjecture that the U.S. bishops compared these two initiatives, the NCCL and the Fordham NPC, to the already existing National Advisory Council. Their conclusion? The grass on the other side of the hill was not greener.

The Laity Council

Let us start with the first of our missteps, the National Council of the Catholic Laity. Supporters of the NCCL began with a somewhat tendentious interpretation of paragraph 26 in the Vatican II Decree on the Apostolate of Lay People, especially the phrase about establishing councils "on the national and international plane."[5] Some interpreted this paragraph as authorizing a national lay council. Foremost among these interpreters were the leaders of the National Council of Catholic Men (NCCM) and the National Council of Catholic Women (NCCW). The leaders viewed their two organizations as the already-existing incarnation of the lay coordinating councils that the bishops of Vatican II had recommended.

Justification for the Proposal

The justification for their proposal lay in the text of the Laity Decree. To that text the council fathers had appended a footnote referring in positive terms to the national councils of men and women.[6] From the footnote, one could conclude that the NCCM and the NCCW are indeed the councils envisioned at Vatican II for assisting the church's apostolic work. Taking this hint, representatives of the NCCM and NCCW in the United States began discussions in the late 1960s, and on November 12, 1971 formed an organization known as the National Council of Catholic Laity.[7]

They had received a letter from the Vatican Secretary of State, encouraging the establishment of their organization,[8] and believed that they were acting in the spirit of Vatican II and with Vatican approval.

Two members of the National Council of Catholic Laity, Richard H. Dement and Thomas J. Tewey, promoted parish councils throughout the U.S. in the early 1970s. The NCCL also published at least three books, on subjects such as coresponsibility and parish life. The last of these books— William Maher's 1974 *A Question of Values*—was written in a deliberately provocative style designed to stir up a dialogue about the relation between church and society.[9] After reviewing pre-publication copies, the bishops of the U.S. registered disapproval, and the NCCL agreed to halt distribution. Gradually the local chapters of the men's and women's councils reduced their support for the NCCL. New officers elected by the men's and women's councils were not as committed to the NCCL as those who created it in the first place. Eventually the laity council ceased to be an effective organization.

Its failure led to the demise of the NCCM, whose members were torn between support for the lay council and the original men's council.[10] The women's council continued, however, because its strength lay in its local and regional affiliates, not in its connection to the National Council of Catholic Laity.[11] There is no evidence of strong support for exclusively lay councils among the United States bishops.[12] For that reason, the NCCL can be described as a "misstep" in the council movement.

Independence of the NPC

From the distance of thirty years, two reasons for the failure of the NCCL emerge with clarity. One is the independence of the proposed laity council from the Catholic hierarchy. Martin H. Work, a lay auditor at Vatican II who became Executive Director of the National Council of Catholic Men, advocated this independence at a March 15-17, 1970 conference in Dayton, Ohio. His mental image for the councils recommended in the Laity Decree was the virtually independent national councils of Catholic men and of Catholic women.[13] Work's emphasis on the independent lay nature of these councils, which in his imagination would coordinate a network of parish councils throughout the United States, might well have created anxieties for those who feared a division between priests and people.

Another reason for the failure of the National Council of Catholic Laity was the fear that such a council might blur the lines of jurisdiction and authority. In Work's proposal, independent laity councils would coordinate parish councils. Lay coordinating councils at the diocesan level, he said, will focus on "action, programming, servicing, and training." They will even train parish councils and provide them with programs.[14] Work contrasted these lay diocesan coordinating councils with the pastoral councils advocated by the Vatican II Decree on the Pastoral Office of Bishops. Pastoral councils are advisory councils, he said, concerned merely with dialogue and planning. The "coordinating" councils he envisioned were more muscular than the strictly advisory "pastoral" councils. Because they were to train parish councils and provide them with programs they would have a significant influence over the governance of parishes. To the extent that Work's proposal represents the thinking of those who framed the National Council of Catholic Laity, one can surmise that the proposal aroused some anxiety in both the clergy and in conservative Catholics about the surrender of church leadership to lay councils.

Lay Trusteeism

Work's proposal for laity councils may well have raised in the minds of many readers the ghost of lay trusteeism. Lay trusteeism was a movement in the Catholic Church that began shortly after the American Revolution. Its principal feature was lay Catholics taking on the legal responsibility for buying land, erecting church buildings, and securing the services of a parish priest. The trustee system itself was acceptable in a frontier land without clearly defined church-state relations. Indeed, some have argued that it marked an exemplary chapter in the history of lay initiative in the U.S. church. But when the trustee system came to be regarded as the ideal, when the clergy were excluded from the control of all church concerns except the purely spiritual, and when lay trustees appealed to civil law for protection of their claims against church authority, then trusteeism became a threat to church unity. That is the way it is usually treated in scholarly literature.[15] Doubtless the proposal for diocesan councils of the laity, bodies that would coordinate and direct parish councils, fell considerably short of lay trusteeism. But some saw a potential connection between lay trusteeism and the councils advocated at Vatican II and gave a warning.[16]

In short, the apparent reason for the failure of the National Council of Catholic Laity was its lack of grass-roots support, and one can conjecture why the grass roots withheld that support. Martin Work, the leader of the NCCM in 1970, outlined a vision for diocesan laity councils that, in the light of subsequent history, proved out of step. He regarded the laity councils as independent of the hierarchy and as bodies that would have a strong influence upon parish governance. The Vatican Congregation for the Clergy's "Private" or Circular Letter of 1973 made it clear that pastoral councils are consultative to pastors, not independent of them, and are advisory in nature.[17] A quite different idea underlay the proposal for the NCCL, and the contradiction between the two may have helped spell defeat for the laity council.

The Canonists' Vision

A second proposal that proved out of step with the emerging rhythm of parish councils, and may have dampened enthusiasm for a national pastoral council, was made at an April 3-5, 1970 symposium at Fordham University sponsored by the Canon Law Society of America. The participants, mostly canonists and theologians, not only called for a National Pastoral Council, but recommended that it have power to elect bishops and enact legislation for the U.S. church. Had this recommendation been accepted, it would have given the proposed NPC far more power than what the existing National Advisory Council exercised.[18]

When Bishop Rausch in 1973 announced that the U.S. bishops were suspending efforts to create a national *pastoral* council, he stated that the existing National *Advisory* Council is now doing "many of the things" that an NPC might be expected to do. But the press release does not say what further things the advocates of an NPC proposed, namely, those things that the National Advisory Council could not or would not do. The proceedings of the Fordham convention identify what some of the NPC advocates wanted. In comparison to the advisory council's actual responsibility to review and reflect on the bishops' committee work, the proposals to involve laity in electing bishops and enacting legislation were more ambitious and democratic. At the time, they merited serious consideration.[19]

The canonists and theologians who supported such a democratic national pastoral council used historical and theological arguments. Historically, they claimed that the U.S. church is heir to a substantial tradition of councils and collegiality. The tradition included the election by priests of John Carroll as first bishop in the United States in 1789, and the establishment by Charleston Bishop John England of a series of diocesan conventions from 1823-1842, conventions with a House of the Clergy and of Lay Delegates.[20] These events, ran the historical argument, were part of the evolution of the church, and one can expect further evolutions. These include a national pastoral council, a council based on American precedents.[21]

Theologically, the arguments for a national pastoral council rested on appeals to Christian freedom and shared responsibility. NPC advocates could cite theologians for whom freedom meant affirming the diverse viewpoints of the people of God as a collective gift to the church, and for whom shared responsibility meant giving the laity a voice and vote as an expression of the Catholic community.[22] Doubtless, these arguments breathed the air of the late 1960s and early 1970s. They display an openness to experimenting with new forms of church governance, an openness that today seems quaint. But they also suggest why a proposed national pastoral council that, among other duties, might participate in the election of a bishop or actually enact legislation, not only seemed plausible, but could be taken seriously.

The Road Not Taken

The idea of a national pastoral council was taken seriously, but it did not prove persuasive. The optimistic words of Monsignor O'Connor, namely, that an NPC "is necessary and inevitable," were an unfulfilled prophecy. Today we are better able to understand why the U.S. bishops suspended their efforts to form an NPC. Contrary to the statement of Bishop Rausch, there is much evidence of popular support for an NPC in the early 1970s. The National Council of Catholic Men, the Canon Law Society of America, and the U.S. bishops' own National Advisory Council, all held conferences in 1970 to discuss the possibility of establishing one. But none of these groups could agree about what a national pastoral council ought to be. That is the key to understanding the words of Bishop Rausch. There was little popular support, he meant, for any *one* kind of national pastoral council.

To tell the truth, at least three kinds of councils were being considered. The National Council of Catholic Men, through their 1970 president, Martin Work, endorsed one kind of NPC. It was a council that would be a clearing house and training center for parish councils throughout the nation. Another potential prototype for an NPC was the National Council of Catholic Laity, established in 1971. It wanted to speak as an independent voice for lay Catholics, and by 1974 had alienated many bishops. Yet another proposal was the 1970 "Consensus Statement" of the Canon Law Society of America. It called for an NPC that would pass legislation for the U.S. church and elect bishops. These proposals enable us to understand why Bishop Rausch said that the NPC proposal lacked public and episcopal support. One can surmise that the bishops read what the National Council of Catholic Laity and Canon Law Society of America proposed and got cold feet. If popular support meant that there was a resounding call for a single NPC model, then popular support was missing. No single model could boast a clear mandate.

The connection between parish councils and these efforts is indirect. Parish councils did not develop as they did solely in reaction to one national proposal or another. But the national proposals illuminate early parish councils by exposing directions in which parish councils did not go. The indirect consequences for parish councils of these unsuccessful proposals can be briefly stated. First of all, parish councils never became laity councils. The argument that Vatican II intended independent councils of the laity never prevailed. Second, parish councils were never trained by national or diocesan lay councils, at least not to an appreciable extent. The dream of Martin Work never materialized. Third, parish councils never became the clergy-electing or legislation-enacting bodies for which some canonists and theologians had argued. There was too much suspicion of lay trusteeism. The unsuccessful proposals can be called American missteps in the evolution of councils.

Eventually, parish councils began to see themselves in terms of the "pastoral" council idea of the Decree on Bishops as affirmed in the 1973 Circular Letter by the Congregation for the Clergy. By the late 1980s, parish councils commonly spoke of themselves as "pastoral" councils, referring to no. 27 of the Vatican II Decree on Bishops. Number 26 of the Decree on the Apostolate of Lay People, the original charter for parish councils (as well as for the National Council of Catholic Laity and for the national pastoral council), fell into obscurity. The reasons for this will be explored in the next chapter.

Chapter Ten

The Circular Letter

When Bishop James Rausch of Phoenix, speaking in 1973 as General Secretary of the National Conference of Catholic Bishops, suspended the conference's efforts to create a national pastoral council, he gave three reasons. We discussed the first two reasons, namely, the lack of episcopal and popular support, in the previous chapter. Bishop Rausch's third reason for suspending efforts to create an NPC was the lack of Vatican support. For that he could rely upon a 1973 publication by the Vatican's six-year-old Congregation for the Clergy. The publication was a "circular" or private letter to the world's bishops.[1] It is remarkable in that it remains, to this day, the only Vatican document wholly devoted to pastoral councils. It declared the creation of national pastoral councils "inopportune"—and thus signaled official disapproval of them. On this basis, Bishop Rausch could say there was no Vatican support for a national pastoral council.

The Circular Letter not only poured cold water on the proposed national pastoral council, but also proves indispensable for understanding the history of parish councils. For the letter marked the first time that "pastoral" councils were mentioned at the parish level. No official document had ever mentioned them before, and so the official use of the term "parish" pastoral council, we can say, began with the Circular Letter. Yet the term did not enter popular parlance until after the publication of the Code of Canon Law in 1983. This raises an important question: what was the intention of Vatican authorities in introducing the new terminology?

In this chapter, we will see how the Circular Letter emerged as a reprimand, however indirect, to the Dutch National Pastoral Council. The Dutch council, with its emphasis on co-responsibility and its democratic style, had posed a problem to the Vatican authorities. The authorities not only expressed their reservations directly to the Dutch bishops, but also began drafting their letter on pastoral councils to the world's bishops. Even before the letter was published, the Dutch bishops had deferred to the Vatican authorities. They recast their pastoral council as a "national dialogue." The eventual publication of the letter sent a clear warning to pastoral councils worldwide: pastoral councils are consultative, dependent on the pastor, and limited in scope.

Finally, we will see that the letter was a bellwether: it applied the "pastoral" council idea to parishes. It signaled the approach to parish councils that the 1983 Code of Canon Law would take. Before the publication of the Code, the Decree on the Apostolate of Lay People was considered the Vatican II "source" for parish councils. Afterwards, the Laity Decree faded from the consciousness of council members. The Vatican II Decree on the Pastoral Office of Bishops, with its reference to pastoral councils, replaced it. The Circular Letter, which ignored the Laity Decree in favor of the Bishops' Decree, was a hint of the change to come.

First Reference to the Parish "Pastoral" Council

As we have seen, the earliest councils at the parish level were called "parish" councils. They took as their charter the Vatican II Decree on the Apostolate of Lay People, which in section no. 26 called for councils to assist the church's "apostolic" work (without mentioning "pastoral" work). These "apostolic" councils, envisioned primarily at the diocesan level, were the aim of the Laity Decree, no. 26. The document added, however, that apostolic councils should also be found, "if possible, at parochial, inter-parochial, [and] inter-diocesan" levels, as well as "on the national and international plane." Since this paragraph of the laity decree was the only mention of "parochial" councils in all of the Vatican II documents, every early writer cited it as the main warrant for parish councils.[2] Almost no one, in the 1960s and 1970s, spoke of parish *pastoral* councils.

In those days, the term "pastoral council" was reserved exclusively to councils at the diocesan level. Two Vatican II documents, the Decree on the Pastoral Ministry of Bishops and the Decree on the Church's Missionary Activity, spoke of diocesan pastoral councils.[3] Of these documents, the fuller reference is Decree on Bishops, published October 28, 1965. It treats the pastoral council in detail. On August 6, 1966, less than a year after the Bishops Decree, Pope Paul VI issued an apostolic letter on its implementation. The letter expanded the treatment of pastoral councils.[4] But in none of these documents was there any reference to "pastoral" councils at the parish level. The pastoral council idea seemed irrelevant to parish councils.

To tell the truth, at least two early authors, David O'Neill and Martin Work, criticized the type of councils envisioned by the Bishops Decree. They disparaged diocesan pastoral councils in favor of the apostolic councils envisioned by the Laity Decree. From their viewpoint, the councils of the Bishops Decree were merely advisory, seemingly without any real strength. The councils of the Laity Decree, by contrast, would actually coordinate lay undertakings, and so had a more powerful role.[5] In their preference for the Laity Decree as the basis for parish councils, O'Neill and Work represented the majority of early thinkers.

Of all the writers in the 1960s, only the Swiss theologian Hans Küng saw the potential for parish councils of the "pastoral" council idea. He stated in an article from 1969 that the parish council ought to "parallel" the diocesan pastoral council. Only the DPC, he said, gives the laity a say about decision making in the church.[6]

The councils described in the Laity Decree, by contrast, focus on decision making for apostolates in the world. Contrary to Küng's expectations, few of the earliest writings about parish councils sought to confine their scope to temporal matters. We saw that the scope of early parish councils was virtually unlimited. But Küng was remarkably prescient. He saw that the pastoral council, at whatever level, aimed at giving the laity a voice in specifically ecclesial decision making.

Shortly after the 1973 publication of the Circular Letter, another article acknowledged the relevance of the "pastoral" idea for parish councils. James Buryska, who was executive secretary of the pastoral council in the Diocese of Winona, also spoke of "pastoral" councils at the parish level. Buryska used the term "pastoral" to refer to those councils that are truly "representative" of the Catholic people—councils that included clergy, laity, and religious—as distinct from laity councils and priests' senates.[7] Like Küng he saw that the "pastoral" council, far from being less effective because of its explicitly consultative nature, might have a strength all its own. Its strength lay in its inclusion of priests, religious, and laypeople.

No other early writers apparently saw what Küng and Buryska saw. The Laity Decree was the basis for parish councils, almost everyone agreed, and the Bishops Decree was irrelevant to parish councils, if not a distinctly weaker proposal. Not until 1973, with the publication of the Circular Letter on pastoral councils by the Vatican's Congregation for the Clergy, was the word "pastoral" applied to parish councils. By the mid-1980s, references to parish "pastoral" council had become common-place. Indeed, people contrasted the supposedly outdated "parish" coun-cils with the new and preferred "parish pastoral" councils. Did the Circular Letter intend to alter the direction of the parish council move-ment? To answer this question, let us review the events that gave rise to the Circular Letter.

The Origin of the Circular Letter

For seven years after the 1965 promulgation of the Decree on the Laity, the Vatican preserved a relative silence on councils at the parish level. About diocesan councils, however, there were signs of concern. On August 15, 1967, Pope Paul VI created the Congregation for the Clergy, giving to the congregation responsibility for pastoral councils.[8] On May 5, 1969, John J. Wright, the Pittsburgh bishop who had written the introduction to Bernard Lyons' 1967 Parish Councils, was elevated to the rank of Cardinal and made Prefect of the Congregation for the Clergy. One of Cardinal Wright's first concerns was the Dutch National Pastoral Council. Consisting of the seven Dutch bishops and 80 elected priests, religious, and laity, and assembled as a "representative" body of the faithful, the Dutch NPC had been meet-ing on an experimental basis since 1966. By 1970, the Dutch had drawn up a charter for a permanent national structure, a charter that attracted the attention of Cardinal Wright's Congregation for the Clergy.

In the winter of 1970-71, the congregation wrote a letter to the world's various bishops' conferences, including the Dutch. The letter presented the congregation's own draft guidelines for diocesan councils. Writing in reference to the Dutch council, John Coleman summarized the draft guidelines as follows:

> The Roman document presumed that members of diocesan councils would be appointees of the bishop, not elected. Secondly, such councils would have no juridically permanent character; each bishop was to be free to erect a pastoral council for his diocese or not. Further, every diocesan council was to avoid the appearance of being a representative body of the faithful; individual members of such councils were to be considered acting strictly as individuals. Again, the Roman document proposed that it was somehow confusing to combine, as the Dutch models did, priests and laity in a single episcopal advisory council.[9]

In each of these areas, Coleman reports, the proposed charter for a permanent Dutch national council took the opposite point of view. Members of the Dutch council would be elected, the council would be permanent, priests and laity would be combined, and the council would be co-responsible for policy and statutes. The authors of the "Roman document" (namely, the Vatican's Congregation for the Clergy) and the Dutch bishops had distinctly different ideas for a pastoral council.

The Congregation for the Clergy consulted the presidents of the world's conferences of bishops in order to evaluate local experiments with diocesan pastoral councils and to recommend norms. It almost certainly shared the concerns reflected in the November 30, 1971, Synod of Bishops assembled in Rome. The world synod grappled with the nature of the ministerial priesthood. The priesthood's distinctive character was being obscured, the bishops feared, by ecclesial activities in which lay and ordained members had similar roles.[10] The bishops mentioned catechetics, administration, and liturgy, but they could have mentioned pastoral councils as well. Pastoral councils, especially the Dutch National Pastoral Council, had become a source of tension.[11]

On March 15, 1972, the Congregation for the Clergy hosted two other Vatican Congregations (those for Bishops and for Religious and Secular Institutes), as well as the Vatican Council of the Laity, at a "plenary combined congregation" on pastoral councils. The conclusions of this group were published in 1973 as a Circular or Private Letter to the world's bishops and became the Vatican's official policy.[12] But the Dutch bishops retreated from their proposal before the conclusions were published. In a communiqué dated August 13, 1972, they abandoned their plan to establish a permanent pastoral council at the national level, settling instead for a national pastoral "dialogue." The reason given by the Dutch bishops was that the Vatican's "curial organs" (i.e., the Congregation for the Clergy) were preparing their own document on pastoral councils. The Roman authorities considered that the Dutch plan had not sufficiently safeguarded the authority of bishops.[13] By giving up their plan for a permanent national pastoral council, the Dutch bishops deferred to the congregation's authority. They had accepted the judgment, later expressed in the Circular Letter, that the formation of national pastoral councils was "inopportune."

The Rebuke to the Dutch Council
So the 1973 Circular Letter emerged both from the experience of the Dutch bishops in forming a national pastoral council, and the Congregation for the Clergy's desire to prevent other episcopal conferences from making the same apparent mistakes. But what was the primary motive for the letter? Was it a surreptitious effort to extinguish the Dutch and other national councils under the guise of a general letter about diocesan councils? This does not appear likely. First of all, the Sacred Congregation for the Clergy originally issued the letter in English, rather than in the customary Latin.[14] One would think that if the Dutch bishops were the primary audience in the mind of the congregation, the communication would have been made in Dutch.

Second, the earliest commentary on the Circular Letter did not mention the Dutch church. That commentary was written by Father Donald W. Wuerl (later Bishop of Pittsburgh), who in 1973 was Cardinal Wright's secretary. Wuerl put the ban on national pastoral councils in ecclesiological perspective. The "local church" is the diocese, he said, not a national organization or ethnic group. National church organizations (such as national pastoral councils) exist to serve the local or diocesan church.[15] Diocesan pastoral councils must be established before national ones become "opportune."

Finally, there is the editorial evidence of the 1973 text itself. The Circular Letter, rather than a heavy-handed and undeserved blow to the Dutch council, seems to have been the product of revision and compromise. The primary evidence for this is the history of the letter's composition. The guidelines for pastoral councils published by the congregation in the 1973 Circular Letter differed from the draft guidelines that the congregation had proposed in 1970. For example, the 1970 draft guidelines apparently called for separate councils of priests and laity, suggesting that it was confusing to combine them.[16] By 1973, however, the Circular Letter backed away from this position. It reaffirmed the mix of priests, religious, and laity on pastoral councils recommended in the Vatican II Decree on Bishops.

To give another example, the early draft guidelines apparently said that DPC members were to be appointed, not elected as they were in Holland. In the 1973 Circular Letter, however, there was no prohibition against elections. Elections were not even mentioned. The Circular Letter distinguished between appointment and "selection," leaving the manner of selection to the diocesan ordinary. All of this suggests that the Circular Letter published in 1973 was a product of some revision. The consultations done by Cardinal Wright's congregation in 1970, 1971, and 1972 resulted in a circular letter that differed significantly from the draft of winter, 1970-71.

So we can confidently say that the 1973 Circular Letter was not a thoughtless and ill-conceived reaction to the Dutch NPC. The editorial evidence of consultation and revision is too extensive to allow that interpretation. But it *was* a rebuke, however indirect, to the Dutch. The Circular Letter insisted that pastoral councils are consultative and impermanent. They are consultative in that, while their recommendations are to be esteemed, no bishop is bound to accept them. Pastoral councils cannot infringe upon a bishop's freedom or authority. This marked a criticism of the Dutch council, which was "co-responsible" with the bishops for pastoral policy.[17] "Co-responsible" is more than consultative.

Furthermore, said both the early draft and the 1973 final document, pastoral councils are impermanent. Councils are not self-perpetuating entities. They serve when convened by bishops. Once an episcopal see is vacant, the pastoral council is not to meet. The Dutch, by contrast, were contemplating a charter for a permanent national council. This troubled Cardinal Wright's congregation in 1970, and the congregation discouraged permanent pastoral councils in 1973. On the consultative nature of councils, and on their temporary service when convened by the bishops, the congregation agreed. All of this suggests that the Dutch experience was a catalyst for the 1973 Circular Letter. The letter concluded that the establishment of pastoral councils at the national level was "not opportune"—the very judgment that the congregation had rendered earlier against the Dutch.

To be sure, the congregation offered no evidence or justification for the judgment that national councils were inopportune. Indeed, one could argue that the virtual prohibition against national councils contradicts the Vatican II Decree on the Apostolate of Lay People. The Decree called at no. 26 for "apostolic" (if not "pastoral") councils on the national plane. But the Circular Letter did not even allude to Laity 26. To that extent, the congregation's judgment appears to have been an exercise of unwarranted censorship and reaction.[18] It ignored a text that had hitherto been considered essential. The disapproval of national pastoral councils was an administrative fiat, not the conclusion of a fully articulated chain of reasoning.

The congregation's 1973 Circular Letter reveals traces of compromise in the realms of pastoral council membership and selection. It was not merely an authoritarian reaction to Dutch experiments. Cardinal Wright was a proponent of councils. The main purpose of the Circular Letter was not to extinguish the Dutch council which, by the time of the letter's publication, had already been reconstituted. The purpose of the letter was to strengthen the foundation for pastoral councils at the diocesan level. The permission it granted to allow pastoral councils at the parochial level was a mere afterthought.

Commentaries on the Circular Letter

By allowing pastoral councils at the parish level, the Circular Letter introduced a new terminology. It was the beginning of the parish *pastoral* council. But there was no call for existing parish councils to become parish pastoral councils. Nor did it even make a distinction between the two. Indeed, the letter made only a one-sentence reference to councils at the parish level. Commentaries on the letter confirm that its reference to "parochial" pastoral councils was marginal and did not signal a new direction for councils. Not one of the three commentaries published in the twelve months after the appearance of the Circular Letter did any more than quote the letter's reference to "parochial" councils. Not one suggested that parish councils should reform themselves and henceforth be "pastoral" councils.[19]

Commentators observed that the Circular Letter defined the composition, consultative nature, and scope of pastoral councils. In these areas the letter has had important consequences for parish councils. But these consequences would not be felt for more than a decade. Most early commentators thought they applied to diocesan, not parish, councils.

For example, two commentators noted that the Circular Letter speaks of the pastoral councils as "representing" the people of God, but not representing them in a juridical sense.[20] This is a significant advance beyond Pope Paul VI's Apostolic Letter, *Ecclesiae Sanctae*, of August 6, 1966. *Ecclesiae Sanctae* did not use the word "representative" or distinguish a juridical from a consultative use of the word. The 1973 Circular Letter, by speaking of councils that are "representative" in a non-juridical sense, introduced a broad democratic resonance. But it also suggested that political and ecclesial representation are two different things.

One commentator drew attention to the Circular Letter's statement that bishops "should greatly esteem its [the pastoral council's] propositions and suggestions and seriously consider the judgments on which they [the council members] agree."[21] To be sure, the letter insists that councils have only a consultative voice, and cannot infringe on the bishop's freedom and authority, but it also makes plain that the advice of the council is not to be taken lightly. Consultative does not mean insipid.

Finally, the Circular Letter makes a stab at limiting the scope of the pastoral council. It does so by suggesting areas in which the council can provide help: apostolic initiatives, the ministries of Word and sacrament, aid to priests in the diocese, and determining public opinion. It also excluded four areas. Councils may not consider general principles of faith, orthodoxy, morality, or church law.[22] Practical wisdom and prudence, not theology or ethics, are the province of councils. Theirs is the realm of contingent decision making: a wide field indeed.

Conclusion: The Circular Letter as Bellwether

The 1973 Circular Letter was momentous because it marked the first time the word "pastoral" was applied officially to parish councils. But the momentous event was little heralded. Indeed, the issues that gave rise to the Circular Letter in the first place overshadowed it. The letter apparently did not intend to alter the direction of parish councils. Its focus was "pastoral" councils, mainly at the diocesan level. The one reference to "parochial" pastoral councils was unelaborated.

Although the Circular Letter focused mainly on diocesan pastoral councils, it eventually had enormous consequences for parish pastoral councils. The consequences were not felt, however, until after the 1983 publication of the Code of Canon Law. There the canons that refer to diocesan and parish pastoral councils affirmed the teaching of the Circular Letter. They stated that pastoral councils are consultative, dependent on the pastor, and reflective of the people of God. The canons use the language of the Vatican II Decree on Bishops, not the Decree on the Laity. All of this shaped parish councils after 1983.

So we can say that the Circular Letter was a bellwether. It served as a kind of lead ram in a flock, the one whose bell sounds the direction in which others are to follow. The ambiguities of the Decree on the Laity—ambiguities about whether councils should be solely composed of laypeople, about whether they have deliberative authority, and about whether the council is permanent and independent of the office of pastor—these ambiguities simply played no role in the Circular Letter. It avoided Laity 26 altogether. Instead, the Circular Letter concentrated on the "pastoral" councils of the Decree on Bishops. In so doing, it presented a simplified doctrine about councils. For better or worse, this was the direction that official teaching on councils was to take: away from the ambiguities of Laity 26 and toward the more circumscribed role for councils in Bishops 27. But it was ten years before the teaching of the Circular Letter registered at the popular level. In the meantime during the 1970s—a period of great ambiguity about the meaning of consultation—councils spread rapidly throughout the U.S.

Chapter Eleven

The Growth of Councils in the 1970s

The 1970s were a time of tremendous growth for parish councils in the United States. The number of councils rose dramatically. National organizations for planning and councils emerged. Dozens of articles and books about councils were published. The decade after the Second Vatican Council witnessed an impressive flowering of the council movement.

With all this growth, however, there were problems. In the fall of 1974, for example, the parish council of Good Shepherd Church in the Diocese of Arlington got into a dispute with its pastor, Father John P. Hannan. The council wanted to institute the practices of female eucharistic ministers and the reception of Communion in the hand. Father Hannan objected to these practices, arguing that Bishop Thomas Welsh had not given permission for them. Things reached such an impasse that Father Hannan dissolved the council. Bishop Welsh backed him up. Two months later, after reconciliation efforts, the council and its committees were re-established, this time as consultative to the pastor. It was a relatively small crisis, but the occasion of a pastoral letter from Bishop Welsh.[1] Good Shepherd's council stood out because it was a noteworthy failure in a time of notable successes.

Given the unresolved tension about the consultative nature of councils, why did they spread so rapidly? The answer lies in the overwhelming climate of support for them. By the 1970s, the bishops of the U.S. had generally embraced the idea of councils. They promoted councils in their dioceses by means of pastoral letters, the publication of guidelines, and the hiring of personnel. Bishops believed that councils were worth having, despite the tensions. There was a sense that councils were fulfilling the spirit of Vatican II.

This chapter will first examine the growth of councils in the seventies. Although no official count of the number of councils has ever been made, the evidence for a meteoric rise is hard to deny. A significant motive for this growth is the support for councils by the U.S. bishops, and this chapter will briefly examine that support. Next, the chapter will study the emergence of two national organizations related to councils. These national organizations offered two distinct ways of understanding councils and deepened the council idea. Finally, the chapter will look at the council tensions that emerged in the 1970s. The fusion of consultative practices and the church's hierarchical structure proved difficult.

The Number of Councils in the 1970s

How many councils were there? In 1970, Charles Fecher of the National Council of Catholic Men estimated that there were 10,000 councils in the U.S. If his figure was accurate, it meant that more than one-half of all U.S. parishes had councils. Six years later, Robert G. Howes estimated that councils existed in three-fourths of U.S. parishes. The estimate of Howes was confirmed in 1986, using the methods of social science research, by the *Notre Dame Study of Catholic Parish Life*. It too stated that councils exist in three-fourths of U.S. parishes. The *Notre Dame* study was ten years later than Howes' estimate, but lends support to the conjecture that councils grew tremendously in the 1970s.[2]

Another measure of council growth is the number of articles in church publications. The index to *Origins*, the documentary service of the Catholic News Service, is a barometer of interest. In the period from 1973 to 1982, the index contains 89 references to news items about parish and diocesan councils. By contrast, the index shows only 31 references for the period 1983 to 1992. The seventies were not only a time of growth in the number of councils, but a time of growing intellectual interest in them as well.

Anecdotal evidence also supports the thesis of growth. For example, important episcopal sees began establishing archdiocesan pastoral councils: Baltimore (1973), Omaha (1974), and Milwaukee (1979). The period also witnessed the appearance of groups such as the National Pastoral Planning Conference (1972) and Diocesan and Parish Council Personnel (1974). Individuals such as Thomas Tewey and Richard Dement of the National Council of Catholic Laity, the Denver Archdiocese's Cyndi Thero, and William Rademacher of the Diocese of Lansing, travelled throughout the U.S., giving workshops about councils. American Catholics in the 1970s began to regard councils as essential to parish life. As councils increased, so did the need to organize, support, and understand them.

Episcopal Support
One of the major reasons for this growth was the support from the U.S. bishops. Bishops were convinced that councils would share responsibility, promote ministry, and foster teamwork. One bishop, Christopher Weldon of Springfield in Massachusetts, spoke of the 1970s as the "era of the parish council."[3] Bishops published guidelines for councils[4] and issued pastoral letters.[5] These documents suggest that the bishops embraced the general idea of councils, the idea sketched by their advocates in 1967 and 1968. The bishops saw councils as instruments of participation, instruments with a task of coordinating, with decision-making authority, and with a mission-centered spirituality. Let us look at each of these in turn.

Participation
The bishops indicated that parish councils are, first of all, a means for lay participation and involvement.[6] Of eight guidelines published in *Origins* between 1972 and 1977, the guidelines of the Diocese of Columbus provide the best illustration. They stated that, in the past, ministry was "performed" by priests; the laity were the "recipients" of this ministry. Now the laity are active, and the parish council shall "embody the communal ministry of the people of God."[7]

A further indication of this participative viewpoint lies in the bishops' prescriptions for open meetings and elections. Many dioceses stated that parish council meetings are to be open to all parishioners. Indeed, the Springfield and Boston guidelines went so far as to say that all parishioners are non-voting members of the parish council. Many bishops also agreed that most council members are to be elected, rather than appointed or *ex officio*. These episcopal directives were meant to guarantee the democratic and participatory flavor of councils.[8] By involving laypeople in parish life, suggested the bishops, councils would build community, share responsibility, and renew the parish.

Task

Because the bishops regarded councils as instruments of participation, they spoke of coordination as the councils' principal task. "Coordinating" was the very word used in number 26 of the Vatican II Decree on the Apostolate of Lay People.[9] What councils coordinated was most often a structure of standing committees or commissions. Many dioceses specified an exact number of such committees or commissions for each parish.[10] They were to carry out parish policy, as formulated by the council. Moreover, the scope of councils was enormous. Virtually no attempt was made (the sole exception is the Archdiocese of Boston) to confine the council to administrative matters. Councils could address almost any topic. Few bishops imposed any limits whatsoever on the scope of parish councils.[11] Indeed, quite the opposite was the case. Diocesan guidelines seemed to multiply the tasks, giving councils responsibility for planning, communicating, leading, and implementing.[12]

Authority

The authority of councils is another area in which the bishops of the 1970s reflect the writers of 1967-68. Many agreed that councils are "decision-making" or "policy-making" bodies. They help pastors govern parishes.

More than one bishop was displeased with pastors who refused to establish a council.[13] Many wanted pastors to give the laity a bigger role. In the eyes of at least some bishops, decision-making councils were a powerful instrument for updating parishes—and for updating pastors as well.[14]

At the same time, however, bishops were adamant that parish councils make decisions subject to the veto of the pastor. Pastors can withhold ratification of council decisions. And in the case of pastor-council disagreements, there was little possibility of appeal.[15] Councils were decision-makers, yes, but not in an absolute sense. Decisions were subject to the pastor's approval. This ambiguity led parish councils down a rocky road of future difficulties. Father Hannan's troubles with the Good Shepherd parish council testify to that.

Spirituality

When we turn from the task and authority of parish councils to the area of spirituality, we see once again a confirmation of the earliest writers. The guidelines from 1972 to 1977 usually did not recommend any specific and formal discipline of council prayer.[16] Instead, we see a spirituality of participation and shared responsibility. By participating in councils, the guidelines said, lay Catholics share responsibility for the church's mission.[17] But there was almost no link between the work of the council and liturgical prayer. In these guidelines, pastors played the role of chairman, member, or partner. Rarely were they called presider or president.[18] Spontaneous lay-led prayer, not the Liturgy of the Hours, characterized council meetings. The spirituality of parish councils, as reflected in the guidelines of 1972-1977, was not a liturgical spirituality. Its focus was lay members who by their involvement assume greater responsibility for the parish, not those who find their identity in a corporate act of worship.[19]

In short, the bishops of the United States accepted a view of parish councils that originated after Vatican II and was reflected in American publications from 1967-1968. That view was incorporated in parish council guidelines published in the 1970s. Early parish councils apparently saw themselves as instruments of lay participation. Their principal task was parish coordination, particularly of standing committees or commissions. On behalf of such committees and commissions, or with their cooperation, councils made decisions and set policy—subject, however, to ratification and possible veto by the pastor. Their spirituality was not liturgical but participatory. They were serving God by serving the parish and the mission of the church. There were tensions; but tension was an acceptable price to pay for greater participation.

Pastoral Planning

As the number of councils grew, the level of reflection deepened about their meaning and purpose. Pastoral planning soon emerged as one way of describing what councils do, one among other tasks such as coordinating committees and making policy. It was a long time, however, before many council leaders would argue that pastoral planning was *the* major task of councils. In the early years of the council movement, pastoral planning was a discipline usually reserved for professional planners at the diocesan level. Dioceses began to establish offices of planning in the 1960s, and soon diocesan planners were organizing conferences and bishops were consulting professional planners.[20]

Bishops and their consultants began to introduce councils to the vocabulary of the managerial sciences. Parish councils, some bishops said, should heed the advice of professional planners. Councils should pay attention to both the *task* of the council and to *relations* among council members—a distinction drawn from management theorists. Councils should commit themselves to regular evaluations of the parish. Councils should plan, set goals, and establish standards.[21] With this vocabulary, the U.S. church began to move beyond a naive concept of the parish council as merely the arena of participation and involvement. Church leaders and pastoral planners had begun to see councils as one element among others in decision making. As a pastoral planning perspective emerged, it led to the development of a national organization.

We should note the date and place at which this national organization was born. On the night of June 16, 1972, while five burglars were breaking into the Watergate complex in the Northwest section of Washington, D.C., Father Bernard Quinn was hosting a party at his home in the same quadrant of the city. Father Quinn was Research Coordinator of the Town and Country Department of the Center for Applied Research in the Apostolate (CARA). During that summer, he and Father Robert G. Howes (a colleague at CARA) had been collaborating on a summer course for diocesan planners at the Catholic University. During the party, Fathers Quinn and Howes, along with two other priests, Charles J. Giglio and John D. Dreher, formed a plan to create a national organization for church planners.[22] From that seed grew the National Pastoral Planning Conference (NPPC). The NPPC's "First National Pastoral Planning Conference" took place at the Jesuit Retreat House in Cleveland on December 3-5, 1973. For many years afterward the NPPC distinguished itself with annual conventions and efforts to promote pastoral planning throughout the United States.[23]

It did not take NPPC members long to see how relevant pastoral planning is to councils. Councils, with their goal of sharing responsibility for church decision making, were a breath of the Holy Spirit. NPPC members saw that pastoral planning was an effort to follow the lead of the Spirit more faithfully.[24] The Synod of Bishops in 1971, and the Vatican's Congregation for Bishops in 1973, had spoken of diocesan pastoral councils as instruments of planning. The same, argued NPPC members, can be said for parish councils.[25] Councils develop pastoral plans. Councils set goals and objectives for the parish. Councils keep the planning process in motion.[26] NPPC members were among the first in the 1970s to advocate a pastoral-planning role for councils. They saw councils as a Spirit-led initiative, sanctioned by the Vatican, and dedicated to shared responsibility.

Not every NPPC member, however, realized the planning potential of councils. Most planners focused on diocesan, rather than parish issues. For them, parish councils were but one slice of the planning pie. Pastoral planning was dedicated to the development of the entire church as an organization, not just to parish councils. It aimed at the realization of a future for which comprehensive action was necessary, not the piecemeal efforts of parish volunteers. It required thorough research by trained professionals, research that could not be accomplished even by gifted amateurs. For these reasons, few planners saw the potential of parish councils. They believed that pastoral planning was the work of professionals. Councils could make a contribution to planning, but it was a partial one. Catholics dedicated to councils soon developed their own organization.

A National Organization for Councils

As one group of church professionals deepened its grasp of planning, another group was deepening its grasp of councils. We saw earlier how the National Council of Catholic Laity, especially Richard Dement and Thomas Tewey, promoted parish councils in the early 1970s. From October 21-23, 1974, the NCCL and the "New England Conference on Parish Councils" sponsored the First National Conference for Diocesan Parish Council Personnel at The Cenacle in Brighton, Massachusetts.[27] With that, a new national organization—Diocesan Parish Council Personnel (DPCP)—was born.

DPCP members did not define their organization in terms of an academic discipline or administrative science, as did NPPC members. Nor did the DPCP publish proceedings, as the planners did from 1974 to 1982. But like the planners, DPCP held a series of lively annual conferences.[28] Members heard presentations with titles such as the following: "Diocesan Pastoral Councils: What Are They Doing?" and "Spirituality = Ministry (Ours)" and "Self-Image of Today's Volunteer."[29] In a time when the number of councils was rising and bishops were creating offices to support them, the DPCP provided opportunities for the new office-holders to meet and share information. To understand the beliefs of DPCP members, let us look at the work of the group's chief writer, William J. Rademacher, and at the group's views on council decision making.

William J. Rademacher

The DPCP did not see itself as a professional organization. Its members had no common academic background or single theoretical perspective. But the organization could boast the membership of Rademacher, who in the 1970s was Professor of Systematic Theology at St. John's Provincial Seminary in Plymouth, Michigan. Rademacher wrote five books about councils (one of which was extensively revised and published under the same name) and co-authored a sixth.[30] Although he claimed that his "300 plus workshops across the U.S. did more for the formation of parish councils" than his books,[31] nevertheless his written work offers a snapshot of beliefs about councils in the 1970s and 1980s.

Rademacher's books present parish councils as the fulfillment of the promise of the Second Vatican Council. Showing how the parish is a realization of the people of God, examining the relevance of leading conciliar thinkers, and affirming the ecumenical movement, he popularized the teachings of Vatican II. At the same time, Rademacher created a synthesis of church teaching and the participative spirit of American democracy. In councils, he believed, Catholics would fully share parish responsibilities. Although he was cautious about presenting councils as representative bodies in the parish, nevertheless he emphasized the popular election of councillors, the decision-making authority of councils, and the pastor as a voting member. Rademacher, who as a Catholic priest had served as pastor, was also an early advocate of councils as pastoral planners. His view of pastoral planning was not that of a professional planner, however, but of a pastor. Rademacher emphasized the need for close interpersonal relation, emotional support, and sound group dynamics. His books manifest a desire to embody the teachings of Vatican II in U.S. parishes.[32]

At the same time, Rademacher's work also reveals some of the weaknesses of the parish council movement. This is apparent in the changed positions he took during his writing career. In one early book he spoke of councils as decision-making bodies who were not merely advisory. Later he would speak of councils as "primarily" decision making but also "advisory."[33] In his 1979 *Practical Guide* Rademacher stated that councils assign goals for committees to implement and hold those committees accountable. In the 1988 *New Practical Guide* he conceded that councils could not be expected to implement policies. At one point he emphasized that pastors are voting members on councils. Eventually he spoke of the pastor as a ratifier of council decisions, giving to the pastor more than merely a vote. These corrections in Rademacher's course suggest that even he, the foremost thinker about councils in the 1970s and '80s, had not fully resolved the tension between the roles of council and pastor.[34] Perhaps his very gifts as a pastor, his confidence and strong personality, made him feel that any further clarification of the pastor's role was unnecessary. But the obscurity in which he left the relation between pastor and council anticipated weaknesses in the council movement.

Reaching Decisions

Rademacher reflected not only the convictions of the council movement, but also its changes of opinion. A good example is his attitude toward parliamentary procedure. He praised it in his early writings but later expressed doubts about it.[35] By the end of the 1970s many American Catholics were frustrated with council decision making. Tentative questions about the value of parliamentary procedure started to show up in council guidelines. Guidelines began to explore the value of reaching consensus, even citing St. Ignatius Loyola's treatment of spiritual discernment as a model for parish councils. This suggests that council members had begun to see the limits of parliamentary democracy as a means of conducting themselves.[36] They were searching for ways to make the experience of councils more productive and less rancorous. They tried to do so by improving the way councils made decisions.

Two approaches to council decision making offered hope. The first can be called the group dynamics approach. Many council writers believed that knowledge of the methods of group facilitation and leadership would lead to more satisfying and decorous meetings. If only council members understood the general principles of group behavior, and if only leaders were effective, council meetings would be more harmonious. Many writers in the 1970s educated council members about the predictable crises of council life and how to negotiate them.[37]

A second approach to council decision making underscored the council's spiritual goal and motive. If council members understood that they were participating in the mission of Christ, then they would (following this approach) bring a deeper sense of purpose to meetings. Redemptorist Father Earnest Larsen articulated this viewpoint in his 1977 book, *Spiritual Renewal of the American Parish*. There he criticized a preoccupation with material accomplishment and a corresponding lack of attention to Christian mission.[38] Larsen advocated a mission-centered spirituality that would draw councillors' attention to the specifically Christian reasons for parish existence. Councils are to promote the spiritual renewal of the parish, he reminded his readers, and demand a similarly spiritual mode of operation.

The work of Rademacher, the group dynamics approach, and the mission-centered spirituality of Larsen, have one point in common. They illustrate the thinking of Diocesan and Parish Council Personnel, the first national organization for councils. DPCP members were aware of the tension between councils and pastors, tensions arising whenever councils made decisions. The DPCP emphasized that councils were to make decisions, but also acknowledged that pastors could exercise a veto and were more than mere voting members. Recourse to the group dynamics approach, or to deeper spirituality, was insufficient to alleviate the tension. It persisted and was not resolved. The DPCP, in the interest of promoting lay participation and shared responsibility, was unwilling to overstate the obvious point that church law granted juridical power in parishes to pastors alone.

Conclusion: The Fulfillment of a Promise?

The growth of parish councils in the 1970s was spurred by an overwhelming confidence in them as the fulfillment of Vatican II. Praise from bishops in their pastoral letters, support from dioceses in the form of council guidelines, and the rise of national organizations dedicated to planning and councils were a powerful testimony. Councils sprang up in parishes of the 1970s because almost the entire U.S. church advocated them. Even at the end of the decade the overall mood about consultation was one of great expectations.[39]

But as councils flourished, tensions grew. Decision making in the council was the most difficult issue. Pastors and councillors stumbled over the legal status of councils, over parliamentary procedure, and over whether councils are entitled to implement the policies they made. The church presupposed a unity between pastor and people. That presupposition was hard to reconcile with the American experience of democracy, an experience indispensable for discussing the spirit of councils in the 1970s.

Efforts to lower the tension by means of better group dynamics and by a renewed emphasis on the spiritual mission of councils were not always efficacious. Bishop Francis Shea of Evansville found out about this the hard way. His diocesan pastoral council undertook a large number of tasks. Each task required a committee and the committee's own process of consultation. Shea discovered that the DPC had spawned such a bureaucracy, and that consultation had become so laborious, that the DPC was more trouble than it was worth. Needing a solution, he turned to the Vatican II Decree on the Pastoral Office of Bishops, which stated that DPCs are strongly commended but not mandatory. He dissolved the DPC and explained his decision in a pastoral letter.[40]

The publication in 1983 of the new Code of Canon Law affirmed the teachings of Vatican II about DPCs. The Code recommended (but did not mandate) them as strictly consultative bodies. The Code became a tool in the hands of those who wanted to reform parish councils by calling them "pastoral" and by limiting their scope. The controversy about the use of the Code is the topic of the next chapter.

Chapter Twelve

The New Code

The parish pastoral council entered the law of the church in 1983, with the publication of the Code of Canon Law. The Code included a single canon, number 536, about parish pastoral councils. The canon marked the entry of the term "parish pastoral council" into common parlance. Although official documents referred to the parish pastoral council as early as 1973, nevertheless the term was practically unknown prior to the Code.[1] That changed after 1983. There was, first of all, a publication of the Canadian Catholic Conference, *The Parish Pastoral Council*, in 1984.[2] Thereafter, commercial and diocesan publications (as well as videos) with *parish* pastoral council in the title began to appear more regularly. At least eleven separate titles were published between 1988 and 1993. So we can say that, with the 1983 publication of the Code, and not with the 1973 Circular Letter, the term "parish pastoral council" came into widespread use in the United States of America.

Since 1983, the term has acquired a distinctive popular meaning. That popular meaning will be the topic of the next chapter. But what about its official meaning? Does the term "parish pastoral council," as used in canon 536, simply reinforce the church's teaching on councils that began at Vatican II? Or does the canon about parish pastoral councils change the meaning of that teaching? These are the questions we hope to answer in this chapter.[3]

Were Early Councils Wrong?

Some early commentators on canon 536 did not notice any fundamental changes. In their opinion, the canon simply followed what the Vatican documents had already said regarding the parish pastoral council. To be sure, some were unenthusiastic about it.[4] Some authors wished that the Code had treated councils differently, or that it had ignored them entirely. But none of them noticed any fundamentally new ideas about councils in the 1983 Code.

A different view soon emerged. In the late 1980s and the early 1990s, some authors began to suggest that the intentions of Vatican II regarding parish councils had been widely misunderstood. Vatican II, they said, had not intended the kind of parish councils that appeared in the immediate postconciliar period, and parish council pioneers had misread the church's official documents. The pioneers' belief that the Vatican II Decree on the Apostolate of Lay People was a source for parish pastoral councils was mistaken. And matters relating to parish administration, these authors said, were outside of the scope of pastoral councils. They suggested that canon 536 intended to restore Vatican II's original intention. That intention had become obscured, and the new Code meant to clarify it.

This point of view strongly challenged the common opinion about parish councils. It hypothesized an enormous misunderstanding of Vatican II, a failure to correctly interpret its teachings, and a need to drastically curtail the scope of councils. Moreover, the viewpoint was not advanced by critics outside the mainstream of Catholic opinion, but by reputable churchmen. Before we weigh their claims, let us examine them in some detail.

The Thesis of Homogeneous Intent: A Clarification of Vatican II?

The authors of this view included a professor of canon law, a former *officialis* and seminary rector, a diocesan bishop, a Jesuit professor, and a diocesan vicar general. They were all scholars with pastoral experience as parish priests.[5] Their main argument was that the 1983 Code clarified Vatican II's intentions regarding parish councils.

The five authors advanced a questionable thesis that I call the thesis of constant homogeneous intent. The thesis holds (without persuasive evidence) that the bishops at Vatican II had intended two types of council, the apostolic and the pastoral, from the very start. The five agreed that councils of the "pastoral" type, as described in the Decree on the Pastoral Office of Bishops (no. 27), were the intention of Vatican II. The intention could have been expressed more clearly, they conceded, but it was discernible from the beginning. Moreover, the five agreed that the Decree on the Laity (no. 26) did not call for pastoral councils. Those who claimed it did were wrong. Finally, they agreed that canon 536 expressed the intention of Vatican II regarding councils. The teaching of the 1983 Code on parish pastoral councils is homogeneous with the teaching of Vatican II. To be sure, the five authors disagreed on some particulars, as we shall see. But they agreed that Bishops 27 is the proper source for pastoral councils, that Laity 26 is not, and that canon 536 expressed what Vatican II envisioned.

The church's constant homogeneous intent, so their thesis goes, was the proper yardstick by which to judge the development of actual parish councils. And by that yardstick, most parish councils did not measure up. The Catholic world had misinterpreted the direction indicated by the Second Vatican Council, according to this thesis, and had to be put back on course. A clear Vatican II intention, and a widespread misinterpretation of it, were the two components the five authors used to rewrite the history of parish councils. The arguments of the five have not proven persuasive, but they deserve attention.

Elements of their Thesis

The thesis of constant homogenous intent begins with the Second Vatican Council. The thesis maintains that Vatican II intended parish pastoral councils. These councils, intended from the 1960s, were explicitly authorized in 1973. Finally, the thesis holds that the 1983 Code merely reinforced the intention of Vatican II. Each of these three points is highly questionable. Let us examine each in turn, beginning with the original intention of Vatican II.

The authors we are considering held that Vatican II intended to recommend parish councils of the pastoral type. It wanted councils to advise the parish priest on pastoral matters. The clearest evidence presented by the authors lies in the Dogmatic Constitution on the Church, *Lumen Gentium*. Number 37 of *Lumen Gentium* speaks of the laity's right to advise pastors.

"This should be done," it states, "through the institutions established by the church for that purpose."[6] Parish councils, the thesis goes, were among these institutions. Their main purpose, the one sketched in *Lumen Gentium* 37, was to advise pastors, but not to coordinate apostolic works. Our authors argued that such consultation accords better with the "pastoral" councils envisioned in Bishops 27 than with the "coordinating" and "apostolic" councils of Laity 26. Hence pastoral-style parish councils were the fundamental intention, however indirectly expressed, of Vatican II. Some pastors and parishes, according to the thesis we are considering, were able to rightly discern the intention. They created pastoral-style councils on the parish level, in imitation of diocesan pastoral councils, even before church officials had officially called for them.[7] But these discerning few were the exception.

Another clue to the intention of Vatican II, according to this thesis, was the bishops' clear differentiation between types of councils. Laity 26 and Bishops 27 speak of "apostolic" councils and of "pastoral" councils respectively. The different language of the two documents was clearly noted by early commentators.[8] Laity 26 recommended that councils should be established to assist the church's apostolic work and possibly to coordinate lay associations at all levels, including the parish level. This was not (according to the thesis) a call for parish pastoral councils.[9] We are told that the Laity Decree intended something quite different. It recommended councils for individual apostolic activities, or councils to coordinate diocesan institutions, or councils to coordinate autonomous apostolates.[10] Not the coordination of the parish, but the coordination of autonomous groups (so the thesis goes), was the intention of Laity 26. In support of this view, Peter Kim even suggested that parishes ought to have three kinds of councils, apostolic, financial, and pastoral.[11] To be sure, it seems almost indisputable that the bishops of Vatican II distinguished between the councils recommended in Laity 26 and Bishops 27. The words "coordinating" and "pastoral" are not the same. But what did the difference mean?

Our authors suggest that the whole church should have seen the difference and understood it. They acknowledge, however, that the supposedly clear distinction was generally overlooked and that parish council pioneers misunderstood the intent of Vatican II. The pioneers did not clearly see that Vatican II had called for two types of councils, only one of which was a "pastoral" council. And in the absence of good models for a parish pastoral council, the pioneers turned to whatever was close at hand, however inappropriate. They imitated representative democratic government or the management style of corporate business, not the model of Vatican II.[12] The problem word was "coordination." Laity 26 had expressed a desire for apostolic councils to coordinate lay associations, and this was misinterpreted as a desire for parish councils to coordinate parish ministries.[13]

So, say these writers, in order to accomplish this coordination, many fledgling councils unrealistically expected pastors to surrender to them all responsibility. Henceforth, nothing would be done at the parish without consultation and the council's approval. "Parish councils as envisaged by the Second Vatican Council," wrote William Dalton, "did not materialize in the way intended by the Council Fathers."[14] He believed that the pioneers never even grasped the bishops' intention.

An Erroneous Interpretation?
Did the council pioneers fail to grasp the bishops' intention? If so, how did this happen? The simplest answer is that the Catholic world did not immediately fathom the intention of Vatican II. The authors we are considering believed that the intention for parish pastoral councils was discernible from 1965 on. And as if that intention were not clear enough, it was affirmed in 1973. That was the year in which the Congregation for the Clergy issued its "Circular Letter on 'Pastoral Councils.'" It stated that there is nothing to prevent the institution of such pastoral councils, the very councils that had been recommended in Bishops 27 at the diocesan level, for parishes as well.[15] This was not a departure from Vatican II, according to the thesis, but homogeneous with the intention expressed in Bishops 27 and *Lumen Gentium* 37. The Circular Letter merely expanded the earlier documents and confirmed the church's experience of councils.[16] The letter did not, however, mention the "apostolic" or "coordinating" councils of Laity 26. Since the Circular Letter was the first official document to explicitly mention parish pastoral councils, and was the only post-conciliar document to deal exclusively with pastoral councils, its silence regarding Laity 26 was deafening. For those who maintain the thesis of constant homogeneous intention, it meant that Laity 26 was never intended as a basis for parish pastoral councils.[17] The vast majority of pioneers, those who cited that text as a basis, had misread the intention of Vatican II.

The 1983 publication of the Code of Canon Law rectified that mistake, according to the thesis we are considering here. Canon 536 wrote into law what was implicit in the documents of Vatican II and was first explicitly permitted in the 1973 Circular Letter. By allowing parish pastoral councils, canon 536 followed *Lumen Gentium's* grant to the laity (in no. 37) of the right to freely express opinions and to unite lay energies to the work of pastors. By applying the word "pastoral" to parish councils, canon 536 endorsed the pastoral-style council recommended for dioceses in the Vatican II Bishops' Decree.[18] It ended a period of experimentation on parish councils by affirming one model above others, namely the pastoral council.[19] In this way (according to the thesis), canon 536 stopped the mistaken reliance upon Laity 26 as the basis of parish councils.

Canon 536, so goes the thesis, also corrected two widely held errors about the authority and scope of parish councils. The first was the misconception that parish councils have a deliberative (as distinct from a consultative) role. "The parish council," wrote Bishop Keating, "is not a legislative body."[20] Those who believed that parish councils had been empowered by Laity 26 to "coordinate" parishes must henceforth reconsider. The pastoral council is consultative only. Moreover, the Code provided for a second parish council, the parish finance council. This corrected the mistaken focus on temporalities of many parish councils, so the thesis goes, and limited the scope of the emerging parish pastoral council.[21] Canon 537, by requiring finance councils to "aid the pastor in the administration of parish goods," seemed to restrict the administration of temporalities to the finance council. So, says the thesis, no longer may pastoral councils concern themselves with the administration of the parish.[22] That had become the province of finance councils.

The thesis of constant homogeneous intent, in short, expressed a belief about the relation between Vatican II and the 1983 Code of Canon Law. It argued that canons 536-537 on parish pastoral and finance councils are homogeneous with the Vatican II intent regarding councils. That intention had been widely overlooked, say the proponents of the thesis, but the 1983 Code broadcast the Vatican's intention to the world.

What's Wrong with This Approach?
The trouble with the thesis of constant homogeneous intent is that it does not hold up to scrutiny. To be sure, the authors who hold it unanimously maintain that Bishops 27 is the proper source for pastoral councils, that Laity 26 is not, and that canon 536 expressed what Vatican II envisioned. Nevertheless they do not agree on particulars. The task of parish councils,

the number of councils recommended for each parish, the scope of councils—all of these are areas of disagreement. More to the point, there is ample evidence to suggest that the bishops of Vatican II were ambiguous about "pastoral" councils and about councils at the parish level. To claim that the Code of Canon Law is homogeneous with the intention of Vatican II regarding councils, and that such an intention has remained constant, is fraught with difficulties. It would be more accurate to say that the Code of Canon Law, in its treatment of parish councils, was selective in its use of Vatican II documents and innovated by extending the "pastoral" council idea to parishes.

It is important to see that the five interpreters do not agree about the task, number, and scope of councils. The task of councils is a particularly knotty problem. Many interpreters say that early parish councils were correct in finding their origin in the Vatican II Decree on the Laity. Parish councils, in their view, may coordinate lay apostolates.[23] (We will pursue this viewpoint in Chapter Seventeen.) Others say, however, that the Laity Decree is no basis for parish pastoral councils. Instead, their origin is the Vatican II Decree on Bishops. In the view of these interpreters, pastoral councils are not to coordinate apostolates. The task of councils is disputed. If the task of parish pastoral councils had been clearly articulated at Vatican II, no one would disagree about it.

The number of parish councils is a second area of disagreement. Some interpreters say that apostolic and pastoral councils form a unity. They believe that only one parish council (apart from the finance council) was intended, namely, the parish pastoral council. Others say that Vatican II intended two types of non-financial councils, the apostolic and the pastoral. So how many non-financial councils did Vatican II intend?

There is no agreement, moreover, about the scope of councils. Some interpreters say that Canon Law limits pastoral councils to pastoral matters. They interpret this to mean that financial and administrative matters are off limits. Others say that the coordination of apostolates is beyond the scope of pastoral councils. But no consensus exists. Still others say that Canon Law does not prohibit pastoral councils from taking up financial and administrative matters. From this point of view, nothing of practical parish consequence is off limits to the council.

Ambiguity about Councils at Vatican II
When experts cannot agree on the task, number, and scope of councils,

one can be sure that the bishops of Vatican II were not of one mind about councils either. The bishops did not, for example, use a consistent terminology about councils. They assigned both "pastoral" and "apostolic" functions to diocesan pastoral councils, at least in the preparatory documents leading to the Decree on Bishops.[24] The ambiguity about pastoral and apostolic functions persisted, even in the final draft of the Vatican II documents. For example, the Decree on the Church's Missionary Activity assigned an "apostolic" function (including the "coordination" of lay apostolates) to diocesan pastoral councils in mission lands.[25] This suggests that, even in the final draft of the Vatican II documents, the pastoral/apostolic distinction was not hard and fast. Moreover, at least one later Vatican document failed to maintain the pastoral/apostolic distinction.[26] In light of this evidence, it seems at least questionable whether the difference between pastoral and apostolic councils has been clear and distinct in the eyes of Vatican authorities.

To be honest, one need not conclude that apostolic and pastoral councils are mutually exclusive. There is nothing to prevent an "apostolic" council from doing what "pastoral" councils do (i.e., studying pastoral problems and proposing conclusions). Nor is there any obstacle to "pastoral" councils doing the work of "apostolic" councils (i.e., promoting the apostolate or coordinating lay initiatives). Apostolic councils can still be pastoral, pastoral councils can still be apostolic. Two apparently clear and distinct kinds of councils may more properly be described as two functions that a single council can perform. (Chapter Seventeen will treat this argument at greater length.)

But after 1983, the year of the publication of the Code of Canon Law, the term "parish pastoral council" came to eclipse the so-called parish ("apostolic") council. "Pastoral" councils were seen as a new kind of parish council. The "parish pastoral council" acquired a distinctive popular meaning. That meaning is the subject of the next chapter.

Chapter Thirteen

Popular Meanings of the Word "Pastoral"

On March 9, 1985, I flew to Baltimore for a convention entitled "The Catholic Church in the United States: Foundations and Futures." Jesuit Father Joseph Carroll, who was one of my mentors at the Diocese of Oakland, flew with me. Joe was Oakland's director of pastoral research, and he introduced me to many of the attendees, such as Bishop James W. Malone of Youngstown (who at that time was Chairman of the National Conference of Catholic Bishops) and Richard Schoenherr, the prophetic chronicler of the priest shortage. It was the first national Catholic convention I ever attended, a joint convention of the NPPC, the National Pastoral Planning Conference, and PADICON, the Parish and Diocesan Council Network.

On the opening day of the convention, I received an "orientation" to PADICON offered by Marliss Rogers and Father Mike Hammer of the Archdiocese of Milwaukee. Marliss Rogers was coordinator of the parish councils office and had begun collaborating with William Rademacher on *The New Practical Guide for Parish Councils*. Mike Hammer was a dynamic presenter and experienced pastor. The two explained how PADI-CON had developed in 1983 as a more formal "network" from the less formal group called "Diocesan Parish Council Personnel" (DPCP).[1]

Hammer and Rogers also described the common features of the parish "pastoral" council. Until the publication of the Code of Canon Law in 1983, few referred to parish councils as "pastoral." But in their 1985 orientation, Hammer and Rogers had already identified the parish pastoral council's key features. It was a planning body, first of all, a body concerned about the parish's future. Second, it treated "pastoral" matters, matters such as evangelization and mission, and avoided the temporal affairs of daily administration. It also had a prayerful style. Hammer and Rogers taught that one-third of a council meeting should be devoted to prayer. In their focus on planning, on pastoral matters, and on prayerful discernment, they sketched the popular hallmarks of the parish "pastoral" council.

But in the course of their orientation to PADICON, they also said two things that disconcerted me. One was that pastoral councils coordinate a system of standing committees. The other was that the finance council is a sub-committee of the pastoral council. These ideas were new to me. Although I was a novice to councils, I knew that the new Code of Canon Law said nothing about standing committees or about the finance council as a sub-committee. Were these proposals universally accepted, and how had they developed?

The Application of Official Teaching

Eventually I saw that the Milwaukee proposals were local applications of the church's official teaching. Council practitioners took the Vatican II recommendations and applied them as they saw fit. Although the church's official teaching does not specifically recommend that councils coordinate standing committees, it certainly allows them to. Local practices spread from one diocese to another and gradually became common. We saw in Chapter Four how frequently councils regard themselves as the coordinators of standing committees. Making the finance council a committee of the pastoral council is a similar innovation. No Vatican document recommends it, but some practitioners have found it useful.[2] In the absence of more specific and official Vatican guidelines, council practitioners innovated and experimented. They applied the church's teaching, and so "invented" the pastoral council. But in 1985 I did not yet realize how fluid the situation was, or appreciate the enormous variety of parish councils.

My lack of experience, however, was not the only reason why I felt disconcerted by the Milwaukee proposals. The new Code of Canon Law, with its innovative and selective application of the Vatican II texts, had changed the church's official teaching about councils. In 1985, few had yet felt the effect of the change. No one had yet fully weighed the Code's teaching about the consultative nature of councils, or the effect of its application to parishes of the "pastoral" terminology. No one knew why the 1983 Code had ignored references to parish councils contained in the Vatican II Decree on the Apostolate of Lay People. But everyone could see that there were differences between what the sources said and what councils in fact did. Those differences were disconcerting. It took me years to distinguish between the church's official teaching and the pastoral application of it.

In this chapter, we will survey the popular literature about the "pastoral" parish council in the 1980s and 1990s. We have already traced the church's official teaching about councils in the Code. We rejected the thesis that canons 511-514 and 536-7 simply re-stated the intention of Vatican II regarding councils. There is no evidence that Vatican II envisioned "pastoral" councils at the parish level. Despite this, the Code's emphasis on the "pastoral" (as distinct from the "apostolic") council precipitated a tremendous effort of reflection. The popular literature about councils in the past twenty years is in many ways an attempt to digest and apply the teachings of the Code.[3] When it recommended parish "pastoral" councils, it called into question many practices common to the early years of the council movement. Today's popular emphasis on planning, on prayerful discernment, and on pastoral matters, is an interpretive response to the Code.

The Council as Pastoral Planner

To begin, let us recall that there is no reference to pastoral planning in the documents of Vatican II or in Canon Law. Apart from a brief allusion to planning in the 1971 *Synod of Bishops* and the 1973 *Directory on Bishops*, the word does not appear in the church's official teaching about councils.[4] But planning can be used as a synonym for the threefold task of pastoral councils. Canon 511 states that councils are to investigate pastoral matters, to ponder them, and to make practical recommendations.

This was the language of the Vatican II Decree on the Pastoral Office of Bishops. Canon 511 endorsed this concept of the pastoral council, and so indirectly affirmed the pastoral planning role for councils.

As a role for parish councils, however, pastoral planning predated the 1983 Code. As early as the mid-1970s, council theorists and diocesan guidelines were promoting the idea that the parish council should plan by setting goals and objectives.[5] In 1981, Father William Harms, a leader in the National Pastoral Planning Conference, clearly proposed a comprehensive planning role for parish councils.[6] By the late 1980s, the idea that parish councils were pastoral planners was well accepted. But pastoral planning at that time remained one among many roles assigned to the council.[7] Very few leaders in the council movement argued that planning is the primary role of councils.[8]

The publication of the 1983 Code gave a new impetus to the parish council as pastoral planner. The Code's statement that the parish pastoral council has a "consultative only" vote was startlingly blunt. If the council is not a "deliberative" body, that is, if it cannot make legally binding decisions on behalf of the parish, what is its role? Some cynically said that councils exist to share responsibility, but not to share leadership. Through councils, Catholic pastors give an illusion of dialogue and collegiality, but no real power.[9] This, however, was a minority view. Although councils do not have the final say, they do influence pastors.

Indeed, many people in the council movement were satisfied with (or at least resigned themselves to) a distinction between decision making and choosing. Councils help decide, but pastors choose. Although the final choice lies with the pastor, the literature suggests that the work of a council lays an indispensable foundation for wise decisions.[10] Even councils with a "consultative only" vote can speak authoritatively in their planning role. Canonists agreed with the council practitioners. In 1993, John Renken made a detailed argument that pastoral planning was just what Canon 511 meant when it said that councils investigate, ponder, and recommend. Planning had begun to emerge as the primary role of councils.[11]

Practical experience, not Canon Law, proved to be the decisive factor in the acceptance of the pastoral planning role for councils. By the early 1980s, writers had begun to register complaints about coordinating councils. Bertram Griffin spoke of "the growing sense of boredom on parish super councils where the only action month after month is hear-

ing reports from committees, commissions, and organizations, each having a reserved seat on the board."[12] Dissatisfaction had set in. Doubtless
the Laity Decree said that apostolic councils may coordinate lay initiatives. But lay initiatives are not the same thing as standing ministerial
committees, and the Laity Decree did not say that councils are to coordinate ministries.

Many began to envision pastoral planning councils as an alternative
to coordinating councils. Planning councils would enable the parish to
envision its mission and goals, it was said, leaving the implementation
of those goals to ministry groups coordinated by the pastor and his
staff.[13] Writers started to imagine planning councils without the task
assigned to them since the late 1960s—the task of ensuring the participation of parishioners. One does not need a council to communicate
with and coordinate volunteers.[14] If the goal is active participation by
Catholics in parish life, many said that councils should only plan (and
not coordinate) such participation. Planning is an enormous task in
itself.

In short, the motive for the pastoral planning role was less official
teaching than practical experience. The documents of the church did not
state that councils should do pastoral planning. But when the official
teaching said that councils investigate, ponder, and recommend, people
associated those tasks with pastoral planning. Pastoral councils became
planning councils.

Decision Making and Discernment

A focus on pastoral planning, then, was the most important feature of
the post-1983 "pastoral" council. The word pastoral also came to imply
a deeper insight into decision making and discernment. Recall that, in
early parish councils, decisions were usually reached by parliamentary
procedure, and councillors were elected by a popular vote. In the 1980s,
both parliamentary procedure and popular elections were subjected to
ever-increasing criticism. As we saw in Chapter Four, several diocesan
guidelines for parish councils discourage the use of parliamentary procedure. It gave an unfair advantage to its adepts, they said, and treated a
decision as settled if a bare majority could be mustered to support it. The
popular election of council members, once a fundamental principle of
the council movement, also came under fire. Several diocesan guidelines,
we saw in Chapter Seven, encouraged a process of "discerning" council

members for membership. These new ways of decision making and member selection can also be called hallmarks of the pastoral council.

It is worth remembering that Vatican documents say almost nothing about how councils are to select members and make decisions. To be sure, Pope John Paul II's apostolic exhortation of 1987, *Christifideles laici,* endorsed pastoral councils as a resource for decision-makers.[15] But the Exhortation did not say when or how councils are to make decisions. Vatican documents have even less to say about the selection of council members. True, the 1973 Private Letter about pastoral councils from the Vatican Congregation for the Clergy made general comments on member selection. It emphasized that council members should be diverse and gifted.[16] But it said nothing in practical terms about how they are to be selected. In the almost complete absence of Vatican direction about this topic, U.S. practitioners have shown great inventiveness. The shift away from the general election of councillors to discernment processes has been connected, in the popular mind, with the rise of the pastoral council.

Three Related Topics
Council decision making and member selection are complicated issues. The literature since the publication of the new Code has indirectly linked them to three topics: leadership, the priest shortage, and collaborative ministry. Let us look at each of these, starting with the topic of leadership.

Leadership
Before the 1980s, councils were often viewed as elected parish leaders who, as councillors, exercised collective leadership. Partially as a result of the new Code's statement that councils possess a vote that is "consultative only," leadership by councils came into question. Are councils indeed leadership bodies, or does leadership belong to the pastor alone?

Some maintained that councils do have a position of leadership, a new kind of decentralized, cooperative leadership.[17] Others distinguished between the pastor's official role as presider at the council and the charismatic leadership exercised by the church's laity, leadership that does not depend on one's membership in a council (or, for that matter, whether or not one is ordained).[18] The relation between official and charismatic leadership continues to remain problematic. Councils undoubtedly "lead."[19] But they do so indirectly, by contributing to decisions that belong ultimately to the pastor.

The Priest Shortage

In the 1980s and 1990s, U.S. Catholics became aware that the number of priests was falling, that the average age of priests was climbing, and that the ordination of seminarians was not keeping up with resignations, retirements, and deaths.[20] At the same time, there was great rise in the number of lay church professionals. In a church of fewer ordained leaders, laypeople increasingly assumed positions formerly held by priests.[21]

This has complicated the question of decision making and membership on councils. Councils now have to relate, not just to authoritative pastors, but to authoritative lay staffs as well. There is evidence to suggest that the relation between volunteer councillors and professional lay staff members is not always smooth sailing.[22] Lay professionals find it no easier to take the advice of pastoral councils than do the clergy. They may feel trapped between the pastor who employs them and the council that advises him. Each of the three (pastor, lay professionals, and councillors) wants to know where in the group true wisdom resides.

Collaborative Ministry

Collaborative ministry is a third topic. It emerged as an answer to the question of how lay volunteer and professional ministers are to relate to priests. No longer, it was said, would ministers exercise leadership according to their hierarchical position. Henceforth, lay and ordained would collaborate, working together in an atmosphere of mutual respect. The literature on collaborative ministry describes how lay and ordained ministers work together, warns about the dangers, and offers advice drawn from theology, psychology, and the planning sciences.[23] A good example is Robert G. Duch's *Successful Parish Leadership*. Borrowing insights from Jungian psychology and organizational behavior, the book describes the wise leader—priest or lay—as one who correctly diagnoses the personality type of the follower and tailors a leadership style to his or her measure.[24] For the parish council, this kind of literature signaled a shift. Councils began to focus as much on *how* they worked as on *what* they did.

A greater attention to group process fueled the critique of parliamentary procedure. Many saw that a heavy-handed use of rules of order could destroy a group's cohesiveness. Some writers began to emphasize the importance of reaching consensus in the council. Consensus, they said, is a call to holiness. It does not polarize the council into winners and losers, but creates a sense of cohesiveness. Hence it is best suited to councils.[25] To be sure, not everyone saw the benefits of the consensus approach. Some preferred parliamentary procedure, and some warned that the search for consensus can be time-consuming and a hindrance to ministry.[26] The issues are undoubtedly complex. But diocesan guidelines and popular publications since the 1980s have generally extolled the search for consensus. It is a popular feature of the pastoral council.

The emphasis on group process has also changed council member selection. Popular elections have not always guaranteed a high quality of parish councillors. As an alternative, many writers have suggested the "discernment" of councillors as an alternative to popular elections. We shall examine discernment at greater length in Chapter Fifteen. For now it is enough to say that discernment means a thorough weighing of the potential council member's gifts for the ministry. Proponents of discernment view service on the council as a vocation that must be tested by the community and that requires formation. They advocate a series of parish meetings, to which interested parishioners are invited to learn about the council, discuss whether they would serve well on it, and receive training.[27]

To be sure, popular election remains the norm throughout the U.S., as we saw in Chapter Seven, and some parishes prefer to draw council members from parish standing committees.[28] But since the 1980s, guidelines and popular literature have increasingly recommended the "discernment" of council members. Discernment and consensus are identified, in the popular mind, with the pastoral council.

Pastoral as Spiritual

The pastoral council of this period was, first of all, a planning body. Second, it was an office whose group process received great attention. But its most distinctive feature, in the popular imagination, was its spirituality. For many, pastoral meant spiritual (in contrast to temporal). This direction could be seen as early as 1982 in Bernadette Gasslein's *Parish Council: New Parish Ministries*, a Canadian book that was later reprinted in the U.S. Published before the revision of the Code of Canon Law, the book did not use the expression "pastoral council." But its emphasis on the "ministry-type Parish Council" foreshadowed the pastoral council. Gasslein's ministry-type council focused on "nourishing and building up the Christian community." It sought to identify priorities that are "pastoral" or "spiritual" and then to involve people in ministry by "discerning" their gifts and inviting them to serve. To be sure, this kind of council had many of the features of older councils. Its members were elected, for example, and Gasslein envisioned a system of permanent committees. But the ministry-type council did not focus on political representation, on the coordination of committees, or on greater ministerial efficiency. It was rather a council in which members would "help one another discuss individual and common visions, and to translate them into action."[29] The terms ministry, community, spirituality, discernment, and vision—all of these came to be associated in the popular mind with the "pastoral" council.

Once again, we should recall that in canon law the word "pastoral" does not mean "spiritual" as opposed to "temporal." Instead, the adjective pastoral describes all those things pertaining to the pastor and his concerns. The canonist Roch Pagé expressed it this way: "Everything depends on the pastor" in the realm of pastoral councils, including their "establishment, direction, resources, effectiveness and dynamism."[30] A pastoral council is not a more spiritual council, in terms of canon law, but a council consulted by the pastor in order to serve his people better. Its scope is not limited to one or another aspect of the church's apostolate or spirituality. Indeed, canon law implied that councils may advise the pastor on any practical aspect of parish life to which he might draw its attention.

In the popular mind, however, pastoral councils were concerned about ministry and spirituality. The very titles of books from this period indicate what "pastoral" was coming to mean. Councils were to help create "a vision for parish life, mission, and ministry," to be places for "implementing spirituality," and to become "communities of spiritual leaders."[31] Many called for a more spiritual content in council meetings. If councils are to plan for the parish, said these authors, then they should get in touch with the spiritual dimensions of Christian community. How were they to do this? The literature of the period recommended that councils study the Scriptures, undertake pastoral planning as a kind of ministry, and clarify the mission of the parish.[32] This would make them more pastoral.

The form of meetings changed as well as the content. Judging from the literature of the period, people began to see the far-reaching effect of participation on a council. Such participation means more than a perfunctory commitment to a narrow aspect of the church as an institution. Rather, it embraces the very lives of participants. Writers began to advocate group processes designed to engage councillors at a personal level: by telling auto-biographical stories about faith, by theological reflection, by prayerful discernment, and by efforts to imagine the parish's future. People responded to the invitations of those who, like Mike Hammer and Marliss Rogers, wanted councils to spend one-third of their time in prayer. They began to explore the many various forms of prayer available to councils.[33] To be sure, some were careful to point out that the pastoral council differs from a prayer group or small Christian community.[34] Councils must do more than pray. But writers who promoted a prayerful style in council meetings were registering changes in councils and expanding the meaning of the word pastoral.

It is easy to satirize the spiritual rhetoric of pastoral councils in the 1980s and 1990s. Their focus on prayer almost overshadowed their specific task, their emphasis on group process tended to obscure their product (i.e., sound advice), and their rhetoric of visioning seemed to render planning less precise. But a look at the motive for these changes makes satire unnecessary. Council writers of this period had begun to see that participation on a council touched the deepest chords of the Christian life. Pastoral matters included every theme from parish finances to the affective life, faith, and ecclesiology of parishioners. For that reason, writers recommended that council discussions sound a more profound note in a more refined style. They used the word pastoral to designate that style.

The Marriage of Planning and Councils
The destiny of the professional planning and council organizations, NPPC and PADICON, illustrates the popular transformation of the word pastoral. The two merged in 1989 to become a new organization. It was a merger not just of people but of values. The NPPC was a professional organization originally composed of experienced researchers and pastoral planners, many of whom had academic credentials in planning and related fields. PADICON was a network of council advocates with little formal training but a wide range of expertise and experience. Many of them (at least at first) did not see themselves as professionals. Although the two organizations held joint conventions from 1985-89, and although members of each organization frequently belonged to the other, nevertheless there was always tension between them.

A "white paper" written after an October 1, 1986 meeting of the steering committees of the two organizations described the tension. The white paper described the two groups as having different self-images—professional planners and practical council advocates. The planners emphasized the tasks involved in planning. The council advocates emphasized the importance of group process and the need to develop grassroots leaders for sharing responsibility. The planners saw consultation via councils as one aspect of planning. The council advocates regarded planning as one aspect of the council task. One planner recalled that the tension between the two was so great that, after the decision was made in 1984 to jointly sponsor the Baltimore convention, an NPPC steering committee member resigned. Despite the tension, however, the October 1 meeting ended with a commitment to further discussions about the possibility of merger.[35]

The fashion of the times called for a thorough discernment of major decisions. Accordingly the NPPC and PADICON discussions were thorough and well-planned (and for some, exhausting). The organizations discussed the possibility at their 1987 joint convention and, in 1988, approved a process for reaching a decision. The process proved successful at the 1989 convention in Los Angeles, where on March 8 the members voted for the merger of the two organizations. The new organization was eventually called the Conference for Pastoral Planning and Council Development (CPPCD). Arthur X. Deegan, II, who was chairman of the NPPC in 1989, was elected the first chairman of the CPPCD.[36] He recalled that "There was an air of absolute relief that a final vote had been taken, with next to no opposition, although there were a few doubting Thomases."[37] Even the doubting Thomases, or at least most of them, remained with the new organization.

After his term as first CPPCD chairman expired, Deegan was chosen to be its executive director, the first and only salaried position in the CPPCD, NPPC, or PADICON. He served in that capacity from 1992 to 1997. During his tenure, the CPPCD gained a firm financial basis, published two books, and established awards to honor notable people in the fields of planning and councils. Deegan oversaw what he called the "wedding" of NPPC and PADICON with a minimum of tears and to great applause.[38]

For our history of parish pastoral councils in the U.S., the creation of the CPPCD marked a watershed in the popular meaning of "pastoral." It shows how the pastoral council has come to mean a planning council focused on the church's mission. Doubtless the word pastoral also refers to a style of decision making and to spirituality. But the planning function is paramount. Before the merger of NPPC and PADICON, some viewed pastoral planning as a broad endeavor within which councils played a minor role. Others regarded the work of councils as leadership development, with some attention to pastoral planning. But after the merger, the pastoral planning role of councils emerged with ever greater clarity. It was practical and realistic, and it harmonized with the church's official teaching.

To be sure, some of the doubting Thomases at the NPPC/PADICON wedding rightly believed that parish councils cannot possibly do the work of professional planners. One of the doubters was the NPPC veteran Robert G. Howes. The result of the merger, he wrote, "would be an emulsion in which the form and maturation of at least NPPC would be obscured and necessarily watered down."[39] Some things, Howes believed, should not be mixed. But even a doubting Thomas could see the logic of the planning role for councils. Howes devoted the 1990s to writing books about them and parish planning. Before 1980, councils saw planning as one among their many tasks. By the end of the 1990s, it was their main task.

If planning is the main task of parish pastoral councils, then other tasks are subordinate to it. How do the other tasks commonly assigned to the pastoral council, such as the coordination of parish standing committees, fit into the planning paradigm? And if planning is the council's main task, how do we attract council members who are good at it? These are among the questions we will treat in this book's final part, "Building an Effective Council."

Part 3

Building an Effective Council: *Representation, Purpose, Consultation*

The history in Part II of this book began by describing council pioneers from the period 1967-68. These pioneers established the first councils, based on slim hints from paragraph 26 of the Vatican II Decree on the Apostolate of Lay People. The councils rapidly spread throughout the United States. The 1983 publication of the Code of Canon Law put the achievement of the pioneers into question. Canons 511-514 and 536-537 do not refer to the Laity Decree. They quote paragraph 27 of Vatican II's Decree on the Pastoral Office of Bishops. It had recommended diocesan "pastoral" councils, and the new Code applied the "pastoral" council terminology to parish councils. Many critics argued that the new parish pastoral councils spelt the end of the old parish councils.

Part III of this book offers a theory of councils refuting that argument. References to councils in the new Code do not supersede Vatican II, but have to be interpreted in its light. In particular, the Code's "pastoral" council terminology cannot be taken to negate the provisions of Laity 26. Parish pastoral councils should continue to assist the church's apostolic work and may coordinate various lay initiatives. Nor does the Code's mandate of parish finance councils limit the scope of pastoral councils as described in Bishops 27. The main task of such councils is to examine and consider all that relates to pastoral work—even matters of parish administration. The documents of Vatican II are superior to the Code, not vice versa.

The following theory of councils articulates a trio of themes: representation, purpose, and consultation. Representation is the topic of Chapters 14-16. The church teaches that pastoral councils should be representative, but it does not say exactly how. The popular (but uninformed) election of councillors can lead to bad choices. The selection of councillors by an informed (but narrow) group denies the greater parish any say in their appointment. Chapter Fifteen sheds light on this situation by defining ecclesial representation. The church does not intend pastoral councils to represent primarily a parish's demographic profile, but rather to make present the practical wisdom of the people of God. Chapter Sixteen advocates the popular and discerning participation of the greater parish in the selection of councillors.

The purpose of pastoral councils is our theory's second theme. Chapter Seventeen rehabilitates the concept of coordination of lay initiatives by the pastoral council. Coordination was the term used in Laity 26 to describe a possible activity of parish apostolic councils. Far from being superseded by the language of the new Code, coordination remains a possibility, but it must be rightly understood. Coordination does not mean that the council directs lay initiatives or parish committees as would an executive body. Rather, it offers them a service, working to promote their success and good order as defined by their proper leaders, putting their concerns (rather than its own desires) first. The pastoral council's main purpose, however, is not coordination. Chapter Eighteen contends that its main purpose is the threefold task of studying, reflecting on, and concluding about pastoral matters. The U.S. church calls this pastoral planning. Coordination is a subordinate function.

The final theme in our theory of councils is consultation. This fundamental topic gets to the heart of the church's vision for councils. If the church meant—with its statement that councils have a "consultative only" vote—that pastors should distance themselves from parish opinion, consultation would have no future. Chapter Nineteen insists upon a different meaning. It proposes shared responsibility as the basic premise of ecclesial consultation. All Catholics share responsibility for the parish in the manner proper to each, and pastoral planning is the proper function of councillors. Those who prevent the council from accomplishing its proper function, laypeople as well as pastors, deserve to be called dysfunctional. Pastors consult their people because they seek practical wisdom. Parishioners join councils in order to put their gifts at the service of the parish. The one motive of pastors and people, according to Chapter Twenty, resides in the gospel. In their search for practical wisdom, they help make the gospel credible.

Chapter Fourteen

Problems with Selecting Councillors

I once served on a pastoral council with rotating membership. The year after I was elected, two members completed their term of office. It was time to conduct another election. We council members took responsibility for the elections and followed our usual practice. Parishioners were invited to submit nominations. The council chairwoman asked nominees if they were willing to stand for elections and, if so, to submit a description of their qualifications to the parish community. We posted these descriptions in the vestibule. The ushers distributed ballots at the start of each Mass and collected them at the preparation of the gifts. That was our standard operating procedure.

One of the newly elected council members, however, proved to be a problem. Theresa (not her real name) was a single mother. She had two constant preoccupations, which she expressed before, during, and after each council meeting. One topic was the difficulty she faced as a single mother, and how much the parish ought to do for women like her. The second topic was how little the parish actually did. Whatever subject the council discussed, Theresa would return to her favorite topics. We grew to expect them. Whenever she began to ride her hobbyhorse, we other councillors would roll our eyes.

The pastor liked her no better than we did. When she tried to refocus our meeting on her agenda, he would ask her to return to the subject at hand. When she insisted upon her favorite themes, he would remind her of the broader parish picture. When she continued unabashed, he would try to rein her in. Then she would berate him and the rest of us for our callous insensitivity. One evening she was particularly vociferous. The pastor tried to steer her back to the council's agenda, but she resisted his every suggestion. Finally, she lost her temper.

"You just don't like me, do you?" she said, glaring at the rest of us. "This parish talks the talk about charity but won't walk the walk." Then she turned to the pastor and threw down the gauntlet. "What is it you don't like about me?" she asked. "Is it because I'm a single mother?" The pastor looked at her coolly, but we could tell he had passed the point of no return. "I'll tell you what I don't like about you, Theresa," he said. "You're loud, you're boring, and you're a whiner—three strikes and you're out!" There was a moment of silence. Then Theresa got up and left the room, slamming the door. She never attended another council meeting.

The story of Theresa reveals a problem with selecting council members by popular ballot. Most of us parishioners who elected Theresa did not know her well. We had not worked with her in a committee or ministry. We did not really understand her or the council ministry. A popular election can create enormous problems if parishioners are unfamiliar with the work of the council or the gifts of nominees. This chapter will offer a critique of popular elections. But one alternative to the popular ballot, namely, a private selection by the pastor of his councillors, is no better. This chapter will also illustrate the problems that arise when a pastor hand-picks his council. It will show that the absence of popular participation can profoundly disturb a parish. Neither a popular ballot, plain and simple, nor a private selection, will suffice for the selection of pastoral council members.

The Problem with Theresa

We parishioners had elected Theresa in the usual way. She had been nominated. She had accepted her nomination. She had submitted a statement about herself. We cast our ballots for her. Theresa joined the council via procedures common to thousands of parishes, as we saw in Chapter Seven. Theresa was a baptized Catholic, confirmed, and a regular communicant. In that sense, she met the spiritual and religious criteria stated in most pastoral council guidelines throughout the U.S. And Theresa was fairly knowledgeable about the parish. She was active in the social justice ministry. Her children were enrolled in the parochial school. She was a fixture of parish life.

But Theresa was ineffective as a council member. Her preoccupation with being a single parent left her unable to consider many parish matters. Her responsibilities left her without leisure to give any other subject its due. Furthermore, she irritated the pastor and the other council members. Theresa was incapable of listening to and absorbing their opinions. She could not think a matter through with a group, keeping track of other viewpoints and adding her own. In short, she could not join with others in constructing a common project. When the group reached a conclusion, she was hurt if the conclusion was not her own. She could not integrate herself into the group.

The Problem of Representation

The case of Theresa is not typical. But it illustrates a problem with the way many parishes elect councillors. The typical process emphasizes "representation" in a very limited sense of the word. It suggests that we want councillors to represent us, our beliefs, our culture, and our neighborhoods. They represent us, we tend to think, in the same way that our elected political leaders represent us. They stand in our place and express our views. We imagine them doing what members of Congress or of the Senate do. We imagine them giving speeches, taking sides, and advocating our cause, the cause of those who elected them.

The church, however, differs in significant ways from the world of politics. To be sure, the church recommends that pastoral council members be representative. They are representative, the church states, but not in a juridical sense.[1] Pastoral council members do not legislate. They do not make laws for the parish or the diocese. They cannot compel the pastor or the people to follow their recommendations.

Pastoral council members are representatives in a limited sense. They make present, after a fashion, the wisdom of the People of God. That is the clear import of Canon 512 (about diocesan pastoral council members). It states that council members "are to be so selected that the entire portion of the people of God which constitutes the diocese is truly reflected."[2] Hence the church's paradigm of representation is not democratic in the American political sense. It does not regard councillors as legislators or as advocates of the popular will.

Sovereignty of the People?

The reason for this is clear. The church's legislation and other official documents do not presume the sovereignty of the people. They do not envision a heterogeneous society in which decisions are made on the basis of majority rule. Instead, they presume unity in Christ. A pastor does not consult his people because he needs to be checked and balanced. He consults because he wants to know his people and serve them better. The good pastor is like Socrates, who (if we believe Plato's *Republic*) was no fan of raw democracy. The good pastor knows that rule by the majority can be despotic, unfair, and even cruel. The meaning of representation, as we understand it in the United States, is not wholly compatible with the church's vision.

The story of Theresa and the teachings of the church may lead us to the conclusion that we should not ask parishioners to elect councillors. Problem councillors seem to suggest that parishioners often know little about what it takes to be a good councillor and less about the people nominated for council membership. One might infer that popular participation in the selection of councillors is unnecessary. Then one could take a further step and say that only knowledgeable officials should be involved in the selection of council members. This is sometimes the case with diocesan pastoral councils,[3] and is not unknown among parish pastoral councils. But I disagree with those who argue against popular participation. Excluding popular participation has its own problems. The following story (fictionalized but based on a real example) illustrates them.

Santa María's Appointed Council

The Church of Santa María is a suburban parish less than fifteen years old. Located in an Arizona city where developers have built new housing tracts, the church complements the city's original parish. The original parish is traditional in its orientation and serves the city's older inhabitants, many of whom are Mexican-Americans. Santa María Church serves the residents in the recently developed, northern part of the city. To be sure, the northern part has some older residents. There are two large trailer-park communities, a retirement village, and a Mexican-American district. But the new tract homes purchased by young families are the center of vitality. They are the source of the parish's growth. The founding pastor, Father Padraig Twomey, is an industrious man with an attractive, engaging personality. He has a background in education and a flare for the dramatic. He used to host a local Catholic television program and understands the value of symbols.

The Early Years

When Santa María was established, its only asset was a wooded lot owned by the diocese. Father Twomey rented an office and a space for worship in a warehouse area on the north side of town. With the cooperation of the pastor of the original parish, he explained that Santa María would serve the city's northern inhabitants. His aim was first to develop a community and eventually to build a church. He worked hard, and his efforts were very successful. He hired a director of religious education and established a religious education program in which small groups of children met in various homes. This effort was very popular with parents and stood in marked contrast to the traditional classroom catechesis of the original parish. Father Twomey also hired a director of liturgy. The liturgy director was a clever and ambitious man. He wanted to distinguish the Santa María liturgy from that of the city's older parish, with its traditional devotions and Spanish-language Masses. He strove for large-scale participation in the liturgy, including greeters, ushers, boy and girl altar servers, trained lectors, professional cantors, choirs, numerous eucharistic ministers providing Communion under both species, and free coffee and donuts after Mass. Father Twomey came to rely on these two directors. They helped him realize his dreams for the parish.

Within a few years, Santa María Church was flourishing. On the first Sunday of Advent hundreds of parishioners would walk from the city's original parish to what Father Twomey called the "sacred space," that is, the wooded lot where the new church was to be built. There they decorated the "Jesse Tree," a stately pine, with ornaments and symbols of the season. The parish also was known for its "living Stations of the Cross" in Lent. Some 300 children were enrolled in home centers for catechesis, and the warehouse was overflowing with people during Sunday Mass. Father Twomey established a fund-raising committee and hired an architectural firm. The committee, chaired by the pastor, won many pledges from parishioners. The architects developed an attractive scheme for a new church and parish office. At Father Twomey's direction, they presented plans to parishioners after Mass and invited them to state what they most wanted in the new buildings. Father Twomey also chaired a building committee that reviewed parishioner suggestions. He closely supervised every aspect of fund-raising and design. After seven years, half of the construction money had been raised. The diocese extended a loan for the other half. Site preparation began, and the new church opened its doors in the summer of the parish's eighth year.

Hand-Picked Councillors

When the parish began, Father Twomey was reluctant to establish a pastoral council. He knew parishes in which the council bullied the pastor, virtually forcing him to embark on projects in which the pastor had neither confidence nor success. But Father Twomey appreciated the symbolic value of a pastoral council. It was a sign to parishioners of shared responsibility. So when Father Twomey decided to establish a pastoral council, he tried to avoid the problems that other pastors encountered with their councils by personally selecting the members himself. This was not the norm for parish pastoral councils in his diocese, but there was a precedent. The bishop appointed all the members of the diocesan pastoral council, based on the recommendations of a nominating committee. Father Twomey decided to follow the bishop's example.

With his director of religious education and the liturgy director, he drew up a list of potential councillors. They were influential parishioners (the mayor, the editor of the local newspaper, and generous contributors to the building fund). Father Twomey personally telephoned each of them, inviting them to be a member of his pastoral council. He told them that the council would meet every other month. The council would advise him, he said, but apart from this he added little about the actual work of the council. The parishioners felt honored, and most of them accepted his invitation.

Father Twomey personally set the agenda for each 90-minute council meeting. There he would usually review the progress of the parish's efforts to pay off the diocesan loan, the growth of the religious education program, and upcoming liturgical celebrations. He would note the comments of the council members, taking their advice in some cases, and explaining his reservations when he disagreed. None of the councillors had had experience in other parish pastoral councils. They were satisfied with their role at Santa María Church.

Cracks in the Façade

The pastoral council was not widely publicized. If other parishioners knew of it, they generally applauded it. They saw it as a sign of parish participation and shared responsibility. But eventually cracks appeared in the smooth façade of the Santa María Council.

One crack was a result of Father Twomey's efforts to create a parish mission statement. He had heard about another parish's success with a Sunday afternoon assembly to discuss the parish's mission. He decided to use a similar process. With the help of the religious education director, he created a parish committee to run the assembly, provide refreshments, and keep track of parishioner discussions. There was, however, one important difference between the Santa María assembly and that of the other parish. In the other parish, the pastoral council had run the assembly. It also dedicated three subsequent meetings to a discussion of the assembly's findings. At Santa María, the parish committee ran the assembly. The council had almost nothing to do with it. After the assembly was over, Father Twomey reviewed the comments of parishioners and drafted a parish mission statement himself. Two months later, he presented the draft to the pastoral council. The council made some minor adjustments and affirmed what Father Twomey had written. This statement was then publicized in the parish bulletin.

The publication of the parish mission statement generated criticism. Some parishioners felt that the mission statement was too bland. It spoke about discipleship in such general terms that it could have been the mission statement of any church in the diocese. The critics were also unhappy that the statement said nothing about the parish's mission to its older inhabitants, many of whom were widows living in trailer parks and in the retirement village. Nor did it say anything about parish responsibility to the Mexican-American residents, many of whom spoke Spanish as their first language. The critics wanted to know why the pastoral council had failed to acknowledge these important aspects of parish life.

A second and wider crack soon appeared. One of the ushers who helped count the weekly collection discovered irregularities in the liturgy budget. He mentioned it to Father Twomey. The pastor discovered that the liturgy director was taking parish money for his own private use. Wishing to avoid further scandal, Father Twomey forced the director to resign, but did not pursue legal action against him. He feared the public embarrassment and its impact on efforts to retire the parish debt. But some people knew of the director's misdeeds. The word spread. Parishioners wanted to know the extent of the fraud. They approached the pastoral council, asking for a full accounting. The council members, however, took Father Twomey's point of view. They chose not to pursue the matter. They did not want to publicly acknowledge the scandal. This hurt the council's credibility. Many people felt that the councillors confused loyalty to the pastor with loyalty to the parish.

The scandal about the liturgy director was never publicly acknowledged. Some parishioners felt that this was a sign of poor stewardship. As a consequence, they stopped contributing, and some never paid their pledged contributions. This slowed the retirement of the parish debt. More important, it caused a split in the parish. Some parishioners remained loyal to the pastor, honoring his desire to avoid scandal. Others wanted more financial accountability and more shared decision making (for example, about the parish mission statement). They wanted the pastoral council to be a forum for their concerns and to take a more active role in the parish. They were disappointed when it did not. For them, the council had ceased to be a symbol of shared responsibility, and many lost faith in the pastor.

Unrepresentative Councils

The separate stories of Theresa and of Santa María Church illustrate the problem of representation. The church envisions pastoral councils that are representative, but not in a juridical sense. They are representative in that they make present the wisdom of the people of God.

Theresa

Theresa, the ineffective councillor, hindered the effort to make parish wisdom present. She was not able to pay careful attention to other council members, to give full consideration to their thoughts, or to integrate them into a whole. Her own concerns were a constant distraction. She had little free time, and she viewed everything in terms of her own preoccupation with her children. When Theresa criticized those who did not see things her way, she irritated the council and prevented it from doing its work.

Yet Theresa was elected to the council in the way that most parishes in the United States select members. She accepted nomination and, on the strength of the brief statement she wrote for the vestibule, she was elected. Her story shows what happens when there is not enough information for parishioners to make a good decision. Most parishioners do not know what takes place in a pastoral council meeting. Most lack an understanding of the qualities needed to be a good councillor. When parishioners do not know the candidates for whom they are voting and what qualities are needed, it is easy to elect ineffective councillors. They are ineffective because they cannot represent or make present the wisdom of the parish.

Santa María

The story of Theresa may suggest that popular participation in the selection of council members is not a good idea, but the story of Santa María illustrates why such participation is important. Father Padraig Twomey did not ask his parishioners to help him select councillors. He chose them himself, relying on his two directors to make nominations. The two directors shared Father Twomey's implicit point of view, namely, that the pastoral council has mainly a symbolic function. At Santa María it symbolized that parishioners share responsibility in parish decision making, but their share was minuscule. The parishioners had no responsibility for selecting councillors, and the councillors, once selected, were content with their largely passive role.

The lack of popular participation in selecting the Santa María council led to problems. Their causes and effects were numerous. Father Twomey's failure to adequately prepare his councillors for their role, and his lack of a clear vision for the council (apart from its symbolism), led to a conflict of expectations. He expected the council to be content with meeting every two months, and he never suggested that the council could take a more proactive role. This satisfied his councillors, whose expectations were no different from Father Twomey's own. But it did not satisfy the parishioners. Many expected the council to take the initiative in developing a mission statement, and they expected it to investigate the resignation of the liturgy director. These parishioners were frustrated with the council's refusal to do so.

Opposite Conclusions?

In short, the stories of Theresa and of Santa María Church seem to suggest opposite conclusions. An ineffective member like Theresa may suggest that we avoid popular participation in the selection of councillors. Because popular participation can lead to poor choices, it may seem reasonable to conclude that only knowledgeable people, such as the pastor, should select councillors. But the selection of councillors by the pastor alone is also problematic. He may not get wise counsel but only a reflection of his own prejudices. A select group like the Santa María council does not inspire confidence in the parishioners and may not understand its role. Without popular participation in the selection of councillors, there is little opportunity to clarify parish expectations and build trust in the council.

The stories of Theresa and of Santa María Church illustrate the complexity of council membership. The selection of wise councillors hinges on the question of representation. If councillors are to represent the parish, then parishioners must know them. If they are to represent the wisdom of the parish, then they must know what this wisdom is. The ecclesial meaning of representation is the topic of the next chapter.

Chapter Fifteen

Ecclesial Representation

As we saw in the previous chapter, popular participation in the selection of pastoral council members may lead to poor choices. Theresa, the ineffective councillor, was elected in an open parish ballot, but could not contribute much to the council. The parishioners who chose her were uninformed about its ministry. They could not rightly discriminate between her and more gifted potential councillors.

The private selection of council members by the pastor, however, is not preferable to an open parish ballot. That was the lesson of Santa María Church. The pastor chose influential parishioners without preparing them or the parish for their ministry.

These stories present us with seeming contradictions. They suggest irreconcilable and unattractive opposites. Either we select pastoral council members by a general ballot (and risk the choice of poor councillors), or the pastor and his closest associates select members privately (leaving both members and parishioners uninformed and uncommitted). That is one apparent contradiction. Another contradiction concerns the pastor. It seems that either the pastor should choose councillors himself (so he can have confidence in them) or that parishioners should choose them (so that councillors might have a constituency). The contradictions involve discrimination and trust. How are parishes to resolve them so as to choose a wise council in whom the pastor has faith? In this chapter, we will not treat the practical question of how to select councillors. That is the topic of the next chapter. This chapter focuses rather on the nature of representation.

In order to define this word we will first review the church's teaching and empirical findings about representation. They say that the pastoral council is to be representative, but do not explain this with sufficient clarity. The guidelines are vague for a good reason. The task of councils depends on the knowledge of contingent matters. We will examine this knowledge with concepts drawn from philosophy, second of all, and show that the concepts express the church's aims. They enable us to speak of an "ecclesial meaning of representation." The third section amplifies this ecclesial meaning and connects it to theology. We will see that popular participation in the selection of councillors is not in contradiction with wise discrimination. Nor is the pastor's trust in the council incompatible with the council's ability to represent the parish.

Official Teaching about Representation
The official teaching of the church about representation is not extensive, but it sheds light on the qualities of good councillors. When we speak of official teaching, we refer to two distinct sources. One source is Vatican documents. At the highest level of authority, these documents include the teachings of the Second Vatican Council and other episcopal directives, especially the treatment of diocesan pastoral councils in the Decree on the Pastoral Office of Bishops. At the next level, there are canons pertaining to pastoral councils in the Code of Canon Law. And finally there is the 1973 Circular Letter of the Vatican Congregation for the Clergy on pastoral councils. These documents say very little about representation, but they articulate general principles and enjoy worldwide authority.

Guidelines for pastoral councils published by individual dioceses constitute a second source of official teaching about representation in the pastoral council. These guidelines treat the qualities of councillors in much greater detail than do the Vatican documents. But their authority is limited to the diocese from which they come. They are the official teaching of a bishop, but they pertain only to his diocese. In what follows, I will sketch Vatican teaching in general terms[1] and then summarize the guidelines.

Vatican Documents

The first of the Vatican documents pertaining to pastoral councillors is the Vatican II Decree on Bishops. Paragraph no. 27 states that diocesan pastoral councils should include priests, religious, and laity.[2] This reinforces the church's later teaching that pastoral councils should make the wisdom of the entire people of God present. This highlights the representative nature of councils, but does not define it.

More descriptive of councillors than the documents of Vatican II is the 1983 Code of Canon Law. It identifies certain criteria for diocesan pastoral council membership. Unfortunately, canon 536 (the only canon pertaining to parish pastoral councils) says nothing about the qualities of councillors. The treatment of diocesan pastoral council members is more thorough. They are to be in full communion with the church, according to canon 512, and "of proven faith, good morals, and outstanding prudence." Canon 512 also sheds particular light on the criterion of representation. The pastoral council is to "reflect" the entire people of God. The canon states that council members:

> are to be so selected that the entire portion of the people of God which constitutes the diocese is truly reflected, with due regard for the diverse regions, social conditions and professions of the diocese as well as the role which they have in the apostolate, either as individuals or in conjunction with others. (Canon 512, §2)

Canon 512 suggests one reason why popular participation in the selection of pastoral council members is important. Popular participation may help the pastoral council "reflect" the people of God. To be sure, it cannot guarantee it. The example of Theresa proves that. But popular participation prevents the selection of councillors who are only the pastor's friends and confidants.

The most important Vatican document about the qualities of council members is the Circular Letter, the letter that first applied the "pastoral" council idea to parishes.[3] Published in 1973, the Circular Letter anticipated the 1983 teaching of Canon 512 about the representative nature of the pastoral council.[4] It said that the council should "present a witness or sign" of the people of God "in such a way the diocese is truly represented." The letter amplified the concept of representation. It stated that pastoral council members should include people who "expound various requirements and experiences," "who possess noteworthy prestige and prudence," and it added that "most" members should belong to the laity. In the Circular Letter, representation means that pastoral council members generally should be gifted laypeople of diverse but suitable backgrounds.

Vatican documents insist that councillors are non-juridical representatives. But the documents are somewhat abstract. They do not say how to identify these gifted people, nor how they manifest their gifts. They do not answer our question about representation. Diocesan guidelines have far more to say about that subject.

Diocesan Guidelines

Another source of official teaching is the guidelines for pastoral councils published by U.S. dioceses. In Chapter Seven we saw that most guidelines want representative councillors. They link the concept of representation with popular elections. The guidelines say that the purpose of elections is to make the pastoral council representative, diverse, or balanced. Representation, we saw in the guidelines, can mean many things. It can mean that the council mirrors a demographic profile, reflects a range of opinions, or includes a variety of gifts. To be sure, the guidelines are not of one mind. Representation, they suggest, can refer to ethnicity, culture, race, attitude, knowledge, or competence. No two guidelines concur about what representation is. All of them affirm it, however, as a criterion or principle.

When they say that the pastoral council is representative, they do not mean that it represents the parish in exactly the same way as public officials represent the electorate. This is implicit in the proviso, contained in most guidelines, that pastors can appoint pastoral council members. The widespread practice of appointment by the pastor is a tacit critique of the concept of "representation" we know from civic life. Appointment suggests that an elected pastoral council may represent the parish but still lack diversity or balance. The guidelines suggest that a pastor can appoint members to the council if he desires the presence of a minority point of view.

Councillors should not only be representative, diocesan guidelines say, but also should have various dispositions and skills. Dispositions include a number of moral and spiritual qualities. Open-minded, involved, willing to serve, and active in other ministries—good councillors, say the guidelines, are disposed in these ways. The guidelines include more about skills than about dispositions. Some skills are very general. The good councillor is informed, knowledgeable, skillful, experienced, and understanding. Other guidelines more specifically speak of pastoral expertise and competence. Guidelines recommending the discernment of councillors call for the "process skills" of listening, cooperating, creativity, and spirituality.

In short, diocesan guidelines list a number of desirable qualities in the potential councillor, far more than the Vatican documents list. The list is impressive, and may prove daunting to council nominees who fear they do not have all the qualities on the list. One cannot escape the conclusion, however, that even diocesan guidelines are rather abstract. When we ask what the qualities really mean, there is no clear answer. For example, the good councillor is supposed to be knowledgeable. But how are we to measure knowledge? Must councillors have a degree in, say, theology or administration? Or take, as another example, the criterion of creativity. What does it mean, in the context of the pastoral council, to be creative? How is the councillor to represent the parish's knowledge and creativity? About this, the guidelines are unsatisfactory.

Requirements for the Council Ministry

The list of desirable qualities in the potential councillor is abstract for a good reason—the task of the pastoral council, and the qualities of the good councillor, are contingent. They depend on a number of factors that cannot be specified in advance. They depend, first of all, on the *pastor*. He consults the council with a specific intention. That intention cannot be predicted because it depends on a second factor, namely, the *situation of the parish*. That situation differs from parish to parish. It is the subject matter about which the pastor consults. He wants to tap the wisdom of *parishioners*. They are a third factor upon which the work of the council depends. They have various viewpoints, but membership in the church unites them. The parish wants both to benefit from their viewpoints and to preserve their unity. In summary, the qualities of the good councillor are vague because the council's work is contingent. It requires a special kind of knowledge, the knowledge of contingent things.

"Knowledge of contingent things"—this phrase may strike readers as strange. But it is a common philosophical term.[5] Aristotle described it as "practical wisdom," and St. Thomas Aquinas treated it under the heading of "prudence." It seeks what is best to do, not in general or in the abstract, but in a changing situation. Councillors need to represent or make this practical wisdom present in the pastoral council. The church's official documents about councils do not speak of the knowledge of contingent things, but the church speaks of councils that ponder pastoral questions, synthesize many viewpoints, and limit their scope to practical matters.

They imply that the church seeks councillors with practical wisdom. Is this the kind of knowledge that the church intends councils to seek? Let us follow the arguments of philosophers.

Knowledge of Contingent Things—Aristotle, Plato, Thomas Aquinas

It was Aristotle's *Nicomachean Ethics*—written in the fourth century B.C. and supposedly edited by his son, Nicomachus—that first treated the "knowledge of contingent things." Some kinds of knowledge can be strictly demonstrated, said Aristotle, and others hold true as a general rule, but not always. The knowledge that can be strictly demonstrated deserves to be called "science." It is always and everywhere true. But it is not the only kind of knowledge. Another kind depends on the situation and aims at what is best to do for a community. In Book VI of the *Nicomachean Ethics* Aristotle calls it practical wisdom.

Practical wisdom concerns action. It focuses on those deeds that we may or may not want to do. People with practical wisdom, says Aristotle, have a capacity for seeing what is good. They exercise this capacity in dialogue. In conversation they are able to judge what the situation demands. They listen to others and express their own opinion, integrating and synthesizing a variety of viewpoints. On the basis of what emerges in the dialogue, on the basis of common sense, they choose this action or that. So the rightness of a given action, which is the subject matter of practical wisdom, can never be always and everywhere true, as empirical science is. Action is contingent. It depends on the choices we make, choices that may or may not be wise.

The search for knowledge of contingent things proceeds by deliberation. It has no fixed-and-firm scientific method because what it deliberates about—in our case, the changing needs of the parish—follows no unchangeable rules. Instead, it applies a capacity for seeing the community's good. This capacity, skill in deliberation, enables people to choose from among a number of actions, all of which are good in themselves.

Is this way of proceeding unscientific? Plato considered this question in the dialogue entitled *Phaedo*. In Plato's dialogue, Socrates says that he once thought that he could explain all things empirically, that is, by observing and quantifying data. But when this proved unsuccessful, he decided that he must have "recourse to theories." That is, he had to express his views to others and seek agreement or disagreement. According to Socrates, there is no other way to get at the truth of some things than to put forward an argument and subject it to scrutiny. The knowledge of contingent things is scientific (i.e., having to do with knowledge) but not empirical. It emerges in dialogue.

The ability to get at the knowledge of contingent things is a special gift. St. Thomas Aquinas called it a virtue. It is the virtue of people who are prudent. St. Thomas treated prudence in the second part of the *Summa Theologica's* Part Two. In question 47 he defined it as thought applied to action. Prudence concerns not only making a good decision, but understanding the decision as well. It not only disposes us to want the good, but it teaches us what good can be accomplished by our actions. Prudence is, as Thomas says in article four, an intellectual as well as a moral virtue.

Prudent people can deliberate well, take counsel, inquire, and judge shrewdly. How can we discern who they are in the parish? The only way is to watch parishioners using their gifts in dialogue. They are the ones who express their opinions well. They listen attentively to the opinions of others. They are able to synthesize their opinions, clarifying them and making sound recommendations. They exercise self-control, preserving their ability to judge what is good. These are the people, in short, who are able to get at the knowledge of contingent things. There is no other way of reaching this knowledge. It is not always and everywhere true, but depends on the situation of the community. Practical wisdom is the knowledge that pastoral councils seek.

Representatives of Practical Wisdom

The 1973 Circular Letter stated that pastoral council members should be prudent, but it did not specifically mention practical wisdom or the knowledge of contingent things. Is there any evidence to suggest that this knowledge is what the church has in mind for councils? I believe there is. Vatican documents imply it by describing the scope of pastoral councils.

The church's official documents concur that pastoral councils in general have a threefold task. It is, in the words of the Vatican II Decree on Bishops, "to investigate and consider matters relating to pastoral activity and to formulate practical conclusions concerning them" (no. 27). Subsequent treatments of the pastoral council in Vatican documents repeat this formula virtually without change.[6] The documents state, first of all, that this threefold task is to be accomplished in a council. A council implies dialogue, as does the work of "investigating" and especially of "considering." The church envisions the give and take of conversation. It takes a group effort to arrive at the meaning of a concrete situation.

The Circular Letter's treatment of representation (at no. 7) offers further evidence that practical wisdom is what councils seek. It says that pastoral council members are to represent "the entire composition of the People of God." This implies that everyone has an opinion worthy of consideration. There is no univocal point of view. Pastors consult councils because the truth of a situation needs to be investigated and pondered. This suggests that true knowledge of a pastoral situation is contingent knowledge. It is not always and everywhere true, like empirical science, but depends on the convictions of the people of God.

The Circular Letter offers a further piece of evidence when it describes the scope of the pastoral council. The council offers "proposals and suggestions" about a number of matters. The letter gives examples of them. Speaking of pastoral councils at the diocesan level, it states (at no. 9) that the work of the council may include:

> missionary, catechetical and apostolic undertakings within the diocese; concerning the promotion of doctrinal formation and the sacramental life of the faithful; concerning pastoral activities to help the priests in the various social and territorial areas of the diocese; concerning public opinion on matters pertaining to the Church as it is more likely to be fostered in the present time; etc.

This list is practical. Each item has to do with action and with contingent affairs, precisely the subject of practical wisdom. The Circular Letter confirms this practical focus by defining what is outside the scope of the pastoral council. The letter says (also at no. 9) that it is "beyond the competence of this council to decide on general questions bearing on faith, orthodoxy, moral principles or laws of the universal Church." These are the matters that belong to the science of theology. About them, a pastor does not consult a council, but instead needs expert advice. Councils treat contingent things and avoid the domain of theological science. Councillors seek practical wisdom, one can conclude, the truth about matters contingent on a changing situation.

To sum up, the knowledge of contingent things is precisely the kind of knowledge that the church seeks from pastoral councils. The good councillor is not the person who is an expert in theology or pastoral administration, but rather the one who has skill in deliberation and prudence. He or she knows how to listen carefully, speak clearly, and integrate a variety of opinions about what the church is to do. So Theresa, whom we met in the previous chapter, was ineffective as a councillor because she could not aid the search for practical wisdom. She was intelligent, but lacked the ability to deliberate well. She could not apply her intelligence to anything apart from her own preoccupations. In that sense she could not represent the parish.

The Ecclesial Meaning of Representation

Pastoral councils represent to pastors the practical wisdom of the people of God. This is the "ecclesial meaning" of representation. Councillors make the community's wisdom present. What does ecclesial representation mean for our question of popular participation in councillor selection? Let us recall from the last chapter the story of Santa María Church. Father Padraig Twomey hand-picked his pastoral council. He did not believe that the popular participation of parishioners was necessary. If we had asked him about it, he would have said that a pastoral council election is more trouble than it is worth. His goal was to share responsibility by convening the council every two months, according to his agenda, and to make it a symbol of the style of parish he was trying to build. Popular participation in councillor selection, he would have said, is unnecessary.

In the absence of a diocesan guideline for pastoral councils that explicitly insists on popular participation, Father Twomey was free to appoint. But I believe that his practice was not fully consistent with the ecclesial meaning of representation. Popular participation in the selection of pastoral council members better accords with ecclesial representation than the mere appointment of councillors.

In order to substantiate this thesis, we must first recall what the church teaches about popular participation. Then we have to see its harmony with the notion of ecclesial representation. The church affirms popular participation, I believe, precisely because participation enables councils to represent the practical wisdom of the people of God.

The Church and Popular Participation

Vatican documents do not insist upon popular elections of pastoral council members. But they do allow them. The main thrust of the Vatican documents has to do with the representative nature of councils. They are to be a sign of the entire people of God. A hand-picked council may be able to signify this people. But more likely it signifies the will of the pastor. This is the risk that hand-picked councils run.

Diocesan guidelines for councils are less ambiguous than the Vatican documents. They overwhelmingly support the idea of popular elections for pastoral council members. They link representation with popular election. In the next chapter, we will show how popular elections can be more discerning. Here it is enough to affirm that parishioners can judge the abilities of potential councillors. They can identify those parishioners who meet the criteria for council membership, that is, those who are representative, suitably gifted, and well-disposed.

The philosophical concept of practical wisdom provides an additional motive for popular participation. Parishioners with skill in deliberation, not outside experts, are the most reliable source of practical wisdom. Parishioners know one another and know the actual situation of the parish. They are more able than outsiders to judge the contingent affairs of the parish. Their gift is the capacity to judge, from among all the things that a parish might do, those particular actions that the parish ought to do. Not all parishioners have this gift. But even those who do not have it can recognize the gift. By their participation they can contribute to the selection of councillors.

Father Padraig Twomey undoubtedly broke no laws by appointing his council, but he was not fully consistent with the church's idea of representation. He did not allow popular participation in councillor selection. Church documents emphasize that councillors should come from different walks of life, should have various roles in the apostolate, and should be prudent and worthy of respect. Pastors who appoint their councils without popular participation run the risk of gaining a council too narrow in its outlook. An appointed council may represent the pastor's prejudices more than the wisdom of the people of God.

Theology and Practical Wisdom

At the heart of the church's teaching about representation and popular participation dwell three convictions of faith. They are the link between councils and the dignity of the person, the unity of the parish, and the participation of parishioners in God's love. Each of these motivates the search for practical wisdom. Let us look at each of these convictions in turn.

When the American colonies declared their independence from Great Britain, they asserted that "all men are created equal." The founders of the country emphasized that God had created human beings with fundamental rights that deserve respect. Undoubtedly, not everyone is equally gifted. Some opinions are better than others, some arguments have more merit, some voices are more reasonable. But every opinion, argument, and voice expresses something fundamentally human. And that human something has dignity. This is the basic assertion of the Vatican II Decree on Religious Liberty. It expressed the church's belief that people are free to worship as they see fit and this freedom must not be infringed.[7] To be sure, not all convictions are truthful. But we honor the people who maintain them. This principle also holds in the parish, which contains a variety of viewpoints. Some conflict with others. The council aims to discriminate among them, to discover what is wise, and to recommend it to the pastor. If the council wants to be representative, it must acknowledge the dignity of all viewpoints. They express the equal dignity with which each person has been created.

The dignity of the person is our first conviction of faith about representation. The second has to do with the unity of the parish. The church recommends councils because it believes that they express the practical wisdom of the people of God. This presupposes a real unity. It is not just the empirical unity of faithful people who worship regularly or who constitute a parish majority. It is also the unity of everyone who finds in the parish a public expression of their communion with God, a communion in the name of Father, Son, and Holy Spirit. We believe that Jesus Christ founded the church in the sense that our faith has its origin in him. Being a Christian means membership in his body.[8] To be sure, this unity is not always apparent. Sometimes the unity of the church is unity-in-difference. We express this fractured unity by being faithful in our opposition to a parish policy or practice. But the church remains convinced that its unity is real. It recommends councils because they represent a unity that already exists, a unity that has its origin and end in God. Imperfectly, incompletely, inadequately, every aspect of the church's life reflects this unity—including pastoral councils.

A third conviction is the love of God. The church recommends councils because the search for practical wisdom is a participation in God's love. Love motivates both the pastor and the council. The pastor consults because he loves his people and wants to serve them better. He seeks councillors with practical wisdom. Councillors put their gifts at the service of the church so as to participate in the love of God. Participation in God is an ancient theological idea.[9] It refers to the way in which we gradually appropriate or take on the very being of God. The life of the Father, with which the Son enjoyed a perfect unity and which abides as the Holy Spirit, becomes our own life. The work of the council is one aspect of this participation. There both pastor and council represent and make present the love of God, the love that expresses itself in practical wisdom.

Theological convictions dwell at the heart of the church's recommendation of councils. The church teaches that the pastoral council is to reflect the entire people of God. This affirms human dignity, the dignity inherent in every member of the community. Everyone deserves respect, and the council accords parishioners that respect by attending to their opinions and weighing them carefully. Not every opinion, however, can prevail. The fact that some proposals succeed and others fail may seem to detract from the unity of the church. But ecclesial unity does not hinge on the attainment of this or that individual goal. The church is not united because the council unites it. Ecclesial unity is rather the achievement of God. In this unity the council seeks practical wisdom. It seeks this wisdom as an expression of its desire to participate in God's very life. These theological convictions lend support to the idea of popular participation in councillor selection. They motivate parishes that want to be consistent with the ecclesial idea of representation.

Conclusion: The Motive for Popular Participation

Our reflection on the ecclesial meaning of representation enables us to give an answer to Father Twomey, the pastor of Santa María. When Fr. Twomey had personally appointed his council, he had not realized the importance of popular participation in the selection of members. Neither his parish nor his councillors understood the particular task of the council, namely, the search for practical wisdom. Had Father Twomey invited popular participation in the selection of councillors, he would have been more consistent with the church's idea of representation.

The church's official teaching about the selection of pastoral councillors is vague because councillors seek a kind of knowledge that cannot be predicted in advance. It is the knowledge of contingent things. This knowledge, defined in philosophy as practical wisdom, has a deep relationship with theology. It is connected to the dignity of every human being, to the unity of the church, and to Christian participation in the love of God. All of these suggest the importance of popular participation in the selection of councillors. At the beginning of this chapter, we supposed that popular participation might have been in contradiction with wise discrimination. We hypothesized that a pastor may not be able to trust a council chosen with popular participation. This hypothesis does not hold. The participation of informed parishioners in the selection of councillors may lead to a better council. The advice of a representative council is more worthy of a pastor's trust.

Chapter Sixteen

Discerning Councillors

The ecclesial meaning of representation enables us to dissolve—in theory, at least—two apparent contradictions. The first is the tension between popular participation and wise choice in the selection of councillors. We have seen that the popular participation of an educated parish may yield better councillors. The second apparent contradiction is the tension between the pastor's trust in the council and the council's representation of the parish. A good pastor knows that a representative council may be better than a hand-picked group of friends. Popular participation is indeed preferable, at least in theory.

The purpose of this chapter is to move from theory to practice. It aims to show how to discern councillors in a way preferable to an uninformed election or an exclusive selection. We will begin with a review of church teaching about the selection of councillors. Church teaching does not say how to choose councillors, but it indicates the value of popular elections and the need to attract gifted people. Next we will explain what it means to discern councillors. Discernment is an informed choice, a choice using our best resources and consonant with our Christian tradition. It requires a clear pastoral intent, the awakening of interest, and the development of commitment. Finally, we will show how parish discernment intimately expresses the community's faith.

The Option for Discernment

What does the church teach about selecting councillors? This teaching is not unanimous. Vatican documents, for example, endorse the practice of election but also speak of the appointment of councillors by a pastor. Most diocesan guidelines for parish councils recommend popular election, but some also encourage a discernment that may or may not include a popular election. On this topic, both Vatican documents and diocesan guidelines deserve a closer look. I am convinced that the diocesan advocates of discernment are on the right track. A knowledgeable, reflective, and popular choice of councillors by the parish is better than an uninformed or exclusive choice. So after a review of official teaching about council selection, we will explain discernment and see what its advocates recommend.

Vatican II's Support for Elections

The Vatican II Decree on Bishops was the first to recommend pastoral councils, but it did not say how to select the members. After publishing the Decree, Pope Paul VI wrote an apostolic letter about how to implement it. His instructions scarcely address the selection of the diocesan pastoral council. They state only that such councils "may be established in different ways."[1] Paul VI left the means of selecting members to the bishops.

But the Decree on Bishops was not the only Vatican II document that spoke of pastoral councils. The Decree on the Church's Missionary Activity spoke about them also. It referred to diocesan pastoral council members as "delegates" of the people who have been "selected."[2] The selection of delegates includes the possibility of popular election. Eight years later, the 1974 Directory on Bishops also endorsed the value of elections. Although it did not say how parish councillors are to be selected, it implicitly encouraged the election of diocesan pastoral council members. Parish pastoral councils, it said, may "choose their representatives to serve on the diocesan council."[3] In brief, there are a variety of ways to choose councillors, of which popular election is one.

Although the 1973 Circular Letter on Pastoral Councils spoke about the number of members, their term of office, and rotating membership, it did not endorse any particular way of choosing members.[4] It simply left the selection of them to the free choice of the bishop. It even neglected to mention the Decree on Missionary Activity and its reference to "delegates." In Chapter Ten, we saw that a first draft of the Circular Letter recommended appointment instead of election. This recommendation, however, was dropped in the final draft. Not everyone supports popular elections, but they have been an option for selecting pastoral councillors since Vatican II.

Election in Diocesan Guidelines
Diocesan guidelines have much to say about the selection of parish pastoral councils, as we saw in Chapter Seven. More than two-thirds of the 26 guidelines surveyed in 1990 and 1995 recommend the election of councillors. Most guidelines endorse the election of councillors at large. A few recommend (as an alternative to parish-wide elections) that ministerial standing committees elect councillors as representatives of the various ministries. But whether through elections at-large or by committees, popular participation is the U.S. norm for selecting pastoral councillors.

Most guidelines provide for the appointment of pastoral council members by the pastor for the sake of representation, that is, for diversity or balance. This is an implicit critique of the civic concept of political election. The appointment of councillors by the pastor indicates that the pastoral council expresses something other than the sovereignty of the people. It seeks to express the practical wisdom that has its source in God.

Most diocesan guidelines also allow for the presence on the pastoral council of *ex officio* councillors. *Ex officio* councillors are parish staff members who bring a special knowledge or competence to council meetings. About them, some guidelines express a word of caution. They say that the staff members are merely a "resource" or are "non-voting" members. Staff members should not dominate council meetings or stifle the voice of elected members. In brief, the common practice of election of pastoral council members by the parish is supplemented by *ex officio* councillors and by the pastor's appointment of other members.

The Meaning of Discernment
Some guidelines advocate a process of discernment as an alternative or adjunct to parish-wide elections. Three out of thirteen guidelines surveyed in 1995 recommend it. Discernment refers to a process designed to give parishioners knowledge of council nominees and of the council

ministry. It tests the ability of nominees and plumbs their commitment to council membership. Guidelines say that it may take place in one or more open meetings or by a select group of parishioners. In the meetings, parishioners weigh the gifts of potential councillors and probe whether they have a real calling for the ministry. Guidelines distinguish between the discernment proper and the actual choice by appointment or balloting.

The recommendation that parishes "discern" their council members emerged in the late 1970s. It was a response to the critique that general elections had become a "popularity contest," that is, a superficial way of choosing councillors. Thinkers in the pastoral council movement stated that discernment has its roots in the church's spiritual tradition and the practices of many religious congregations. They wanted to employ that tradition in the pastoral council and discourage the comparison of council elections to political contests. By the mid-1990s, references to discernment in pastoral council guidelines were common.[5]

Although most guidelines do not treat the process of discernment at length, it deserves such a treatment. A thorough discernment solves many problems in councillor selection. Unlike some popular ballots (that fail to educate parishioners about councils and that offer a merely superficial acquaintance with nominees), discernment aims at more profound knowledge. It explores the role of the council and offers an opportunity to watch potential councillors exercise their gifts. Unlike the private selection of council members by a pastor or by his staff (which leaves parishioners in the dark about the criteria for the choice of councillors), an entire parish may discern together. This can build up the community and inspire the confidence of everyone, including the pastor. Discernment helps provide the knowledge required for selecting wise councillors.

The practice of discernment generally includes four stages. It begins with the sharing of information about the council. The discernment proper takes place in a series of parish meetings. In these meetings, people are nominated, and the participants examine and weigh the nominations in dialogue. Finally, there is the act of selection, usually by ballot.[6] The first step, the sharing of information, lays a foundation for the remaining steps. It expresses the pastor's intention, awakens the parish's interest, and builds commitment to the council.

Intent, Interest, Commitment

Before a parishioner can make a commitment to service on a parish pastoral council, he or she needs to know about the ministry. We saw in the last chapter that the church's official teaching about the qualifications of councillors is vague because the work of the council is contingent. It cannot be described in the abstract because it depends on the parish's situation. It also depends on the pastor. He has a reason for consulting his people, but others may not know what the reason is. To attract good councillors, he must tell them. He must share his intentions and awaken parish interest.

Ultimately, the goal is to choose councillors who are best for the ministry and to help the parish see why they are best. This is the heart of discernment. Sound discernment expresses church unity and is a participation in God's love. It builds commitment to the council. The sharing of pastoral intent, the awakening of interest, and the building of parish commitment—these are essential to councillor discernment.

Father Parise and Pastoral Intent

In 1995, an article by Father Michael Parise appeared in *The Priest*. Entitled "Forming Your Parish Pastoral Council," the article described how Father Parise's Boston parish chose council members.[7] The parish, a busy place with fifty projects and programs, used a process of discernment. Father Parise announced a series of three Sunday evening meetings with the explicit purpose of choosing a pastoral council. All parishioners were invited, and Father Parise sent personal invitations to a number of parishioners whom he especially wanted to consider council membership. In the meetings, he spoke in general about the purpose he envisioned for the council. He also did some work in small groups about the church, discipleship, and the personal formation of the pastoral councillor.

The third meeting emphasized the importance of personal formation in Christian life. It also included a process of nomination, discernment, and balloting. Father Parise invited the participants into the sanctuary of the church. There, in a climate of prayer, he led them through a process of discernment, asking them to nominate and vote for council members. None of the nominees were excluded. "All those who had received votes during the nomination process," Father Parise wrote, were invited to the next meetings. Later we read that the council included eleven members of the parish staff and 22 lay councillors. The 22, we can presume, were the ones who received votes.

Father Parise's article illustrates the four stages of discernment: information, education in a series of meetings, nomination, and balloting. It also describes the formation of councillors after they were selected. It says that they reviewed an archdiocesan report about the parish, examined the structure of the parish staff, and created a parish vision. The article, however, does not explicitly state why everyone who received a vote was allowed to participate in the council. Nor does it explain why the pastor wanted a council of 33 members. Father Parise's expectations for the council—what he hoped it would achieve—were not clear, at least not from the outset.

One sentence toward the end of the article, however, hints at Father Parise's pastoral intent. After the councillors were chosen and formed, he wrote, they began their proper work. It was "to envision the parish of the future and to evaluate the 50 projects and programs now in place, to determine their evangelical potential and perhaps to recommend consolidation, elimination of old programs and the creation of new efforts to serve the People of God." This sentence implies that his parish, with its 50 initiatives, may have lost its focus. Some projects and programs had more evangelical potential than others. Some were more worthy of parish support. Some deserved to be consolidated or eliminated. Father Parise wanted a council to help him examine and reflect on them in the light of the parish mission.

This purpose falls squarely within the church's threefold intention for pastoral councils, namely, the work of investigating, pondering, and recommending. Such a purpose is clear and important. Father Parise, I believe, should have stated it more explicitly from the outset. To be sure, he did not want to create needless anxiety about the future of the 50 projects and programs. And by choosing councillors in an open series of meetings and excluding no one, he defused the fear that his new council was out to close down beloved parish initiatives. But he was less than perfectly candid about his intentions. Had he been clearer, he might have attracted better councillors.

The first stage in the discernment of councillors is to express the pastor's intention. He has a reason for wanting a council. The more clearly he can express the intention, the more he can help his parishioners understand the council ministry. The clearer the pastoral intent, the better the chance of attracting suitable councillors.

Awakening Interest and Different Cultures

Robert Howes, a priest of the Diocese of Worcester, has vividly expressed the principal motive for parishioners to join the pastoral council. They want red meat, he wrote, substantial and nourishing fare.[8] People want an opportunity to study pastoral matters, to reflect on them for the sake of achieving the parish's mission, and to make wise recommendations to the pastor. When pastors clearly state their intentions for the council, they help people see why council membership is an important and rewarding ministry. This is essential to awakening parish interest.

For immigrant parishioners, especially parishioners whose first language is not English, participation in a pastoral council is not easy. But a wise pastor will want to attract the immigrant community's leaders. These are the people who speak for the community and enjoy its respect. They have prudence and skill in deliberation. Such immigrants typically do not enjoy the leisure of more established parishioners. They may find the council's work of study and reflection time consuming and without immediate rewards. Participation in an English-speaking council may be strenuous for them.

I witnessed this directly in the Diocese of Oakland. The diocese sought the participation of various ethnic communities at its pastoral conventions in 1985 and 1988. The first convention taught a lesson that proved instructive in the second convention. The 1985 plan called for the selection of two delegates by each of the diocese's ethnic pastoral centers. These centers were offices, sponsored by the diocese, that employed pastoral workers to promote a sense of community among immigrant groups. When the plans for the diocesan convention were finalized, I assumed that it would be enough to write a letter to each of the center directors, inviting them to choose convention delegates from their communities. I presumed that they shared my ideals of participation in the church. Based on my American experience, I took for granted what such a diocesan convention might mean. I believed that they took it for granted as well.

What I found, however, was that there were many ideas of participation in a diocesan convention. Each ethnic pastoral center had its own way of examining issues, raising concerns, and forming consensus. I discovered that my assumptions were not the only ones. But they prevailed because they were the assumptions of the dominant culture in the diocesan church. These assumptions gave delegates from the dominant culture—those who spoke English as their native language and were familiar with U.S. forms of political discourse—a decided advantage. They were more prepared to voice their issues than were immigrant delegates. As a result, some pastoral center members felt that the 1985 convention did not sufficiently heed their concerns.

In planning the 1988 convention, diocesan officials were able to avoid some of these problems. Part of their success was due to the efforts of Felicia Sarati, a Sister of St. Joseph. Sister Felicia had participated in the 1985 convention, and thereafter had become the ethnic pastoral center coordinator. She knew firsthand the frustrations felt by the ethnic pastoral center delegates. Long before the second convention, she began to prepare them. She held meetings with the leaders of each of the pastoral centers. She asked them to name the contribution that their immigrant group made to the diocese. She invited them to identify the most pressing issues facing their communities, the issues that the diocese should address. She asked them to discern from among their members those who could deliberate well, who could best contribute to the convention. Her efforts paid off. The ethnic pastoral centers participated effectively in the 1988 convention. They successfully brought their concerns to the attention of the diocese.

Oakland's experience offers a lesson to the pastor who wants to awaken the interest of the parish, especially immigrant parishioners, in the pastoral council. No pastor should presume that his people grasp the council's purpose. The very idea of a council, which a pastor consults but whose advice he is not obliged to follow, is difficult. Not everyone understands the concept of practical wisdom and the knowledge of contingent things. Immigrants may not see the importance of participation in a council whose language may be utterly foreign and whose benefits are not immediately obvious. Special effort is needed to ensure their participation. Awakening interest in the council requires not only a clear pastoral intent, but also a convincing promise that participation will be nourishing and fulfilling.

Developing Commitment

Advocates of discernment agree that it takes a series of meetings to adequately prepare a parish for the selection of councillors. If they are to accomplish this purpose, however, parish meetings cannot consist of mere lectures in which parishioners are passive. Instead they must begin to engage the entire parish in the work of the council.

This was what Father Jim Keeley did at Our Lady of the Snows Church in rural Utah. He recently opened a new church, constructed to seat 700, with magnificent views of the Rockies. On any given Sunday, he can look out upon his growing congregation, many with young families, and take justifiable pride in the parish's new sanctuary. But with a construction debt of more than a million dollars, Our Lady of the Snows is cash poor. Father Keeley and Sister Carmen Braga (the names have been changed) are the parish's only paid staff members. They made a deliberate decision to keep personnel expenses low in order to retire the debt. But this has hindered the parish from developing other initiatives, such as youth ministry. Doubtless Our Lady's Church needs a youth ministry, said Father Keeley, but where are the resources to undertake it? Father Keeley had no pastoral council. He wanted to establish one to help him address the youth ministry question.

In order to engage the parish's interest in the question, and to help select council members, Father Keeley called for a series of four parish meetings. In them, he invited parishioners to envision the kind of youth ministry that they desired. Did they want weekly youth meetings or a drop-in center? Would youth ministry include religious education and sacramental preparation? Was the youth minister to work exclusively with young people or would the minister recruit and train adult volunteers? Father Keeley also presented the parish's financial situation and challenged participants to estimate the resources a youth ministry requires.

Having laid this foundation, Father Keeley clarified the tasks for which he needed a pastoral council. He hoped the council would reflect with him on what parishioners had said, define the hoped-for youth ministry, draw up a job description for a youth minister, and plan ways to develop new resources. By clarifying his intentions, Father Keeley engaged the interest of the whole parish. Parishioners helped him envision the future, restructure the parish's ministry, and solve problems.[9] At the end of the third meeting, Father Keeley invited them to nominate people for his ten-member pastoral council. During the fourth meeting, participants chose the new councillors.

Parish meetings at Our Lady of the Snows achieved the purpose of selecting the pastoral council. They were able to do this because they raised the interest of the whole parish. The meetings explained Father Keeley's intention, educated parishioners about the pastoral situation faced by the parish, and asked them to share their insights about youth ministry. As they did this, parishioners learned about the pastoral council and the qualities that councillors should have. They were able to discern these qualities in their fellow parishioners. They grew in commitment to the council and its work.

Choosing Councillors

Council experts agree that the selection of councillors is an act of faith in the church, in the pastor who seeks the parish's wisdom, and in the parish members.[10] It touches the deepest chords of Christian life. It should be intimate and prayerful. It should recall the purpose of the parish and allow members to speak truthfully to one another. The intimacy of the selection of councillors and the role of prayer deserve a special word.

The Intimacy of Discernment

Benedictine Sister Mary Benet McKinney emphasizes the importance of intimacy and interaction in discernment. The author of *Sharing Wisdom*, she says that parish meetings allow people to match their own gifts and talents with the needs of the council. This process should not be hurried. It should involve conversation, reflection, and prayer.

Instead of impersonal or secret nominations, Sister Mary Benet suggests that parishioners speak up about those they want to see on the council.[11] If they have participated in several meetings, they are in a good position to judge who has the ability to serve on the council. A good discernment process invites them to express their views. They should be able to say, "I nominate Stephen," and give their reasons. "Stephen is thoughtful, a careful listener, good at stating his views, and able to compromise." In this way, they honor Stephen, expressing their faith in him and in the church. Others should also be able to affirm his nomination. If they disagree, they may nominate another.

After the nominations and the affirmations, the nominees need to speak. They must indicate whether they accept nomination. "I accept the nomination," Stephen should be able to say. "I have a deep interest in the parish and the council and I believe that I can make a good contribution." After the nominees have accepted or declined, the parishioners need further discussion. Sister Mary Benet calls this testing or confirming the group's wisdom. People should be able to express doubts ("Stephen has just started a new job and may not have time to serve on the council") or affirmations ("I was impressed by what Stephen said about the parish's youth ministry"). These reflections help the group arrive at a common understanding of the nominees.

Once the discernment of nominees is complete, writes Sister Mary Benet, "the process of final selection can vary according to the experience and expectations of the parish or diocese: election, appointment, or a combination of the two."[12]

This does not mean, however, that popular participation is unimportant. Sister Mary Benet rightly implies that the discernment is more important than the means by which participants indicate their judgment. But her underlying assumption is that those who discern are fair-minded sharers of wisdom. Popular participation is one way of ensuring that the discerning group is not exclusive and close-minded. In addition, the discernment should be unhurried. By means of it, the parish discovers its representatives and expresses its faith. When the discernment is complete, parishioners should learn its results and celebrate it publicly.

Prayer of Discernment

Some writers about parish councils in 1967-68 did not refer to prayer in the council meetings and did not advocate a discerning style of decision making. That changed by the 1980s and 1990s. Those years gave rise, as we saw in Chapter Thirteen, to the idea of a *pastoral* council. That is the council, many said, that understands itself as ministry, studies the Scriptures, and focuses on the parish mission. All of the literature about discernment emphasizes the importance of prayer.

What is the prayer of discernment? It originates in contemplation, the simple recognition that God is the foundation of all reality. Christian tradition calls this adoration. Prayer is next an act of praising God. It acknowledges the difference between God and creatures and celebrates the way God has disposed all things. Next comes thanksgiving. The prayer of Christians gives thanks for their relationship with God. Adoration, praise, and thanksgiving—these are the context for the prayer of petition, the request that God come to the community's aid. Whether the petition is conducted spontaneously, or based on the Scriptures, or according to the liturgy, it has a proper context, namely, faith in the God who is always present.

The discerning community should be cautious about a prayer of petition that expresses hope in a miraculous intervention. Some prayers imply that the outcome of the discernment is God's will. Without prayers, they suggest, God might not guide the discernment. We saw in Chapter Seven that some guidelines for pastoral councils recommend the final selection of parish council members by drawing lots. A parishioner can misread these guidelines and conclude that drawing lots expresses God's will. But God is not a link in a chain of causes that ends with a lucky draw.[13] To be sure, there is nothing wrong with lots, provided that every nominee for the pastoral council is equally gifted and the community is willing to leave the final selection to chance. The drawing of lots, however, is no substitute for a thorough discernment. Our petitions express the faith that God is already working through the community and will continue to do so.

Discernment and Wisdom

Official documents do not concur on how to select pastoral councillors. Although most pastoral council guidelines in the United States favor popular elections and do not require a process of discernment, the process helps to ensure the success of elections. Parishes should not regard discernment and election as alternatives. Rather they are aspects of one and the same process of selection. Discernment without the participation of interested parishioners may yield unrepresentative councils. Elections without discernment may yield poor councillors. When parishes educate people about the council ministry, begin to engage them in the council's work, and invite their participation in selecting councillors, they express the faith of the church.

The discernment of councillors expresses faith in the church's vision of shared responsibility. It allows parishioners to understand the role of the pastor and his search for practical wisdom. It reveals the parish as God's instrument, an instrument with a mission and a future. It invites people to honor one another and speak the truth. The discernment of council members expresses a common faith that the parish is indeed God's people and that God will continue to work through them.

Chapter Seventeen

Misunderstandings about Coordination

aul Steinmetz is the youth minister at St. Alphonsus Church in
southern California. Twenty-six years old and recently married,
Paul works hard at his part-time parish job. He conducts a weekly
youth group, plans skiing trips, coordinates events with the other youth
ministers from the town's Protestant churches, and has even taken parish
youth over the border for "encuentros juveniles," that is, meetings with
Mexican youth leaders. Paul has a degree in philosophy from a Catholic
college, but no formal degree in theology or catechesis. He relies on a
youth ministry team, a group of young people and adults who help him
carry out the ministry. One of the adults on his team is the youth ministry representative to the pastoral council. Paul is popular, and his ministry is growing. The pastor, Father Andrea Chirico, appreciates the way
he relates to parish youth.

The director of religious education at St. Alphonsus Church is Sister
Susan Flanagan. A veteran catechist, she has been a parochial school

teacher, a catechist trainer at the diocesan level, and an administrator with her religious congregation. Sister Susan works full time at St. Alphonsus, coordinating a large team of volunteer home catechists and organizing the confirmation program. She is a confidant of Father Chirico, and has worked with him for many years. The confirmation program is designed for freshmen and sophomores in high school. They meet every month. In the course of the two-year program, they receive an overview of church teaching. One of Sister Susan's most trusted catechists is the religious education representative on the pastoral council.

At St. Alphonsus, the pastoral council serves to "coordinate" the various parish ministries, such as youth ministry and confirmation. Each ministry has a representative on the pastoral council. The council helps to set policies, and the ministries follow them.

The practice of St. Alphonsus (this story has been fictionalized) is a common one. Many parishes in the U.S. define the work of the pastoral council as coordination. In this chapter, we will see how this practice works, its basis in the documents of Vatican II, and the dangers that coordinating councils encounter—and can avoid.

The Ministries Collide

The youth ministry and confirmation programs at St. Alphonsus sometimes collide. There are occasional scheduling conflicts, for example, like the time when one of Paul Steinmetz's Mexican outings prevented a number of young people from attending an important confirmation meeting. Paul and Sister Susan are friends, but their philosophies differ. When young people ask Paul about Christian doctrine, for example, he will often say that doctrine is less important than life and faith. This bothers Sister Susan. She has told him (as well as the pastor, Father Chirico) that she would like more support from Paul, who is a role model for young people in the parish. As for Paul, he feels that the confirmation program is too much like a school. Both Father Chirico and Sister Susan know that Paul prefers more interaction, such as role-playing, case studies, group process, and less doctrinal instruction.

Father Chirico met with Paul and Sister Susan to talk about better coordination between the youth ministry and confirmation programs. The two ministry heads agreed that better cooperation would help the two programs, but they acknowledged that their differences in philosophy were significant. The differences prevented them from being objective about their programs. They wanted help. Father Chirico suggested that he would take up the matter with the pastoral council. He had trust in the group, which contained a representative from each ministry. Paul and Sister Susan agreed.

In a series of meetings, some attended by Paul and Sister Susan, the council studied the two programs, youth ministry and confirmation. They saw a number of ways in which the two could cooperate better. They could establish an annual calendar. Youth ministry meetings could take up themes explored during the confirmation classes. Classes on prayer, social justice, and personal morality could include more discussion and hands-on experience. The council drafted a proposal that included these suggestions.

When the proposal was complete, Father Chirico thanked the council but said that he wanted to discuss it with the religious education and youth ministry teams. They needed time to absorb it, and he did not want to rush the changes. Some councillors were disappointed and even indignant when Father Chirico failed to insist on the proposal's immediate implementation. They had worked hard on it. They had done so at the direct request of the ministry heads. The coordination of ministries, they felt, was the council's explicit task. The council represented the ministries. Why propose ways for them to cooperate, some councillors asked, if the proposals were not to be implemented?

This anecdote illustrates the difficulties involved in coordination by a pastoral council. Should councils coordinate parish ministries? And if so, how should they coordinate them? To answer this question, let us review our empirical study.

Evidence of Coordination

Most of the 15,000 pastoral councils in the United States coordinate standing committees or ministerial commissions. This generalization is based on our survey of council guidelines in Chapters Three and Four. More than two-thirds of these guidelines assign to councils the task of coordinating. Education, liturgy, and social justice committees, for example, need to cooperate. Councils aim to help them. Guidelines describe councils as promoters of committee member participation. They say that councils ensure cooperation among ministries. Many explicitly state that such councils develop committee policy. Some even announce that committees are accountable to the council, which ensures that the committees implement the council's policies. The coordination of committees is one of the council's most common tasks.

But coordination by councils can be easily misunderstood. For example, council members may draw the mistaken conclusion that when they coordinate parish ministries, they act as an executive body, not as the pastor's consultants. They may wrongly believe that ministerial committees or commissions originate in the council, not the parish. They may labor under the false impression that the council is a governing body and that committees implement its directives. Some guidelines imply these false conclusions.

Coordination at Vatican II

The council's role as coordinator was sanctioned in the documents of Vatican II and has a venerable history. Two documents in particular express the idea that councils may coordinate. The Decree on the Apostolate of Lay People has the distinction of being the only Vatican II document to speak of councils in the parish. It does not speak of parish pastoral councils, however, but of apostolic councils that can be established at many levels, including the parochial. Its recommendation of such councils was certainly a source for the later development of parish pastoral councils.[1]

The second document is the Decree on the Church's Missionary Activity. It does not speak of councils in parishes, but in dioceses, and it calls them "pastoral" councils. We shall see that both councils, the apostolic and the pastoral, use the word coordination to describe part of their work. This suggests that they may not be two different types of councils after all, or if they are, that their functions overlap. It also suggests what the bishops of Vatican II meant by coordination.

The Laity Decree

The Laity Decree of Vatican II recommends councils "to assist the Church's apostolic work." "These councils," it said, "can take care of the mutual coordinating of the various lay associations and undertakings, the autonomy and particular nature of each remaining untouched."[2] What does it mean that councils "can take care" of the coordination of associations and undertakings? The Latin verb is "poterunt . . . inservire." It means that councils are "able to" serve by coordinating. Councils can coordinate, but they need not do so. Coordination is a possibility, but is not their main purpose. Their main purpose is to assist the church's apostolic work. Councils may coordinate if it enhances the apostolate.

The Latin verb also suggests that coordination "serves" the various lay associations and undertakings. Coordination is subordinate to their proper task and may not infringe on it. In order to serve lay associations and undertakings, the council needs to understand them. True understanding arouses a desire for their success. Once the council understands them, it is able to offer help in the form of coordination. But the council may not interfere with their autonomy and particular nature. To be sure, it wants them to succeed. But success is defined by the lay associations and undertakings under their rightful leaders. The council serves them, not vice versa.

The hints in no. 26 of the Laity Decree suggest that coordination of lay initiatives by councils was indeed a recommendation of Vatican II. We saw in Chapter Twelve the arguments of certain authors that this text does not refer to parish pastoral councils. These authors were right in one sense only. The Laity Decree does not refer to pastoral councils. It refers to apostolic councils. Apostolic councils were the only parish councils of which Vatican II spoke. And these apostolic parish councils are undoubtedly able, in the words of Laity 26, to serve the coordination of associations and undertakings. Coordination does not impose order or dominate. It serves by understanding and desiring to promote success as the laity and their proper leaders define it.

The Missionary Decree
The other Vatican II text that spoke of coordination by councils was the Decree on the Church's Missionary Activity. It stated that the bishop's responsibility is "to promote missionary activity, guide and coordinate it, so that the spontaneous zeal of those who engage in this work may be safeguarded and fostered." A diocesan pastoral council, according to the decree,[3] may be of help. "For better coordination, the bishop should, as far as possible, establish a pastoral council in which clergy, religious and lay people would have a part through elected delegates." What did the Missionary Decree mean when it spoke of coordination by councils?

The text uses two verbs to describe what coordination can do for the "spontaneous zeal" of missioners. It "safeguards" and "fosters" that zeal. "To safeguard" means to protect. Poor guidance and lack of cooperation threaten the zeal of missioners. Their efforts may interfere with one another or be frustrated by miscommunication and disorganization. Coordination can prevent those problems. The second verb, "to foster," implies knowledge, appreciation, and support. A bishop wants his missioners to succeed. A diocesan pastoral council can help him guide and coordinate their activity. But the primary goal is not guidance and coordination for their own sake, but rather the success of the missionary activity. Coordination that discourages the zeal of others is misguided and dangerous. True coordination expresses the church's desire to promote evangelical activity.

Unlike the Laity Decree, the Missionary Decree does not speak of parish councils. Its focus is rather the diocesan pastoral council. This "pastoral council" idea was not applied to parish councils until 1973. Some would have us believe that the work of pastoral and apostolic councils is totally separate. I disagree. The fact that the Missionary Decree uses the same word as the Laity Decree to describe one aspect of the work of councils—the aspect of coordination—suggests that the bishops of Vatican II did not intend two wholly separate types of councils. Apostolic and pastoral councils alike may coordinate. The two decrees imply that coordination does not impose order on subordinates, whether on lay associations and undertakings or on missioners. It respects their autonomy and particular nature. It serves, protects, and safeguards them.

Misunderstandings about Coordination

When the Vatican II recommendations about councils were applied in the United States, they took on a distinctive form. Americans sought primarily to involve parishioners and foster participation. This commonly gave rise to a system of ministerial commissions or standing committees, such as education, liturgy, and social justice, all coordinated by the council. There was a close relation between committees and the council, with council members often elected by standing committees as their representatives. When the various committees or commissions needed to coordinate their activities, they had a ready forum in the parish council. All of this was a legitimate application of Vatican II teaching about coordination by councils.

Coordination as the Main Task?

Three developments, however, are tangential to or clearly incompatible with the teachings of Vatican II.[4] One tangent is the proposal, found in some diocesan guidelines, that the council's main work is to coordinate a system of parish standing committees and ministerial commissions. We saw that coordination in the Laity Decree is a possibility of the apostolic council, but not its main work, which is to promote the church's apostolate. The Laity Decree did not speak of parish committees or commissions. It focused rather on lay associations and undertakings (e.g., the national councils of Catholic men and women), independent of parishes. It insisted that their autonomy and particular nature are to remain untouched. The establishment of parish committees and commissions, all coordinated by the council, is tangential to what the Laity Decree proposed.

Accountability to the Council?
Another development in the United States is the proposal in diocesan guidelines that standing committees and ministerial commissions are accountable to the council. This can suggest that committees and commissions are no longer autonomous. It can imply that they must take direction from the council, which ensures that they carry out its policies. If so, this development is incompatible with the Laity Decree. It clearly stated that the council may coordinate groups but not in such a way that it infringes upon their autonomy and particular nature. A forced coordination may crush the "spontaneous zeal" of which the Missionary Decree spoke.

Executive Authority?
The executive authority of the council is a third development among U.S. councils and incompatible with Vatican II teaching. Many diocesan guidelines state that committees and commissions implement the policies of the council. They say that these groups are the council's working arms. Implementation may connote an executive role for the council, as if it directed parish ministries independently of the pastor. It may suggest that the council, rather than the pastor, supervises ministry. When it does, it contradicts the teaching of Vatican II, which stated that councils are consultative bodies.[5]

In short, the word coordination is ambiguous. It describes a proper task of councils, but a task that can be misinterpreted. Coordination clearly expresses the hope of Vatican II that councils might assist lay associations and undertakings as well as missioners. Councils exist in part to serve the purposes of these groups, taking care not to frustrate them or impose upon them. That is the rightful meaning of coordination. At the same time, coordination can be wrongly interpreted. Some have mistakenly proposed that councils must oversee a system of ministries, that these ministries are accountable to the council, and that the council enjoys executive authority. These proposals contradict the spirit and the letter of Vatican II.

Correcting False Developments

Some took the 1983 publication of the Code of Canon Law as an opportunity to correct these false developments. The Code referred to pastoral, not apostolic councils. In that connection it ignored the Laity Decree. It did not say that councils can coordinate. It was silent about standing committees and ministerial commissions. It emphasized that councils enjoy a consultative vote only. Some suggested that the 1983 Code was a better interpretation of the ecumenical council's intentions than the documents of Vatican II themselves, and that it required a correction in the course of parish councils.

Their argument, as we saw in Chapter Twelve, had two presuppositions. First, it presupposed that the bishops of Vatican II had intended parish pastoral councils, not apostolic councils. Second, it presupposed that the teaching about coordination in the Laity Decree did not apply to pastoral councils. These presuppositions led to the conclusion that pioneers in the parish council movement had misunderstood Vatican II. Henceforth, the critics argued, parish councils (of the "apostolic" type) needed to reconstitute themselves as "pastoral" councils.

This argument, however, does not hold water. The documents of Vatican II relating to councils are ambiguous. They do not speak of parish pastoral councils. In the one place where they speak of councils at the parish level, they speak of apostolic councils that may coordinate. Coordination is not reserved for some hypothetical apostolic council recommended by the Missionary Decree, but belongs to pastoral councils as well.[6] It is simply false to say that the Code of Canon Law (with its silence about coordination) is superior to the documents of Vatican II or better expresses the intention of the bishops regarding parish councils. Those who seek to understand parish councils should not exclude some Vatican II texts in favor of others.

A Faithful Interpretation of the Code

The proper answer to false developments is, first of all, a faithful interpretation of the Code in the light of Vatican II, not the other way around. The Code speaks, in canon 536, of parish pastoral councillors who "give their help in fostering pastoral activity." How do they give this help? The primary way was defined in the Decree on Bishops and subsequent official publications. Pastoral councils investigate and consider matters relating to pastoral activity and formulate practical conclusions concerning them. The threefold task of investigation, consideration, and formulation is the primary business of pastoral councils.

The threefold task is not, however, the only business of pastoral councils. They can also coordinate. This is clearly stated in the Decree on Missionary Activity, as we saw above. It stated that missionary bishops should establish diocesan pastoral councils precisely for better coordination. So coordination is within the purview of DPCs. It is also within the purview, I believe, of parish pastoral councils. When the Vatican II Laity Decree recommended councils at the parish level to assist the church's apostolate, it gave them a coordinating function. That is implicit in the Laity Decree's statement (at no. 26) that councils "may" (but need not) coordinate. To be sure, the Laity Decree recommended "apostolic," not "pastoral" councils. But if we interpret the language of Laity 26 as a precursor of parish pastoral councils, then PPCs may also coordinate. Coordination is subordinate to their main work, but remains a legitimate activity.

A proper grasp of coordination offers a second answer to the false developments we have described. The council that wrongly sees itself as the official supervisor of parish ministry, or as an executive body to which all ministries are accountable, misunderstands coordination. Coordination is a service to parish ministries. It begins by appreciating their nature. It wants to promote the well-being and success of ministries as they (under the pastor's supervision) define them. It honors the principle of subsidiarity, namely, that no decisions should be made for ministries that the ministries can make for themselves. Maintaining the spirit and enthusiasm of others is fundamental to coordination. That is the way the church understands it.

Coordination and Autonomy

Father Chirico, the pastor of St. Alphonsus Church whom we met at the beginning of this chapter, properly understood the principle of coordination. He showed this when he told the pastoral council that youth ministry and religious education needed time to absorb its proposals for enhanced cooperation. Some of his councillors expressed disappointment (and even indignation) when their proposals were not immediately implemented. Their view of the pastoral council was mistaken. They believed that its main task was coordination and that the two ministries were answerable to it. But Father Chirico's idea of coordination is better. He recognized that cooperation is a service that cannot be imposed. He wanted to discuss the proposals with his youth minister and religious education director. He saw that the council's work of coordinating the two ministries could only succeed if it honored their own right to govern themselves.

The coordination of standing committees and ministerial commissions, common to pastoral councils in the United States, needs to be rightly interpreted. These committees and commissions have their origin and source of being in the parish, not in the council. They express the ministerial aims of parishioners, for whom the pastor is the proper spokesman. They implement *parish* initiatives, properly speaking, initiatives of the parish whose practical wisdom the council seeks. When councils coordinate, they do so as the pastor's consultants. They offer a service to the pastor and the parish, recognizing that sound coordination respects the right of ministries to govern themselves.

The task of coordinating ministerial efforts is an inalienable right of councils, according to Vatican II. But it is not their main work. Vatican II did not describe the principal work of councils as coordination, but allowed coordination as a possibility. It is subordinate to the main work, namely, assisting the apostolate or the work of pastors. That work deserves to be called pastoral planning and is the subject of the next chapter.

Chapter Eighteen

The Main Purpose
of the Council

What should be the main work of the parish pastoral council? The clearest answer comes from the church's official documents. The main work of the pastoral council in general, they say, is the threefold task of investigating pastoral matters, reflecting on them, and recommending practical conclusions to the pastor. To be sure, most official references to the threefold task of the pastoral council speak of such councils at the diocesan, not the parish level. But if we define the pastoral council as a distinct type of council that may exist at various levels, then I would argue that the threefold description of its task applies to parish as well as diocesan councils. Vatican documents almost unanimously describe the pastoral council as a body that investigates, ponders, and draws practical conclusions.[1]

One may respond that Canon 536 defines the parish pastoral council without reference to this threefold task. It states that pastoral councils merely "give their help in fostering pastoral activity." In my view, the language of this canon is vague and unsatisfactory. All Christians are to give such help, we could say. What is unique to the parish pastoral council? I answer that it helps by doing what pastoral councils in general do. It studies pastoral matters, reflects on them, and draws appropriate conclusions.

Council practitioners in the United States increasingly tend to describe the threefold task of pastoral councils as pastoral planning. Planning has not been, generally speaking, the terminology of Vatican documents.[2] But the threefold task they assign to councils is fully consistent with pastoral planning. Practitioners have spoken about pastoral planning by parish councils since the mid-1970s. In the mid-1980s, they began to describe a comprehensive planning role for councils. The 1989 creation of the Conference for Pastoral Planning and Council Development signified that pastoral planning was the main task of councils, at least for many diocesan professionals with responsibility for planning and councils.[3] The professionals say that investigating parish matters, reflecting on them, and proposing practical conclusions "is" pastoral planning.

To say *that* parish councils ought to do pastoral planning, however, does not explain about *what* councils plan. Yes, they investigate, reflect, and propose. But about what? It does not suffice to say that they plan regarding "pastoral matters." Efforts to define pastoral matters as more visionary than practical, more spiritual than material, and more consensus-oriented than parliamentary, have not been satisfactory. They do not reflect the church's official documents, which indicate that "pastoral" means pertaining to the pastor. To be sure, there are many suggestions about the proper focus of pastoral councils—parish ministries, planning themes, and topics taken from canon law. These recommendations about the scope of pastoral planning are helpful, but they cannot settle the matter.[4] No one can predict with certainty what situation a parish will face.

The scope of pastoral planning is hard to describe because it concerns contingent matters, as we saw in Chapter Fifteen. Pastoral councils seek to represent practical wisdom, wisdom about what a community should do in a given situation. In this chapter we will see that practical wisdom is the key to defining the council's main work. No one can fully predict it because the situation is constantly changing. What the council needs to plan for depends on the parish and the pastor. The idea of contingent knowledge suggests that we cannot describe with certainty the topics about which a parish must plan.

We can clarify the task of the pastoral council, however, by contrasting it with the finance council. Canon 537 obliges every parish to have one. Finance councils aid the pastor in the administration of parish goods. What is the difference between the finance council and the pastoral council? As an illustration, let us consider the Church of All Hallows where the pastor, Father Roger LaBonte, faces an enviable situation.

The Church of All Hallows
All Hallows Church (this story has been fictionalized) lies in a north-eastern city that, for many years, suffered an economic depression. Employment was low, and the population fell. Then a major drug company decided to move its corporate headquarters to the city. It built a huge campus with an administrative center, research facility, and factory. Within a decade, the fortunes of the city changed. Employment rose, the tax base swelled, and the population grew. Under the direction of Father LaBonte, All Hallows built a new church according to the latest liturgical principles, with the altar in the midst of the congregation. After years of belt-tightening to erase the debt, the income at All Hallows now exceeds its operating expenses. Father LaBonte wants to know what to do with the surplus. He consulted his pastoral and his finance council about where should he put it and how he should spend it.

The finance council advised Father LaBonte, first of all, that the excess income is not "excess" at all. The councillors reminded him that the parish rectory needs a new roof. Unforeseen emergencies may arise. The so-called extra income, they said, belongs in the bank. It is only prudent to have parish savings.

The pastoral council took a different tack. The councillors opposed the idea of simply banking the excess. They argued that ministry should take precedence over financial security. After years of saving to pay off the debt, they asked, how could Father LaBonte even think of establishing a savings account? Religious education needs books. The choir needs new music. The youth ministry program needs a full-time director. Ministry budgets always lag behind fixed and operating expenses. Extra income belongs in the ministry budgets.

Father LaBonte was dismayed to receive two different opinions about what to do with the extra income. To be sure, he took some consolation in knowing that disputes about a surplus are better than disputes about a deficit. But he realized the danger of serious disagreement about parish income. His finance and his pastoral councillors represented two differ-

ent viewpoints, each of which is reasonable, each of which has its supporters in the parish. To which should he listen?

If he were to pay more attention to the finance council, he would
become a fiscal conservative. Under its influence, he would save for capital improvements and avoid additional ministry expenses. But Father
LaBonte knows that there is more to parish administration than money
in the bank. Pastoral council members were quick to remind him of that.
If he were to accept their advice, he would appear more responsive to
parishioner needs. With the pastoral council's recommendations, ministries might grow and flourish. But should this happen, he asked himself, at the expense of fiscal security?

The Proper Task of the Two Councils

If we want to better understand the task of the pastoral council, we need
to distinguish it from that of the finance council. This distinction is not
easy. To be sure, the church's documents speak about the task of these
councils in different ways. Pastoral councils have the threefold task of
investigating pastoral works, pondering them, and proposing practical
conclusions. Finance councils aid the pastor in the administration of
parish goods. On the surface, the tasks are quite different.

Two kinds of difficulties, however, can produce confusion. One difficulty is about the scope of the two councils. Are "pastoral" matters really distinct from the "administration" of parish goods? Or is administration part of the pastoral task? The second difficulty involves the relation
between the two councils. Are they independent, or is the finance council subordinate to the pastoral council? In order to solve these difficulties
(and define more clearly the task of the pastoral council), let us look at
each in turn.

The Finance Council

The church's law includes a single canon on parish finance councils.[5]
Canon 537 describes their task as follows:

> Each parish is to have a finance council which is regulated by universal law
> as well as by norms issued by the diocesan bishop; in this council the
> Christian faithful, selected according to the same norms, aid the pastor in
> the administration of parish goods.

Aiding the pastor in the administration of parish goods—that is the work of the finance council. Does this mean that pastoral councils have nothing to do with administration? Such was the interpretation of the late John Keating, Bishop of Arlington. He said that, according to canon 537, the administration of parish goods is the province of the finance council. He drew the conclusion that temporal matters belong to the finance council, and pastoral matters belong to the pastoral council. No pastoral council, he maintained, should deal with parish administration.[6]

Bishop Keating's view has proven unpersuasive, however, because it unduly restricts the scope of the pastoral council. That scope has been consistently described as "pastoral matters." To be sure, Vatican documents distinguish between the exercise of jurisdiction or governing power and the consultative role of the pastoral council. But that does not mean that questions of governance or administration are off-limits for the pastoral council. Indeed, the Congregation for the Clergy's 1973 Circular Letter on Pastoral Councils made this explicit. It stated that pastoral councils may consider acts of governance that belong specifically to the pastor as the one who legally acts on behalf of the parish.[7]

Few canonists would admit Bishop Keating's sharp distinction between pastoral matters and parish administration.[8] To say that the administration of the parish does not fall within the scope of "pastoral matters" curtails the pastor's freedom to consult as he sees fit.

In short, we cannot divide the pastoral and the finance council on the basis of their scope or subject matter. But canon 537 suggests another avenue when it describes how finance councils are regulated. It says that finance councils are "regulated by universal law as well as by norms issued by the diocesan bishop." If we want to know more about finance councils, we have to examine what diocesan bishops say about them.

Diocesan Guidelines on Finance Councils
The intentions of bishops regarding finance councils are expressed in the norms for finance councils published by various dioceses. In 1994, I examined seven different guidelines for finance councils, published by the dioceses of Harrisburg, Richmond, Cleveland, Milwaukee, St. Louis, San Antonio, and Los Angeles.[9] Each states that finance councils should help the pastor prepare the parish budget. Six out of seven recommend that finance councils assist the pastor in making periodic financial reports. Four state that finance councils advise the pastor on major

expenditures or long-term contracts, oversee the parish's accounts and financial record-keeping, recommend parish investments, and monitor the parish's financial security and collections.

About the relation between the finance and the pastoral councils, however, there are some disagreements. To be sure, all agree that the two councils should coordinate their work. But coordination means different things. In some dioceses, coordination means that finance councils are subordinate to pastoral councils. I cannot say how many dioceses in the U.S. endorse this, but the finance council guidelines for the dioceses of Milwaukee, Harrisburg, and St. Louis (for example) recommend it.[10]

The superiority of the pastoral council, however, is not universally acknowledged. The finance council guidelines of the dioceses of Richmond, Cleveland, and Los Angeles state that the relation between finance and pastoral councils should be "cooperative."[11] One council is not subordinate to the other. Indeed, many could argue that an attempt to make one council superior to the other contradicts the consultative nature of church councils. How can one consultative group demand that another conform to its wishes, as if the finance council were merely consultative and the pastoral council had administrative authority? The ploy of making one council superior to the other not only lacks universal acceptance, but may well violate the very soul of consultation.

To sum up, there have been two efforts to distinguish between the proper work of finance and pastoral councils. One effort, that of Bishop Keating, has been to distinguish between the two councils on the basis of their subject matter. "Pastoral" concerns belong to pastoral councils, and "administration" belongs to finance councils. This effort, however, does not reflect the intention of Vatican II and unduly restricts the pastor's freedom to consult. In diocesan guidelines we see another effort to clarify how the two types of councils may cooperate. Some guidelines recommend that pastoral councils coordinate finance councils as ministries of the parish, and are superior to them. Others describe the two as relatively independent. There is no single point of view.

An Aristotelian Solution
Past attempts to coordinate finance and pastoral councils by curtailing their subject matter or defining their relationship have not been entirely successful. We have seen that administrative concerns belong as much to the pastoral council as to the finance council. Diocesan guidelines do not

agree that one council is subordinate to the other. Since defining the relationship between the two on the basis of subject matter or a hierarchical relationship do not suffice, another effort is required. I would like to propose a "new" way to correlate the two councils. It is based on the type of knowledge that each council seeks, on the method of each, and on the gifts of councillors.[12] This "new" attempt is grounded on very old principles, the principles laid down by Aristotle.

In Chapter Fifteen we treated the question of ecclesial representation with the help of Aristotle's *Nicomachean Ethics*. Aristotle distinguished in Book VI between two types of knowledge. One is always and everywhere true, and Aristotle called it "science." The other seeks what is best in a concrete situation. Aristotle called it "practical wisdom," namely, the knowledge that people seek by means of dialogue. This is what pastoral councils seek. They aim at a particular kind of truth, the truth about contingent matters, the truth about how a parish should act in a changing situation. Pastoral councils are "representative" in that they seek to "represent" this practical wisdom of the People of God. Finance councils, by contrast, are concerned about the sciences of finance and accounting. They apply these disciplines to the tangible goods of the parish.

Aristotle's distinction between practical wisdom and science can help us understand finance and pastoral councils. The two councils not only seek different kinds of knowledge, but employ distinct methods and require different gifts in councillors. We will first examine the types of knowledge that the two councils seek. Then we will show that each proceeds according to its own method, the two methods of demonstration and deliberation. Finally, we will see that each council requires different abilities in its members. Distinguishing between them will help us understand the proper role of the pastoral council.

Types of Knowledge
Science, for Aristotle, does not refer to the "scientific method" as we know it today. It is not merely the work of formulating hypotheses and testing them in a laboratory. To science (the Greek word is *theoria*) belongs every kind of knowledge that is always and everywhere true. It is the knowledge of the expert. Science is the knowledge of those things that cannot be other than what they are.

Practical wisdom, on the other hand, has to do with action. Practical wisdom (in Greek: *phronesis*) concerns deeds that we may or may not want to do. People with practical wisdom, says Aristotle, have a capacity for seeing what is good. The good that they see is not an abstraction, but rather the best choice of action in a given situation. It is contingent on the pastor and the parish. Those with practical wisdom are able to rightly judge how matters stand with a particular community.

Finance councils are concerned with the realm of what is always and everywhere true. No matter how the finance council categorizes the budget, income can never be more than what the parish has collected. Expenses can be no less than what the parish has spent. This is not mere opinion. The finance council can actually demonstrate its knowledge with collection receipts and check stubs.

Pastoral council members, by contrast, focus on something other than what is presently the case. Their concern is the future: what can and should be. A parish can make many different choices about religious education, liturgy, social justice, parish renovation, and care for the elderly. Everyone will admit that no parish can do everything. That is where practical wisdom comes in. The council with practical wisdom helps a pastor decide what the parish ought to do with limited resources.

So finance councils are scientific, in Aristotle's sense of the word, and pastoral councils are practically wise. Aristotle enables us to distinguish between them. But what are the consequences for the way the two councils run?

The Method of the Two Councils

Aristotle states that scientific knowledge can be demonstrated and taught. If we apply his insight to the finance council, we see the council's fundamentally scientific nature. Finance councils have two main tasks: they make periodic reports, and they help a pastor prepare the parish budget. In making reports, they show what has been collected and spent. And in budgeting, they project next year's income from a history of the last year's income. This is the basis for the following year's payroll, operating expenses, and capital improvements. The goal of the finance council is straightforward. It is to demonstrate the parish's finances and to teach what will happen if income and expenses are as projected. The basic principles of accounting are fixed, unchangeable, and (as Aristotle would say) scientific.

In the pastoral council, however, there is no "scientific" way to proceed. Without a doubt, pastoral councils amass facts, study issues, and calculate with regard to worthwhile ends. They proceed scientifically in the sense that their goal is knowledge. But the knowledge that pastoral councils seek is not the demonstrably scientific knowledge of finance councils. It is rather a kind of wisdom: the knowledge of what is good for a community and the ability to discriminate about what the community desires. "Reasoning must affirm what desire pursues," wrote Aristotle. The pastoral council must hold up to the light of reason the desires of the parish community, affirming what is good and recommending it to the pastor.

So finance councils proceed by demonstration, that is, by showing and making clear. They manifest the financial reality of the parish, projecting it into the future. They demonstrate this financial reality on the basis of scientific principles of accounting.

Pastoral councils, by contrast, proceed by deliberation. They have no fixed-and-firm scientific method. Why? Because what they deliberate about—namely, the changing needs of the parish—follows no fixed rules. Pastoral councils apply a capacity for seeing the community's good. This capacity, practical wisdom, enables them to consider a number of actions, all of which are good in themselves. Their wisdom is "practical" because it aims at choice and action. Pastoral councillors choose—from among all the good things the parish could *possibly* do—what it should *actually* do.

The Gifts of Councillors
Not only do the tasks of pastoral and finance councils differ; the councillors themselves ought to have different gifts. Finance council members should have expert knowledge. They should be familiar with the science of accounting, should be able to rigorously demonstrate the parish's finances, and should be able to express their conclusions to the pastor. Financial knowledge is the primary criterion for selecting finance councillors.

Pastoral council members, however, need not be scientific experts. Their gift is deliberation. They should know the parish. They should be able to judge how it will respond to new initiatives. They should be able to express their opinions well and to listen attentively to the opinions of others. Above all, they should be able to synthesize the various opinions, clarifying them and making sound recommendations. Their goal is not to gain an advantage for one group at the expense of another, but to seek the common good. By controlling their passions, Aristotle said, the wise preserve the ability to judge correctly.

Ordinary parishioners can discern among themselves, as we saw in

Chapter Sixteen, about the gift of deliberation. It is wise to involve the parishioners in the choice of pastoral councillors. But no guideline suggests a popular election of finance councillors. They are experts and should be chosen for their expert ability. Not everyone can serve as pastoral and finance councillors. People without scientific knowledge of accounting should decline the invitation to be finance council members. Those who are impatient with discussion, who lack the ability to consider all sides of a question, and who want to impulsively "get on with the job" of the parish, need not apply for the pastoral council.

Whose Advice?

Father LaBonte received conflicting opinions from his finance and pastoral council about what to do with the surplus at All Hallows. He had two questions: where should he put the surplus and what should he do with it? About the first question, I agree with the finance council. Extra income belongs in the bank, at least until the pastor decides to spend it. The finance council was able to demonstrate the extent of the surplus and to recommend an account in which to put it.

Banking the surplus was an appropriate recommendation for the finance council. It recognized that its job is not to decide how to spend the money, but to keep track of it. Finance councillors knew that their goal was the application of the principles of finance and accounting, scientific principles that are always and everywhere true. They were wise not to recommend spending the money, for that is a question of right action, and beyond the finance council's scope.

Father LaBonte's second question was about how to spend the money, namely, a question about action. This was an appropriate question for the pastoral council. Since there is no scientific rule about how best to act, Father LaBonte wanted to deliberate about it. He did well to consult the pastoral council, because its members are good at deliberation. The councillors know that there are many opinions among parishioners about where the parish should spend its money. These opinions have to be collected, understood, and weighed. Only then is it possible to wisely discriminate among them.

Father LaBonte was aware that some parishioners resented the constant fund-raising efforts necessary to pay off the parish debt. At the same time, he knew that parish donations were still high and there was a good esprit among the people of All Hallows. He wanted to maintain that esprit, and did not want to simply spend the parish money on this or that good idea. With the parish debt gone, his church was in a fundamentally new situation and enjoyed a freedom that it had not known for years. Father LaBonte wanted to know more about this new situation. He asked the pastoral council to help him conduct a series of parish assemblies. Their purpose was to listen to parishioners, inquire about how the parish mission had changed, and build commitment to that new mission. In this way, he recognized the fundamental purpose of the pastoral council, namely, to deliberate and so to make present the community's practical wisdom.

Conclusion: Science and Practical Wisdom

Pastors should consult the finance council in order to know the parish's financial reality. They should consult the pastoral council when they want to deliberate about what to do in a particular situation. That is the lesson of Aristotle.

Pastors who distinguish between pastoral and finance councils along Aristotelian lines may still receive conflicting advice. But if they know what each council is good at, they can ask the questions that pertain to each. There are, of course, no impermeable borders between the two councils. Aristotle himself recognized that discussions of truth admit only the precision that the subject at hand allows. Scientists aim at strict demonstration, he said, and the practically wise aim at what is probably good. By distinguishing between the two, a pastor can invite his councillors' best efforts. The doctrine of Aristotle suggests that each council pursues a different goal, proceeds in a different way, and requires different talents. Pastors should be aware of this and tailor their questions to the abilities of each council.

The pastoral council seeks practical wisdom, that is, the knowledge about what the parish ought to do in its concrete situation. When the church asks councils to investigate pastoral matters, ponder them, and propose practical conclusions, it invites them to seek such wisdom. Catholics in the U.S. call this search "pastoral planning." It is the main task of councils.

Chapter Nineteen

The Meaning of Consultation

William Rademacher, with six books about parish councils to his credit, was the foremost thinker of the council movement in the 1970s and 1980s. After years of writing about councils, he shifted his focus in the 1990s to lay ministry.[1] Then, at the end of a decade of relative silence about councils, he returned to them. In 2000 he published an article that criticized the phrase "consultative vote only," the phrase from Canon 536 that circumscribes the legal authority of councils. His article was a vigorous attack on the church's doctrine about councils. By limiting their legal authority, Rademacher suggested, the church robs the power of councils to express the Holy Spirit, distorts the proper relation between pastors and people, and reinforces an inadequate form of church governance.[2]

Rademacher argued that the "consultative vote" of councils, namely, the teaching that they only advise the pastor, tends to muzzle the truth. It doubts the presence of the Spirit in the people of God and gags the prophetic impulse. This was implicit in Rademacher's description of the

Holy Spirit and ecclesiastical law as two opposing "power systems" between which "there is bound to be a conflict." A class conflict between pastors and parishioners, he suggested, was inevitable. In Rademacher's view, many pastors do not want advice. They want unlimited power to command the parish.

Instead of giving unlimited power to pastors, Rademacher would oblige them to listen to their people. Consultation, he said, does not suffice. He stated that the consultative-only clause reduces the laity's participation in Christ's prophetic office "to mere advice-giving." Preferable to consultation, he said, is prayerful discernment. If we could only compel pastors to sit down and work out their differences with a council in a spiritual atmosphere, pastoral matters would improve. The laity's word is less robust, spiritual, and prophetic, implied Rademacher, because the pastor is not obliged to take it.

In his article Rademacher went so far as to criticize the hierarchical model of Roman Catholic governance. The council's consultative-only vote depends on this model, which, Rademacher wrote, "serves poorly, if at all." He stated that he would like to phase it out and recover "the patriarchate, presbyterial, or synodal models" of governance. In other words, he would like to see a number of apostolic patriarchs (rather than Roman primacy), or boards of elders, or rule by councils. "Many good Catholics in their personal faith life have selectively phased out the hierarchy," Rademacher wrote. For that reason, he suggested, the current system of governance has outlived its usefulness.

No one can protest that the problems identified by Rademacher are imaginary or unreal. Pastors do not always work well with councils. When a pastor's failure to consult alienates parishioners, it is tempting to look for other forms of governance. But Rademacher's proposed solutions to these problems are shortsighted. Difficulties with consultation do not render it useless. To be sure, the "consultative only" doctrine may appear to demean councils. But there is more to consultation than its superficial appearance.

In this chapter, we will first look at the ecclesial meaning of consultation. Our goal is to manifest the church's intention. The church intends consultation in a proper context—the context of mutual appreciation, charity, and dialogue—and this context gives councils a clear goal. They enable us to distinguish between council functions, properly speaking, and dysfunctions.

Ecclesial Consultation

To say that councils have a "consultative" role may suggest to some read-ers an understanding that is legalistic, narrow, and unappreciative. The word "consultative" means that the vote of councils is not deliberative or legally binding. Councils cannot overrule the pastor. Church law limits their authority. The insistence that councils are consultative-only may appear legalistic. It may also seem narrow-minded. This book has argued that the main purpose of parish pastoral councils is the threefold task of investigating and reflecting on pastoral matters and proposing practical conclusions. Other purposes, such as fostering pastoral activity and assisting the church's apostolic work (with the possibility of coordinat-ing lay initiatives), are distinctly secondary. This narrows the council's role. Indeed, it may seem to disparage councils, minimizing their share in responsibility for the parish.[3] Readers may conclude that this book pays insufficient attention to the "pastoral" attributes of the council, popularly understood as visionary, consensus-oriented, and spiritual. Is this true? Are we being legalistic, narrow-minded, and unappreciative when we emphasize the consultative role of councils?[4]

I do not think so. Ecclesial consultation implies shared responsibility. This is the idea that every faithful Christian shares responsibility for the church's well-being, each according to his or her own gifts.[5] Shared respon-sibility is anything but legalistic, narrow-minded, and unappreciative. It suggests a more adequate understanding of ecclesial consultation. In this more adequate understanding, the pastor takes a leading role. He consults with particularly Christian motives, wanting to know his people more deeply and love them more fully. We will examine his motives in the next chapter. For the present, it is important to see how he employs a broad repertoire of consultative styles. He adapts them to his council, depending on the members' readiness to undertake its work. Shared responsibility also implies the council's commitment to a mode of inquiry that is profoundly Christian and appreciative. It grasps the proper method of councils, the method of dialogue. This chapter will look at the pastor's repertoire, at sit-uational and appreciative leadership, and at the meaning of dialogue.

The Pastor's Repertoire

Bishop John Cummins of Oakland, as we saw in Chapter Five, had a wide repertoire of consultative styles. He knew, first of all, that he was not bound by the recommendations of his pastoral council. He could invite the council to express its opinions without legally committing himself to them. At the same time, however, he recognized that the council possessed a certain authority. This recognition was a second style in his consultative repertoire. He knew that the council exercised a persuasive power in its work of investigating, reflecting, and proposing conclusions. He had invited it to undertake its work. He felt bound intellectually and morally to honor it.

Throughout his work with the pastoral council, Bishop Cummins sought consensus, that is, a common understanding. This was a third consultative style. He presupposed rightly that he and his councillors were engaged in a search for practical wisdom. Together they sought the truth about pastoral situations, using the method of dialogue to discern the reality and to enrich one another's grasp of it. In the formation of this consensus, Bishop Cummins asked questions, sought clarifications, and posed challenges, all with the goal of deepening the common understanding.

When the council reached consensus with the bishop and proposed it in the form of a recommendation, the bishop usually accepted it. He ratified (a fourth style of consultation) what the council proposed. Often the viewpoint of the bishop and the council were so close that the formalities—namely, a separate recommendation and acceptance—were not observed. The two actions became one. To be sure, the bishop was not surrendering authority to the council. He was in fact accepting its recommendations. But a casual observer might think that it was the council who was making policy, rather than proposing it to the bishop. This fifth style was also part of Bishop Cummins' consultative repertoire.

When we speak of the council as "consultative only," we are tempted to imagine an impersonal relationship between pastor and councillors. He consults. They advise. Regarding their advice, he can take it or leave it. We may even suppose that councillors are akin to hired consultants. They sell their knowledge, and the buyer's relation to them may be purely financial. In ecclesial consultation, however, nothing could be farther from the truth. This was the lesson of Bishop Cummins. A pastor's councillors are not hired hands. In the church's view they are brothers and sisters. The good pastor treats them with honor and love. The bad pastor—the one who treats them impersonally, casually, or without serious attention—betrays the idea of ecclesial consultation.

Situational Leadership
New councils are often unable to offer a pastor the wisdom he most

needs. The members may be novices at consultation. They may not be aware of the problems the pastor faces. They may lack confidence in their capacity to study pastoral matters and reach a sound conclusion about them. This may frustrate a pastor who expected his council to immediately plunge into pastoral planning. Councillors may sense his frustration, feel inadequate to the task, and resent the pastor's overblown expectations.

The management concept of situational leadership can remedy this problem.[6] At the heart of situational leadership is the principle that good leaders adapt themselves to the readiness of their followers. Pastors recognize that, whenever people are new to a job, they usually lack knowledge and confidence. With an inexperienced council, the good pastor should take charge and offer clear directions. Inexperienced councillors will not resent strong leadership, according to this theory, but appreciate the pastor's willingness to direct them. They want to know what to do, and he can tell them.

Later, as pastoral councillors become veterans, the pastor should change his style. He should become less directive and invite the council to take the initiative. Eventually, when he is confident of their abilities, he can pay more attention to interpersonal relations. He can confide in them and invite their confidence, trusting in their loyalty. Finally, when he feels completely secure about their abilities, he can simply delegate many tasks to them, knowing that they will perform them in a competent manner. An experienced council challenges the pastor to refine his delegating skills.

It is important for pastors to remember, however, that councillors are not unpaid parish staff members. The council's role is not to carry out the administration of the parish, but to advise the pastor. He may delegate certain tasks to them, but his ultimate goal is to tap their wisdom. To do this, he needs to be with them, to attend their meetings, to engage them in dialogue. If he fails to make the distinction between staff and council, delegating to them as he would to his staff, he does councillors a disservice. To be sure, there are many things that council members must do on their own. They must study, attend meetings, talk to parishioners, and write reports outside of the pastor's presence. But they undertake these tasks so that they can reflect with the pastor on a deeper level and draw sound conclusions. Although he may delegate tasks to this council member or that, the heart of consultation is the dialogue of the council. A pastor who absents himself from council meetings may give councillors the impression that he does not want to work with them.

A pastor is a mediator. In the vision of the Letter to the Hebrews, the priest stands between the faithful and God, offering prayers and sacrifices on their behalf. His effectiveness depends on their willingness to grant him that privilege. When we translate this into the terms of the pastoral council, we see that the pastor enjoys a profound relationship of trust. Councillors trust him to speak his mind and share with them his concerns. He trusts the council to speak the truth. Although a pastor is the bishop's delegate, and his legal authority does not stem from his people, nevertheless his success depends on them. He should adapt his consultative style to their knowledge and level of confidence. Situational leadership enables him to understand this necessary adaptation.

Appreciative Inquiry
Ecclesial consultation is an encounter with faith. Some of the most satisfying moments I ever spent with Oakland's diocesan pastoral council were in prayer. I remember one meeting when the work of the Oakland council was nothing more exciting than to review a draft report on youth ministry. Bishop Cummins had asked the DPC to study youth ministry and recommend ways to strengthen it. The subcommittee had done its work, the report had been mailed out, and the DPC's task was to assess it.

Instead of rushing into a point-by-point critique, the council prayed for more than an hour. It began with Joel's prophecy of the time of the Spirit: "The old shall dream dreams, and the young shall see visions." Then Bishop Cummins invited the council members to recall their own memories of the church when they were young, and to express how they felt that God's Spirit was "speaking" through the youth ministry report.

What followed was an extraordinary outpouring of memory, self-revelation, anecdote, appreciation of the sub-committee, critique, and discernment. By the end of the prayer the council had not only "prayed," but also accomplished the most important part of its "work" regarding the report. The members had expressed, in their prayer, what the report meant to them and connected it with their own experience. The sub-committee members who sat on the council were gratified to see the report's effect. Having also heard the few reservations that had been expressed, they were ready to start work on a second draft. And Bishop Cummins had begun to reflect on what the report's recommendations could mean for the diocese. He had led us in a prayer that was much more than prayer—or better said, was truly prayer.

"Appreciative" is the word that describes the good pastor's leadership and the council's mode of inquiry. He appreciates his people. He encourages councillors to recall their experiences of faith. He invites them to connect their faith with the fabric of parish life.

The concept of appreciative inquiry has a venerable ancestry. It is connected to the Pauline doctrine of justification by faith. When pastors and councillors show their appreciation for the parish, they acknowledge the faith that is its reason for being. Before any council reflects on a problem, evaluates a ministry, or discusses a policy, it is, at the most fundamental level, an assembly of faithful people. The appreciative pastor begins with that acknowledgment. No matter what work has brought the group together, it is first a communion in the Body of Christ. That communion is more important than (and is the basis for) any mission the group undertakes.

Appreciative inquiry[7] measures success not by the number of problems one can name and attempt to solve, but with a question. It asks about what gives life to those who are gathered. The application to church councils is obvious. If a pastor believes in his council, its meetings will cease to be a depressing litany of problems to be solved. Instead the meetings can become what they should be, namely, moments of encounter with the mystery that formed the group in the first place. Every council meeting is potentially a rekindling of faith. Appreciation ought to be the heart of council prayer. When pastors consult their councils, they never merely seek answers to problems. They are also putting those problems into their proper context. That context is the faith that has formed the parish community and sustains it. Consultation presupposes faith.

The Method of Dialogue

It is worth noting that the Second Vatican Council, in its texts about apostolic and pastoral councils, did not speak of a method. Vatican II did not say how pastoral councils were to accomplish their threefold task, or how apostolic councils were to assist the church's apostolic work. But the Decree on the Apostolate of Lay People, apart from its recommendation about councils, spoke about how priests and people were to work together.[8] It said:

The laity should develop the habit of working in the parish in close union with their priests, of bringing before the ecclesial community their own problems, world problems, and questions regarding man's salvation, to examine them together and solve them by general discussion.

The phrase "by general discussion" is a translation of the Latin word "consiliis," that is, council. The text suggests that laity and priests should "take counsel" together. In this way they can examine questions and solve them. Although this passage does not recommend the formation of councils per se, it intimates a conciliar method. In recent years, this passage has been cited as a source for parish councils.[9] Their "method," we can say, is the common examination of questions in order to solve them. It is the method of dialogue.

Pope Paul VI affirmed this method in his first encyclical letter, *Ecclesiam Suam*. The encyclical, published in the summer before the Laity Decree, was undoubtedly one of its sources. The third section of the encyclical is entitled "Dialogue." Dialogue is the means, according to the encyclical, by which the church becomes more aware of itself and reforms itself. When priests and people discuss their common concerns, they better understand the church and their own role in the drama of salvation. A dialogue among the faithful can lead to deeper faith. "By introducing the notion of dialogue (human dialogue leading men into divine dialogue)," wrote Gregory Baum, "the Pope seeks . . . a more unified understanding of the church's mission."[10] A seemingly "human" dialogue has "divine" consequences. Dialogue encompasses all activities in the church. When we deepen our relationship with one another in a dialogue about pastoral matters, we deepen our relationship with God.

Dialogue is the method of ecclesial consultation. It examines questions and solves them, but not by some impersonal, "scientific," and narrowly empirical process. Rather in dialogue we express opinions and subject them to an examination that is both critical and appreciative. The council assembles in a spirit of inquiry. It acknowledges its standing before God and the parish community. It affirms the insights of its members and puts them into play, holding them up to the light of reason informed by faith, committing themselves to the truth, anticipating that members will gain a deeper insight from one another. This, said Paul VI, is the kind of human dialogue that leads to dialogue with God. It is the method of ecclesial consultation.

A properly "ecclesial" consultation refutes the critique of William Rademacher, discussed at the beginning of this chapter. He said that the consultative-only doctrine deprived councils of courage in the face of pastors who do not want to listen. He argued that pastors ought to be compelled to reach consensus with their councillors. He suggested that the church's mode of governance, in which pastors consult their people but are not legally bound by the advice, has outlived its usefulness. The idea of ecclesial consultation suggests that Rademacher has misrepresented the church's view. The church wants consultations that are sensitive to a contingent situation, respectful and appreciative of council members, and committed to the method of dialogue. Rademacher does not give this its due weight. But he does speak from experience. His critique has an element of truth. Like any family, councils occasionally have problems. What can a council do when it encounters dysfunction?

Council Dysfunction

There are two kinds of dysfunctions in a pastoral council. The first is psychological dysfunction. This term implies an understanding of the normal function of pastors and councils, a function that has become abnormal. In a normal relationship, for example, pastors have questions about how best to plan and carry out the parish's mission. They consult their councils to ensure a well-planned pastoral program, a program appropriate to the parish. These are the proper tasks of the pastor-leader, as we saw in Chapter Six. But when a pastor does not consult his council, consults it poorly, or misleads the council about the consequences of its deliberations, the normal relationship breaks down. The pastor is said to be "dysfunctional." Councillors, to give another example, normally put their gifts at the service of the pastor and the parish. They seek practical wisdom about what is best to do in a concrete situation. But occasionally they fail to contribute properly, instead using the council to express anger, nurse a grudge, or pursue a private goal. They are acting "dysfunctionally."[11]

Dysfunctional councillors are not interested in or capable of studying pastoral matters and making sound recommendations. Like Theresa, the ineffective councillor in Chapter Fourteen, they are preoccupied with private matters. They do not function properly. Dysfunctional pastors are equally troubled. They do not obey the norms that govern the parish council family. Instead of consulting the council and encouraging it to discuss a matter, the dysfunctional pastor cuts off discussion and prevents the council from airing an issue. Instead of posing a question with the hope of an answer, he has no clear expectations, and the council drifts aimlessly. Instead of praising the council when it completes its work and recommends a solution, he never allows it to exercise its competency and reach closure. The normal functions of consulting, probing, and praising become dysfunctional.

Besides psychological dysfunction, there is another, a sociological, aspect of the word. The council can be sociologically dysfunctional when it meets regularly but no longer serves a meaningful purpose. Pastors contribute to this dysfunction by not giving the council meaningful work. A functional council investigates, reflects, and proposes conclusions. A dysfunctional council does not have a clear task. To be sure, the pastor may convoke it regularly. But if his purpose is merely to show that he is "open-minded" and "consultative," he makes the council sociologically dysfunctional.[12] We saw this in Chapter Fourteen with Father Padraig Twomey and the Church of Santa María.

Deliberate Dysfunction

Up to this point we have presumed that dysfunctions are not deliberate. Pastors and councillors often display a kind of invincible ignorance. They create dysfunction because they do not know how to correct it or are incapable of doing so. They do not understand the council's proper function.

Deliberate dysfunctions, on the other hand, arise when people know how to improve the council, but choose not to because of hostility or laziness. Council members, for example, may resent the pastor for some injury, real or imagined. In order to retaliate, they may consciously refuse to allow the council to accomplish its proper functions. The pastor, to give another example, may have developed a dislike for the council or may be unwilling to correct its problems. He intentionally prevents the council from doing its job or he maintains it in a function that no longer has meaning. Councillors and pastors are both to blame. Dysfunctional councillors may use council meetings to achieve their private ends. A dysfunctional pastor may write off a council because, without his instruction, it does not do things the way he would do them. Such people create problems for the council family.

Due Process

What can be done when pastors and councillors function badly? There are three kinds of remedies. The first is an appeal, that is, a kind of due process. Many dioceses at one time described such processes in their published parish council guidelines.[13] These guidelines allowed councils to appeal a pastor's decision when two-thirds of council members disagree with it. Councils may appeal to the chancellor, regional vicar, conciliator, or even the bishop. This official then meets with pastor and council in order to resolve the dispute.

Two persuasive arguments, however, weigh in against the process of appeal. The first is canonical. Canon 536 describes parish pastoral councils as consultative to the pastor. Pastors are not obliged to take their advice. When some diocesan guidelines grant councils the right to appeal a decision "over the head" of the pastor, they seem to imply that councils are more than consultative. The guidelines appear to wrongly give councils a juridical status that they do not possess.

Another reason why guidelines do not universally grant the right to appeal stems from the church's wariness of litigation. St. Paul sounded this note in First Corinthians. There he speaks of the impropriety of Christians settling disputes in a pagan court of law. "To have lawsuits at all with one another is defeat for you," he wrote. "Why not rather suffer wrong?" (1 Cor. 6:7). Paul concludes that Christians should settle their grievances among themselves, rather than going to an external authority. An appeal can pit one official in the church against another.

Conflict Management

A second remedy to dysfunction falls under the heading of conflict management. When there are conflicts in a council, the pastor may exercise his role as presider and try to defuse the conflict. A pastor can manage conflict by identifying the issues, examining the assumptions of disputants, and exploring alternatives to their conflict. He can be the conflict manager *par excellence*.[14] But what if the pastor is unable or unwilling to guide this process? What if he himself is the source of conflict?

In this case, council members themselves can exercise the principles of conflict management. Its goal is to help disputants see the conflict in an objective light and approach it with the tools of rational problem solving. Conflict management frees disputants—councillors and pastors alike—to face the issues that divide them. Wider knowledge leads to reduced tension and better decisions. Conflict management is a skill that can be learned.[15] But to describe it in this way seems to make it an impersonal exercise of skill, like piloting a sailboat or oil painting. The reality is quite different. Conflict management is intensely personal. It includes every color in the palette of diplomacy, from private conversation and dinner invitations to personal notes and the doing of favors. I once cajoled an unwilling pastor to attend a meeting by reminiscing about my boyhood when I was his altar server. Conflict management is a personal art.

So far we have spoken of remedies for indeliberate dysfunctions, dysfunctions caused by a lack of freedom to function normally or by ignorance of the norms of the pastor-council relationship. There are also remedies for intentional dysfunctional behavior. Frustrated pastors and council members should first make efforts to clarify the issues among themselves and express their consensus in good faith. They should strive to understand the disputants' point of view. If disputants reject the opinion of the majority, different measures are justified. Frustrated participants in the council should test the rightness of their opinion with other parish leaders. The leaders may shed light on a seemingly intractable problem. The fundamental principle is to maintain communion among the people of God. Rarely will a pastor or a council member reject an opinion that is the considered opinion of all.

The Boston canonist Richard C. Cunningham has described the extreme remedy in the case of deliberate dysfunction by the pastor. He describes the moral power of the laity in this way: "Ultimately they still possess the power of numbers, of finances, of public opinion, of *sensus fidelium*, of conscience and the radical power of shaking the dust from their feet as they exit."[16] Laypeople are not powerless. They can express their opposition by finding another parish or by withholding contributions. This is no substitute, however, for rational problem solving. The tools of conflict management are extensive and effective. One should appeal to diocesan officials only when these tools fail. Rupture with the parish is a means of last resort in pastor-council conflict.

The Norm of Ecclesial Consultation

Dysfunction, however, is not the norm in parish pastoral councils. The norm is expressed in the threefold task of study, reflection, and recommendation. That is what councils are supposed to do. The steady growth of U.S. councils suggests that they are doing it. If councils were generally a waste of time, pastors would not establish them and people would refuse to participate in them.

Pastoral councils have problems at times. These problems can be serious and debilitating. They led a veteran like William Rademacher to his rejection of the consultative-only approach. In its place he proposed a mandatory search for consensus and novel forms of governance. This chapter has argued that his view of consultation differs from that of the church. A truly ecclesial consultation is not compulsory. It preserves the freedom of pastors to consult, and councillors to advise. Novel forms of governance, attractive from afar, are no less problematic than the present forms. Just because parish problems are real does not mean that ecclesial solutions are inadequate.

Pastoral councils ought to be what the church says they can be, namely, "the principal form of collaboration, dialogue and discernment," helping to "broaden resources in consultation and the principle of collaboration and in certain instances also in decision making."[17]

The consultative-only approach is legal but not legalistic. If we suggest that the pastoral council is something other than what the church's documents say, we run the risk of not thinking with the church and of raising false expectations. By trying to say exactly what the church expects councils to be, we are not proposing anything narrow-minded. We are being precise. All Christians are to build community, pray, collaborate with the pastor, lead by example, and be spiritual. But only pastoral councils investigate, ponder, and propose. They do so, not in an impersonal process, but in a relationship. It is a relationship with a pastor who knows their readiness and wants their help, with fellow parishioners whose wisdom they seek, and ultimately with the God whom they glimpse in dialogue.

Chapter Twenty

The Motive
for Consultation

F ather George E. Crespin was the chancellor of the Diocese of
Oakland in 1982 when it started planning for a diocesan pastoral
council. An experienced pastor, former *officialis* in the diocesan tri-
bunal, and leader in the national Hispanic *Encuentro*, Crespin knew a
great deal about consultation. His first act was to establish a task force
within the senate of priests. The task force recommended to Bishop John
S. Cummins that the DPC be elected at a diocesan convention. Next,
Crespin established a committee, composed of a number of priests, sisters, and lay Catholics. The committee sketched the general features of
the convention, such as the number of delegates, location, date, and general task. With the consultation in Crespin's hands, Bishop Cummins
was confident of firm and collaborative leadership.

The diocesan pastoral council was chosen on January 13, 1984 at the
conclusion of the first diocesan convention. Among the new councillors
was Gesine Laufenberg. A veteran parish councillor, university graduate,

and homemaker, she quickly proved herself as a leader. The DPC chose her to serve as its chairwoman for the first three years. She cultivated a firm working relationship with the other councillors, diocesan staff members, and the senate of priests. She and Crespin developed committees to study lay leadership, youth ministry, social justice, evangelization, and Christian formation. The recommendations of these committees were persuasive. Bishop Cummins eventually accepted them and put them into practice.

Crespin and Laufenberg are good examples of cooperation in ecclesial consultation. In the previous chapter, we saw what ecclesial consultation is. It is the search for wisdom by means of an appreciative and critical dialogue. In this chapter, we are going to examine the motives for consultation. Why do pastors establish councils? Why do parishioners engage in them? These are not idle questions. Pastors at times find councils more trouble than they are worth. They have serious disagreements with them, needing occasionally to overhaul or even suspend them. Laypeople, for their part, can find working on councils dispiriting and boring, and may prefer shaking the dust from their feet and walking away.[1] I believe, however, that these bad experiences are the exception. The steady growth of U.S. councils suggests that they in fact accomplish what the church intends them to accomplish.

Motivation offers a fundamental insight about the participation of lay Catholics in councils. One might well ask why the laity should participate when they have merely a consultative vote. In a secular society, many Catholics do not readily assume that pastors have a divine right to govern their people. Instilled with the concept of the sovereignty of the people, many American Catholics prefer the church as the people of God to the church as a hierarchy. The consultative-only vote of pastoral councils appears to contradict our secular and democratic principles.

In this chapter, we will see why it does not. After a review of the principles of leadership contained in diocesan guidelines for councils, we will examine the leaders' motives. The goal is to find out why they follow the church's recommendations. The examples of George Crespin and Gesine Laufenberg offer a point of reference. They illustrate what the guidelines imply but do not say explicitly, namely, that the motives for council participation are rooted in the very nature of the church.

Leadership and Motivation

Leadership provides an entrée into our question. We saw in Chapter Six that pastoral council guidelines speak of leadership by the pastor "in" the council and leadership "by" the council. Pastors lead by presiding. Councils lead, we commonly read, in governance and decision making. Council committees may even claim to "run" the parish. The same word, leadership, is used for councils and pastors. Is this inconsistent? Do both of them "lead"?

Leadership means helping followers attain a goal.[2] This implies motivation. Leaders must understand and desire the goal. They know that they cannot attain it without followers. Their motive is to attain the goal with the followers' help. The followers must affirm the goal, each according to his or her own capacity. If they are not committed to the goal, they will not follow. Dedication to the goal is the motive of leaders and followers alike. The concept of leadership "in" and "by" the pastoral council begins to reveal participants' motives. After reviewing what pastoral council guidelines say about leadership, we can apply it to the question of motivation.

The Pastor as Leader
The pastor leads the council in two ways, as we saw in Chapter Six. He helps the council accomplish its task, and he fosters the good relationships needed to do so. He and the council do their work—primarily the threefold task of studying pastoral matters, reflecting on them, and proposing sound conclusions—in a variety of ways. In one example suggested by the guidelines, the council achieves its goal by following the pastor's strong lead. Our example was Father Sweeney's response to the influx of Hispanic parishioners. He set the council's agenda, consulted it, received proposals, and made decisions.

Father Colman provided a second example of task-centered leadership. In his parish, he let the council develop its own initiatives. Eventually the council proposed the assessment of youth ministry, the creation of a children's liturgy of the Word, and the establishment of a food pantry. Father Colman led the council by encouraging it to develop its own proposals and by ratifying them. This is an equally valid example of the pastor's leadership of the council task.

In addition to helping the council accomplish its task, the pastor also has a concern for relationships. Council guidelines say that he strives to create and maintain them. He searches for consensus, serves as a spiritual leader, creates a climate of trust, and builds community. His actions help to cement the pastor–council relationship. By alluding to the pastor's relationship-building efforts, diocesan guidelines suggest how important these relationships are. But none of the guidelines examined in Chapter Six describe the pastor's efforts in great detail. Nor do they examine why the pastor cultivates good relationships. They tell us what he does, but not why he does it. If we want to understand the pastor's motives for consultation, we have to look more deeply.

Leadership by Councils
The council "leads" in a different way than the pastor does. To be sure, guidelines say that the council provides direction for the parish. Some guidelines even describe the lay chairperson as the "president." But the council does not usurp the pastor's functions. The pastor is the presider. Lay members lead by contributing to the council's task. They lead when their advice is so persuasive that pastors accept it.

The guidelines try (without much success) to distinguish between the role of the pastor and that of the council chairperson. Undoubtedly the two share many of the same tasks. In fact the guidelines use the same verbs—namely, to communicate, collaborate, facilitate, shape the agenda, and develop consensus—in describing the role of the pastor and the chairperson. But the chairperson has a subordinate role. He or she has more to do with the council task, the guidelines suggest, than with building relationships. The chairperson organizes, coordinates, and "chairs" the meetings. To be sure, the chairperson may also support council relationships by leading prayer and resolving conflict. But in building relationships, the guidelines suggest, the pastor is primary.

The primacy of the pastor—that is the real import of the guidelines' emphasis on the pastor's relationship-building duties. It is another way of speaking about the pastor as presider. Councils and lay leaders, in short, do not lead without pastors. They cooperate and collaborate with them. Pastors, in turn, lead by sharing responsibility. They consult councils in a search for practical wisdom. It is not inconsistent to speak of leadership by the laity in councils. But pastors and councils exercise leadership in a different way. When we apply the word leadership to both, we do not mean that they have the same role. We mean that they share the same motive. Motivation, not leadership, is the common reference point.

The Motive of Pastors
The pastor's primary motive in establishing a pastoral council is to elicit

the practical wisdom of the people of God. Theirs is the contingent knowledge of how to act in a changing parish situation. The pastor consults parishioners because they can judge, even better than outside experts can, what is best for the parish community. No one parishioner has all the wisdom. But together, using the method of dialogue, pastor and councillors can reach prudent decisions.

The pastor's consultation of the council is public. It culminates in his reception of the council's recommendations. The pastor's motive, however, is more private. His motive leads him to consult in the first place. It inspires the questions that he poses to the council. The pastor asks questions, not out of weakness or ignorance, but for an essentially Socratic reason. Socrates claimed, in the description of his trial known as the *Apology*, that he had a special kind of wisdom. Unlike his enemies, he recognized his limitations and desired to know more. This recognition was not shameful. Rather, Socrates' insight into the limits of his knowledge enabled him to explore the unknown by consulting others. To gain wisdom is the essential motive for consultation.

But the motive for consultation is not just a desire to know more. It includes a desire to develop a common viewpoint with others. In order to understand this motive, let us look more closely at the example of George Crespin.

Crespin's Example

George Crespin, the Oakland chancellor, understood that the purpose of consultation was to gain practical wisdom. But he also wanted the diocesan search for practical wisdom to build community. That was his guiding principle at the first diocesan convention, for which he served as chairman. He led the convention to a successful conclusion with the election of a diocesan pastoral council. At first, after the convention ended in January of 1985, we members of the diocesan staff were euphoric. The convention delegates had produced an admirable mission statement. They had challenged the diocese with a well-crafted list of goals, goals that provided a direction for the diocesan pastoral council. The DPC had expressed its commitment and had been celebrated with joy and hope. Crespin and his staff had good reason to be happy.

In the weeks that followed, however, the enormity of the DPC task began to settle in. The statement of the diocesan mission seemed excessively complex. The goals seemed overly ambitious and ambiguous. Some of us began to have second thoughts. Should we have simplified the mission statement? Should we have permitted ambiguities to remain?

Crespin's replies were confident and steady. Of course the diocesan mission statement was overly long and complex, he said. It was not written by English majors or managerial experts. It was written by parishioners. They were trying to express something as intricate and profound as faith. The words on paper were important, he told us, but more important was the experience of the convention. The medium, he said, is the message. The medium of the diocesan convention, in which people had shared faith and expressed hope, was indeed its most important result.

To be sure, Crespin told us, there was a lot more to do. The DPC, elected on January 13, was to begin its monthly meetings in March. Its job was to reflect on the mission and goals, studying and simplifying. We staff members could not do that work for the DPC. We had to prepare for it, establish a rhythm, develop relationships, and create a work plan. There, in the actual work of the council, the DPC would become more realistic about its task. Once the meetings began the councillors could clarify the ambiguities of the diocesan goals. There was plenty of work to do, Crespin told us, but no reason to be discouraged.

Motive and Spirituality

Crespin's example reveals much about the good pastor's motives. He is concerned, first of all, with more than expert opinion. He knows the value of experts, to be sure, but he also seeks the contingent knowledge that resides in the community. His goal is not merely to gain philosophic knowledge and make correct decisions. It is also to make wisdom present, the wisdom that Christians identify with the Word and the Spirit. This first motive entails a second. It concerns the upbuilding of community. This upbuilding is not a separate task from the search for wisdom. The two belong together. The good pastor knows that when he serves the community in its search for wisdom, he gains more than wisdom. In a word, he gains community—its trust, commitment, and love.[3]

Many guidelines for pastoral councils blur their focus. Instead of concentrating on the threefold task given to them by Vatican II's Decree on Bishops, these guidelines overwhelm councils with a lengthy list of spiritual purposes. Councils, they say, are to develop themselves as Christian communities, be models of prayer, promote parish leaders, and provide a witness of unity to the parish. These spiritual purposes, however, are not specific to pastoral councils. They are the responsibility of all Christians. Their presence in diocesan guidelines can seem misleading or at least distracting. Why do the guidelines include them? The example of Crespin offers an explanation. When the good pastor consults well, he not only gains practical wisdom, he also builds community. When he helps councillors accomplish their threefold task, Christ is present.

Catholic Christians speak of the priest as a representative of Christ. This doctrine can be easily misunderstood. It may seem to put the priest on a pedestal and crown him as a demigod. The portrait of the historical Jesus corrects this misunderstanding.[4] Jesus' use of parables, his preaching of the kingdom of God, and his directness of speech, suggest the properly human way in which the priest represents Christ. The parish situation, for example, is like a parable. It needs to be properly interpreted. The priest presents it to his councillors because he wants them to help him unlock its meaning. Pastoral planning by councils, to give a second example, recalls Jesus' preaching about the kingdom. He did not teach that the kingdom was a future event at the end of the world, but said it was breaking in as he spoke. Jesus challenged his followers to put away distractions, focus on what is most important, read the signs of the times, and remain vigilant. The good pastor exhorts the council in the same way.

The historical Jesus is also a model in his direct relations with others. Despite his preference for his "true mother and brothers," namely, the ones who do God's will (Mk 3:35), Jesus never severed ties with his family. His dialogues with disciples and with those he cured suggest that Jesus did not assume for himself an institutional role that formalized his relations with others. Leadership never deprived him of intimacy. Good pastors know this. They do not represent Christ by insisting on their authority. The would never arrogate to themselves the words, "I and the Father are one." Rather, they consult their councils because they appreciate parish unity and want to cultivate it. They seek practical wisdom. This is not the impersonal advice of experts with whom the pastor has no relationship, but the recommendations of his own people, his own family.

The Motive of Councillors

The example of George Crespin tells us something about the motive of pastors. But what about the motive of lay councillors? For this, let us look more closely at the example of Gesine Laufenberg, the chairperson of

Oakland's first diocesan pastoral council. Most revealing was how little emphasis she put on the actual business of chairing the meetings. To be sure, Laufenberg was adept at procedure. She had a businesslike manner, calling meetings to order, recognizing speakers, and summarizing arguments. She knew how to field questions and to maintain a focused conversation. But these talents were not her most important contribution.

Chairing was not uppermost in Laufenberg's mind because the Oakland DPC enjoyed the services of a professional facilitator, Sister Marcia Frideger. She was a faculty member at Holy Names College and a member of the priests' senate task force that had planned Oakland's diocesan convention. An expert in group dynamics, Frideger had designed the actual convention processes. Laufenberg often relied on her to do tasks ordinarily reserved to chairpersons, such as conducting discussions, eliciting judgments, and polling for consensus. Laufenberg's most important contribution lay elsewhere. She devoted herself, in a phrase, to enhancing the DPC's credibility.

Laufenberg and Credibility

Laufenberg understood that the proof of the DPC was its persuasive power with the Bishop of Oakland, John Cummins. A council's power does not spring from compelling arguments that bowl a pastor over. Its source is altogether more subtle. It is the power to win people's allegiance—allegiance to a comprehensive vision, to concrete action, and ultimately to one another. Laufenberg appreciated the importance of compromise. For the sake of unity, she knew, people are sometimes able to exchange deeply-held ideas for ones they consider merely acceptable. They can do so when others appreciate their viewpoint and incorporate it. They have made a concession but not abandoned their commitments.[5] Genuine consensus, reached by those who have freely and wholly accepted a compromise for the common good, is indeed persuasive.

I recall an especially heated meeting in 1986.[6] The bishop had asked the DPC to study the diocese's general goal about promoting evangelization. The DPC had formed a committee under the direction of a very knowledgeable and strong-willed priest. He was a powerful advocate for parish renewal and had initiated a renewal program in his own parish. He wanted to extend it to every parish and steered his committee toward that conclusion. He hoped that the DPC would eventually recommend the renewal program to the bishop. His committee, however, interpreted his strong direction as coercion. In a heated meeting, the members voted not to recommend the program.

The committee, Laufenberg knew, did not object strenuously to the renewal program itself. Parish renewal is important, and the priest's program was as good or better than many others. The committee objected, rather, to the priest's overbearing leadership. He did not have the patience to allow the committee to reach its own conclusions. For that reason the members resisted him. They felt that he was imposing his views on them. When the committee finished its work, he was greatly disappointed.

Laufenberg heard about the committee's decision and recognized the danger to the DPC. Dissension within a committee might do more than threaten its work. A delayed report was a tolerable inconvenience. In addition to a delay, however, the dissension jeopardized the council's esprit. Committees wracked by ill-will might imperil the DPC's search for consensus. The bishop would have to decide between contending parties. The DPC's final recommendations, Laufenberg feared, might not be persuasive.

She telephoned the priest. She invited him to lunch. She allowed him to express his frustration. She listened to his arguments for the renewal program. She helped him see that his committee did not oppose parish renewal, but was simply unprepared to affirm the particular program he advocated. Her efforts encouraged him. And, in fact, she proved prophetic. Two years later, the diocese established a second committee precisely to investigate parish renewal. In 1986 the second committee recommended the very program that the priest had advocated.

Laufenberg enhanced the DPC's credibility. She realized that credibility means more than well-written and logical reports. Doubtless, sound thinking and reasonable proposals are essential. Without them a pastoral council fails in its duty. But credibility is more than correct conclusions. It has to do with spirit, a spirit that unites a group and lends credence to its recommendations. Laufenberg realized that every aspect of a pastoral council bears on its credibility, from the hospitality it shows its members to the technical details of its reports. Upon the credibility of the council, she knew, ultimately depended the bishop's ability to affirm it with the church's credo, its "I believe."

Motive and Gift

Does compromise mean a dilution of the truth? The example of

Laufenberg may wrongly suggest that conclusion. If credibility depends solely on consensus, and if councils settle for half-truths in order to reach an apparent harmony, then they do not serve the gospel. They merely seek a superficial accord. But this was not the case with Oakland's council, nor is it true for councils as a rule. In order to show why not, let us recall the first pastoral council, the so-called "Council of Jerusalem," in which the early church distinguished Christian faith from fidelity to the Jewish Law.

We know about the Jerusalem Council from two independent New Testament sources. The first and closest to the event is that of St. Paul in the Letter to the Galatians (2:1–10). The second and later account is by St. Luke in the Acts of the Apostles (15:1–22). Paul came to Jerusalem, he wrote, to explain "the gospel as I present it to the Gentiles" and "to make sure that the course I was pursuing, or had pursued, was not useless" (Gal. 2:2). He came as an apostle, that is, an equal to James and Cephas—but also as one seeking their approval. They were the authorities, the elders of the church.

Paul submitted to them a crucial issue. Jerusalem Christians who had witnessed Paul's Greek (that is, non-Jewish) Christians in Antioch insisted that the Greeks become Jews. The Jewish Christians demanded that the Gentiles submit to circumcision. Paul disputed their claim. He argued that the gospel superseded the requirements of the Jewish Law. A believer did not have to become a Jew, Paul insisted, in order to worship the God of Jesus Christ. At stake was the very meaning of the gospel. If circumcision were essential, faith in Christ is not enough.

Storm and stress marked the council. Certain Jerusalem Christians—Paul said they were merely "claimants to the title of brother"—suggested that the freedom of Paul's community was licentious. Paul, with his associates Barnabas and Titus, replied that the external adherence to law was no substitute for the Spirit of God. To be sure, Paul ultimately won the approval he sought. The prominent leaders affirmed his understanding of the gospel. But the two parties struggled. "It makes no difference to me how prominent they were," wrote Paul about the leaders; "God plays no favorites" (Gal. 2:6). Paul wanted their approval, but he sought it pugnaciously.

The New Testament accounts do not reveal exactly how the elders came to affirm the credibility of Paul's gospel. Luke presents the council as a historic occasion in which great decisions were amicably made. Paul writes with the passion of one for whom the battle is not yet over. But he was not averse to compromise. He was willing to negotiate. The elders affirmed Paul's gospel, but they also insisted that his congregations should be solicitous about the Jerusalem poor. Paul, for his part, agreed to this. He said that the poor were his concern all along. Ultimately the council reached a unanimous decision about Christian freedom. Adherence to the Jewish Law, the council decreed, is no longer a condition for membership in the church. A reflection on the council members' experience led to a decision that became normative for the entire church.

A Common Faith

The elders did not go along with Paul to preserve a façade of unanimity. They went along because he articulated their faith. Although James and Cephas enjoyed the authority of apostles who had seen Jesus, and although they were the acknowledged leaders of the church, they were not the only authorities at the council. Paul too proclaimed the gospel with authority. Without a doubt, he was less prominent than they. He was not an elder. He had not known the earthly Jesus. But he had a gift that they recognized. The gospel Paul proclaimed was not merely his gospel. It was *the* gospel. It was the faith of the church.

The power of the Jerusalem Council did not lie simply in the cogency of Paul's arguments, as if they had an impersonal but compelling logic. Its power lay in the gospel. Paul's arguments expressed the truth of the gospel. That expression won the allegiance of the entire church. Therein lies the power of pastoral councils and the motive for lay participation in them. Laypersons like Gesine Laufenberg do not possess a pastor's authority of office. But they have their own charismatic authority, the authority stemming from the gifts that God has given. They put their gifts at the service of the church, confident that their gifts contribute to it, seeking a credible expression of faith, motivated by the gospel.

The Credibility of the Gospel

The documents of the church treat the purposes of the pastoral council briefly but clearly. They tell us what it does. But they do not tell us much about why Catholics engage in the task of studying, reflecting, and making recommendations about pastoral matters. This is an important question. In a secular and democratic society, the value of the pastoral council, a consultative-only institution, is questionable. It may seem to prop up the outmoded view that pastors know more than laypeople. It may seem to falsely suggest that, because the power of pastors comes from the church and ultimately from God, they can be indifferent to God's people.

Pastors consult councils not simply to imitate the techniques of management. To be sure, these techniques are of great value. By consulting parishioners, a pastor can enhance council relationships, contribute to the quality of parish life, and build commitment to the church. But consultative pastors are not merely managing. They are seeking practical wisdom. They desire knowledge about how the parish can best serve God. The Christian search for wisdom presupposes a unity between God, the source of all wisdom, and the people of God, who seek to participate more fully in God's own life. When a pastor consults, he is seeking the truth that will unite his people.

Parishioners do not participate in councils to prop up beliefs that they no longer hold. Participation in a consultative-only institution does not mean that one subscribes to the belief that the pastor knows more than his people. Nor does it signify a belief that he has a divinely given right to ignore them. When councillors devote themselves to consultation, they do not surrender their common sense. They are expressing faith. They are insisting that, in the church, they have found something supremely good. Despite the difficulties of faith in an age of secularism and democracy, they are acknowledging the credibility of the church. A secular viewpoint need not deny the sacred, but may instead affirm the importance of intelligence and judgment. Democracy need not reject hierarchy, but may instead insist upon popular participation in decision making. Councillors want to participate because councils enable them to share responsibility for the church. That helps to make the church credible.

Pastors and councillors both have a stake in maintaining the credibility of the council. Both search for accord by means of dialogue. Wise pastors want not just an apparent unity, not just a superficial absence of strife, but a genuine unity that stems from the truth. Wise councillors share the same desire, even when they negotiate compromise. Compromise does not necessarily dilute the truth, but may attain it in a more profound way. This is especially the case when people are willing to surrender their private aims for the sake of a common good. In short, the pastor's and the councillors' motive for consultation stem from the same root. Both search for practical wisdom. Both believe that God, the source of wisdom, enables them to seek it by means of dialogue. Both believe that, in their search for wisdom, they are participating in the wisdom of God.

Chapter Twenty-One

A Foundation Document

I n the Introduction to this book I described an encounter in 1992 with a gentleman at a workshop sponsored by the Diocese of Dallas. The gentleman was peeved with me because I used the term "parish" council. He said that in his parish a "pastoral" council had replaced the parish council. He suggested that old-fashioned parish councils were focused on day-to-day administration, used parliamentary procedure, and were preoccupied with temporal matters. His parish's pastoral council, by contrast, looked to the future, was more discerning in its style of decision making, and was more spiritual in orientation. The change from parish to pastoral councils was the intention of the church, he said, and I ought to know better.

This book has argued that the gentleman was wrong. We have shown that, when the church introduced the terminology of parish "pastoral" councils, it did not repudiate the type of councils that went before. Nor did it define the word "pastoral" in terms of future events, a style of decision making, or a more spiritual subject matter. Rather it linked parish councils to the Vatican II Decree on the Office of Bishops, which at no. 27

recommended diocesan pastoral councils. Eventually the Vatican allowed that pastoral councils might be established at the parish level. No rejection of older style parish councils was ever expressed. The church never disparaged the so-called "apostolic" councils recommended in the Vatican II Decree on the Apostolate of Lay People (no. 26), which were the original source for parish councils.

That does not mean, of course, that old-fashioned councils cannot be improved. They certainly can be. But the improvement should come by trying to be faithful to the church's vision and by reflecting on experience, not by making false claims about the church's intention. This book has tried to dispel false claims. We have seen that church documents never advocated a single style of decision making or member selection. They never forbade councils from coordinating lay initiatives. They never declared parish administration off-limits to councils. Those who make these claims for parish pastoral councils should re-examine the evidence.

A Basis for Improvement

Faithfulness to the church's vision and reflection on experience are the most reliable bases for improving councils. If that is true, then how can we give new councils a good start and renew existing councils? I propose that councils re-examine their foundation documents. These are the constitutions and by-laws that spell out the purpose of councils and their operating procedures. Re-examining these documents forces us to consider whether the written word describes what the council actually is and does. This can improve them.

The terms "constitution" and "bylaw," however, can create a false impression. They can wrongly suggest to councillors that the council is a governing body independent of the pastor. Nothing could be further from the truth. What we ordinarily call constitution and bylaws are really the agreements that underlie a pastoral council. They signify the relationship of trust that is meant to exist between the council and the pastor who consults it. Foundation documents do not take the place of that trust. They are meant to reflect the bonds of Christian faith, hope, and love that bind pastor and council together.

With that in mind, let me offer the following "foundation document." It describes the kind of council I would like to see. My document differs from other constitutions and by-laws in two important ways. First, it is solidly rooted in the church's documents, and assigns no more to the pastoral council than what the documents allow. Doubtless the council I foresee is by no means the only type of pastoral council. There are as many types as there are parishes. But mine is fully consistent with church teaching.

Second, my foundation document is distinctive in that it proposes a council whose members have a three-year term. The document does not require the staggered election of council members. Each three-year term constitutes a planning cycle. At the end of the cycle, the document recommends the selection of a wholly new set of councillors and the beginning of a new planning cycle. With these two distinctive features in mind, consider the following "Introduction" to the foundation document.

1. Introduction

Recognizing that sound pastoral decisions are informed by the wisdom of the People of God, Father _____ established the pastoral council of _____ Church on June 1, 2002. The documents of the Second Vatican Council recommended the establishment of such councils. They state that Catholics have a right and duty to express their opinion on what pertains to the good of the church. Pastors should willingly consult their people and use their prudent advice. By establishing a pastoral council, the pastor acknowledges the wisdom of his parishioners and expresses his desire to share with them his responsibility for the governance of the parish.

This introduction is direct. It states that pastors consult councils because they seek wisdom. Councils offer advice, and do not govern parishes. We have seen, however, that certain pastoral council guidelines published by U.S. dioceses do not preserve this insight as clearly as they should. They occasionally describe the pastoral council as the coordinator of parish ministries and standing committees, and do so in such a way that it appears as if the council is a governing body independent of the pastor. This can mislead the parish.[1] A good foundation document clearly describes the council's consultative vote.

Some authors intend to honor pastoral councils by giving them a high profile. They emphasize the primacy of the council. They say that it supersedes other parish organizations, boards, and committees, including the finance council. For example, Robert Howes says that the purpose of the council is "to constitute the primary consultative voice of the people of God."[2]

He means that the pastoral council is primary and other committees and councils are secondary. But this proposal goes beyond canon law, which does not assign first place to the pastoral council and second place to the finance council. Apart from what diocesan norms may specify, no parish consultative body is necessarily superior to any other.

One reason why some authors emphasize the primacy of the pastoral council is that they assign to it the task of implementing its own recommendations through a system of standing committees. In many parishes, the council's liturgical recommendations are implemented through the liturgy committee, for example, and the education committee implements recommendations about education. I believe that this tends to obscure the council's proper role. That role is not to implement but rather to investigate, ponder, and recommend. This is the threefold description that the Vatican first applied to diocesan pastoral councils and then extended to parish pastoral councils. It brings me to my second point, the purpose of the council.

2. Purpose

The purpose of the parish pastoral council is to investigate pastoral matters, to consider them thoroughly, and to propose practical conclusions about them. In this way the council fosters pastoral activity. The council's task is, first of all, to study those matters brought to its attention and shed light on them. Its second task is to reflect on them thoroughly, to discern their true nature, to evaluate and to ponder them. Its final task is to draw sound conclusions. The council presents these conclusions to the pastor in the form of recommendations. This threefold task of the council—investigating, considering, and recommending conclusions—is called pastoral planning. After the pastor has accepted the recommendations of the council, he directs their implementation. Council members may assist him, but strictly speaking, implementation is the responsibility of the pastor, not the council.

Some authors obscure the line between recommendation and implementation. They do this, for example, when they give the pastoral council the duty of coordinating a system of standing committees. To be sure, coordination is a service that councils may render, provided that they respect the autonomy of the committees they are coordinating. It is not the primary task of councils, as we saw in Chapter Seventeen, but it has been a responsibility that councils have had the possibility of exercising since Vatican II.

Trouble can arise, however, when councils understand coordinating as an executive function. This may happen when councils see themselves as directly implementing their own decisions, rather than implementing the recommendations that a pastor has accepted.[3]

Such implementation goes beyond the council's official duty of studying, reflecting, and recommending about pastoral matters. What are these pastoral matters? The following section gives an answer.

3. Scope

The scope of the council is pastoral matters. These may include everything that pertains to the pastor's ministries of proclaiming God's word, celebrating the sacraments, caring for the faithful, promoting the mission of the church to the world, and being a good steward of parish resources. The scope includes all the practical matters of parish life. There is nothing practical about which the pastor may not consult the council, apart from faith, orthodoxy, moral principles or laws of the universal church.

Pastoral councils cannot change canon law or church doctrine, but practical matters are their bread and butter. Robert Howes stated that "no major area of pastoral concern should be segregated away from a council's right and obligation to overview it."[4] I affirm his viewpoint. We have seen that efforts to artificially restrict the scope of the pastoral council, either by excluding parish administration or by giving councils an exclusively spiritual focus, have not been successful. The church gives pastors a great deal of latitude in the subject matter about which they are consulting.

Some writers distinguish between "policy" and "daily administrative decisions." They say that councils make policy but not administrative decisions. This is a well-meaning effort to limit the scope of the council. But I dislike it. It wrongly suggests that a council makes policy on its own, rather than offering recommendations to the pastor. The church intends for pastoral councils to make recommendations. But their advice can be more or less persuasive. Its persuasiveness depends on the quality of the members' work. No council can force a pastor to do what he believes will harm the parish. A pastor would be foolish, however, not to accept good advice from his councillors. What are the criteria for good council members?

4. Criteria for Membership

Pastoral council members are chosen, above all, for their ability to accomplish the main task of the council—the work of investigating, considering, and recommending practical conclusions. They are baptized Catholics, in good standing with the church, who reflect the parish's various neighborhoods, social and professional groups, and apostolates. Finally, they are parishioners noted for their faith, good morals, and prudence.

These are the criteria for council membership implicit in the church's official documents. We have seen that they offer a corrective to the general silence about criteria for council membership in private and diocesan publications. Rademacher and Rogers, for example, offer a list of ten qualifications for pastoral council members. Among other things, they say that the potential councillor should be a praying Christian who desires to reconcile the parish and who accepts the teachings of Vatican II. But apart from a few general words about possessing a "skill, gift, or talent" and the "ability to relate to other members as a team," Rademacher and Rogers say nothing about the ability to accomplish the council's threefold task.[5] They do not say that the qualifications of a council member should include the ability to study, ponder, and recommend. These are essential, I believe, to the selection process.

5. Selection of Members

Twelve pastoral council members are elected every three years. The election takes place on the last of a series of four weekly assemblies during the month of September to which all parishioners are invited. The **first** assembly introduces parishioners to the work of the pastoral council. The pastor explains his motives for establishing it and invites parishioners to express their hopes for it. Participants at the **second** assembly identify the strengths of the parish and those areas in which the council may help it to develop. The **third** assembly is devoted to a reflection on the qualities of a good councillor and it culminates with nominations. In the **fourth** assembly, participants elect, in an atmosphere of prayer and discernment, the twelve new councillors.

My foundation document specifies twelve councillors. The precise number, however, is not important. Robert Howes, for example, recommends fifteen members. The council should be large enough to include wise advisors and not so large (according to the Vatican) as to be unable to carry out effectively the work committed to it.[6]

More important than the size is the way in which councillors are chosen. Official documents about pastoral councils state that they should be "representative," but not in a juridical sense. They exist to make present the wisdom of the people of God. Three things are needed in order to attract such "representatives." First, parishioners should receive a thorough orientation to the work of the council. Second, they should have an opportunity to nominate parishioners who are willing and able to do the council's work. Finally, they should have an opportunity to elect them. Orientation, Nomination, Election—Rademacher and Rogers call this the O.N.E. process.[7] These elements are essential for the selection of representative councillors.

In my ideal council, members are selected during a series of four weekly assemblies at the beginning of the three-year planning cycle. This allows parishioners to learn about the council, to reflect on one another's gifts as potential councillors, and to actually elect the council. Assemblies require an investment of time, but the payback is more clarity about the council's task, a better-formed council, and greater motivation in council members. My ideal council works together as a stable team for three years without staggered elections and a major turnover of members.[8] At the end of the planning cycle, the old council celebrates its accomplishments and a new council is chosen. The new councillors choose their own officers. They develop the agenda with the pastor.

6. Officers

The pastor presides at every meeting of the council. He consults, he accepts or rejects recommendations, and he develops the agenda with the council officers. The pastor and councillors select three officers from among their number. They are the chairperson, vice-chairperson, and secretary. With the pastor they develop the council agenda. The chairperson facilitates council discussions, making sure that everyone speaks and is heard. The chairperson also monitors the work of the councillors between regular meetings. The vice-chairperson assists the chairperson and facilitates meetings in the chairperson's absence. The secretary keeps the minutes. He or she ensures that they are sent, along with the agenda and supporting documents, to each councillor at least one week before every meeting.

Vatican documents do not speak of the role of officers in the pastoral council. But diocesan publications describe these roles at ample length. Although the pastor is the presider, he shares leadership of the council with its officers. To be sure, the pastor has legal responsibility for the parish. He alone has the legal right to speak on its behalf. But his final decision, as Robert T. Kennedy has observed, is only one part of decision making. The other parts include brainstorming, data gathering, planning for implementation, and evaluation.[9] And in these parts, the officers of the council may exercise leadership. They aid in the operation of the council.

7. Operation
The pastoral council has a three-year planning cycle, and members are selected for a three-year term. The pastor defines the theme of the planning cycle during the September assembly at which the council is selected. In the beginning of the council's second and third year, the members facilitate a parish assembly to report on the council's progress and to elicit the advice of parishioners. At the end of the third year, the council completes its work. Then a new council is selected and a new planning cycle begins.

The definition of a three-year planning cycle is the most distinctive feature of the "foundation document" I am proposing here. It assumes that the council is creating a plan at the pastor's direction. It may be a plan to evangelize the community, to improve the liturgy, to expand the existing parish, to merge with another nearby parish, or to develop a youth ministry. Whatever it is, creating the plan is the council's main task.[10]

At the end of its three-year term, the council will turn its work over to the pastor and a new planning cycle will begin. The advantages are twofold: a clear task and an established deadline. This kind of council will never have to ask what its agenda is.

8. Agenda

The pastor develops the agenda with the council officers. It states the goals for each meeting, the means and group process for reaching the goals, and the materials needed to accomplish them. The agenda guides the meeting. It begins with a review of the minutes of the previous meeting and concludes with a brief evaluation. If the pastor is dissatisfied with the consultation, he expresses his reservations and asks the council to clarify whatever remains obscure. When he is satisfied with the consultation, he formally accepts the council's recommendations. He may then ask the parish staff or other parishioners to implement them.

Nothing is more important to the council than a well-prepared agenda. Father Howes assigns it to an "executive committee," and Rademacher and Rogers recommend an "agenda committee."[11] Whatever we call the group, the members must develop the agenda in concert with the pastor. After all, he is doing the consulting. The agenda should say what the council hopes to do during its meeting and describe how it hopes to do it. If the council was not able to do what the agenda said it would do, the agenda was probably too ambitious. The council may have been trying to do what rightly belongs to the staff or the finance council.

9. Relation to the Staff and Finance Council

The pastor consults others besides the pastoral council about parish governance. He relies upon the parish staff for their expertise and consults them daily about the management of parish operations. Indeed, he may occasionally ask parish staff members to attend council meetings in order to put their knowledge at the service of the pastoral council. Moreover, the pastor relies on the finance council to develop, monitor, and report on the parish budget. Finance council members are chosen for their technical skill in realms of accounting and finance. The pastoral council, by contrast, offers practical wisdom. That is the ability to investigate pastoral matters in a general way, to reflect on them deeply in dialogue, and to propose conclusions appropriate to the parish.

As parish staffs grow, they often take on jobs formerly done by the pastoral council. Each is in danger of stepping on the toes of the other. The solution is sound leadership by the pastor. He must distinguish between those technical questions that require expert opinion (i.e., the opinion of his trained staff or the expertise of the finance council) and the more general questions that do not require expert advice.[12] If the questions are technical, he should consult technical experts. But if the pastor wants to know what decisions will unify the community, increase its momentum, and make best use of parish volunteers, he should consult the pastoral council.

10. Meetings

The pastoral council meets once a month from September to May. Meetings are two hours in length. Between the monthly meetings, council members are expected to follow up the previous meeting and prepare for the next. This usually entails work on ad hoc committees. The first meeting of the new pastoral council is dedicated to the call and mission of the newly chosen members. The council's second and third year begin with a parish assembly. After each assembly, the council assimilates the assembly results. During the final meeting of each year, the councillors assess the progress of the three-year planning cycle. The pastor thanks them for their service and reflects on the progress made by the council toward reaching its goals.

Some pastoral councils try to get by with quarterly meetings. Some try to intersperse regular meetings with gatherings of the heads of all parish ministries. This is the recommendation, for example, of William J. Bausch. He recommends that the parish council proper meet every other month. In between he holds meetings of the parish assembly, composed of the heads of ministries and organizations, to share information and to lobby for particular projects.[13] I believe, however, that bimonthly or quarterly meetings are too infrequent. And gatherings with the heads of all ministries can prevent the council from doing its main work, the work of investigating, reflecting, and drawing practical conclusions. That is why I recommend monthly meetings and a three-year planning cycle. When a pastor meets the council on this kind of regular basis, he helps to make the consultation credible.

Empirical Reality, History, Theory

The three-year planning cycle and the selection of new councillors every three years makes this "foundation document" different from the constitutions and bylaws of most pastoral councils. It envisions a pastoral council that does not monitor or supervise existing ministries. Rather, it is planning for the future and has a single theme. Its success hinges upon the desire of a pastor to examine an issue thoroughly. Such a pastor will find collaboration with this kind of council creative, deliberate, and reflective.

This book's empirical survey of diocesan guidelines reveals that pastoral councils take many forms. Each guideline is different. Our chapters about the purpose, committee structure, understanding of consultation, leadership, and selection of members, suggest that Americans have adapted the pastoral council idea in a variety of ways. They adapt it according to the needs of local churches. Recommended by the universal church, pastoral councils have planted themselves in a variety of American soils and climates. Diversity is to be expected. My ideal pastoral council, represented in the foundation document above, is meant to contribute to the diversity.

The history of councils in this book contends that it is simplistic to contrast today's "pastoral" council with the supposedly outmoded "parish" council. Parish councils—or more precisely, the kind of councils that developed in the late 1960s under the inspiration of the Vatican II Decree on the Apostolate of Lay People—were not simply an early and now obsolete stage in the development of pastoral councils. Our analysis of documents from 1967-68 showed that early councils were broad in scope, supported by pastors, and motivated by a profoundly spiritual desire to share responsibility for the parish. The foundation document I present here does not repudiate early "parish" councils or the "pastoral" councils of the 1990s. It highlights, however, the insights gained from a history of councils in the U.S.—insights into the fundamental importance of pastoral planning as a shorthand term for what Vatican II envisioned.

This foundation document respects the theoretical insights of both canon lawyers and council practitioners. The two have not always spoken the same language. Chapter Twelve, for instance, refuted the dubious thesis that canon 536 meant to exclude coordination and administrative matters from the pastoral council agenda. But a consensus is growing that parish pastoral councils are about pastoral planning. Canonists have shown that planning is what the church means when it speaks of study, reflection, and recommendation. Council practitioners tend to agree. For that reason, the foundation document emphasizes pastoral planning more than it does the coordination of committees.

The practice of consultation expresses a specifically Christian spirituality. It gives the lay councillor a deep participation in the parish's continuing quest to embody the gospel. It fosters the pastor's assimilation of the identity of Christ the servant leader, the one who helps the parish achieve its quest.[14] When consultation succeeds—as it so obviously did for the gentleman from Dallas with whom I began this chapter—we can only rejoice.

This success is not due, however, to a rejection of one teaching from Vatican II and the replacement of it with another. Rather, it is due to our faithfulness to the church's search for wisdom. In 1965, that search took the form of a recommendation about councils to assist the church's apostolic work. In more than thirty years of experience, reflection, and further teaching, Catholics have embraced that recommendation. They have helped to make pastoral councils a firm fixture of U.S. parish life.

Notes

Chapter One: The Number of Councils

1. Mark F. Fischer, "Parish Pastoral Councils: How Many Are There? How Do Bishops Support Them?" in Ruth T. Doyle, Robert E. Schmitz and Mary Beth Celio, Editors, *Parish Laity and Ministry*, Monograph no. 1 in the series *Research Monographs of the Catholic Research Forum* of the Conference for Pastoral Planning and Council Development (New York: Archdiocese of New York, 1999), pp. 82-106.

2. Charles A. Fecher, *Parish Council Committee Guide* (Washington, D.C.: National Council of Catholic Men, 1970), p. 10. Robert G. Howes estimated that three-fourths of U.S. parishes have councils in "Parish Councils: Do We Care?" *America* 135: 17 (November 27, 1976), p. 371.

3. David C. Leege, "Parish Life Among the Leaders," Report No. 9 of the *Notre Dame Study of Catholic Parish Life*, edited by David C. Leege and Joseph Gremillion (Notre Dame, IN: University of Notre Dame, 1986), p. 6.

4. P.J. Kenedy and Sons, *The Official Catholic Directory: 1994* (New Providence, New Jersey: P. J. Kenedy and Sons in association with R. R. Bowker, a Reed Reference Publishing Company, 1994).

5. A survey of 6,762 parishes out of 19,181 stated that "More than nine in ten parishes report having a parish pastoral council." That suggests that there are more than 17,263 parish councils. See Bryan T. Froehle and Mary L. Gautier, *National Parish Inventory Project Report* (Washington, D.C.: Center for Applied Research in the Apostolate, Georgetown University, October, 1999), p. 22. The same authors repeat this figure in their more recent *Catholicism USA: A Portrait of the Catholic Church in the United States,* Center for Applied Research in the Apostolate, Georgetown University (Maryknoll, NY: Orbis Books, 2000), p. 59. Data from the newest wave of the Inventory (based on preliminary results from 8,942 parishes and reported by Froehle and Gautier at the April 2-5, 2000 annual convention of the Conference for Pastoral Planning and Council Development in Orlando) suggest that 82% of parishes have a council, for a total of 15,728 councils

6. One of my early studies suggested that the average council size is fifteen members. See Mark F. Fischer, "Parish Pastoral Councils: Purpose, Consultation, Leadership," *Center Papers,* No. 4 (New York: National Pastoral Life Center, 1990), Table 1, p. 2. Based on a 1995 survey of guidelines, I now believe the average is eleven members.

7. National Conference of Catholic Bishops (Committee on Priestly Life and Ministry, Committee for African American Catholics, Committee for the Diaconate, Committee on Hispanic Affairs, Committee on Home Missions, Committee on Pastoral Practices, Committee on Vocations, and Sub-Committee on Lay Ecclesial Ministry), *The Study of the Impact of Fewer Priests on the Pastoral Ministry,* Supplementary Document "D," including research conducted for the Bishops by the Center for Applied Research in the Apostolate (CARA), Spring General Meeting, June 15-17, 2000, Milwaukee, WI (Washington, D.C.: NCCB, 2000 [Unpublished]).

The bishops found the percentages of dioceses that employ the strategy of a single pastor caring for more than one parish (56%) and the strategy of entrusting parishes to deacons and laypeople (22%). They also stated that there are 437 Latin and Eastern Rite parishes out of 19,181 that operate out of this second model.

Seventeen percent of this number of parishes is administered by non-resident pastors or entrusted to someone other than a priest, according to Froehle and Gautier, *Catholicism USA*, p. 58. If we multiply 19,181 parishes by 17 percent, we get 3,261 parishes. And if 437 of these are administered by a deacon or layperson, that means that 2,824 parishes (14.72 % of the total) have pastors who serve more than one parish. "The Midwest has 28 percent of parishes with no resident pastor, the highest percentage of all five regions," state Froehle and Gautier; "Sixty-two percent of all parishes for which a non-resident pastor is not available are entrusted to women religious" (p. 58).

8. Canon 536 states that the pastor presides over the council. See John Paul II, *Code of Canon Law*, Latin-English Edition, Translation prepared under the auspices of the Canon Law Society of America (Washington, D.C.: Canon Law Society of America, 1983). The code also states that "the care of several neighboring parishes can be entrusted to the same pastor due to a dearth of priests or in other circumstances" (c. 526, §1). Further, it states that, when there is a dearth of priests, a parish may "be entrusted to a deacon or to some other person who is not a priest or to a community of persons" (c. 517, §2). "Parish coordinator" and "priest moderator" are the terms of John A. Renken, "Parishes without a Resident Pastor: Comments on Canon 517, §2," in Edward G. Pfnausch, editor, *Code, Community, Ministry: Selected Studies for the Parish Minister Introducing the Code of Canon Law*, second revised edition (Washington, D.C.: Canon Law Society of America, 1992), pp. 100-108.

Chapter Two: Support by the Bishops

1. Canadian Conference of Catholic Bishops, CCCB Laity Commission, *The Parish Pastoral Council: Guidelines for the Development of Constitutions* (Ottawa: CCCB, 1984).

2. Mark F. Fischer, "Parish Pastoral Councils: How Many Are There? How Do Bishops Support Them?" in Doyle et al., Editors, *Parish Laity and Ministry*, pp. 82-106.

3. Fourteen dioceses out of 64 employ officials who devote 60 percent or more of their time in council support. Fourteen out of 64 employ council support staff members who work less than 10 percent of their time on councils. The median full-time equivalent is 25 percent. That is, half of the dioceses with support staff for councils devote a quarter or more of an official's time to councils. Half devote a quarter or less. See Fischer, "Parish Pastoral Councils: How Many Are There? How Do Bishops Support Them?"

4. Mary P. Burke and Eugene F. Hemrick, *Building the Local Church: Shared Responsibility in DPCs* (Washington, D.C.: United States Catholic Conference, 1984), pp. 65-66.

5. Fischer, "Parish Pastoral Councils: How Many Are There? How Do Bishops Support Them?" found that 62 percent out of 98 dioceses have DPCs.

6. The Committee on the Laity of the National Conference of Catholic Bishops, in collaboration with the NCCB Committee on Doctrine and Pastoral Practices, formed a "Steering Committee" on shared responsibility as exercised in DPCs. With replies from every U.S. diocese, it found that there are 91 DPCs in the U.S. See Bryan T. Froehle, *Diocesan and Eparchial Pastoral Councils: A National Profile*, undertaken by the Center for Applied Research in the Apostolate (CARA) at Georgetown University (Washington, D.C.: United States Catholic Conference, June 1998). Among the committee's members was Bill Broderick, a layman from the Arlington diocese whose writing had reawakened the question. See Bill Broderick, "Does Your Diocese Have a Council?" *Commonweal* 122 (Oct. 20, 1995): 12. See also John P. Kavanagh, "Yes, We Have a Council" [letter to the editor from Lansing, Michigan], *Commonweal* 122 (Dec. 15, 1995): 4, 24.

7. Not surprisingly, the 81 U.S. dioceses in which parish councils are mandated have a higher percentage of parishes and missions with councils (81.7 percent) than those 17 dioceses in which councils are not mandated (60.2 percent). See Fischer, "Parish Pastoral Councils: How Many Are There? How Do Bishops Support Them?"

8. Christopher Weldon, "Era of the Parish Council," *Origins* 2:2 (June 1, 1972): 21.

9. Roger Mahony, letter of April 25, 1991, in the Los Angeles Archdiocesan publication *Together in Mission: Parish Pastoral Council Guidelines* (Los Angeles: Pastoral Councils Office, 1991), p. ii.

Chapter Three: The Purpose of Councils

1. "Council of Ministries" is the term of Thomas Sweetser and Carol Wisniewski Holden, *Leadership in a Successful Parish* (San Francisco: Harper and Row, 1987), p. 124. This type of council (though not described as such) is also the recommendation of William J. Rademacher with Marliss Rogers, *The New Practical Guide for Parish Councils*, Foreword by Most Rev. Rembert G. Weakland, OSB (Mystic: Twenty-Third Publications, 1988).

2. Councils of the pastoral planning type are recommended by Robert G. Howes, *Creating an Effective Parish Pastoral Council* (Collegeville: The Liturgical Press, 1991); by Robert R. Newsome, *The Ministering Parish: Methods and Procedures for Pastoral Organization* (New York and Ramsey: Paulist Press, 1982); and by Loughlan Sofield and Brenda Hermann, *Developing the Parish as a Community of Service* (New York: Le Jacq Publishing, 1984). Newsome's *The Ministering Parish* was supposed to be the first of a three-volume work (see pp. 7-8), but the later volumes, to my knowledge, never appeared.

3. Diocese of Fargo in North Dakota, *Handbook for Parish Councils in the Diocese of Fargo* (Fargo: Diocese of Fargo, 1983), pp. 29-30. Cf. Rademacher and Rogers, which in chapter 4 assigns to councils fourteen purposes, seven characteristics, and ten functions.

4. Mark F. Fischer, "Parish Pastoral Councils," p. 3. This publication compared the guidelines of Boston, New York, Harrisburg, Raleigh, Louisville, Cleveland, Milwaukee, Fargo, Omaha, Brownsville, San Bernardino, Portland in Oregon, and Cheyenne. Further information about them can be found in the appendix, "A Bibliography of Pastoral Council Guidelines."

5. Three guidelines surveyed in 1995 state that planning is the main task of the council (guidelines of Philadelphia, Detroit, and Seattle). Eight guidelines state that planning is one of several council tasks (Hartford, Ogdensburg, Baltimore, Nashville, Green Bay, Salina, Fort Worth, and Sacramento). Only two guidelines did not name planning as a council task (Bismarck, Denver). Further information can be found in the appendix entitled "A Bibliography of Pastoral Council Guidelines."

6. Nine guidelines surveyed in 1995 state that the parish council is to coordinate a system of standing committees (Hartford, Ogdensburg, Baltimore, Nashville, Detroit, Green Bay, Salina, Fort Worth, and Seattle).

7. For example, the Hartford guidelines state that the primary task of a pastoral council is "to develop itself into a praying, unified Christian community" (p. 4), the Baltimore guidelines state that councils are "to listen to where the Spirit is leading" (p. 6), and councils in the Archdiocese of Detroit are to "be sensitive to the movement of the Spirit" ("Guidelines," p. 11).

The Nashville guidelines say that councils "act as a line of communication to and from the people" (p. 8); and the Seattle guidelines state that the council's third purpose (after forming community and planning) is "to promote communication" (p. 29).

8. The Ogdensburg guidelines state that the council "assists in developing a spiritual unity" (p. 8); the Salina guidelines refer to the pastoral council as "an energizing, coordinating and unifying organism" (p. 2); and the Seattle guidelines state that councils are to be "a sign and witness of unity" (p. 28).

9. John P. Flaherty, editor, *Diocesan Efforts at Parish Reorganization* (Clearwater, FL: CPPCD, 1995), Appendix 3.

10. Jerome Hanus, *Vision 2000: A Vision and Plan for the Archdiocese of Dubuque in the Twenty-First Century*, directed by a 17-member Planning Task Force and composed by a Writing Committee, including Mary Montgomery, OP, Director of Strategic Planning (Dubuque: Office of Archbishop Jerome Hanus, OSB, 1999), p. 15.

11. See Flaherty, Editor, *Diocesan Efforts at Parish Reorganization*, p. 88.

12. Hanus, *Vision 2000*, p. 65. See also p. 16 about "the emotions involved in the clustering process."

13. Mary Montgomery, "Sharing More than a Pastor," Chapter Nine in Mark F. Fischer and Mary Raley, Editors, *Four Ways to Build More Effective Parish Councils: A Pastoral Approach* (Mystic, CT: Twenty-Third Publications-Bayard, 2002).

14. Sacred Congregation for the Clergy, "Patterns in Local Pastoral Councils" (January 25, 1973), paragraph no. 12, *Origins* 3:12 (9/13/73): 186-190. This document was also published as "Pastoral Councils" in James I. O'Connor, Editor, *The Canon Law Digest*, vol. VIII: Officially Published Documents Affecting the Code of Canon Law 1973-1977 (Mundelein, IL: Chicago Province of the Society of Jesus, St. Mary of the Lake Seminary, 1978), pp. 280-288. It will be discussed at length in Chapter Ten below.

Chapter Four: Committees and the Council

1. Mark F. Fischer, "Parish Pastoral Councils," Table 6, p. 7.

2. My 1995 survey revealed that the guidelines for Hartford, Green Bay, and Fort Worth specify five committees. Salina and Seattle call for three, which is the smallest number specified in the guidelines surveyed. Others have as many as six (Ogdensburg), seven (Baltimore), or even ten (Bismarck).

3. For a good introduction to parish committee work, see Thomas Baker and Frank Ferrone, *Liturgy Committee Handbook* (Mystic, CT: Twenty-Third Publications, 1998). The recruitment of volunteers, including committee members, to accomplish the parish mission is treated at length by William J. Bannon and Suzanne Donovan, *Volunteers and Ministry: A Manual for Developing Parish Volunteers* (New York and Ramsey: Paulist Press, 1983). The interplay of chairperson, facilitator, and recorder (in a non-Church milieu) is the topic of Michael Doyle and David Straus, *How to Make Meetings Work: The New Interactive Method*, second printing of the 1976 edition (New York: Jove Books, 1983). The human dynamics of a group and its leader are treated by Barbara J. Fleischer, *Facilitating for Growth: A Guide for Scripture Groups and Small Christian Communities* (Collegeville, MN: The Liturgical Press, 1993). The *process* of committee work, especially the discernment of potential committee members and a non-adversarial way of promoting consensus, is outlined by Mary Benet McKinney, *Sharing Wisdom: A Process for Group Decision-Making* (Allen, Texas: Tabor Publishing, 1987). A spiritual approach to meetings which includes story telling, theological reflection, discernment, and envisioning of the future is the focus of Charles M. Olsen, *Transforming Church Boards Into Communities of Spiritual Leaders* (New York: The Alban Institute, 1995). A very basic book about the importance of a clear goal and a well-planned agenda is Medard Laz, *Making Parish Meetings Work* (Notre Dame, IN: Ave Maria, 1997).

4. Of 13 council guidelines surveyed in 1995, those of Philadelphia, Sacramento, and Denver, for example, do not advocate standing committees. Among the authors who question the system of standing committees, see William J. Bausch, *The Hands-On Parish* (Mystic, CT: Twenty-Third Publications, 1989), Sofield and Hermann, *Developing the Parish* (1984), Newsome, *The Ministering Parish*, and Howes, *Creating an Effective Parish Pastoral Council.*

5. Of thirteen guidelines surveyed in 1995, three "mandate" standing committees (Hartford, Detroit, Salina), six "recommend" them (Ogdensburg, Baltimore, Nashville, Green Bay, Fort Worth, and Seattle), and three merely "allow" them (Philadelphia, Bismarck, Denver). Only the Sacramento guidelines do not treat the topic of committees.

6. In thirteen council guidelines studied in 1995, the most common standing committees are education/formation (recommended in ten guidelines), social justice (eight guidelines), liturgy (seven guidelines), spiritual life (five guidelines), administration or stewardship (four guidelines), and evangelization or outreach (four guidelines). Other recommended standing committees are family life, social life, vocations, ecumenism, building and grounds, development, and planning.

7. Even the two best-known books on the "council of ministries" style of council are not in full accord with the majority of council guidelines published by dioceses. Rademacher and Rogers' *The New Practical Guide* recommends a standing committee on "Parish and Community Life" (p. 115 ff.), and Sweetser and Holden's *Leadership in a Successful Parish* recommends a standing committee on "Community Building" (p. 127). These committees

have some responsibility for evangelization, and may perhaps be classified as "evangeliza-tion" committees, which are commonly recommended in the thirteen guidelines. But none of the thirteen guidelines recommend a standing committee on "community."

8. Green Bay, "Commentary and Resources," p. 23. The clearly "executive" function (ital-ics in the original) given to the council, however, is contradicted in the first section of the Green Bay guidelines. There one reads that it is the pastor who is "in charge of implementa-tion" ("Norms," p. 5). The same ambiguity can be seen in the Detroit guidelines. First one reads that the council sets goals and the commissions set objectives, implementing them with the help of the parish staff ("Guidelines," pp. 11, 14, 19-21; "Handbook," p. 40). But then one reads that commissions implement objectives under the "oversight" of the pastor ("Handbook," p. 13).

9. Salina, p. 9; Nashville, p. 10; Detroit, "Guidelines," p. 19.

10. Four guidelines describe the committee role as "planning," "planning and imple-menting," or "recommending."

11. This is envisioned in the Baltimore guidelines, which state that "the parish council rec-ommends these goals to the pastor, who assigns them to staff and/or committees" for imple-mentation (p. 19).

12. The guidelines of Baltimore (p. 21), Green Bay ("Norms," p. 6), and Seattle (p. 33) state that the committees are "accountable" to the council.

13. Hartford, p. 4; Nashville, p. 32; Detroit, "Guidelines," p. 12.

14. Ogdensburg, p. 11; Salina, p. 10; Fort Worth, "Practical Suggestions," p. 3.

15. The Denver guidelines state that committees implement policy, but they implement "parish" policies, i.e., recommendations of the council that have been accepted by the pastor.

Chapter Five: Five Types of Consultation

1. Sacramento guidelines, p. 3. Denver guidelines, p. 4. The language is taken from John Keating, "Consultation in the Parish," *Origins* 14:17 (October 11, 1984), p. 264.

2. James H. Provost, "The Working Together of Consultative Bodies—Great Expectations?" *The Jurist* 40 (1980): 257-281; at p. 261.

3. Thus Hartford councils both "advise" pastors and "give direction" to the parish (p. 4). Bismarck councils have "consultative authority" (p. 37) subject to the pastor's "veto" (p. 40). Fort Worth Councils have both a "consultative" and a "leadership" role ("Guidelines," pp. 2, 5). Management texts refer to this kind of authority as "centrality," the power that comes from being central to important decisions. See David A. Whetten and Kim S. Cameron, *Developing Management Skills* (Glenview, Illinois: Scott, Foresman and Company, 1984), p. 250 ff.

4. Robert T. Kennedy, "Shared Responsibility in Ecclesial Decision-Making," *Studia Canonica* 14:1 (1980): 5-23.

5. See the Ogdensburg guidelines on prayer (p. 5), the Baltimore guidelines on shared wisdom rather than Robert's Rules (p. 23), and the Seattle guidelines on discernment (pp. 33-35). The Nashville guidelines include ten pages of council liturgies, the Bismarck guide-lines include twelve pages.

6. Robert G. Howes, *Creating an Effective Parish Pastoral Council*, p. 50. See Henry M. Robert, *Robert's Rules of Order Revised, Seventy-fifth Anniversary Edition* (Chicago: Scott, Foresman and Company, 1951). Participative decision making (such as a search for consen-sus) is not desirable unless the problem is a general one and all need to accept the decision to make it effective. See Victor H. Vroom and Phillip W. Yetten, *Leadership and Decisionmaking* (Pittsburgh: University of Pittsburgh Press, 1973).

7. The Detroit guidelines speak of the pastor as one who, for the sake of consensus, grants or withholds ratification ("Guidelines," pp. 13-14); the Salina guidelines also link ratifica-tion and consensus (pp. 8-9). The guidelines of Nashville (p. 7) and of Bismarck (p. 40) also give pastors the task of ratification and the right to veto, but this legal approach is seen by them as an exception. On the pastor as ratifier of council decisions, see Rademacher with Rogers, *The New Practical Guide*, pp. 75 ff.

8. Nashville guidelines, p. 32; Green Bay guidelines, "Commentary and Resources," p. 23. The Green Bay guidelines, however, are not univocal about the council "making" policy. They elsewhere state that the council offers "recommendations," and "assists in setting policies" rather than making them directly ("Norms," p. 5). At another point, the Green Bay guidelines note that the pastor is the real decision maker ("Commentary and Resources," p. 29).

9. Nashville guidelines, p. 4. The Green Bay guidelines, however, are not so sanguine. "Norm VI" states that the pastor will ordinarily affirm a council's recommendations "if he is one with the people and active in the deliberative process" ("Norms," p. 4). Needless to say, this condition of unity is not always met.

Chapter Six: Leadership in the Council

1. The principle that only a pastor can convoke the pastoral council is articulated in canon 514 of the Code of Canon Law, referring to diocesan councils. See Pope John Paul II, *Code of Canon Law*, Latin-English Edition. The source for the canon is the apostolic letter of Pope Paul VI, "Ecclesiae Sanctae I" (August 6, 1966), written *motu proprio*, on the implementation of the Vatican II Decree on Bishops, translated by Austin P. Flannery, in *The Documents of Vatican II*, edited by Flannery (New York: Pillar Books, 1975), no. 16, p. 601.

2. The exceptions are the Archdiocese of Hartford, whose guidelines describe the pastor as "leader" and "supervisor" (p. 5) and which speak of the lay "President/Chairperson" (p. 8); and the Diocese of Nashville, whose guidelines describe the pastor as one who delegates authority to the council (p. 4) and ratifies its decisions (p. 7).

3. The Bismarck guidelines connect the pastor's role in the council to the pastor's "presiding" over the Eucharistic assembly (p. 40). My earlier study of council guidelines found that the guidelines of Louisville and of Cleveland make the same connection. See Fischer, "Parish Pastoral Councils" (1990), p. 9.

4. On setting the agenda, see the guidelines of Philadelphia (p. 4) and Sacramento (p. 5). On consulting, see Hartford (p. 5) and Denver (p. 5). On receiving proposals, see Philadelphia (p. 4) and Baltimore (p. 19). On deciding, see Detroit ("Guidelines," p. 13) and Green Bay ("Commentary and Resources," p. 29).

5. These guidelines are also an anomaly in that they allow the lay vice chairperson to "preside" in the pastor's absence (Ogdensburg, p. 10; Philadelphia, p. 7). Presiding (as distinct from chairing) is a pastor's role, and these guidelines envision a council that may meet in the pastor's absence.

6. On ratifying, see Nashville (p. 7), Detroit ("Guidelines," p. 14), Bismarck (p. 40), and Salina (p. 15). On participating, see Detroit ("Guidelines," p. 13), Green Bay ("Norms," p. 9), and Bismarck (p. 40). On listening, see Bismarck (p. 40), Sacramento (p. 5), and Seattle (p. 42). Pastors may chair councils in Green Bay ("Commentary and Resources," p. 10), Bismarck (p. 40), Fort Worth ("Guidelines," p. 2), and Seattle (p. 19). On helping the executive committee prepare the agenda, see Baltimore (p. 22), Detroit ("Guidelines," p. 17), Green Bay ("Norms," p. 6), Salina (p. 6), Fort Worth ("Guidelines," p. 3), and Seattle (p. 42).

7. For a description of how the good leader in general (and not just the priest-leader) helps his followers achieve their goals, see Robert K. Greenleaf, *Servant Leadership: A Journey into the Nature of Legitimate Power and Greatness* (New York, Ramsey, and Toronto: Paulist Press, 1977).

8. The distinction between task and relationship behavior in leaders is a commonplace in the managerial literature. See Robert R. Blake and Jane S. Mouton, *The Managerial Grid* (Houston: Gulf Publishing, 1964).

9. On consensus-building, see Ogdensburg (p. 4), Philadelphia (p. 5), Nashville (p. 7), Seattle (pp. 13-14), and Denver (p. 9). On spiritual leadership, see Hartford (p. 5), Baltimore (p. 29), and Salina (p. 2). On creating trust, see Philadelphia (p. 5), Salina (p. 8), and Fort Worth ("Guidelines," p. 3). On building community, see Bismarck (p. 40) and Fort Worth ("Guidelines," p. 3). On serving, see Detroit ("Guidelines," p. 13) and Seattle (pp. 13-14). Most pastors meet their councils on a monthly basis. Eight out of thirteen guidelines recommend monthly meetings (Philadelphia, Baltimore, Detroit, Green Bay, Bismarck, Salina, Fort

Worth, and Seattle). Three do not specify the frequency of meetings (Nashville, Sacramento, Denver). Two guidelines recommend four or four to six meetings per year (Hartford and Ogdensburg).

10. Ogdensburg, p. 8; Detroit ("Guidelines"), p. 15; Bismarck, p. 18.

11. David C. Leege, "Parish Life Among the Leaders" (December, 1986), Report no. 9 in Leege and Joseph Gremillion, Editors, *The Notre Dame Study of Catholic Parish Life,* 10 reports in total (Notre Dame, Indiana: University of Notre Dame, 1984-1987), Report no. 9, pp. 2, 7, and 14.

12. Although in two guidelines the lay "vice chairperson" may, at times, actually "preside" (Philadelphia, p. 7; Ogdensburg, p. 10), nevertheless this is not the norm today. The earliest parish council publications, however, would typically speak of the elected lay leader of the council (not the pastor) as the "president." See Robert C. Broderick, *The Parish Council Handbook: A Handbook to Bring the Power of Renewal to Your Parish* (Chicago: Franciscan Herald Press, 1968), p. 45; Bernard Lyons, *Parish Councils: Renewing the Christian Community* (Techny, Illinois: Divine Word Publications, 1967), p. 135; and Edward E. Ryan, *How to Establish a Parish Council: A Step-by-Step Program for Setting Up Parish Councils* (Chicago: Claretian Publications, 1968), p. 27.

13. Lay chairpersons are described as "facilitators" in the following guidelines: Hartford (p. 8), Baltimore (pp. 41-42), Detroit ("Handbook," pp. 45-46), Green Bay ("Commentary and Resources," p. 10), Salina (p. 6), Fort Worth ("Practical Suggestions," pp. 13, 22), and Seattle (p. 43). Lay chairpersons appoint the heads of parish standing committees, according to the guidelines of Baltimore (p. 42) and Bismarck (p. 48).

14. On prayer, see Hartford (p. 8), Detroit ("Handbook," pp. 45-6), and Green Bay ("Commentary and Resources," p. 10). On motivation, see Detroit ("Handbook," pp. 45-6), Bismarck (p. 18), and Salina (p. 6). On developing consensus and resolving conflict, see Baltimore (p. 35), Detroit ("Handbook," pp. 45-6), Fort Worth ("Practical Suggestions," p. 37), and Seattle (p. 32).

15. Denver, p. 4, Sacramento, p. 3.

16. Leege, Report no. 9; see Castelli and Gremillion, p. 107.

17. Nashville (p. 6).

18. On consensus, see Nashville (p. 2), Baltimore (p. 23), Salina (p. 7), and Fort Worth ("Guidelines," p. 1). On conciliation, see Nashville (p. 7). On appeals, see Detroit ("Guidelines," p. 14) and Green Bay ("Norms," p. 5). In my earlier study of pastoral council guidelines, nine out of thirteen guidelines provide for appeal in cases of pastor-council conflict. See Fischer, "Parish Pastoral Councils" (1990), p. 9. On prayer, see Hartford (p. 4), Baltimore (p. 10), and Detroit ("Handbook," pp. 6 ff.); on trust, see Philadelphia (p. 5), Salina (p. 8), and Fort Worth ("Guidelines," p. 3).

Chapter Seven: The Selection of Council Members

1. See William J. Rademacher, *The Practical Guide for Parish Councils* (West Mystic, CT: Twenty-Third Publications, 1979), p. 118; and McKinney, pp. 6-8.

2. Of the 13 guidelines surveyed in 1990, five exclusively recommend at-large elections (Harrisburg, Boston, Raleigh, Fargo, and San Bernardino). Five others recommend elections either at-large or from parish standing committees (Cleveland, Milwaukee, New York, Omaha, and Portland). See Fischer, "Parish Pastoral Councils" (1990), Table 5, p. 6.

3. Of the 13 guidelines surveyed in 1995, nine recommend the election of most council members (Hartford, Ogdensburg, Philadelphia, Baltimore, Nashville, Bismarck, Salina, Sacramento, and Seattle). Three others allow the selection of councillors by drawing lots as an alternative to parish-wide elections (Detroit, Green Bay, and Fort Worth). One guideline (Seattle) allows for election of members by the pastoral council itself or by ministerial committees as an alternative to parish-wide elections.

4. The guidelines of Hartford (p. 6), Philadelphia (p. 6), Baltimore (p. 40), Salina (p. 7), and Seattle (p. 41) mandate or allow the appointment of council members for the sake of representation, diversity, or balance. Five other guidelines (Ogdensburg, Green Bay, Bismarck, Fort

Worth, and Sacramento) allow appointment but are less explicit about the rationale.

5. *Ex officio* members are provided for in the guidelines of (1) Hartford, (2) Ogdensburg, (3) Philadelphia, (4) Baltimore, (6) Detroit, (7) Green Bay, (8) Bismarck, (9) Salina, (10) Fort Worth, and (12) Seattle. They specify the clergy (guidelines 1, 2, 3, 4, 6, 7, 8, 9), trustees (guidelines 1, 2, 7, 8), and financial councillors (guidelines 1, 3, 7) as council members.

6. Parish staff may serve on the council according to the guidelines of Hartford, Ogdensburg, Baltimore, Detroit, Green Bay, Bismarck, Fort Worth, and Seattle.

7. The council membership of the parish staff is qualified in the guidelines of Detroit ("Guidelines," p. 15), Green Bay ("Norms," p. 9), and Baltimore (p. 40).

8. McKinney, pp. 79-81.

9. Discernment is a necessary adjunct to elections in Fort Worth ("Practical Suggestions," pp. 15-21), and an option in Detroit ("Handbook," pp. 24-26) and Green Bay ("Commentary and Resources," p. 31; and Appendix G).

10. Demographic representation is a primary concern in the guidelines of Hartford (p. 6), Ogdensburg (p. 8), Philadelphia (p. 6), Baltimore (p. 40), Nashville (pp. 5, 9), Detroit ("Guidelines," p. 15), Green Bay ("Norms," p. 9), Salina (p. 6), and Seattle (p. 41).

11. On the criterion of "balance" see Baltimore, p. 40. On reflecting concerns and needs, see Detroit ("Guidelines," p. 15). On seeking a representation of attitudes, see Salina (p. 4).

12. Hartford (p. 7), Ogdensburg (p. 10), Philadelphia (p. 6), Baltimore (p. 40), Green Bay ("Norms," p. 9), Bismarck (p. 47), Salina (p. 4), Fort Worth ("Guidelines," p. 3), and Seattle (p. 40).

13. Guidelines call for council members with the following skills: experience (Hartford, p. 6), knowledge (Green Bay, "Commentary and Resources," p. 30), skill (Fort Worth, "Guidelines," p. 3), understanding (Seattle, p. 40), expertise (Ogdensburg, p. 8), and competence (Baltimore, p. 40).

Chapter Eight: The Earliest Parish Councils

1. Parish pastoral council guidelines, for example, commonly define the role of today's council by contrasting its elements with those of the earlier parish council. The contrasting elements cited by these guidelines may differ, as they do in Greensburg and Fort Worth, but in both cases the old becomes merely a foil to the new. See the Diocese of Greenburg's *New Wine, New Wineskins: Revisioning the Parish Through the Ministry of the Parish Pastoral Council* (Greensburg: Office of Parish Life and Ministry, Mary Ann Gubish, Director, 1996), pp. 13-14; and the Diocese of Fort Worth's *Handbook for Consultative Bodies*, Part II: "Practical Suggestions" (Fort Worth: Office of Parish Planning and Stewardship, Mary Raley, Director), 1995, p. 8.

2. Dennis J. O'Leary, "Parish Pastoral Councils: Instruments of Visioning and Planning," in Arthur X. Deegan, II, Editor, *Developing a Vibrant Parish Pastoral Council* (New York and Mahwah: Paulist Press, 1995), p. 20. John Heaps, an auxiliary bishop in New South Wales, illustrates the "temporal order" critique of earlier parish councils in his *Parish Pastoral Councils: Co-responsibility and Leadership* (Newtown, NSW, Australia: E.J. Dwyer, 1993), pp. 1-2.

3. O'Leary, p. 20.

4. Robert D. Newsome, *The Ministering Parish*, pp. 79-80.

5. Newsome's critique was indirectly confirmed by Loughlan Sofield and Carroll Juliano, "Developing a Pastoral Council," *Today's Parish* 19:4 (April/May 1987): 17-19, who stated that "Parish councils have frequently been the cause of frustration, conflict, and tension," p. 17.

6. Earnest Larsen, *Spiritual Renewal of the American Parish* (Liguori, MO.: Liguori Publications, 1977), pp. 42-43.

7. McKinney, *Sharing Wisdom*, p. 6.

8. Robert C. Broderick, *The Parish Council Handbook*; Bernard Lyons, *Parish Councils*; David P. O'Neill, *The Sharing Community*; The National Council of Catholic Men, *Parish Councils: A Report on Principles, Purposes, Structures and Goals* (Washington, D.C.: NCCM, 1968); and Edward E. Ryan, *How to Establish a Parish Council.*

9. O'Neill spoke of "community" councils (p. 17). Lyons described the parish as a "litur-

gical community" (chap. 2). Ryan said that council members are "partners in the running of the parish" (p. 22). Broderick spoke of renewing the world for Christ on p. 36. The National Council of Catholic Men spoke of partnership on p. 2.

10. Broderick, p. 41. Lyons, p. 124. O'Neill, p. 46. NCCM, p. 5. The exception was Ryan, who saw the council's primary role as administration (pp. 9, 14, 22). His book was a revision of a 1967 Louisiana State University thesis entitled "Lay Participation in Parish Administration."

11. O'Neill (p. 46) would only exclude the "private area of personal relationship between parishioners and their priests" from the scope of council discussions. He uses the word plan (pp. 32, 41), but does not speak of pastoral planning. Lyons (p. 124) would only exclude, in the financial realm, information about the private donations and offerings of parishioners. In the "Foreword" to Lyons, Bishop John J. Wright spoke of planning (p. viii), but Lyons himself did not. The NCCM spoke of "planning," calling it "the Council's first concern" (p. 3), but subsumed it under the general heading of "coordination." Ryan (p. 24) limited the scope of the council to whatever authority the pastor would delegate.

12. T. Whelan, "Thoughts on Setting Up a Council of Parishioners," *Clergy Review* 52:7 (July 1967), p. 552.

13. Joseph C. Buckley, "Parish Councils," *Clergy Review* 53:4 (April 1968), p. 271. The same point was made by William Rademacher in an article from 1972, who rejected the temporalities/spiritualities distinction as a "false dualism." See William J. Rademacher, "The Parish Council: A Series of Relationships," *The Priest* 27:12 (January 1972), p. 26.

14. These were the tasks of the parish council in, respectively, Broderick (p. 45), Lyons (p. 124), the NCCM (p. 2), O'Neill (p. 30), and Ryan (p. 14).

15. Vatican II, "Decree on the Apostolate of Lay People" (*Apostolicam actuositatem*, November 18, 1965), no. 26, translated by Father Finnian, OCSO, in Vatican II, *The Documents of Vatican II*, Edited by Austin P. Flannery (New York: Pillar Books, 1975), p. 791. See the discussion of this phrase in Chapter Seventeen.

16. Lyons regarded standing committees as extensions of the council and strictly subject to its control (p. 131). Broderick not only called for standing committees in 1968, but then wrote a second volume expounding the committee structure: Robert C. Broderick, *Your Parish Comes Alive* (Chicago: Franciscan Herald Publications, 1970). Ryan (pp. 29-32) viewed committees as an extension of the authority, delegated by the pastor, for coordinating areas of parish life.

17. NCCM, p. 26. But the NCCM publication of 1970, namely, Fecher's *Parish Council Committee Guide*, fully embraced the standing committee ideal.

18. O'Neill, p. 71.

19. Broderick (*Handbook*, p. 45), Lyons (p. 125), NCCM (p. 22), and O'Neill (pp. 40, 66). The exception was Ryan, who states that there are many methods for selecting members, from complete appointment to complete election (pp. 20-22). Lyons (p. 40) raises the question of whether democratic structures are always desirable in a parish where members, for example, are satisfied with racial segregation. He concludes that, yes, they are desirable, because people always "vote" anyway with their contributions to parish collections and by leaving parishes with whose members they disagree.

20. O'Neill, p. 40. The same view is present in Broderick (*Handbook*, p. 46), the NCCM (p. 23), and Lyons (p. 125). See also Robert J. Arquett, "Is the Parish Council Worthwhile?" *Homiletic and Pastoral Review* 67:8 (May, 1967), p. 649, who wanted to forestall the accusation that his council was a "clique." This continued to be a problem, leading one pastor to suggest that councils need to be "overhauled" in such a way that the entire parish (and not just the few elected councillors) would be "in council." See Patrick Fitzgerald, "Overhauling a Parish Council," *Clergy Review* 60:10 (October 1975): 684-691.

21. Lyons (p. 115) gave a list of reasons for using parliamentary procedure. Broderick (*Handbook*, p. 69) and the NCCM (p. 27) encouraged it as well. Of our five authors, O'Neill alone (pp. 73-74) rejected parliamentary procedure as legalistic. He even poked fun at Bernard Lyons, with whom he generally agreed, for the overly formal style of his model constitution.

22. Broderick (*Handbook*), p. 41. Two years later, he repeated a formulation from the

Archdiocese of New York that, however inadequate, influenced a number of later publications. The New York archdiocesan "Guidelines for Parish Councils" state that "the Parish Council should be a decision-making body whose decisions are binding when ratified by the pastor." Quoted in Broderick, *Your Parish*, p. 10. The word "ratify" would appear frequently in later publications about councils to describe how the pastor would receive the council's recommendations.

23. The NCCM stated that parishes can have a "purely advisory" council or a "decision-making" council, and expressed a preference for the latter, but added that decision-making councils are usually subject to a veto (p. 5). O'Neill (pp. 56, 60) criticized Broderick's *Handbook* for granting veto power to the pastor, noting that veto is not a term in church law. He conceded, however, that parish councils have no legal status "as yet" (p. 31). Lyons, the earliest and most adamant about the decision-making role of the council, recommended giving the lay parish council "president" authority to sign checks and legal documents (p. 135). The members of the council, he argued, should be indemnified "out of the funds of the [parish] assembly" against legal action (p. 135). The pastor should have no veto, said Lyons, but should ask for reconsideration of a matter with which he disagrees (p. 134). Ryan took a different tack, emphasizing the advisory nature of councils (p. 24).

24. For that reason, Broderick (*Handbook*) presents two constitutions in his "Appendix II." One constitution gives to the parish council power to initiate programs on its own authority (p. 45). The second limits the council to advising the pastor (p. 55). Not every author in the period would agree, however, that councils should be more than advisory. Jordan Aumann, in an "Editorial: Diocesan and Parish Councils," (*The Priest* 27:1 (1971): 5-7), warned against "rule" by the parish council "aristocracy" (p. 6).

25. On appeals, see Broderick (p. 42); Lyons (pp. 35-36); the NCCM (p. 5), and O'Neill (p. 53).

26. Basil Cole, "Conceiving, Creating and Sustaining the Parish Council," *The Priest* 34:9 (September, 1978): 30-33

27. Broderick (*Handbook*, p. 95) and the NCCM (p. 21) said that the pastor might be given the vote. Lyons (p. 133) opposed giving pastors the vote. O'Neill, one could surmise, opposed the vote for the same reason that he opposed the veto (pp. 56, 60). Ryan said that the pastor is an *ex officio* member of the council (p. 20), but apparently non-voting, since the authority of the council depends on him.

28. Other authors from the period did refer, however, to prayer in the council. George Martin advocated a "prayerful" (as distinct from a "natural") method of conducting the council in "Basic Options for Parish Councils," *Today's Parish* (January 1969), pp. 8-9. The parish council steering committee at Bill Schaeffer's church started its meetings with the Mass, writes Gerry Fitzpatrick, "Diary of a Parish Council," *Today's Parish* (January, 1969), p. 3.

29. William J. Rademacher with Marliss Rogers, in *The New Practical Guide*, stated that, for early "political" councils, "Power was the main concern" (p. 63).

30. Lyons (p. 31); NCCM (p. 2); O'Neill (p. 30). Although Ryan emphasized the administrative role of councils, nevertheless he spoke of "community" and "involvement" (pp. 6-8). Richard McBrien distinguished between the "Catholic Action" ideal of the laity's participation in the apostolate of the hierarchy and the Vatican II ideal of the laity's participation in the mission of the Church itself. See McBrien, "The Place of Parish Councils within the Developing Theology of the Church," p. 19, in William V. Coleman, Editor, *Parish Leadership Today: A Compilation of Writings from* Today's Parish (Mystic: Twenty-Third Publications, 1979), pp. 19-29.

31. Broderick, p. 3. Bernard Lyons, *Leaders for Parish Councils: A Handbook of Training Techniques* (Techny, Illinois: Divine Word Publications, 1971), p. 37.

32. O'Neill (p. 44); Lyons (*Councils*, pp. 19, 32); NCCM (p. 3).

33. On submissiveness, see O'Neill, p. 23. O'Neill anticipated an equality in which parishioners can freely criticize the pastor's preaching (p. 39). On the "atrophied laity," see Lyons (*Councils*), p. 9.

34. O'Neill, p. 60. On the distant professionalism of priests, see Lyons (*Councils*), p. 10.

35. With councils, said Lyons (*Leaders*), "the priest no longer needs to be the corporation executive, no more the bookkeeper, fund-raiser, and employer" (p. 13). Broderick

(*Handbook*) viewed councils as "complementing, helping, and expanding" the mission of the hierarchy (p. 9). The NCCM spoke of the pastor as "in partnership" and "co-responsible" with parishioners (p. 3). Ryan viewed the council as freeing the pastor "from his administrative detail to devote himself fully to the formation and leadership of the Christian community" (p. 9).

Chapter Nine: American Missteps

1. Vatican II, "Decree on the Apostolate of Lay People," no. 26, in Vatican II, *The Documents of Vatican II*, Flannery, General Editor, pp. 791-792.

2. Michael J. Sheehan and Russell Shaw, *Shared Responsibility at Work: The Catholic Bishops' Advisory Council, 1969-1974* (Washington, D.C.: United States Catholic Conference, 1975).

3. United States Catholic Conference, USCC Advisory Council, Steering Committee (to study the feasibility of an NPC), *A National Pastoral Council Pro and Con: Proceedings of an Interdisciplinary Consultation August 28-30, 1970, in Chicago, Illinois*, J. Paul O'Connor, Chairman of the Steering Committee (Washington, D.C.: USCC, 1971). The quotation is from an unsigned essay, "A National Pastoral Council: Some Reservations" (pp. 128-141), presumably written by O'Connor (p. 139). One year earlier, the USCC had published a twelve-page guide for discussions about the proposed NPC, which acknowledged that an NPC in which bishops would have a veto "does not sit well with groups which want to see a radical change in the way church policies and programs are established." See United States Catholic Conference, USCC Advisory Council, Steering Committee, *A National Pastoral Council: Yes, No, and Maybe*, Introduction by J. Paul O'Connor (Washington, D.C.: USCC, 1970), p. 10.

4. James Rausch, "Improving Pastoral Councils," *Origins* 3:17 (Oct. 18, 1973): 262. Russell Shaw attributed the suspension of the NPC to the January 25, 1973 "Private Letter on 'Pastoral Councils'" of the Vatican Congregation for the Clergy and he expressed doubts about shared responsibility in general. See Shaw, "The Pastoral Council that Never Was," *Catholic World Report* 6:9 (Oct. 1996): 40-45.

5. Vatican II, "Decree on the Apostolate of Lay People," no. 26, in Vatican II, *The Documents of Vatican II*, Flannery, General Editor, pp. 791-792. Speaking of councils to assist the Church's apostolic work, the decree states that "Such councils should be found too, if possible, at parochial, inter-parochial, interdiocesan level, and also on the national and international plane."

6. Footnote eight to no. 26 of the Laity Decree refers to the Encyclical Letter *Quamvis Nostra*, 30 April, 1936 of Pope Pius XI, *Acta Apostolicae Sedis* 28 (1936): 160-161.

7. News stories reported that 24 people were named "directors" at a convention of "several hundred" delegates in Cincinnati, with H. G. Rountree as first President and Margaret Mealey (who was Executive Director of the NCCW) as Executive Director of the NCCL. See "NCCL Begins With 24 Directors," *Davenport Messenger*, 25 November 1971. James F. Walsh, Jr., a council veteran and a proponent of parish councils in the Diocese of Nashville during the 1970s, called in 1992 for a revivified National Council of Catholic Laity. See his "Empowering the Laity: A Proposal to Implement Section 26 of the Decree on the Laity" (unpublished paper), March 7, 1992, p. 3.

8. J. Cardinal Villot, letter of November 5, 1971, to the founders of the National Council of Catholic Laity of the U.S.A. A photocopy of this letter is appended to Walsh's "Empowering the Laity."

9. William Maher, *A Question of Values*, Introduction by Richard H. Dement (Washington, D.C.: National Council of Catholic Laity, 1974). Maher's 60-page book skeptically asked, "where was the Church when Fascism and Nazism were on the rise in Europe?" (p. 2), referred to "the abysmal failure of the churches to respond to human need with something besides dogma and self-protection" (19), and concluded that the "institutional Church" of the future "will not tell people that God's law, as interpreted by the Churches, is to be obeyed regardless of human consequences" (55). Other books published by the NCCL were Helen B. Brewer and Thomas J. Tewey, Editors, *Understanding Coresponsibility* (Washington, D.C.:

NCCL, 1974); and Thomas J. Tewey, *Recycling the Parish* (Washington, D.C.: NCCL, 1972).

10. Walsh, "Empowering the Laity," p. 4. The National Councils of Catholic Laity and of Catholic Men, although defunct, are still listed as official national organizations by the U.S. Catholic Conference. On May 19, 1977, Archbishop McCarthy of Miami stated that "Despite great effort and dedication, the National Council of Catholic Laity has been unable to achieve its goals." See Edward McCarthy, "Is a Laity Secretariat Needed?" *Origins* 6:24 (Dec. 2, 1976): 378. Six months later, the U.S. bishops approved the establishment of a laity secretariat at their May 3-5, 1977 meeting in Chicago.

11. Jean Eckstein, letter to James F. Walsh, Jr., October 28, 1990. Ms. Eckstein, a resident of Iowa City, was President of the NCCL in 1975. A photocopy is appended to Walsh's "Empowering the Laity."

12. As early as 1967, Bishop John Wright of Pittsburgh had gone on record as stating that "The parish council is not a *lay* council or *lay* committee." John Wright, "Foreword," to Lyons, *Parish Councils*, p. vii. An exception to the U.S. bishops' general lack of support for exclusively lay councils was the September 15-17, 1978 consultation in Washington DC sponsored by the U.S. Bishops' Committee for the Laity. See Dolores Leckey, "Laity Councils: Developments in Lay Ministry," *Origins* 8:16 (Oct. 5, 1978): 245-248.

13. Work wrote that the "NCCM/NCCW are the equivalent in the United States of the national coordination recommended by the Vatican Council." Martin Work, "Diocesan Pastoral Councils and Substructures," in National Council of Catholic Men, *Diocesan Pastoral Council*, Proceedings of the Bergamo Conference, 15-17 March 1970 (Washington, D.C.: NCCM, 1970), p. 41.

14. Work stated that diocesan lay councils "should have as their parish outlet and local unit of action parish councils." See Work, "Diocesan Pastoral Councils and Substructures," in National Council of Catholic Men, *Diocesan Pastoral Council*, p. 42. In an earlier interpretation of the Laity decree, however, Work did not emphasize the independence of lay councils. He stated rather that they "will be consultative to the pastor; they will also share in some decision-making processes." Martin H. Work, "Commentary" on the Laity Decree, in Vincent A. Yzermans, Editor, *American Participation in the Second Vatican Council* (New York: Sheed and Ward, 1967), p. 465. Broderick, *Parish Council Handbook*, p. 15 also advocated diocesan lay councils.

15. For a general treatment, see Thomas T. McAvoy, *A History of the Catholic Church in the United States* (Notre Dame and London: University of Notre Dame Press, 1969), esp. Chap. Five, "The Trustee Controversy, 1815-1828," pp. 92-122. Negative portraits of trusteeism can be found in Robert F. McNamara, "Trusteeism in the Atlantic States, 1785-1863," *The Catholic Historical Review* 30 (July 1944): 135-154; and in Alfred G. Stritch, "Trusteeism in the Old Northwest, 1800-1850," *The Catholic Historical Review* 30 (July 1944): 155-164. For a positive portrait, see Joseph J. McCadden, "The Specter of the Lay Trustee," *America* 117:6 (8/5/67): 133-136, who believed that the disparagement of lay trusteeism has prevented the church from "sharing responsibility in temporal affairs" (p. 136).

16. Ryan, *How to Establish a Parish Council*, warned against the dangers of lay trusteeism and emphasized that parish councils have only the authority which the pastor delegates (p. 16). For a contrasting view, see Edward Day, "Parish Council: Pastor and People Sharing Christ's Priesthood," *Liguorian* 64:2 (February 1976): 20-25. Day concludes that the pastor's offering of dedicated service is an answer and "safeguard against the bitter battles of trusteeism" (25).

17. The Sacred Congregation for the Clergy issued a private letter to the bishops of the world on January 25, 1973 which was published in the United States as "Patterns in Local Pastoral Councils" (*Origins* 3:12 (9/13/73): 186-190), and also as "Pastoral Councils" in James I. O'Connor, Editor, *The Canon Law Digest*, vol. VIII: Officially Published Documents Affecting the Code of Canon Law 1973-1977 (Mundelein, IL: Chicago Province of the Society of Jesus, St. Mary of the Lake Seminary, 1978), pp. 280-288. For the Latin version, which followed the English, see Sacra Congregatio Pro Clericis, "Litterae circulares ad Patriarchas, Primates, Archiepiscopos, Episcopos aliosque locorum Ordinarios. De Consiliis Pastoralibus iuxta placita Congregationis Plenariae mixtae die 15 Martii 1972 habitae: Normae statuuntur novae circa compositionem, naturam, munera modumque procedendi

Consilii Pastoralis in unaquaque Dioecesi." *Omnes Christifideles*, 25 Januarii 1973. In Ochoa, Xaverius, Editor, *Leges Ecclesiae post Codicem iuris canonici editae*. Collegit, digessit notisque ornavit Xaverius Ochoa (until 1985). Institutem Iuridicum Claretianum. 8 volumes. Vatican City: Libreria Editrice Vaticana; and Rome: Commentarium Pro Religiosis, 1973-1998. See vol. V: "Leges Annis 1973-1978 Editae" (1980), columns 6444-6449.

18. The specific proposals for electing bishops and enacting legislation represented the consensus of an interdisciplinary symposium sponsored by the Canon Law Society of America in cooperation with Fordham University on April 3-5, 1970. See the unsigned "Statement of Consensus" in James A. Coriden, Editor, *Who Decides for the Church? Studies in Co-Responsibility* (Hartford, Connecticut: Canon Law Society of America, 1971), pp. 280-284. Father Coriden, then Assistant Professor in the Schools of Theology and Canon Law at Catholic University of America, edited two other books about Church governance: *The Once and Future Church: A Communion of Freedom—Studies on Unity and Collegiality in the Church* (Staten Island: Alba House, 1971), and *We, the People of God: A Study of Constitutional Government for the Church* (Huntington: Our Sunday Visitor, 1968). In *The Once and Future Church*, he said that subsidiarity is a key issue "in the tension between papal authority and the national conferences of bishops (or national pastoral councils)." The parenthesis, which suggests an equality in dignity of bishops and councils, indicates the authority which supporters of the NPC hoped it would have (see Coriden, "Editor's Preface" to *The Once and Future Church*, p. xii). Coriden expressed his own views more amply in a contribution entitled "Shared Authority: Rationale and Legal Foundation" to the volume edited by Charles E. Curran and George J. Dyer, *Shared Responsibility in the Local Church*, published as *Chicago Studies* 9:2 (Summer, 1970), pp. 171-182. The naivete of these early collections was the point of a review article by Denis Read, who stated that most of the contributors focused on changing the Church institutional structures, rather than the attitude or virtues of Church members. See Denis Read, "Review Article: *The Once and Future Church* and *Who Decides for the Church?" The American Ecclesiastical Review* 166:6 (June 1972): 421-424.

19. The article by James Hennesey, "Councils in America," printed in the proceedings of the 1970 consultation on *A National Pastoral Council* (at p. 60), praised the Canon Law Society of America for its "leading renewal role," especially in regard to the "Statement of Consensus" from the Fordham symposium, printed in Coriden, Editor, *Who Decides for the Church?* (pp. 280-284).

20. On Carroll's election, see John Tracy Ellis, *Catholics in Colonial America* (Baltimore: Helicon Press, 1965), pp. 450 ff., and Ellis, "On Selecting Catholic Bishops for the United States," *The Critic* 27:6 (June-July, 1969): 43-55; see also Francis J. Weber, "Episcopal Appointments in the U.S.A.," *American Ecclesiastical Review* 155:3 (Sept., 1966): 178-191. On England's conventions, see McAvoy, p. 117; and James Hennesey, *American Catholics: A History of the Roman Catholic Community in the United States*, Foreword by John Tracy Ellis (New York and Oxford: Oxford University Press, 1981), p. 114.

21. James Hennesey, "Councils in America," in the United States Catholic Conference, *A National Pastoral Council Pro and Con*, pp. 39-67, esp. pp. 40-41.

22. On diverse viewpoints, see William W. Bassett, "Subsidiarity, Order and Freedom in the Church," in Coriden, Editor, *The Once and Future Church*, pp. 210-213; on the charismata of the faithful, see Thomas F. O'Dea, "Authority and Freedom in the Church: Tension, Balance and Contradiction," in Coriden, Editor, *Who Decides in the Church?*, pp. 247-248; on giving the laity a voice and a vote, see Robert L. Benson, "Election by Community and Chapter: Reflections on Co-responsibility in the Historical Church," ibid., p. 80; and on councils as a communal voice, see Thomas F. O'Meara, "The National Pastoral Council of a Christian Church: Ecclesiastical Accessory or Communal Voice?" in the United States Catholic Conference, *A National Pastoral Council Pro and Con*, pp. 21-34.

Chapter Ten: The Circular Letter

1. Sacred Congregation for the Clergy, "Circular Letter on 'Pastoral Councils'" (January

25, 1973), reprinted in O'Connor, ed., *The Canon Law Digest*, vol. VIII, pp. 280-288. The circular letter was also published in *Origins* 3:12 (9/15/73): 186-190. For the Latin text, see Sacra Congregatio Pro Clericis, "Litterae circulares . . . De Consiliis Pastoralibus" (*Omnes Christifideles*), in Ochoa, editor, *Leges Ecclesiae*, vol. V: "Leges Annis 1973-1978 Editae" (1980), columns 6444-6449.

2. Each of the books by Broderick (p. 2), Lyons (p. 31), the NCCM (p. 2), O'Neill (p. 18), and Ryan from the period 1967-68 cited no. 26 of the Laity Decree.

3. Vatican Council II, "Decree on the Pastoral Office of Bishops in the Church" (*Christus Dominus*, October 28, 1965), translation by Matthew Dillon, Edward O'Leary and Austin P. Flannery, at no. 27; and "Decree on the Church's Missionary Activity" (*Ad Gentes Divinitus*, December 7, 1965), translated by Redmond Fitzmaurice, both in *The Documents of Vatican II*, Austin P. Flannery, General Editor. The missionary decree merely gives a one-sentence encouragement to pastoral councils: "For better coordination, the bishop should, as far as possible, establish a pastoral council in which clergy, religious and lay people would have a part through elected delegates," no. 30, p. 847. For the original texts, see Vaticani II, Cura et Studio Archivi Concilii Oecumenici, *Acta Synodalia Sacrosancti Concilii Oecumenici Vaticani*, "Decretum: De Pastorali Episcoporum Munere in Ecclesia" (Vol. IV, Periodus Quarta, Pars v, pp. 564-584); and "Decretum: De Activitate Missionali Ecclesiae" (Vol. IV, Periodus Quarta, Pars vii, pp. 673-704) (Vatican City: Typis Polyglottis Vaticanis, 1978).

4. Pope Paul VI, "Ecclesiae Sanctae I," nos. 16-17, in Vatican Council II, *The Documents of Vatican II*, Flannery, General Editor, pp. 601-602.

5. David O'Neill said that the call for councils in the bishops decree "has the proper vagueness of an embryo" (*The Sharing Community* [Dayton, Ohio: Pflaum, 1968], p. 18). Martin Work stated that diocesan pastoral councils are merely advisory bodies "to concern themselves with dialogue and planning, rather than with action, programming, servicing, and training" (Work, "DPCs and Substructures," in National Council of Catholic Men, *Diocesan Pastoral*, p. 41).

6. Hans Küng, "Participation of the Laity in Church Leadership and Church Elections," trans. by Arlene Swidler, *Journal of Ecumenical Studies* 6:4 (Fall 1969): 511-533. See p. 528 (on the DPC/parish council parallel) and p. 512 (on the exclusively temporal focus of the councils described in the laity decree).

7. James Buryska, "Four Dilemmas of Pastoral Councils," *Pastoral Life* 23:12 (December 1974): 12-20, at p. 17.

8. Pope Paul VI, "Regimini Ecclesiae Universae, Constitutio Apostolica" (August 15, 1967), *Acta Apostolicae Sedis* 59 (1967): 885-928. Translation: "Roman Curia Reorganized," in T. Lincoln Bouscaren and James I. O'Connor, Editors, *The Canon Law Digest*, Officially Published Documents Affecting the Code of Canon Law, 1963-1967, Vol. VI (New York: The Bruce Publishing Company, 1969), pp. 324-357.

9. John A. Coleman, *The Evolution of Dutch Catholicism*, 1958-1974 (Berkeley, Los Angeles, and London: University of California Press, 1978). Coleman states that the letter was written on November 25, 1970, and he summarizes its contents on pp. 179-180. His source was the *Archief van de Kerken*, XXVII, 40 and 41 (October 3-10, 1972), columns 913-923. The 1973 Private Letter itself gives another date for its consultation of the world's bishops: March 12, 1971. For another treatment of the Dutch council, see Rigobert Koper, "Die Lage der Katholischen Kirche in Holland: das holländische Pastoral-Konzil," *Theologisch-praktische Quartalschrift* 119 (1971): 220-228.

10. Synodo Episcoporum, "De Sacerdotio Ministeriali," *Acta Apostolicae Sedis* 63 (1971): 898-922, at pp. 900-901. Translation: Synod of Bishops, *The Ministerial Priesthood*, November 30, 1971, translation published in reference to canon 329 in James I. O'Connor, editor, *The Canon Law Digest*, vol. VII, pp. 342-366.

11. Sidney J. Marceaux, "The Pastoral Council," Doctor of Canon Law dissertation (Rome: Pontifical University of Studies at St. Thomas Aquinas in the City, 1980), p. 44, points out that the 1971 Synod document implicitly acknowledged the tension.

12. Congregation for the Clergy, "Circular Letter," reprinted in O'Connor, ed., *The Canon Law Digest*, vol. VIII, pp. 280-288. In paragraph no. 5, the letter dates the first request for

advice from bishops as March 12, 1971 (cf. Coleman's date of November 25, 1970); and for the "plenary combined congregation" as March 15, 1972.

13. Coleman, pp. 180-181. In the communiqué, the Dutch bishops reported that the Roman authorities considered "that the time was not ripe to set up a pastoral council at the national level."

14. This was reported in *Christ to the World* 18 (1973): 455-460, which stated that the English version was that of the congregation itself.

15. Donald W. Wuerl, "Pastoral Councils," *Homiletic and Pastoral Review* 73:11-12 (August-September 1973): 21-25, 93-94; at p. 22.

16. Coleman reported that, in the Dutch Diocese of Haarlem, the Diocesan Pastoral Council and the Council of Priests had merged. Coleman, p. 180, footnote 45.

17. Quoting from the statutes of the Dutch council, Coleman defines "co-responsible" on p. 169 and suggests that the term implied a sharing of juridical, deliberative power. The term "co-responsibility" is an elusive one. It was introduced to official Church documents, as far as I know, by the 1971 Synod of Bishops, "The Ministerial Priesthood" (*De Sacerdotio ministeriali*, Nov. 30, 1971), reprinted in James I. O'Connor, editor, *The Canon Law Digest*, Vol. VII: Officially Published Documents Affecting the Code of Canon Law 1968-1972 (Chicago: Chicago Province of the Society of Jesus, 1975), pp. 342-366. The synod wrote, "The more the *co-responsibility* of bishops and priests, especially through priests' councils, increases day by day, the more desirable it is that a pastoral council be established in the individual dioceses" (Part 2, II, section 3, "Relations between priests and lay persons," p. 364). Before the 1971 synod, however, co-responsibility was the subject of a book by Léon-Joseph Suenens, *Co-responsibilité dans l'église d'aujourd'hui* (Bruges: Desclée De Brouwer, 1968), translated as *Coresponsibility in the Church* by Francis Martin (New York: Herder and Herder, 1968). Later discussions include James A. Coriden, Editor, *Who Decides in the Church? Studies in Co-Responsibility* (Hartford: Canon Law Society of America, 1971), and Helen B. Brewer and Thomas J. Tewey, Editors, *Understanding Coresponsibility* (Washington, D.C.: National Council of Catholic Laity, 1974).

18. This is the opinion of Coleman, who at p. 181 quotes Cardinal Alfrink's acknowledgment that Rome, in the matter of the Dutch NPC, was acting in an "authoritarian" way.

19. Frederick R. McManus, "Diocesan Pastoral Councils," *The Jurist* 34 (Winter/Spring 1974): 168-171; Michael Sheehan, "Commentary: The Vatican's Letter on Pastoral Councils," *Origins* 3:12 (Sept. 13, 1973): 190-191; and the commentary by Wuerl entitled "Pastoral Councils." McManus quoted (p. 171) and Sheehan paraphrased (p. 191) the words of the letter—"there is nothing to prevent the institution within the diocese of [pastoral] councils of the same nature and function, whether parochial or regional"—without commentary. Wuerl did not even note the reference to parish pastoral councils.

20. Wuerl, p. 94; Sheehan, p. 190.

21. Sacred Congregation for the Clergy, "Circular Letter on 'Pastoral Councils,'" no. 8; in O'Connor, ed., *Canon Law Digest*, VIII: 285. McManus (p. 170) quotes the Latin version of the passage: "multumque concordi suffragio deferat," which suggests that the bishop should defer to the "vote" of widespread agreement. This is stronger language even than the English.

22. Sacred Congregation for the Clergy, "Circular Letter on 'Pastoral Councils,'" no. 9. McManus, p. 171; Sheehan, p. 191; and Wuerl, p. 93.

Chapter Eleven: The Growth of Councils in the 1970s

1. See Thomas Welsh, "A Parish in Conflict," *Origins* 4:26 (12/19/74): 411-413; and John P. Hannan, "Toward Reconciliation in Good Shepherd Parish," *Origins* 4:33 (2/6/75): 524.

2. Fecher, *Parish Council Committee Guide*, p. 10. Howes, "Parish Councils: Do We Care?" p. 371. Leege, Report No. 9 of the *Notre Dame Study of Catholic Parish Life*, p. 6. See the discussion of Fecher, Howes, and the Notre Dame Study in Chapter One.

3. Christopher Weldon, "Era of the Parish Council," *Origins* 2:2 (June 1, 1972): 19, 21 (first published in the 5/5/72 issue of the Springfield Catholic paper, the "Catholic Observer").

4. Eight of these guidelines were excerpted in *Origins*, the Documentary Service of the Catholic News Service, between 1972 and 1977. The eight dioceses that published guidelines are listed below in chronological order. Hereafter they will be cited as "guidelines" of the particular see, without full publication data.

—Diocese of Springfield, Massachusetts, "Areas of Competence" (parish council "norms"), *Origins* 2:2 (June 1, 1972): 19, 21, 26.

—Archdiocese of Boston, Massachusetts, "Parish Council/Element of Team Ministry," (Parish Council Guidelines), *Origins* 3:3 (June 14, 1973): 35-37.

—Diocese of Buffalo, "The Buffalo Parish Council Guidelines," *Origins* 3:17 (October 18, 1973): 260-261.

—Diocese of Columbus, "Parish Council Rationale: New Level of Ministry" (excerpts from the Parish Council Guidelines), *Origins* 7:16 (October 6, 1977): 241, 243-246.

—Archdiocese of Louisville, "The Parish Council's Role: Appeals Structures/Consensus Decisions," *Origins* 5:36 (February 26, 1976): 571-579.

—Archdiocese of Newark, Office of Pastoral Renewal, "The Parish Council at Work," *Origins* 6:17 (October 14, 1976): 272-276.

—Archdiocese of St. Paul - Minneapolis, "Sharing Responsibility: Parish Councils" (archdiocesan parish council guidelines), *Origins* 5:41 (April 1, 1976): 645, 647-651.

—Diocese of San Diego, "San Diego Guidelines for Parish Councils," *Origins* 7:3 (June 9, 1977): 36-39.

5. In addition to the pastoral letter by Bishop Weldon (mentioned above), the following pastoral letters appeared in *Origins*:

—William Borders (Archbishop of Baltimore), "The Difficult, Practical Phase of Shared Responsibility," *Origins* 6:5 (June 24, 1976): 65, 67-69.

—James Case (Archbishop of Denver), "Evaluating Today's Parish: Pastoral Process/Denver," *Origins* 6:3 (June 10, 1976): 41-44.

—Carroll T. Dozier (Bishop of Memphis), "Strategies for Community and Ministry," *Origins* 3:34 (February 14, 1974): 521, 523-526.

—Louis Gelineau (Bishop of Providence), "Reflections on Pastoral Planning: Discoveries in Renewal," *Origins* 6:27 (December 23, 1976): 421, 423-429.

—Edward D. Head (Bishop of Buffalo), "Sharing Responsibility," *Origins* 3:17 (October 18, 1973): 257, 259-260, 270-272.

6. The exceptions were the 1976 guidelines of Louisville and Newark that, in their emphases on the search for consensus (Louisville) and on pastoral planning (Newark), were more sophisticated than the others. The earlier guidelines' focus on mere involvement had given way (in the Louisville and Newark guidelines) to the harder questions of the "how" and the "to what purpose" of involvement.

7. Columbus guidelines, pp. 243-244.

8. On open meetings, see the guidelines of Springfield (p. 21), Boston (p. 36), Buffalo (p. 261) and St. Paul (p. 648). On elections, see the guidelines of Springfield (p. 21), Boston (p. 36), St. Paul (p. 649) and San Diego (p. 38).

9. On "coordinating" councils, see the guidelines of Springfield (p. 19), Boston (p. 36), Buffalo (p. 261), Louisville (p. 572), St. Paul (p. 647), and San Diego (p. 37). Two of the eight guidelines explicitly refer to the Laity Decree, *Apostolicam actuositatem* no. 26: Buffalo (p. 260) and San Diego (p. 36). By contrast, most bishops avoided the language about "pastoral" councils in the Decree on Bishops, the language about investigating, pondering, and recommending solutions for pastoral problems.

10. See the guidelines of Springfield (6 commissions), Boston (5 commissions), Louisville (4 coordinating committees), and San Diego (6 commissions).

11. The Boston guidelines state that the scope of the council is "parish administrative matters," not "higher level policy" (p. 37). The St. Paul guidelines limit councils from dealing with matters that belong to "archdiocesan jurisdiction" (p. 649), and the San Diego guidelines add diocesan regulations and official Church teachings to the list of forbidden subjects (p. 37).

12. The Louisville guidelines assigned seven "functions" to the parish council: coordi-

nating activities, assessing needs, establishing goals, promoting dialogue, providing leadership, carrying out diocesan directives, and involving parishioners (p. 572). The St. Paul guidelines adapt the first four functions, using almost identical language. The San Diego guidelines reproduce six of the seven functions (p. 37), leaving out Louisville's number three, "to set priorities, to establish goals and objectives."

13. Weldon, "Era of the Parish Council," p. 21.

14. On decision-making or policy-making councils, see the guidelines of Springfield (p. 21), Boston (p. 37), Louisville (p. 573), St. Paul (p. 648), and Columbus (p. 244).

15. Of eight dioceses, only Springfield (p. 19), Boston (p. 37), and Louisville (p. 573) allowed appeals.

16. The three exceptions are the St. Paul guidelines, which emphasize prayer but do not prescribe any particular practice (p. 649); the guidelines of Newark, which emphasize spirituality, prayer, and prayerful reflection while planning and discerning (pp. 273, 276)—again, without specifying any particular practice—and the guidelines of Columbus, which merely state that the steering committee ought to pray (p. 245).

17. This was articulated by McBrien, "The Place of Parish Councils," in Coleman, Editor, *Parish Leadership Today*, p. 26.

18. In Springfield, the pastor is "president" (p. 21), and in Columbus, he "presides" over both the liturgy and the parish team (p. 244).

19. The Vatican expressed this as follows: Laymen "take part in the parish pastoral council and take responsibility for the apostolate proper to them." Sacred Congregation for Bishops, Directory on the Pastoral Ministry of Bishops (*Ecclesiae imago*, May 31, 1973), translation prepared by the Benedictine monks of the Seminary of Christ the King, Mission, British Columbia (Ottawa: Publications Service of the Canadian Catholic Conference, 1974), no. 179, p. 92. Translation of Sacra Congregatio Pro Episcopis, *Ecclesiae imago: Directorium de Pastorali Ministerio Episcoporum* (Vatican City: Typis Polyglottis Vaticanis, 1973).

20. Baltimore and Pittsburgh were the diocesan locations of the earliest pastoral planning offices under the direction of Jack Carr and Kiernan Stenson. From May 16-17, 1972, the Diocese of Pittsburgh's Office for Research and Planning organized and hosted a conference on pastoral planning at Duquesne University and published the proceedings. See Kiernan F. Stenson, "Foreword," to George M. Pope, III and Bernard Quinn, Editors, *Planning for Planning: Perspectives on Diocesan Research and Planning* (Washington, D.C.: Center for Applied Research in the Apostolate [CARA], 1972). As more dioceses in the Northeast began to move into pastoral planning, many began to confer with Dr. Felix M. Lopez, a human resources consultant from Port Washington, New York. See "Appendix B: The National Pastoral Planning Conference: A Chronology," in Eugene F. Hemrick, Ruth Narita Doyle, and Patrick S. Hughes, Editors, *Diocesan Pastoral Planning in the '80s*, with an "Appendix A" entitled "What Is Pastoral Planning" by William C. Harms of the NPPC Coordinating Committee (Oakland, NJ: National Pastoral Planning Conference, Inc., 1983), p. 34.

21. On task and relationship, see the Newark guidelines, p. 274. On evaluations, see Borders, "The Difficult, Practical Phase," *Origins* 6:5 (6/24/76): 68. On planning and goal setting, see Gelineau, "Reflections," *Origins* 6:27 (12/23/76): 421, 423-429.

22. Howes, who was Coordinator of the Department for Church Management and Organization of CARA, had been working with Quinn on planning issues since 1971. See Robert G. Howes and Bernard Quinn, Editors, *Diocesan Pastoral Planning*, the papers from the May 28, 1971 Center for Applied Research in the Apostolate (CARA) symposium on DPCs (Washington, D.C.: Center for Applied Research in the Apostolate, 1971). See also John D. Dreher, "Pastoral Planning for Accountability: Key Assets and Obstacles," *Origins* 3:12 (Sept. 13, 1973): 182-186.

23. The NPPC presidents were Charles Giglio (1974), John Dreher (1975-76), Richard Conboy (1977-79), William Harms (1980-81, 1984), Patrick Hughes (1982-83), Judith K. Shanahan, S.P. (1985), Robert Shearer (1986), James Picton (1987-88), and Arthur X. Deegan, II (1989). All were Catholic priests except Hughes, Shanahan, Shearer, and Deegan. The NPPC held independent annual conferences in Cleveland (1973), Bethesda (1974), Omaha (1975), Providence (1976), Columbus (1977), San Antonio (1979), Hampton (1980), Orlando (1981), Seattle (1982), and Cleveland (1983).

24. Bernard Quinn, "Theological Reflections on the Planning Process," Chapter 4 of Pope and Quinn, Editors, *Planning for Planning*, p. 19.

25. Sacred Congregation for Bishops, *Directory on the Pastoral Ministry of Bishops*, no. 204. The importance of the congregation's reference to pastoral planning was underlined by the Archbishop and Apostolic Delegate to the U.S., Jean Jadot, in a December 3, 1974 address to the NPPC, "Effective Pastoral Planning," *Origins* 4:30 (January 16, 1975): 465, 467-468.

26. On councils developing pastoral plans, see Robert G. Howes, "Guide for Parish Council Members," *Liguorian* 63:5 (May 1975): 49-53.

On setting goals and objectives, see the Archdiocese of Detroit's "Directives and Guidelines for Parish Councils," first published in 1972 (while Arthur X. Deegan, II was Detroit's Director of Planning) and revised in 1974 and 1979 (Archdiocese of Detroit: Ministry to Councils Office, 1979), p. 10. Deegan had published one of the first social science analyses of the Church as an organization: *The Priest as Manager* (New York: Bruce Publishing, 1968). He had also published a leaflet series about councils. See Arthur Deegan, *How to Start a Parish Council*, five-part leaflet series (Fort Wayne, Indiana: Twenty-Third Publications, 1969).

On councils as the promoters of planning, see William C. Harms, *Who Are We and Where Are We Going? A Guide for Parish Planning*, A Parish Project Book copyright by The Parish Project of the National Conference of Catholic Bishops, 299 Elizabeth Street, New York (New York: Sadlier, 1981), esp. p. 21.

27. The First National Conference for Diocesan Parish Council Personnel was announced in the "Datebook" section of *Origins* 4:17 (Oct. 17, 1974): 258.

28. DPCP held independent conferences in Brighton (1974), Cincinnati (1975), Colorado Springs (1976), Clarkston, Michigan (1977), San Antonio (1979), Hampton (1980), Orlando (1981), Seattle (1982), and Cleveland (1983). Its Steering Committee chairpersons were Rev. Henry J. Mansell (1974-75), Rev. Ralph Starus (1976-77), Cynthia S. Thero (1978-1980), Rev. Richard Reis (1981), Sr. Rosalee Burke, N.D. (1982), and Susan Stromatt (1983).

29. These titles are drawn from the program of the October 2-5, 1977 conference in Clarkston, Michigan. The presentations were made by Rev. Henry J. Mansell, Director of the Office for Parish Councils in New York (about DPCs), Rev. Ralph Starus, Associate Vicar for the Laity in Chicago, and Rev. Kurt Gessner, O.F.M.Cap., of Green Bay's Office of Parish Services and Development (about spirituality), and Cynthia S. Thero, Director of Parish Council Services in Denver (about volunteers).

30. William J. Rademacher wrote *Answers for Parish Councillors* (West Mystic, Twenty-Third Publications, 1973); *Starting a Parish Council* (West Mystic, Twenty-Third Publications, 1974); *New Life for Parish Councils* (West Mystic, Twenty-Third Publications, 1976); *Working with Parish Councils?* (Canfield, Ohio: Alba, 1976); *The Practical Guide* (1979); *Answers for Parish Councillors*, with Three Chapters on the History, the Theology, and the Future of the Parish (Mystic: Twenty-Third Publications, 1981); and with Marliss Rogers, *The New Practical Guide for Parish Councils*, Foreword by Most Rev. Rembert G. Weakland, OSB (Mystic: Twenty-Third Publications, 1988).

31. Letter from Wm. J. Rademacher to Mark Fischer, August 24, 1996.

32. On the "People of God," see Rademacher's *Working*, chap. 1; he treated Rahner, Congar, and other conciliar thinkers in *Answers* 1981, pp. 32-33; for his views on ecumenism, see *Answers* 1981, p. 156, and *Working*, p. 11. On representation, see Rademacher's *Practical Guide*, pp. 29 and 121; he emphasized popular elections in *Working*, pp. 48f., and also in the Practical Guide, pp. 60, 143; decision-making councils were treated in Working, p. 92; the vote of the pastor appeared in *Answers* 1981, p. 106, and in the *Practical Guide*, p. 66. Rademacher showed his belief in pastoral planning by calling for parish profiles and goal setting (see *Working*, pp. 33ff, and the *Practical Guide*, pp. 173 ff.). He emphasized group dynamics by offering a typology of council members (*Answers* 1981, pp. 120 ff.), by teaching conflict resolution (*Answers* 1981, p. 142 ff.), and by the use of group process techniques (*Practical Guide*, pp. 53, 143).

33. On the shift to councils that are "primarily decision-making" but also "advisory,"

compare Rademacher's *Working*, pp. 74 and 92, with the *Practical Guide*, p. 59. Rademacher had, as early as 1971, called attention to the inappropriateness of the phrase "decision-making" to describe parish councils. In a eucharistic community, he wrote, council members should not be unduly concerned with their legal power, but should exercise "a certain detachment." See Rademacher, "The Parish Council: A Series of Relationships," p. 25.

34. On the shift from implementing through committees to not implementing, compare Rademacher's *Practical Guide*, pp. 82-83, with the *New Practical Guide*, p. 57. On the voting pastor, compare Rademacher's *Answers* 1981 (p. 106) with the *New Practical Guide* (pp. 75-84).

35. Rademacher approved parliamentary procedure in *Working*, p. 74, but had second thoughts in the *Practical Guide*, p. 143.

36. On the insufficiency of parliamentary procedure, see the Columbus guidelines, p. 245. On the search for consensus, see the Louisville guidelines, pp. 572-573. On St. Ignatius, see the Newark guidelines, p. 275.

37. The group dynamic approach can be seen in Charles J. Keating, *The Leadership Book* (New York and Mahwah: Paulist Press, 1978); Robert McEniry, "Parish Councils and Group Dynamics," *Pastoral Life* 26:9 (October, 1977): 22-29; and Ronald A. Sarno, "Using Group Dynamics to Activate a Parish Council," *Pastoral Life* 24 (September, 1975): 37-44. One can also see it in the 1988 work of Cynthia S. Thero, who was steering committee Chairperson of DPCP from 1978-1980, and owner and president of The Source International, a Catholic leadership consulting service. Thero was the unsigned author of *New Exodus: A Training Experience on Specific Skills Vital to All Catholic Lay Leaders* (Denver: The Source, a Division of Triptych, Inc., 1988), a 212-page manual distributed in a three-ring binder.

38. Earnest Larsen, C.Ss.R., *Spiritual Renewal*, pp. 42-43.

39. James H. Provost, "The Working Together of Consultative Bodies—Great Expectations?" *The Jurist* 40 (1980): 257-281.

40. See Francis Shea, "A Bishop Suspends His Pastoral Council," pastoral letter dated September 9, 1976, in *Origins* 6:15 (9/30/76): 229, 231-232. Bishop Shea may have had in mind the kind of council advocated by John F. Kippley, "Parish Councils: Democratic Process or New Absolutism?" *America* 123:4 (August 22, 1970): 94-97. Kippley recommended a parish council that would be a "governing body" to which all parish organizations answer, so "that co-responsibility does not become no-responsibility" (p. 96).

Chapter Twelve: The New Code

1. Pope John Paul II, *Codex Iuris Canonici*. Translation: *Code of Canon Law*, Latin-English Edition. Prior to 1983, there were hardly any books or articles with the words "parish pastoral council" in the title. Although there was a steady stream of at least 28 books and articles about "pastoral councils" from 1968 to 1976, these referred mainly to diocesan councils, not parish ones.

2. Canadian Conference of Catholic Bishops, Laity Commission, *The Parish Pastoral Council: Guidelines for the Development of Constitutions* (Ottawa: Canadian Catholic Conference, 1984). Roch Pagé, a canonist at St. Paul University in Ottawa, wrote the draft of the final document. He had published an address in 1981 on "The Parish Pastoral Council" in the *Proceedings* of the Canon Law Society of America 43 (1982): 45-61. As early as 1983, the Archdiocese of Portland in Oregon, assisted by canonist Bertram F. Griffin, published its *Parish Pastoral Councils*, which included policies for the archdiocese.

3. See Mark F. Fischer, "What Was Vatican II's Intent Regarding Parish Councils?" *Studia Canonica* 33 (1999): 5-25.

4. Roch Pagé ("The Parish Pastoral Council," pp. 57-60) felt that canon 536 was premature; there is a danger in legislating for the parish pastoral council, he said, before Catholics had developed a familiarity with it. John Lynch ("The Parochial Ministry in the New Code of Canon Law," *The Jurist* 42 (1982): 383-421, esp. p. 403) regretted that the 1983 Code did not encourage the formation of parish pastoral councils more forcefully. Later, William Rademacher and Marliss Rogers (*The New Practical Guide for Parish Councils*, p. 31) expressed disappointment that canon 536 had assigned to the council only a consultative vote; they

would have preferred the 1983 Code to say nothing about councils, allowing them to develop freely without limiting their competence.

5. William Dalton, "Parish Councils or Parish Pastoral Councils?" *Studia Canonica* 22 (1988): 169-185. Orville Griese, "The New Code of Canon Law and Parish Councils," *Homiletic and Pastoral Review* 85:4 (January 1985): 47-53. John Keating, "Consultation in the Parish," Origins 14:17 (October 11, 1984): 257, 259-266. Peter Kim Se-Mang, *Parish Councils on Mission: Coresponsibility and Authority among Pastors and Parishioners* (Kuala Lumpur: Benih Publisher, 1991). John A. Renken, "Pastoral Councils: Pastoral Planning and Dialogue among the People of God," *The Jurist* 53 (1993): 132-154.

6. Vatican Council II, "Dogmatic Constitution on the Church" (*Lumen Gentium*, November 21, 1964), no. 37, translated by Colman O'Neill, in Vatican II, *The Documents of Vatican II*, p. 395. Translation of "Constitutio Dogmatica: De Ecclesia," in Vaticani II, Cura et Studio Archivi Concilii Oecumenici, *Acta Synodalia Sacrosancti Concilii Oecumenici Vaticani*, Vol. III, Periodo Tertia, Pars viii: Congregationes Generalis CXXIII – CXXVII, Session Publica V (Vatican City: Typis Polyglottis Vaticanis, 1976), pages 784-836. Keating (p. 260) describes this passage as "relevant to the creation of parish councils," more relevant even than Bishops 27, which introduced the term "pastoral councils."

7. Griese ("The New Code," p. 48), states that "In a certain evolutionary process, however, and apparently in imitation of the diocesan pastoral council, parish pastoral councils came into being."

8. Ferdinand Klostermann, "Decree on the Apostolate of the Laity," in Herbert Vorgrimler, editor, *Commentary on the Documents of Vatican II*, translated by William Glen-Doepel, Hilda Graef, John Michael Jakubiak, and Simon and Erika Young (Freiburg in Breisgau: Herder; and Montreal: Palm Publishers, 1968), vol. III, p. 388. See also Roch Pagé, *The Diocesan Pastoral Council*, translated by Bernard A. Prince (Paramus, NJ: Newman Press, 1970), pp. 20, 74.

9. Keating (p. 260), states that "Commentators on Vatican II are agreed that this reference [to Laity 26] really does not speak of parish councils"—despite the fact that an entire host of parish council writers cited Laity 26 as the warrant for such councils. Kim concedes this point, stating that Laity 26 was "frequently" cited as the basis of parish councils (p. 33) and that the Vatican II basis for parish councils was "popularly assumed" (p. 73). Griese ("The New Code," p. 47) states that this was indeed a "popular assumption" but a mistaken one. He apologizes (in footnote 1) for making the mistake himself in an earlier article. See Orville Griese, "Pastor - Parish Council Collaboration," *The Priest* 33:2 (February 1977): 19-22, 24. Dalton (p. 171) and Renken (p. 148) agree that Vatican II did not call for parish "pastoral" councils, but insist that such councils harmonize with the intentions of Vatican II better than the parish councils that did emerge.

10. These are the theories of, respectively, Griese ("The New Code," p. 48), Keating (p. 259), Kim (pp. 73, 92) and Renken (p. 148).

11. Kim states that the coordinating council, recommended in Laity 26, has the responsibility for the "development and coordination of parish ministries and apostolic groups" (p. 83).

12. Keating, p. 260.

13. Griese, "The New Code," pp. 47-48.

14. Dalton, p. 170.

15. Sacred Congregation for the Clergy, "Circular Letter on 'Pastoral Councils,'" paragraph no. 9.

16. Renken (p. 138) states that the "circular letter expanded earlier documents and related, at least to some degree, the Church's experience of pastoral councils." Kim (p. 38) calls parish councils "a new ecclesial structure" but not a departure from Vatican II. "Such councils were not created [in the mid-seventies] as an afterthought to diocesan ones," he writes, "but as a consequence of experiments validating their [the parish pastoral councils'] existence."

17. Renken (p. 148); Kim (p. 92) implies the same by stating that Laity 26 intended a coordinating (not a pastoral) council.

18. Griese ("The New Code," p. 52) states that "the prescriptions of the new Code of Canon Law . . . follow closely the concepts . . . from the documents of Vatican II."

19. Keating (p. 259) states that the Code is built on "20 years' postconciliar experience

and experiments." Kim (p. 44) states that the Code "ends experimentation on ecclesial structural changes for a while, including parish councils."

20. Keating (p. 264). Griese ("The New Code," p. 49), Dalton (p. 170), Kim (p. 46), and Renken (p. 153) also emphasize the consultative as opposed to legislative role of the pastoral council.

21. Dalton (p. 172); Griese ("The New Code," p. 48).

22. Keating (p. 264), Griese ("The New Code," pp. 51-2), Kim (p. 48). The same point of view was endorsed by Loughlan Sofield and Carroll Juliano, "Developing a Pastoral Council," pp. 17-19.

23. Most pastoral council pioneers viewed the Laity Decree, no. 26, as a source for councils. See Broderick, p. 2, Lyons, p. 31, O'Neill, p. 18, the NCCM, p. 2, and Francis X. Legrand, "The Parish Council: Reflections on Their Principal Purpose," *Christ to the World* 14:2 (Nov. 2, 1969): 118-120. Many canonists also viewed Laity 26 as a source. Dalton (1988), p. 177 and Renken (p. 141, footnote 3) themselves concede this point. Renken refers to the "coetus" or discussion of April 19, 1980 by the commission preparing the new Code, noting that it cited the Vatican II Decree on the Apostolate of Lay People, no. 26, as a source for parish pastoral councils (he cites the record of the *coetus* or discussion in Communicationes 13 (1981): 146). Among other canonists who view Laity 26 as a source for parish pastoral councils, see the following: Robert J. Ahlin, "Parish Councils: A Theological and Canonical Foundation," Dissertation for the Degree of Licentiate in Canon Law (Washington, D.C.: The Catholic University of America, 1982), pp. 78-79. E. Caparros; M. Thériault, and J. Thorn, Editors, *Code of Canon Law Annotated*, Latin-English edition of the Code of Canon Law and English-language translation of the 5th Spanish-language edition of the commentary prepared under the responsibility of the Instituto Martín de Azpilcueta (Navarra), "A collaboration of the Faculties of Canon Law of the University of Navarra in Spain and Saint Paul University in Canada" (Montréal: Wilson and Lafleur Limitée, 1993), esp. the commentary on Canon 536 by J. Calvo. Mark S. Mealey, "The Parish Pastoral Council in the United States of America: Applications of Canon 536," Doctor of Canon Law Dissertation (Ottawa: St. Paul University, 1989), p. 163. Joseph A. Pereira, "The Juridical Status of the Parish Council," Dissertation for the Degree of Licentiate in Canon Law (Rome: Pontifical Urban University, 1982), reportedly speaks of Laity 26 as a source for parish pastoral councils (at pp. 68 ff.), according to a summary of his paper by Kim (at p. 41).

24. Roch Pagé, The Diocesan Pastoral Council, p. 2. The relevant texts are examined by Egidio Miragoli, "Consejo Pastoral Diocesano – Lombardia," Tesi gregoriana, Serie Diritto Canonico, no. 43 (Roma: Pontificia Università Gregoriana, 2000), pp. 35-37.

25. Vatican Council II, "Decree on the Church's Missionary Activity," no. 30, in Vatican II, *The Documents of Vatican II*, Flannery, General Editor, p. 847.

26. Sacred Congregation for Bishops, *Directory on the Pastoral Ministry of Bishops*, states that the optimum parish is one in which the laity "take part in the parish pastoral council and take charge of the works of the apostolate proper to themselves" (no. 179). The "apostolate" was hitherto the concern of "apostolic" councils as described in the Laity Decree, no. 26.

Chapter Thirteen: Popular Meanings of the Word "Pastoral"

1. On DPCP, see Chapter Eleven. From 1979 to 1983, DPCP held "back-to-back" conventions with the National Pastoral Planning Conference. One group's meeting was immediately followed by the other in the same hotel, so that members of one group could easily attend both meetings. In 1984, the first convention of the newly formed PADICON was held in Houston. Susan Stromatt was the first Chair, followed by Eileen Tabert (1985), Richard Krivanka (1986), Michelle Jones (1987), Mark F. Fischer (1988), and Mary Kay Bailey, O.P. (1989). In Houston the PADICON meeting was not only "back-to-back" with the NPPC, but one day (Wednesday, March 14) was designated a "shared skills" day, attended by both PADICON and NPPC members. The March 10-14, 1985 convention in Baltimore of PADICON and NPPC was the first of five annual "joint" conventions, planned and executed by the steering committees of both organizations. It was followed by conventions in San Francisco (1986), Nashville (1987), New York (1988), and Los Angeles (1989).

2. The Archdiocese of Milwaukee's *Parish Committee Ministry* (1991) states that the finance committee "does not decide priorities for the parish—that is the responsibility of the parish council" (p. 46). The Diocese of Harrisburg's *Parish Council Policy and Guidelines* (1985) state that financial administration is one of the "missions" of the parish, and that the parish council "supersedes every other parish organization, board, and committee" (p. 8), including the finance council. For a further discussion, see Mark F. Fischer, "Should Finance Councils Answer to Parish Councils?" *Today's Parish* (March 1994): 21-23, 32.

3. Marliss Rogers called councils in the 1980s the "second generation" in an article called "Renewing Parish Councils: Five Rules for the Second Generation," *Church* 1:1 (Spring 1985): 34-36. See also Natalie Cornell, "The Parish Council 20 Years After," *Today's Parish* (January, 1986): 26-27. Offering another historical perspective, Bishop Howard Hubbard of Albany said that collaborative lay-pastor relationships were developing from "infancy" to an "adolescence." See his address to the NPPC entitled "Planning in the Church: The People, the Tasks," *Origins* 12:45 (4/21/83): 729, 731-737.

4. See the discussion in Chapter Eleven of the Sacred Congregation for Bishops, *Directory on the Pastoral Ministry of Bishops*, no. 204.

5. See Chapter Eleven's discussion of the functions of parish councils in the 1976 guidelines of the Archdioceses of St. Paul and of Louisville, the 1976 address by Providence Bishop Louis Gelineau ("Reflections on Pastoral Planning"), and the 1975 article by Robert G. Howes, "Guide for Parish Council Members."

6. Harms, *Who Are We and Where Are We Going*, esp. p. 21.

7. Rademacher and Rogers devoted one chapter out of thirteen to pastoral planning in their 1988 *New Practical Guide*. Thomas Sweetser, *Successful Parishes: How They Meet the Challenge of Change* (San Francisco: Winston Press, 1983), showed that councils were doing many kinds of planning activities without calling them "pastoral planning," activities such as prioritizing parish activities (p. 81), restoring the RCIA (pp. 109-112), and coordinating with neighboring parishes (p. 128).

8. An exception is Robert R. Newsome, *The Ministering Parish*, who wanted to see councils function as research and development (i.e., planning) bodies.

9. Richard A. Schoenherr and Eleanor P. Simpson, *The Political Economy of Diocesan Advisory Councils*, Comparative Religious Organization Studies Respondent Report no. 3 (Madison: University of Wisconsin, 1978), p. 98.

10. The distinction between decision making and choosing was suggested in the 1980 article by Robert T. Kennedy, "Shared Responsibility." In 1978, David F. Wall had discovered that supportive leadership by the pastor was a source of high satisfaction for council members, even when they did not have the final decision in pastoral matters. See "Parish Councils in the Catholic Church: Participation and Satisfaction of Members," Unpublished Ph.D. [sociology] Dissertation (Washington, D.C.: Catholic University of America, 1978), pp. 211-213. Collaboration in decision making is a means to "real power," said Edmund Flood, *The Laity Today and Tomorrow* (New York and Mahwah: Paulist Press, 1987), pp. 48-49.

11. Renken, "Pastoral Councils."

12. Bertram J. Griffin, "Diocesan Church Structures," in James H. Provost, Editor, *Code, Community, Ministry: Selected Studies for the Parish Minister Introducing the Revised Code of Canon Law* (Washington, D.C.: Canon Law Society of America, 1983), p. 62. See also Bertram F. Griffin, "The Parish and Lay Ministry," *Chicago Studies* 23 (1984): 45-61, esp. pp. 58-59.

13. One of the earliest arguments for the planning council and against the coordinating council was articulated by Loughlan Sofield and Brenda Hermann, *Developing the Parish as a Community of Service* (New York: Le Jacq Publishing, 1984), p. 13. William J. Bausch, in *The Hands-On Parish*, also envisioned councils that aimed at the discernment of mission more than the coordination of a committee structure (p. 89). The most articulate advocate of the planning council in the 1990s was the veteran pastoral planner, Robert G. Howes. See his *Creating an Effective Parish Pastoral Council; Parish Planning: A Practical Guide to Shared Responsibility* (Collegeville: The Liturgical Press, 1994); and *Bridges: Toward the Inter-Parish Regional Community . . . Deaneries, Clusters, Plural Parishes* (Collegeville: The Liturgical Press, 1998). For an account of how a parish council became a pastoral planning council, see Philip

P. Conley, "The Parish Council: Planning the Mission, Implementing the Vision," Doctor of Ministry Paper (Pittsburgh: Pittsburgh Theological Seminary, 1994), esp. Chapter III, "A New Vision for Parish Councils," in which Conley describes what he and Mary Ann Pobicki accomplished at Holy Family Parish in Poland, Ohio.

14. Ensuring the coordination of volunteers was emerging as a ministry in itself. See William J. Bannon and Suzanne Donovan, *Volunteers and Ministry*; and Marlene Wilson, *How to Mobilize Church Volunteers* (Minneapolis: Augsburg Publishing, 1983). One of the best ways to ensure participation was through the liturgy, and so the 1980s coincide with the rise of the liturgy committee. See Stephanie Certain and Marty Mayer, *Goal Setting for Liturgy Committees* (Chicago: Liturgy Training Publications, 1981); Baker and Ferrone, *Liturgy Committee Handbook*; and Yvonne Cassa and Joanne Sanders, *How to Form a Parish Liturgy Board* (Chicago: Liturgy Training Publications, 1987). By the late 1990s, there was evidence that the liturgy offers more opportunities for participation than does consultative ministry. See Robert E. Schmitz, "Volunteerism: Increasing Sophistication and Complexity," in Ruth T. Doyle et al., Editors, *Laity, Parish, and Ministry* (New York: Archdiocesan Office of Pastoral Research and Planning, 1999), pp. 34-43, esp. 37-40.

15. Pope John Paul II, "Christifideles Laici, Apostolic Exhortation on the Laity," January 30, 1987, *Origins* 18:35 (February 9, 1989): 561, 563-595; see no. 25, p. 573 (about diocesan councils); compare no. 27, p. 574 (about parish councils).

16. Sacred Congregation for the Clergy, "Private Letter on 'Pastoral Councils,'" in O'Connor, editor, *The Canon Law Digest*, Vol. VIII, pp. 280-288. The letter was also published in *Origins* 3:12 (9/15/73): 186-190. See esp. no. 7.

17. This is the viewpoint of Leonard Doohan, who insisted that leadership is not the province of the clergy alone, and so the chairperson of the council can truly be called a "leader." See his *Grass-Roots Pastors: Handbook for Lay Ministers* (San Francisco: Harper, 1989). Doohan described councils as "new forms of leadership," decentralized and interactive, in his *The Lay-Centered Church: Theology and Spirituality* (Minneapolis: Winston, 1984). The leadership role of the council emerges in Ellen Morseth, *Call to Leadership: Transforming the Local Church* (Kansas City: Sheed and Ward, 1993). Baltimore Archbishop William Borders stated that a collegial decision has an authority all its own. See William Borders, "Collegiality in the Local Church," *Origins* 9:32 (January 24, 1980): 509, 511-13.

18. James D. and Evelyn Eaton Whitehead emphasize the charismatic dimension of leadership. They say that lay leaders may lack ordination, but prove themselves dedicated and competent, in *The Emerging Laity: Returning Leadership to the Community of Faith* (New York: Doubleday, 1986). Robert G. Duch also stresses charismatic leadership, but sees the pastor as the one who "selects the right people to be members of the problem solving leadership team," in *Successful Parish Leadership: Nurturing the Animated Parish* (Kansas City: Sheed and Ward, 1990), p. 162.

19. See in Chapter Seven the discussion of Leege, "Parish Life Among the Leaders," Report no. 9 in Leege and Gremillion, Editors, *The Notre Dame Study*, pp. 2, 7, and 14.

20. This was clearly laid out by Dean R. Hoge, *The Future of Catholic Leadership: Responses to the Priest Shortage* (Kansas City: Sheed and Ward, 1987); and by Richard A. Schoenherr and Lawrence A. Young, with the collaboration of Tsan-Yuang Cheng, *Full Pews and Empty Altars: Demographics of the Priest Shortage in United States Catholic Dioceses* (Madison, WI: University of Wisconsin Press, 1993).

21. See Philip J. Murnion et al., *New Parish Ministers: Lay and Religious on Parish Staffs* (New York: National Pastoral Life Center, 1992); and Mary Beth Celio, "Parish Pastoral Staffing: A Case Study," in Ruth T. Doyle et al., editors, *Laity, Parish, and Ministry*, pp. 44-68. See also Philip J. Murnion and David DeLambo, *Parishes and Parish Ministers* (New York: National Pastoral Life Center, 1999); and National Conference of Catholic Bishops, Lay Ministry Subcommittee of the Committee on the Laity, "Lay Ecclesial Ministry: State of the Questions," *Origins* 29:31 (January 20, 2000): 497, 499-512. The NCCB, citing Murnion and DeLambo, states that, in 1992, Murnion "estimated that in parish ministry alone, 21,500 laypersons (including vowed religious) worked full or part time in formal pastoral roles (as distinct from support staff and maintenance roles). . . . A follow-up study titled "Parishes and Parish Ministers" (Philip J.

Murnion and David DeLambo, New York: National Pastoral Life Center, 1999) now estimates that this same group of lay ministers has grown to 29,145—an increase of 35 percent (*Origins*, 29:31, p. 499).

22. Chancery staff members are more ambivalent than bishops about the helpfulness of diocesan pastoral councils. See Froehle, *Diocesan and Eparchial Pastoral Councils*, p. 2.

23. See Loughlan Sofield and Carroll Juliano, *Collaborative Ministry: Skills and Guidelines* (Notre Dame, IN: Ave Maria Press, 1987); Norman P. Cooper, *Collaborative Ministry: Communion, Contention, Commitment* (New York and Mahwah: Paulist Press, 1993); and Howard J. Hubbard, *Fulfilling the Vision: Collaborative Ministry in the Parish* (New York: Crossroad, 1998).

24. Robert G. Duch, *Successful Parish Leadership*, pp. 155-156.

25. These are the positions of, respectively, McKinney, *Sharing Wisdom*, p. 16; Rademacher with Rogers, *The New Practical Guide*, p. 140; Thomas F. Penderghast, "Parish Council: Barriers to Groupthink," *Church* 6:2 (Summer, 1990): 42-44; and Heaps, *Parish Pastoral Councils*, pp. 27-28.

26. The argument for parliamentary procedure as the normal way of making decisions is advanced by Robert G. Howes in his books *Creating an Effective Parish Pastoral Council*, p. 50, and *Parish Planning*, pp. 144-47. The dangers to effective ministry from a time-consuming search for consensus are outlined by Loughlan Sofield, Rosine Hammett and Carroll Juliano, *Building Community: Christian, Caring, Vital* (Notre Dame, IN: Ave Maria, 1998), p. 113.

27. One of the earliest books in this period on discernment was Thomas H. Green, *Weeds among the Wheat. Discernment: Where Prayer and Action Meet* (South Bend, IN: Ave Maria, 1984). Benedictine Sister Mary Benet McKinney was the most eloquent writer on council discernment. She said that service on the council is a ministry with a definite call and the need for formation, and she advised parishes to discern council members in *Sharing Wisdom* (pp. 36-38 and Chapter Eight). Rademacher with Rogers, in *The New Practical Guide*, viewed discernment as an alternative to election, pp. 128 ff. Three meetings of discernment and four meetings of formation are recommended in Michael Parise, "Forming Your Parish Pastoral Council," *The Priest* 51:7 (July 1995): 43-47.

28. On the council of ministries, see Sweetser and Holden, *Leadership in a Successful Parish*, pp. 126 ff.; and Debbie Morrow, "A Parish Council of Ministries," *Church* 6:1 (Spring 1990): 42-44.

29. Bernadette Gasslein, *Parish Council: New Parish Ministries* (Minneapolis: Winston, 1983), p. 10. The first edition was published in Ottawa by Novalis in 1982.

30. Roch Pagé, "The Parish Pastoral Council," p. 48.

31. See Enda Lyons, *Partnership in Parish: A Vision for Parish Life, Mission, and Ministry* (Blackrock, County Dublin: Columba, 1987); David L. Vaughn, "Implementing Spirituality in Catholic Parish Councils," thesis submitted in partial fulfillment of the requirements for certification in the National Association of Church Business Administration at the University of St. Thomas (St. Paul, MN: University of St. Thomas, 1994); and Olsen, *Transforming Church Boards*.

32. On Scripture, see Gasslein, p. 9; on planning as ministry, see Constance Gilder, *The Ministry of Pastoral Planning: A Planning Guide for Parishes in the Archdiocese of Baltimore* (Archdiocese of Baltimore: Division of Planning and Council Services, 1993); on clarification of the mission, see Marie Kevin Tighe, "Council Spirituality: Foundation for Mission," in Arthur X. Deegan, II, Editor, *Developing a Vibrant Parish Pastoral Council* (New York and Mahwah: Paulist Press, 1995), pp. 88-99.

33. For the contrast between the council as an institutional commitment and the council as a life expression, see Klemens Schaupp, *Der Pfarrgemeinderate. Eine qualitative Interview-Analyse zum Thema "Biographie und Institution,"* Innsbruck Theological Studies, Volume 26 (Innsbruck and Vienna: Tyrolia Verlag, 1989). On the variety of processes for councillors, see Olsen, *Transforming Church Boards*, chapters 3-6. On the various forms of prayer, see Kathleen Turley, "The Parish Pastoral Council and Prayer," in Deegan, *Developing*, pp. 100-106; and Marliss Rogers, Editor, *Weekly Prayer Services for Parish Meetings: Lectionary-Based for Cycle C* (Mystic, CT: Twenty-Third Publications, 1994).

34. Unlike a Small Christian Community, the pastoral council is a ministry with a specific interest. SCCs have no other focus than to be an expression of Church for their members. See Arthur R. Baranowski, in collaboration with Kathleen M. O'Reilly and Carrie M. Piro, *Creating Small Faith Communities: A Plan for Restructuring the Parish and Renewing Catholic Life* (Cincinnati: St. Anthony Messenger Press, 1988), pp. 38, 41. Others argue that every ministerial group is potentially a small community. See Patrick J. Brennan, *Re-Imagining the Parish: Base Communities, Adulthood, and Family Consciousness* (New York: Crossroad, 1990), p. 18.

35. The "White Paper" was a six-page typescript, written by Mark F. Fischer, that was eventually distributed to the members of both organizations.

36. Subsequent chairs of the CPPCD were Dennis O'Leary (1991), Mary Kay Bailey, O.P. (1992-93), Robert J. Burke (1994-95), Kathleen Turley (1996), and Rev. Eugene Costa (1997-98).

37. Letter of Arthur X. Deegan, II, to Mark F. Fischer, July 1, 1991.

38. From 1992 until his retirement in 1997, Deegan boosted the CPPCD income from $34,420 to $114,316, having helped secure a number of grants. During his time the CPPCD published two books, one edited by Deegan, *Developing a Vibrant Parish Pastoral Council*, and the other edited by John P. Flaherty, *Diocesan Efforts at Parish Reorganization* (Clearwater, FL: CPPCD, 1995). The Deegan era also saw the establishment of the Lumen Gentium Award, recognizing excellence in pastoral planning and council development by those outside the CPPCD membership, and the Yves Congar Award, recognizing excellence within the membership. Lumen Gentium Award winners include Archbishop William Borders of Baltimore (1993), the Planning Office of the Archdiocese of Seattle (1994), Richard S. Krivanka (1995), Cardinal Joseph Bernardin (1996), Br. Loughlan Sofield, S.T. (1997), and Bishop Howard Hubbard (1999) and Bishop Kenneth E. Untener of Saginaw. Yves Congar winners include Eileen Tabert (1996), Sr. Rosalie Murphy, S.N.D. (1997), Arthur X. Deegan, II (1998), Rev. Philip Murnion (1999), and Sr. Mary Kay Bailey, O.P. (2000). See "Deegan Receives Yves Congar Award," *Conference Call*, the newsletter of the CPPCD, vol. 9:1 (July, 1998), p. 1. Sr. M. Frances Schumer, A.S.C. succeeded Deegan as Executive Director on July 1, 1997. Maria Rodgers O'Rourke succeeded her in July of 2000.

39. Letter of Robert G. Howes to Mark F. Fischer, July 24, 1991. For references to Howes' three books in the 1990s, see footnote 13 above.

Chapter Fourteen: Problems with Selecting Councillors

1. The concept of representation is explained in the Vatican document entitled "Circular Letter on 'Pastoral Councils.'" It stated: "As far as the composition of the pastoral council is concerned, although the members of the council cannot in a juridical sense be called representatives of the total diocesan community, nevertheless, as far as possible, they should present a witness or sign of the entire diocese, and, therefore, it seems extremely opportune that priests, religious and laity who expound various requirements and experiences take part in the council. The persons, then, appointed to the pastoral council ought to be selected in such a way that the entire composition of the People of God within the diocese is truly represented." See Sacred Congregation for the Clergy, "Circular Letter," no. 7.

2. Pope John Paul II, *Code of Canon Law,* Latin-English Edition, Canon 512, §2.

3. Canon 512, §2 states that DPC members are "appointed" by the bishop, even when they have been "elected" by deanery councils (as in the Archdiocese of Newark), by regional councils (as in the Archdiocese of Baltimore), or even by parish councils (as in the Diocese of Baker, where the DPC is an assembly of parish representatives). Popular elections are not the norm, however, for selecting DPC members. More commonly, DPC members are nominated and then screened by a committee. Nominations may come from pastors (e.g., in Brooklyn), by deans (e.g., in New Orleans), by vicars (e.g., in Tucson), by parish councils (e.g., in Superior), or by the Catholic population in general (e.g., in Sacramento). Once potential members are nominated, there are a variety of ways to evaluate and screen them. Usually a committee does this. In some cases, the bishop may ask a dean or vicar to review nominees. Bishops generally rely upon the good judgment of a committee or a trusted priest to review nominations and

recommend people for appointment to the pastoral council. See Mark F. Fischer, "Diocesan Pastoral Council Constitutions," in H. Richard McCord, editor, *Diocesan Pastoral Councils* (Washington, D.C.: National Conference of Catholic Bishops, forthcoming).

Chapter Fifteen: Ecclesial Representation

1. For more technical commentaries about the pastoral council, starting with the most recent, see Renken, "Pastoral Councils"; Marceaux, "The Pastoral Council"; Pagé, *The Diocesan Pastoral Council*; and Joseph F. Hayden, "Diocesan Pastoral Councils," dissertation for the Degree of Licentiate in Canon Law (Washington, D.C.: The Catholic University of America, 1969).

2. See Vatican II, "Decree on the Pastoral Office of Bishops in the Church," no. 27, in Vatican II, *The Documents of Vatican II*, Flannery, General Editor, p. 580.

3. We discussed this letter in Chapter Ten. See the Sacred Congregation for the Clergy, "Private Letter."

4. Sacred Congregation for the Clergy, "Circular Letter," no. 7. See the discussion of the Circular Letter in Chapter Ten. For technical commentaries, see Wuerl, "Pastoral Councils"; McManus, "Diocesan Pastoral Councils"; and Sheehan, "Commentary."

5. For further treatment of the knowledge of contingent things in classical philosophy, see the discussions of Plato, Thomas, and Aristotle (respectively) in Mark F. Fischer, "Parish Councils: Where Does the Pastor Fit In?" *Today's Parish* (Nov./Dec., 1991): 13-15; "Keeping Your Council on Track," *Today's Parish* (March 1996): 31-33; and "When the Parish Council and the Finance Council Disagree," *Today's Parish* 30.1 (January 1998): 8-12.

6. See Vatican II, "Decree on the Pastoral Office of Bishops," no. 27, in Vatican II, *The Documents of Vatican II*, Flannery, General Editor, p. 580. In addition to the "Circular Letter" (no. 9) and Canon 511 of the *Code of Canon Law*, the formula also appears in the Sacred Congregation for Bishops, *Directory on the Pastoral Ministry of Bishops*.

7. See Vatican II, "Declaration on Religious Liberty," *Dignitatis humanae*, 7 December 1965, translated by Laurence Ryan, in Vatican II, *The Documents of Vatican II*, Flannery, General Editor. See numbers 2 (about the dignity of persons and their privilege of bearing personal responsibility, p. 801) and 8 (about the importance of forming people who reach decisions on their own judgment and who govern their activities with a sense of responsibility, joining with others in a cooperative effort, p. 805). See also John Courtney Murray's 1960 title, *We Hold These Truths: Reflections on the American Proposition* (Kansas City: Sheed and Ward, 1988).

8. See the discussion of the "Ecclesial Nature of a Christian" in Karl Rahner, *Foundations of Christian Faith: An Introduction to the Idea of Christianity*, trans. by William V. Dych (New York: Seabury Press [A Crossroad Book], 1978), p. 389 f. Rahner treats the origin of the church in Christ at p. 330.

9. For an analysis of the doctrine of participation in God, see Peter C. Phan, *Grace and the Human Condition*, vol. 15 of the series *Message of the Fathers of the Church* (Wilmington, Michael Glazier: 1988), especially Chapter 5 (on "The Restoration of the Image and Divinization of Humanity" according to Athanasius of Alexandria, pp. 132-138), and Chapter 6 (on "The Cappadocian Fathers," especially Gregory of Nazianzus, pp. 171-176).

Chapter Sixteen: Discerning Councillors

1. Pope Paul VI stated that councils exist so that "the life and activity of the People of God may be brought into greater conformity with the Gospel," thereby implying the concept of representation (i.e., that the work of the council concerns all of the faithful). He did not endorse a particular method of councillor selection. See Paul VI, *Ecclesiae Sanctae* I, no. 16, in Vatican II, *The Documents of Vatican II*, Flannery, General Editor, p. 601.

2. The Decree on Missionary Activity stated that clergy, religious and lay people would have a part in the diocesan pastoral council "through elected delegates" (Latin: "per delegatos selectos"). Vatican II, "Decree on the Church's Missionary Activity," no. 30, in Vatican II, *The Documents of Vatican II*, Flannery, General Editor, p. 847.

3. Sacred Congregation for Bishops, Directory on the Pastoral Ministry of Bishops, no. 204, p. 105.

4. Sacred Congregation for the Clergy, "Circular Letter," no. 7. There the Letter speaks of the number of councillors, term of office, and staggered elections. It states (1) that *"the number of members of the pastoral council* should not be too great so that it is able to carry out effectively the work that is committed to it." This is the only reference in Vatican documents to the number of pastoral council members. The Letter also states (2) that council members, apart from those who serve by virtue of their office, should be "nominated for a period of time determined in the statutes." This is the only Vatican reference to term of office. Moreover, the Letter speaks (3) about staggered elections. "So that the whole council membership will not go out of existence at the same time, it is advisable that for its renewal of membership, *a system of rotation* be employed in such a way that at stated times a certain number end their membership and new members are named in their place." This is the only Vatican reference to such a system of rotation. See the discussion of the Circular Letter in Chapter Ten. For technical commentaries, see Wuerl, "Pastoral Councils"; McManus, "Diocesan Pastoral Councils"; and Sheehan, "Commentary."

5. See the reference to St. Ignatius Loyola's treatment of spiritual discernment in the Archdiocese of Newark's 1976 *Parish Council Guidelines*, p. 275. For a general treatment of discernment, see Thomas H. Green, *Weeds among the Wheat*. For the critique that elections stem from a secular model of decision-making inappropriate for the Church, see Rademacher, *The Practical Guide*, p. 118; and McKinney, *Shared Wisdom*, pp. 6-8. Recent guidelines that make discernment a part of popular elections include the Archdiocese of Cincinnati's *Called to Be Church: A Guide for Parish Pastoral Councils*, prepared by the Office of Pastoral Planning, 1998; and the Diocese of Greensburg's *New Wine, New Wineskins: Revisioning the Parish Through the Ministry of the Parish Pastoral Council*, produced by the Office of Parish Life and Ministry; Mary Ann Gubish, Director, 1996.

6. McKinney defines the four stages of discernment at p. 81 and in her Appendix I, pp. 140-143.

7. Michael Parise, "Forming Your Parish Pastoral Council," describes his parish's voting on p. 45 and the evaluation of the 50 projects and programs on p. 46.

8. Howes, *Creating an Effective Parish Pastoral Council*.

9. Envisioning the future, restructuring work, and solving problems—these are the three major purposes of assemblies, according to Barbara Benedict Bunker and Billie T. Alban, *Large Group Interventions: Engaging the Whole System for Rapid Change* (San Francisco: Jossey-Bass, 1997). The book describes group processes that have worked well with industry, but are also relevant to parishes.

10. See the works by McKinney and Parise. For a variation on McKinney's "shared wisdom" model, see the "election committee" model of Rademacher with Rogers, *The New Practical Guide*, pp. 120-128. This model uses a committee to screen and discern nominees, after which the committee proposes a slate of nominees and conducts a general parish election.

11. See McKinney, p. 81 and her Appendix I, pp. 140-143.

12. Pastors can provide for the participation of certain parishioners, such as immigrants, by appointing them. Appointment does not do away, however, with the need for discernment. Not every discernment must be followed by a parish-wide election, McKinney states (p. 81), but there should be no appointment without discernment.

13 See the discussion of "God's Activity in and through Secondary Causes" in Rahner, *Foundations*, p. 86 ff.

Chapter Seventeen: Misunderstandings About Coordination

1. To be sure, there are some who flatly state that the bishops of Vatican II did not intend pastoral councils to coordinate. This is the assertion of Giuseppe Ceschin, *Il Consiglio Pastorale Parrochiale. Genesi, Natura e Funzionamento*, Dissertation ad Lauream in Facultate Iuris Canonici apud Pontificiam Universitatem S. Thomae in Urbe (Roma: Pontifical University of St. Thomas in the City, 1992), pp. 99, 310. But there is abundant evidence to show that the the Vatican II Decree on the Apostolate of Lay People, no. 26, was a source for parish pastoral councils. See the discussion of the 1983 Code of Canon Law in Chapter Twelve, especially footnote 23.

2. Vatican II, "Decree on the Apostolate of Lay People," no. 26, in Vatican II, *The Documents of Vatican II*, Flannery, General Editor, p. 791. The key phrase is "can take care of the mutual coordinating." This phrase has also been translated more literally as "will be able to promote the mutual coordination." See *The Documents of Vatican II*, Walter M. Abbott, General Editor; translations directed by Joseph Gallagher (New York: Herder and Herder; and Association Press, 1966), p. 515. The Latin original ("Haec consilia poterunt variarum laicorum consociationum et inceptorum mutuae coordinationi inservire salva uniuscuiusque indole propria et autonomia," AAS 58 (1965): 858) suggests future possibility and a condition. Councils can, in the future, serve the mutual coordination of lay associations and initiatives, provided that the councils respect their distinctiveness and autonomy.

3. Vatican II, "Decree on the Church's Missionary Activity," no. 30, in Vatican II, *The Documents of Vatican II*, Flannery, General Editor, p. 847.

4. These three developments are spelled out in detail in Chapter Four: the widespread recommendation of a system of standing committees or commissions, the accountability of these groups to the council, and the council's executive role.

5. Although none of the Vatican II documents that mentioned councils (the Decrees on Bishops, on Laity, and on Missionary Activity) used the phrase "consultative only," the consultative nature of councils is implicit in the Latin term "consilium" (as distinct from the legislative body "concilium"). The consultative nature was made explicit by Paul VI in his Apostolic Letter, *Ecclesiae Sanctae* I, no. 16, in Vatican II, *The Documents of Vatican II*, Flannery, General Editor, p. 601. See James H. Provost, "The Working Together of Consultative Bodies—Great Expectations?" *The Jurist* 40 (1980): 257-281.

6. Peter Kim's proposal that pastors establish a separate "apostolic" council for coordinating parish activities is certainly a legitimate possibility and has worked in Kuala Lumpur. There is no evidence in council guidelines published by U.S. dioceses, however, that this has ever been tried in America. See Kim Se-Mang, *Parish Councils on Mission*, p. 83.

Chapter Eighteen: The Main Purpose of the Council

1. Vatican II first proposed the threefold task of the pastoral council in the 1965 "Decree on the Pastoral Office of Bishops in the Church" at no. 27. Virtually identical language describes pastoral councils in Pope Paul VI's Apostolic Letter "Ecclesiae Sanctae I" at no. 16; in the 1971 document of the Synod of Bishops entitled "The Ministerial Priesthood" (Part 2, II, section 3, p. 364); in the 1973 *Directory on the Pastoral Ministry of Bishops* by the Sacred Congregation for Bishops (no. 204, p. 105); in the 1973 "Circular Letter on 'Pastoral Councils'" by the Sacred Congregation for Clergy (no. 9); and in Canon 511 of the 1983 Code of Canon Law. To be sure, these documents refer mainly to pastoral councils at the diocesan level. Only the 1973 "Circular Letter" (the only Vatican document devoted in its entirety to pastoral councils) explicitly extends the language about Diocesan Pastoral Councils to Parish Pastoral Councils. In my view, however, that is decisive. The consistent threefold description of the "pastoral" council in Vatican documents, and the application of this in the "Circular Letter" to the PPC, suggests that PPCs foster pastoral activity in the same threefold way as pastoral councils in general.

2. Two official documents, from 1971 and 1973, speak of planning as the task of pastoral councils. Using almost identical language, they say that the diocesan pastoral council helps the community "arrange [or "plan"] its pastoral program systematically and carry it out effectively." See the Synod of Bishops, "The Ministerial Priesthood," in O'Connor, editor, *The Canon Law Digest*, Vol. VII, pp. 342-366 (in Part 2, II, section 3, p. 364). See also the Sacred Congregation for Bishops, *Directory on the Pastoral Ministry of Bishops*, no. 204, p. 105. "The Ministerial Priesthood" uses the verb "arrange" (Latin: "praeordinare") and the "Directory" uses the verb "plan" (Latin: "praemoliri"). See also Pope John Paul II, "Novo Millennio Ineunte" (Apostolic Letter "At the Beginning of the New Millennium," January 6, 2001), *Origins* 30:31 (January 18, 2001): 489, 491-508. The letter encourages Christians to esteem "structures of participation" envisioned in canon law, such as pastoral councils, as instruments of communion and planning (nos. 29, 31, 38, 42-3, 45).

3. The development of the pastoral planning role for councils, culminating in the marriage of the National Pastoral Planning Conference and the Parish and Diocesan Council Network, is described in Chapter Thirteen.

4. Chapter Thirteen reviewed popular efforts to define the meaning of the word "pastoral" as visionary, spiritual, and oriented toward consensus. Some diocesan guidelines suggest that pastoral councils should plan and coordinate the parish's ministries, grouped under various standing committees or commissions (this is the "Council of Ministries" model we saw in Chapter Four). Some recent guidelines suggest that pastoral councils do not coordinate parish ministries but develop a comprehensive plan around various themes, such as worship, education, and so forth. (See the Archdiocese of Cincinnati's *Called to Be Church*, 1998; and the Diocese of Greensburg's *New Wine, New Wineskins*, 1996.) Canon law offers a third approach. It suggests that the themes of the pastoral council are those that pertain to the pastor's duties and the activities of the parish community as described in the church's law. See James A. Coriden, *The Parish in Catholic Tradition: History, Theology and Canon Law* (New York and Mahwah: Paulist Press, 1997), especially Chapter Five, "The Parish in Canon Law."

5. Pope John Paul II, *Code of Canon Law*, Latin-English Edition, canon 537.

6. Keating, "Consultation in the Parish." Keating's viewpoint was seconded by Peter Kim and Orville Griese. See Kim Se-Mang, *Parish Councils on Mission*, p. 48; and Orville Griese, "The New Code," p. 53. Their views were discussed in Chapter Twelve.

7. The Vatican II Decree on Bishops (at no. 27) said that diocesan pastoral councils are "cooperators of the bishop in the governing of the diocese." It recommended cooperation between pastoral councils and senates of priests. The Vatican II Decree on the Ministry and Life of Priests suggested that the assignment of "management" to the Senate of Priests does not remove the topic of "administration" from the DPC agenda. See Vatican Council II, "Decree on the Ministry and Life of Priests" (*Presbyterorum Ordinis*, 7 Dec. 1965), no. 7, translated by Archbishop Joseph Cunnane, of Tuam, and revised by Michael Mooney and Enda Lyons of St. Jarlath's College, Tuam, County Galway, in Vatican Council II, *The Documents of Vatican II*, Flannery, General Editor, p. 877.

The Vatican II teaching about cooperation between pastoral councils and senates of priests was amplified in Pope Paul VI's apostolic letter of 1966, "Ecclesiae Sanctae I." It stated (at no. 15) that the priests' senate advises the bishop in matters that pertain to the exercise of jurisdiction or governing power. Bishops may consult their pastoral councils, however, about such jurisdictional matters. Emphasizing this point, the Congregation for the Clergy's 1973 "Circular Letter on 'Pastoral Councils'" stated (at no. 9): "Nothing prevents the pastoral council, however, from considering questions requiring mandates of a jurisdictional act for execution and proposing suggestions regarding them to the bishop, for in such a case the bishop will consider the matter and make his decision after hearing the priests' senate, if the case requires." By extension, nothing prevents the parish pastoral council from considering questions related to parish administration.

8. James H. Provost has written: "Nothing, therefore, escapes the category of *pastoral* if it truly pertains to the Church." See Provost, "Canon Law and the Role of Consultation," *Origins* 18:47 (May 4, 1989): 793, 795-799, at p. 798. John Renken opposes the preoccupation of parish pastoral councils with administration, but concedes that "we can imagine some single issue may involve both [finance and pastoral] councils." See Renken, "Pastoral Councils," p. 15. William Dalton wants parish pastoral councils to be more pastoral, but he gives them the administrative task of coordinating parish activities. See Dalton, "Parish Councils," p. 174. Sidney Marceaux believes that efforts to restrict the scope of the parish pastoral council in light of the 1983 Code are superseded by the broad scope granted to pastoral councils by Vatican II's Decree on Bishops, which "carries a greater force of law" than the Code. See Marceaux, "The Pastoral Council," p. 143. These authors are discussed in Fischer, "What Was Vatican II's Intent?"

9. Fischer, "Should Finance Councils Answer?"

10. Milwaukee's 1991 guideline, entitled *Parish Committee Ministry*, makes the finance council a standing committee of the pastoral council. The finance committee, notes the guideline, "does not decide priorities for the parish—that is the responsibility of the parish council" (p. 46). Milwaukee finance committees prepare the parish budget "based on the

goals and objectives determined by the parish council" (p. 48). Pastoral concerns, not finan-cial, are to remain paramount. The Harrisburg and St. Louis guidelines affirm this view. Harrisburg's *Parish Council Policy and Guidelines* (1985) and St. Louis' *Guidelines for the Ministry of Parish Councils* (1985) insist that finance council members be appointed after con-sultation with the parish council, thereby ensuring the pastoral council's primacy.

11. The 1991 *Parish Pastoral Council Guidelines* for the Archdiocese of Los Angeles describe the responsibility of the finance council as "fiscal stewardship" and make it somewhat inde-pendent of the pastoral council. "While the Finance Council has responsibility for the steward-ship of parish financial resources, it is not the role of the Finance Council to recommend direc-tions, priorities, or programs other than those related to its delegation namely, fiscal stewardship" (p. 18). Richmond's 1991 *Norms for Parish Finance Councils* and Cleveland's 1991 *Parish Finance Council Policy* also agree that finance and pastoral councils should cooperate, because finance councils are not standing committees of the parish council.

12. Fischer, "When the Parish Council and the Finance Council Disagree."

Chapter Nineteen: The Meaning of Consultation

1. William J. Rademacher's *Lay Ministry: A Theological, Spiritual, and Pastoral Handbook* (New York: Crossroad Publishing Company, 1991) marked a break from his council publi-cations, the last of which had been written with the help of Marliss Rogers, *The New Practical Guide* (1988). Chapter Eleven discusses Rademacher's role in the council movement.

2. William J. Rademacher, "Parish Councils: Consultative Vote Only?" *Today's Parish* 32:3 (March 2000): 6-9.

3. The Vatican's 1997 "Instruction on Certain Questions Regarding Collaboration of the Non-Ordained Faithful in the Sacred Ministry of Priest" seems to take a negative view of con-sultation. The absence in the document of any affirmation of councils, and its repeated warn-ings, such as the statement that councils "cannot in any way become deliberative structures" (§ 2) and that their decisions are "null and void" if the pastor is not present (§ 3), may sug-gest that the phrase "consultative only" means "without authority." See Pope John Paul II, "Instruction on Certain Questions Regarding Collaboration of the Non-Ordained Faithful in the Sacred Ministry of Priest," written by a committee representing the Congregation for the Clergy, the Pontifical Council for the Laity, the Congregation for the Doctrine of the Faith, the Congregation for Divine Worship and the Discipline of the Sacraments, the Congregation for Bishops, the Congregation for the Evangelization of Peoples, the Congregation for Institutes of Consecrated Life and Societies of Apostolic Life, and the Pontifical Council for the Interpretation of Legislative Texts, and approved "in forma specifica" by Pope John Paul II and promulgated on August 15, 1997. Posted on the Internet at the Catholic Information Network web site, November 13, 1997.

4. We have already treated the consultative-only vote of councils (Chapters 9 and 12) and the pastor's presidential role (Chapter 6). The threefold task of councils (Chapter 19) may seem nar-row in light of the multiple roles that many theorists have assigned to councils (Chapters 3 and 8). Early advocates of co-responsibility (Chapter 10) and of the popular understanding of "pas-toral" (Chapter 13) may appear to have had more appreciation for councils.

5. Canon lawyers often treat the subject of consultation within the context of "shared responsibility." See Kennedy, "Shared Responsibility." The most important theoretical stud-ies of shared responsibility since the publication of the 1983 Code of Canon Law are by Provost, "Canon Law"; by Kim Se-Mang, *Parish Councils;* and by Renken, "Pastoral Councils." Chapter Ten discussed earlier views of co-responsibility.

6. The theory of situational leadership was developed by Paul Hersey and Kenneth H. Blanchard, *Management of Organizational Behavior: Utilizing Human Resources* (first edition, 1969), Sixth Edition (Englewood Cliffs, NJ: Prentice Hall, 1993). Keating applied it to church governance in *The Leadership Book.* For an explicit application to councils, see Mark F. Fischer, "Parish Councils: Why Good Delegators Don't Always Make Good Leaders," *Today's Parish* (March 1997): 27-30.

7. Appreciative inquiry was first treated by David L. Cooperrider, Suresh Srivastva and oth-

ers, *Appreciative Management and Leadership* (San Francisco: Jossey-Bass, 1990). Other writers have applied the principles of appreciative leadership in David L. Cooperrider, Peter F. Sorensen, Jr., Diana Whitney, and Therese F. Yaeger, editors, *Appreciative Inquiry: Rethinking the Organization Toward a Positive Theory of Change* (Champaign, IL: Stipes Publishing LLC, 2000). The application of appreciative leadership to parish councils was treated in Mark F. Fischer, "Breathe Fresh Spirit into Your Parish Pastoral Council," *Today's Parish* (January 1997): 29-31.

8. Vatican Council II, "Decree on the Apostolate of Lay People," no. 10, in Vatican Council II, *The Documents of Vatican II*, Flannery, General Editor, pp. 777-778. The Latin text is: "Assuescant laici intime cum sacerdotibus suis uniti in paroecia operari; problemata propria ac mundi et quaestiones ad salutem hominum spectantes, collatis consiliis examinanda et solvenda, ad communitatem Ecclesiae afferre; omnique incepto apostolico et missionario suae familiae ecclesiasticae adiutricem operam pro viribus navare." See Vaticani II, "Decretum: De Apostolatu Laicorum," no. 10, in Vaticani II, Cura et Studio Archivi Concilii Oecumenici, *Acta Synodalia Sacrosancti Concilii Oecumenici Vaticani*, Volumen IV, Periodus Quarta, Pars VI: Congregationes Generalis CLVI – CLXIV, Session Publica VIII (Vatican City: Typis Polyglottis Vaticanis, 1978), pp. 609-632, at p. 617.

9. See Pope John Paul II, "Christifideles Laici: Apostolic Exhortation on the Laity" (January 30, 1987), based on the 1987 World Synod of Bishops, *Origins* 18:35 (Feb. 9, 1989): 561, 653-595. It stated, "The [Second Vatican] council's mention of examining and solving pastoral problems 'by general discussion' [footnote reference to *Apostolicam actuositatem*, no. 10] ought to find its adequate and structured development through a more convinced, extensive and decided appreciation for 'parish pastoral councils,' on which the synod fathers have rightly insisted" (no. 27, p. 574).

Thomas J. Green, an American canon lawyer, was among the first (as far as I know) to see *Apostolicam actuositatem* 10 as a source for parish councils. See Green's "Critical Reflections on the Schema on the People of God," *Studia Canonica* 14 (1980): 235-314. Green criticized the lack of attention to PPCs in the draft schema for the revised Code of Canon Law, p. 254. In a footnote about parish councils he wrote, "The schema does not seem to refer to corporate bodies at the parish level," adding that "The thrust of *Apostolicam actuositatem* (nos. 10, 26) and the Directory for the Pastoral Office of Bishops (no. 179) took a different view on the matter."

10. See Paul VI, Pope, *Ecclesiam Suam: Encyclical Letter on "The Paths of the Church,"* (August 6, 1964), with a Commentary by Gregory Baum, OSA (Glen Rock, NJ: Paulist Press, 1964). The sentence by Baum is on p. 11.

11. We are using the word "dysfunction" in the sense pioneered by Murray Bowen's "family systems theory" of the '50s and '60s and presented in Bowen's *Family Therapy in Clinical Practice* (Northvale, NJ: Jason Aronson Inc., 1985). Family systems theory starts with the assumption that spouses ought to have a complementary and cooperative relationship, that parents ought to care for the children who depend on them, and that children ought to respect their parents. When relations break down, for example in the presence of alcoholism, some members of the family cease to function and others try to compensate for the dysfunction. Although a pastor is not the biological father of his parish council, his relation to the council is akin to a family relation. See Mark F. Fischer, "When Your Pastor Is Dysfunctional," *Today's Parish* (September 1994): 11-13, 23.

12. The difference between sociological and psychological dysfunction hinges on effectiveness and freedom. Sociological dysfunction describes the council that is no longer effective. Psychological dysfunction describes those people whose own freedom to enter into a sound relationship with the council is hindered and who therefore hinder the freedom of the council to do its job.

13. A 1990 study noted that council guidelines published by the dioceses of Harrisburg, Raleigh, Louisville, Cleveland, Milwaukee, Fargo, Omaha, and San Bernardino, for example, allowed appeals in the case of pastor-council conflict. See Fischer, "Parish Pastoral Councils" (1990), p. 9. For a critique of the process of appeal, see Basil Cole, "Conceiving, Creating and Sustaining the Parish Council." *The Priest* 34:9 (September 1978): 30-33.

14. Arnold Kurtz describes the pastor's role in "The Pastor as a Manager of Conflict in the Church," *Andrews University Seminary Studies* 20.2 (1982): 111-126.

15. For the basic principle of conflict management, see John W. Lawyer and Neil H. Katz, *Communication Skills for Ministry* (Dubuque: Kendall/Hunt Publishing Co., 1987).

16. Richard C. Cunningham, "The Laity in the Revised Code," in James H. Provost, Editor, *Code, Community, Ministry: Selected Studies for the Parish Minister Introducing the Revised Code of Canon Law* (Washington, D.C.: Canon Law Society of America, 1992), pp. 32-37, at p. 37.

17. Pope John Paul II, "Christifideles Laici" (no. 25), see p. 573. This part of *Christifideles* treats diocesan pastoral councils; parish pastoral councils are treated at no. 27, p. 574.

Chapter Twenty: The Motive for Consultation

1. About pastors' serious disagreements with councils, see Thomas P. Sweetser, "Parish Accountability: Where the People Are At," *Chicago Studies* 12 (Summer 1973): 115-128, esp. p. 119. Fitzgerald, "Overhauling," p. 684-691; and Shea, "A Bishop Suspends," offer examples of the frustrations of pastors. For dispirited councillors, see Morrow, "A Parish Council of Ministries"; about boredom, see Griffin, "Diocesan Church Structures," esp. p. 62; and about shaking the dust, see Cunningham, "The Laity," esp. p. 37.

2. Hersey and Blanchard define leadership as "the process of influencing the activities of an individual or a group in efforts toward goal achievement in a given situation" (p. 95).

3. Daniel M. Buechlein, the Benedictine and Bishop of Memphis, described the priest's essential role as drawing together "all those who, by their baptism, exercise another form of priesthood which is membership in the whole body." Buechlein's "The Sacramental Identity of the Ministerial Priesthood," is in Robert Wister, editor, *Priests: Identity and Ministry* (Wilmington: Glazier, 1990), 139-148, at p. 144. Robert M. Schwartz said that, although priestly identity is essentially different from that of the baptized in general, yet "it is oriented toward the upbuilding of all and has no meaning apart from this task" (p. 132). See Schwartz's *Servant Leaders of the People of God* (Mahwah: Paulist, 1989), p. 132.

4. Mark F. Fischer, "Jesus Never Sought Consensus," *Today's Parish* (March 1993): 23-26.

5. David F. Wall reports that, even when council members do not get their way, they can still experience the council as satisfying, especially when they share the pastor's overall goals and experience his support. See Wall, "Parish Councils," pp. 211-213.

6. Mark F. Fischer, "When Should a Pastor Not Consult the Council?" *Today's Parish* (March 1992): 18-20.

Chapter Twenty-one: A Foundation Document

1. For examples of guidelines that describe the council as a policy-maker and policy-implementer, see Chapter Four's discussion of the council's "Consultative and Executive Functions." Chapter Seventeen presents the proper understanding of the coordination exercised by councils.

2. Howes, *Creating an Effective Parish Pastoral Council*, offers a model constitution and bylaws with this phrase at p. 68. For an example of diocesan guidelines that give councils a superior function, see Chapter Thirteen above, footnote 2.

3. Rademacher with Rogers, *The New Practical Guide* (p. 99), state "The council must also learn to delegate authority and responsibility for implementing portions of the parish mission to its committees; the council can then hold them accountable."

4. Howes, *Creating*, p. 70. For a discussion of the restrictions on the scope of the pastoral council in the 1973 Circular Letter ("faith, orthodoxy, moral principles," etc.), see the section entitled "Commentaries on the Circular Letter" in Chapter Ten above. For efforts to restrict the scope of the parish pastoral council in relation to the parish finance council, see the section in Chapter Twelve above entitled "An Erroneous Interpretation?" On the role of the pastor in determining "pastoral" matters, see the discussion of "Pastoral as Spiritual" in Chapter Thirteen above.

5. Rademacher with Rogers, p. 125. For an overview of what diocesan guidelines actually say about the qualifications of councillors, see the section entitled "The Criteria for Membership" in Chapter Seven, above. For an analysis of what the qualifications ought to be, see the sections above entitled "Requirements for the Council Ministry" in Chapter Fifteen

and "The Gifts of Councillors" in Chapter Eighteen.

6. For the Vatican's view about the number of councillors, the term of office, and the method of selection, see the section entitled "Vatican II's Support for Elections" in Chapter Sixteen above, especially footnote 4.

7. Rademacher with Rogers (pp. 221, 235) draw upon the Archdiocese of Milwaukee's booklet entitled *Orientation/Nomination/Election*. For an analysis of ecclesial representation, see Chapter Fifteen above. For a discussion of the discerning selection of councillors, see the section entitled "Choosing Councillors" in Chapter Sixteen above.

8. Rademacher with Rogers call for staggered elections (p. 122), as does the Vatican's 1973 Circular Letter (at no. 7). The Circular Letter calls such staggered elections "advisable," meaning that they are a recommendation, not a mandate. My experience in Oakland (see Chapter Six above) taught me that a stable three-year term is preferable in many ways.

9. Kennedy, "Shared Responsibility," pp. 10-20. For a discussion of the role of council officers, see the section entitled "Lay Leadership in the Guidelines" in Chapter Six above.

10. For a history of the development of parish pastoral councils into planning bodies, see Chapter Thirteen above. The rationale for councils as pastoral planners is provided in Chapter Eighteen.

11. Howes, *Creating*, p. 69. Rademacher with Rogers, p. 134. For an empirical portrait of consultation in parish pastoral councils, see Chapter Five above. For an analysis of consultation (and remedies for its dysfunctions), see Chapter Nineteen above.

12. For a description of the limited role of parish staff members on pastoral councils, see the section entitled "*Ex Officio* Members" in Chapter Seven above. For a discussion of practical wisdom and a comparison of the roles of the parish pastoral and parish finance councils, see the section entitled "The Method of the Two Councils" in Chapter Eighteen.

13. Bausch, *The Hands-On Parish*, p. 89. Most guidelines for pastoral councils recommend monthly meetings. See Chapter Six, footnote 9. For a discussion of credibility in the council, see Chapter Twenty above.

14. Developing a spirituality of consultation deserves to be a part of seminary formation. Canon 256 states that seminarians should be taught parish administration. But the basic curriculum for seminaries, the *Program of Priestly Formation* published by the U.S. bishops, does not require a course in parish administration, treating it instead under the heading of Field Education, without any mention of pastoral councils or the consultation of parishioners.

Pastoral Council Bibliography

Ahlin, Robert J. "Parish Councils: A Theological and Canonical Foundation." Dissertation for the Degree of Licentiate in Canon Law. The Catholic University of America, 1982.

Arquett, Robert J. "Is the Parish Council Worthwhile?" *Homiletic and Pastoral Review* 67:8 (May, 1967): 645-649.

Aumann, Jordan. "Editorial: Diocesan and Parish Councils." *The Priest* 27:1 (1971): 5-7.

Baker, Thomas, and Frank Ferrone. *Liturgy Committee Handbook:* Mystic, CT: Twenty-Third Publications, 1998.

Balhoff, Michael J. *Strategic Planning for Pastoral Ministry.* Washington, D.C.: Pastoral Press, 1993.

Bannon, William J., and Suzanne Donovan. *Volunteers and Ministry: A Manual for Developing Parish Volunteers.* New York and Ramsey: Paulist, 1983.

Baranowski, Arthur R., in collaboration with Kathleen M. O'Reilly and Carrie M. Piro. *Creating Small Faith Communities: A Plan for Restructuring the Parish and Renewing Catholic Life.* Cincinnati: St. Anthony Messenger Press, 1988.

Bassett, William W. "Subsidiarity, Order and Freedom in the Church." In James A. Coriden, Editor, *The Once and Future Church,* pp. 205-266.

Baum, Gregory. "Commentary." In Paul VI, *Ecclesiam Suam.*

Bausch, William J. *Pilgrim Church.* Mystic, CT: Twenty-Third Publications, 1977, 1981.

Bausch, William J. *The Christian Parish: Whispers of the Risen Christ.* Mystic, CT: Twenty-Third Publications, 1981.

Bausch, William J. *The Hands-On Parish.* Mystic: Twenty-Third Publications, 1989.

Bestard Comas, Joan. *El Consejo Pastoral Parroquial: Cómo dinamizar una parroquia.* Versión castellana revisada y ampliada: Joan Bestard Comas y Joan Darder Brotat. Madrid: Vicarios Episcopales de las diócesis españolas - Promoción Popular Cristiana, 1988.

Blake, Robert R., and Jane S. Mouton. *The Managerial Grid.* Houston: Gulf Publishing, 1964.

Borders, William. "Collegiality in the Local Church." *Origins* 9:32 (January 24, 1980): 509, 511-13.

Borders, William. "The Difficult, Practical Phase of Shared Responsibility," *Origins* 6:5 (June 24, 1976): 65, 67-69.

Bowen, Murray. *Family Therapy in Clinical Practice.* Northvale, NJ: Jason Aronson, Inc., 1985.

Brennan, Patrick J. *Re-Imagining the Parish: Base Communities, Adulthood, and Family Consciousness.* New York: Crossroad, 1990.

Brennan, Patrick J. *The Evangelizing Parish: Theologies and Strategies for Renewal.* Allen, TX: Tabor, 1987.

Brewer, Helen B., and Thomas J. Tewey, Editors. *Understanding Coresponsibility.* Washington, D.C.: National Council of Catholic Laity, 1974.

Broderick, Bill. "Does Your Diocese Have a Council?" *Commonweal* 122 (Oct. 20, 1995): 12.

Broderick, Robert C. *Parish Council Handbook: A Handbook to Bring the Power of Renewal to Your Parish*. Chicago: Franciscan Herald Press, 1968.

Broderick, Robert C. *Your Parish Comes Alive*. Chicago: Franciscan Herald Publications, 1970.

Buckley, Joseph C. "Parish Councils." *Clergy Review* 53:4 (April 1968): 264-274.

Buechlein, Daniel M. (Bishop of Memphis). "The Sacramental Identity of the Ministerial Priesthood." In Wister, editor, *Priests*, 139-148.

Bunker, Barbara Benedict, and Billie T. Alban. *Large Group Interventions: Engaging the Whole System for Rapid Change*. San Francisco: Jossey-Bass, 1997.

Buryska, James. "Four Dilemmas of Pastoral Councils." *Pastoral Life* 23:12 (December, 1974): 12-20.

Burke, Mary P., and Eugene F. Hemrick. *Building the Local Church: Shared Responsibility in Diocesan Pastoral Councils*. Washington, D.C.: United States Catholic Conference, 1984.

Canadian Conference of Catholic Bishops, Laity Commission. *The Parish Pastoral Council: Guidelines for the Development of Constitutions*. Ottawa: Canadian Catholic Conference, 1984.

Caparros, E.; M. Thériault, J. Thorn, Editors. *Code of Canon Law Annotated*. Latin-English edition of the Code of Canon Law and English-language translation of the 5th Spanish-language edition of the commentary prepared under the responsibility of the Instituto Martín de Azpilcueta (Navarra). A collaboration of the Faculties of Canon Law of the University of Navarra in Spain and Saint Paul University in Canada. Montréal: Wilson and Lafleur Limitée, 1993.

Case, James (Archbishop of Denver). "Evaluating Today's Parish: Pastoral Process/Denver." *Origins* 6:3 (June 10, 1976): 41-44.

Cassa, Yvonne, and Joanne Sanders. *How to Form a Parish Liturgy Board*. Chicago: Liturgy Training Publications, 1987.

Castelli, Jim, and Joseph Gremillion. *The Emerging Parish: The Notre Dame Study of Catholic Life Since Vatican II*. San Francisco: Harper and Row, Publishers, 1987. See Leege and Gremillion.

Celio, Mary Beth. "Parish Pastoral Staffing: A Case Study." In Doyle et al., Editors, *Laity, Parish, and Ministry*, pp. 44-68.

Certain, Stephanie, and Marty Mayer. *Goal Setting for Liturgy Committees*. Chicago: Liturgy Training Publications, 1981.

Ceschin, Giuseppe. *Il Consiglio Pastorale Parrochiale. Genesi, Natura e Funzionamento*. Dissertation ad Lauream in Facultate Iuris Canonici apud Pontificiam Universitatem S. Thomae in Urbe. Roma: Pontifical University of St. Thomas in the City, 1992.

Cole, Basil. "Conceiving, Creating and Sustaining the Parish Council." *The Priest* 34:9 (September, 1978): 30-33.

Coleman, John A. *The Evolution of Dutch Catholicism, 1958-1974*. Berkeley, Los Angeles, and London: University of California Press, 1978.

Coleman, William V., Editor. *Parish Leadership Today: A Compilation of Writings from Today's Parish*. Mystic: Twenty-Third Publications, 1979.

Condon, David C., John J. Haggerty, Michael J. Wrenn. *The Interparochial Council: Structure for Renewal*. Collegeville: The Liturgical Press, 1968.

Conley, Philip P. "The Parish Council: Planning the Mission, Implementing the Vision." Paper Submitted for the Degree of Doctor of Ministry. Pittsburgh: Pittsburgh Theological Seminary, 1994.

Cooper, Norman P. *Collaborative Ministry: Communion, Contention, Commitment*. New York and Mahwah: Paulist Press, 1993.

Cooperrider, David L., Suresh Srivastva and others. *Appreciative Management and Leadership*. San Francisco: Jossey-Bass, 1990.

Cooperrider, David L.; Peter F. Sorensen, Jr., Diana Whitney, and Therese F. Yaeger, editors, *Appreciative Inquiry: Rethinking the Organization Toward a Positive Theory of Change.* Champaign, IL: Stipes Publishing LLC, 2000.

Coriden, James A.; Thomas J. Green and Donald E. Heintschel. *The Code of Canon Law: A Text and Commentary.* Commissioned by the Canon Law Society of America. Study Edition. New York and Mahwah: Paulist Press, 1985.

Coriden, James A., Editor. *The Once and Future Church: A Communion of Freedom—Studies on Unity and Collegiality in the Church.* Staten Island: Alba House, 1971.

Coriden, James A. *The Parish in Catholic Tradition: History, Theology and Canon Law.* New York and Mahwah: Paulist Press, 1997.

Coriden, James A. "Shared Authority: Rationale and Legal Foundation." In Charles E. Curran and George J. Dyer, editors. *Chicago Studies* 9 (1970): 171-182.

Coriden, James, Editor. *We, the People of God: A Study of Constitutional Government for the Church.* Huntington: Our Sunday Visitor, 1968.

Coriden, James A., Editor. *Who Decides in the Church? Studies in Co-Responsibility.* Hartford: Canon Law Society of America, 1971.

Cornell, Natalie. "The Parish Council 20 Years After." *Today's Parish* (January, 1986): 26-27.

Cunningham, Richard C. "The Laity in the Revised Code." In James H. Provost, ed. *Code, Community, Ministry: Selected Studies for the Parish Minister Introducing the Revised Code of Canon Law.* Washington, D.C.: Canon Law Society of America, 1983. Pp. 32-37.

Curran, Charles E., and George J. Dyer, editors. *Shared Responsibility in the Local Church.* Published as *Chicago Studies* 9:2 (Summer, 1970).

Dalton, William. "Parish Councils." *The Furrow* 39 (1988): 86-90.

Dalton, William. "Parish Councils or Parish Pastoral Councils?" *Studia Canonica* 22 (1988): 169-185.

Day, Edward. "Parish Council: Pastor and People Sharing Christ's Priesthood." *Liguorian* 64:2 (February, 1976): 20-25.

Deegan, Arthur X., II, Editor. *Developing a Vibrant Parish Pastoral Council.* New York and Mahwah: Paulist Press, 1995.

Deegan, Arthur. *How to Start a Parish Council.* Five-part leaflet series. Fort Wayne, Indiana: Twenty-Third Publications, 1969.

Deegan, Arthur X. *The Priest as Manager.* New York: Bruce Publishing, 1968.

Detroit, Archdiocese of, Office of Planning and Research (Arthur X. Deegan, II, Director). "Insight: Our Faith Today." *Research Report* No. 2. Detroit: Archdiocese of Detroit, 1971.

Detroit, Archdiocese of, Office of Planning and Research (Arthur X. Deegan, II, Director). "1970 Attitudes on Parish Councils in this Archdiocese." *Research Report* No. 4. Detroit: Archdiocese of Detroit, 1971.

Doohan, Leonard. *Grass-Roots Pastors: Handbook for Lay Ministers.* San Francisco: Harper, 1989.

Doohan, Leonard. *The Lay-Centered Church: Theology and Spirituality.* Minneapolis: Winston, 1984.

Doyle, Michael, and David Straus. *How to Make Meetings Work: The New Interactive Method.* Second Printing. Originally Published in 1976. New York: Jove Books, 1983.

Doyle, Ruth T.; Robert E. Schmitz, and Mary Beth Celio, Editors. *Laity, Parish and Ministry.* Monograph no. 1 in the series Research Monographs of the Catholic Research Forum of the Conference for Pastoral Planning and Council Development. New York: Office of Pastoral Research and Planning, Archdiocese of New York, 1999.

Dozier, Carroll T. (Bishop of Memphis). "Strategies for Community and Ministry." *Origins* 3:34 (February 14, 1974): 521, 523-526.

Dreher, John D. "Pastoral Planning for Accountability: Key Assets and Obstacles." *Origins* 3:12 (Sept. 13, 1973): 182-186.

Duch, Robert G. *Successful Parish Leadership: Nurturing the Animated Parish*. Kansas City: Sheed and Ward, 1990.

Ellis, John Tracy. *Catholics in Colonial America*. Baltimore: Helicon Press, 1965.

Ellis, John Tracy. "On Selecting Catholic Bishops for the United States." *The Critic* 27:6 (June-July, 1969): 43-55.

Fecher, Charles A. *Parish Council Committee Guide*. Washington, D.C.: National Council of Catholic Men, 1970.

Fischer, Mark F. "Breathe Fresh Spirit into Your Parish Pastoral Council." *Today's Parish* (January 1997): 29-31.

Fischer, Mark F. "Common Sense about Councils." *Church* 12:4 (Winter, 1996): 10-14.

Fischer, Mark F. "Diocesan Pastoral Council Constitutions." In H. Richard McCord, editor. *Diocesan Pastoral Councils*. Washington, D.C.: National Conference of Catholic Bishops, forthcoming.

Fischer, Mark F. "Jesus Never Sought Consensus." *Today's Parish* (March 1993): 23-26.

Fischer, Mark F. "Keeping Your Council on Track." *Today's Parish* (March 1996): 31-33.

Fischer, Mark F. "Parish Councils: Where Does the Pastor Fit In?" *Today's Parish* (November/December, 1991): 13-15.

Fischer, Mark F. "Parish Councils: Why Good Delegators Don't Always Make Good Leaders." *Today's Parish* (March 1997): 27-30.

Fischer, Mark F. "Parish Pastoral Councils: How Many Are There? How Do Bishops Support Them?" In Doyle et al., Editors, *Laity, Parish, and Ministry*, Pp. 82-106.

Fischer, Mark F. "Parish Pastoral Councils: Purpose, Consultation, Leadership." *Center Papers*, no. 4. New York: National Pastoral Life Center, 1990.

Fischer, Mark F. "Should Finance Councils Answer to Parish Councils?" *Today's Parish* (March 1994): 21-23, 32.

Fischer, Mark F. "What Was Vatican II's Intent Regarding Parish Councils?" *Studia Canonica* 33 (1999): 5-25.

Fischer, Mark F. "When Should a Pastor Not Consult the Council?" *Today's Parish* (March 1992): 18-20.

Fischer, Mark F. "When the Parish Council and the Finance Council Disagree." *Today's Parish* 30.1 (January 1998): 8-12.

Fischer, Mark F. "When Your Pastor Is Dysfunctional." *Today's Parish* (September 1994): 11-13, 23.

Fischer, Mark F., and Mary Raley, Editors. *Four Ways to Build More Effective Parish Councils: A Pastoral Approach*. Mystic, CT: Twenty-Third Publications-Bayard, 2002.

Fitzgerald, Patrick. "Overhauling a Parish Council." *Clergy Review* 60:10 (October, 1975): 684-691.

Fitzpatrick, Gerry. "Diary of a Parish Council." Interview with Bill Schaefer, Head of St. Michael Parish Council Steering Committee, Alberta, Canada. *Today's Parish* (January 1969): 1-3.

Flaherty, John P., Editor. *Diocesan Efforts at Parish Reorganization*. A Report Published by the Conference for Pastoral Planning and Council Development. Clearwater, FL: CPPCD, 1995.

Fleischer, Barbara J. *Facilitating for Growth: A Guide for Scripture Groups and Small Christian Communities*. Collegeville, MN: The Liturgical Press, 1993.

Flood, Edmund. *The Laity Today and Tomorrow*. "A report on the new consciousness of lay Catholics and how it might change the face of tomorrow's Church." New York and Mahwah: Paulist Press, 1987.

Froehle, Bryan T. *Diocesan and Eparchial Pastoral Councils: A National Profile*. Undertaken by the Center for Applied Research in the Apostolate (CARA) at Georgetown University. A

Study Commissioned by the Bishops' Committees on the Laity and Pastoral Practices. Washington, D.C.: United States Catholic Conference, June, 1998.

Froehle, Bryan T., and Mary L. Gautier. *Catholicism USA: A Portrait of the Catholic Church in the United States.* Center for Applied Research in the Apostolate, Georgetown University. Maryknoll, NY: Orbis Books, 2000.

Froehle, Bryan T., and Mary L. Gautier. *National Parish Inventory Project Report.* Washington, D.C.: Center for Applied Research in the Apostolate at Georgetown University, October, 1999.

[Gasslein, Bernadette.] *Parish Council: New Parish Ministries.* Minneapolis: Winston, 1983. [First Edition: Ottawa: Novalis, Saint Paul University, 1982.]

Gelineau, Louis (Bishop of Providence). "Reflections on Pastoral Planning: Discoveries in Renewal." (Address to the National Pastoral Planning Conference, 11/30/76). *Origins* 6:27 (December 23, 1976): 421, 423-429.

Gilder, Constance. *The Ministry of Pastoral Planning: A Planning Guide for Parishes in the Archdiocese of Baltimore.* Archdiocese of Baltimore: Division of Planning and Council Services, 1993.

Green, Thomas H. *Weeds among the Wheat. Discernment: Where Prayer and Action Meet.* South Bend, IN: Ave Maria, 1984.

Green, Thomas J. "Critical Reflections on the Schema on the People of God." *Studia Canonica* 14 (1980): 235-314.

Greenleaf, Robert K. *Servant Leadership: A Journey into the Nature of Legitimate Power and Greatness.* New York, Ramsey, and Toronto: Paulist Press, 1977.

Gremillion, Joseph, and Jim Castelli. *The Emerging Parish: The Notre Dame Study of Catholic Life Since Vatican II.* San Francisco: Harper and Row, 1987. See Leege and Gremillion.

Griese, Orville. "The New Code of Canon Law and Parish Councils." *Homiletic and Pastoral Review* 85:4 (January, 1985): 47-53.

Griese, Orville. "Pastor-Parish Council Collaboration." *The Priest* 33:2 (February, 1977): 19-22, 24.

Griffin, Bertram F. "Diocesan Church Structures," in Provost, Editor, *Code, Community, Ministry,* pp. 53-62.

Griffin, Bertram F. "The Parish and Lay Ministry." *Chicago Studies* 23 (1984): 45-61.

Hannan, John. "Toward Reconciliation in Good Shepherd Parish." *Origins* 4:33 (February 6, 1975): 524.

Hanus, Jerome. *Vision 2000: A Vision and Plan for the Archdiocese of Dubuque in the Twenty-First Century.* Directed by a 17-member Planning Task Force and composed by a Writing Committee, including Mary Montgomery, OP, Director of Strategic Planning. Dubuque: Office of Archbishop Jerome Hanus, OSB, 1999.

Harms, William C. *Who Are We and Where Are We Going? A Guide for Parish Planning.* "A Parish Project Book" copyright by The Parish Project of the National Conference of Catholic Bishops, 299 Elizabeth Street, New York. New York: Sadlier, 1981.

Hayden, Joseph F. "Diocesan Pastoral Councils." Dissertation for the Degree of Licentiate in Canon Law. The Catholic University of America, 1969.

Head, Edward D. (Bishop of Buffalo). "Sharing Responsibility." *Origins* 3:17 (October 18, 1973): 257, 259-60, 270-72.

Heaps, John. *Parish Pastoral Councils: Co-responsibility and Leadership.* Newton, New South Wales: E. J. Dwyer (Australia), 1993. Published in the United States by Morehouse Publishing of Ridgefield, CT.

Hemrick, Eugene F., Ruth Narita Doyle, and Patrick S. Hughes, Editors. *Diocesan Pastoral Planning in the '80s.* With an "Appendix" entitled "What Is Pastoral Planning" by William C. Harms of the NPPC Coordinating Committee. Oakland, NJ: National Pastoral Planning Conference, Inc., 1983.

Hennesey, James. *American Catholics: A History of the Roman Catholic Community in the United*

States. Foreword by John Tracy Ellis. New York and Oxford: Oxford University Press, 1981.

Hennesey, James. "Councils in America." In United States Catholic Conference, *A National Pastoral Council Pro and Con* (1971), pp. 39-67.

Hersey, Paul; and Kenneth H. Blanchard. *Management of Organizational Behavior: Utilizing Human Resources* (first edition, 1969). Sixth Edition. Englewood Cliffs, NJ: Prentice Hall, 1993.

Hoffman, James R. (Bishop of Toledo). "Introduction." In Burke and Hemrick, *Building the Local Church*.

Hoge, Dean R. *The Future of Catholic Leadership: Responses to the Priest Shortage*. Kansas City, MO: Sheed and Ward, 1987.

Howes, Robert G. "A Parish Assembly in Your Parish?" *Pastoral Life* 33 (1984): 16-20.

Howes, Robert G. "Annual Parish Council Evaluation." *Today's Parish* 9 (May-June, 1977): 6-7.

Howes, Robert G. *Bridges: Toward the Inter-Parish Regional Community . . . Deaneries, Clusters, Plural Parishes*. Collegeville: The Liturgical Press, 1998.

Howes, Robert G. *Creating an Effective Parish Pastoral Council*. Collegeville: The Liturgical Press, 1991.

Howes, Robert G. "Guide for Parish Council Members." *Liguorian* 63: 5 (May, 1975): 49-53.

Howes, Robert G. *How to Grow a Better Parish: From Insight to Impact*. A planning book and audiocassette. Canfield, Ohio: Alba House Communications, 1986.

Howes, Robert G. "Parish Councils: Do We Care?" *America* 135:17 (November 27, 1976): 371-372.

Howes, Robert G. *Parish Planning: A Practical Guide to Shared Responsibility*. Collegeville: The Liturgical Press, 1994.

Howes, Robert. G. "Pastoral Councils: Uncertain Future?" *Origins* 3:4 (June 21, 1973): 49, 51-52.

Howes, Robert G. "Pastoral Councils: The Challenge of Shared Responsibility." Address to the National Pastoral Planning Conference, 12/3-5/73. *Origins* 3:27-28 (December 31, 1973): 433-39.

Howes, Robert G. "Priest and Parish Council: Team or Turmoil?" *The Priest* 37 (1981): 7-8.

Howes, Robert G. "Regional Pastor: Regional People." *The Priest* 36 (1980): 19-24.

Howes, Robert G., and Bernard Quinn, Editors. *Diocesan Pastoral Planning*. The papers from the May 28, 1971 Center for Applied Research in the Apostolate symposium on DPCs. Washington, D.C.: Center for Applied Research in the Apostolate, 1971.

Hubbard, Howard J. (Bishop of Albany). *Fulfilling the Vision: Collaborative Ministry in the Parish*. New York: Crossroad, 1998.

Hubbard, Howard J. (Bishop of Albany). "Planning in the Church: The People, the Tasks." Address to he National Pastoral Planning Conference of 3/9/83. *Origins* 12:45 (4/21/83): 729, 731-737.

Hubbard, Howard J. (Bishop of Albany). "Shared Responsibility in the Local Church." *Origins* 8:39 (March 15, 1979): 615-624.

Hubbard, Howard J. (Bishop of Albany). "A Vision for Parish Planning and Restructuring." *Origins* (April 11, 1996).

Jadot, Jean. "Effective Pastoral Planning." Address to the National Pastoral Planning Conference, 12/3/74. *Origins* 4:30 (January 16, 1975): 465, 467-468.

Janicki, Joseph J. "Chapter VI [of Part II]: Parishes, Pastors, and Parochial Vicars (cc. 515-552)." Pages 415-440 of J. A. Coriden, T. J. Green, and D. E. Heintschel, editors. *The Code of Canon Law: A Text and Commentary*. New York and Mahwah: Paulist Press, 1985.

John Paul II, Pope. "Christifideles Laici. Apostolic Exhortation on the Laity." Based on the 1987 World Synod of Bishops, whose theme was "Vocation and Mission of the Laity in the Church and in the World 20 Years after the Second Vatican Council." January 30, 1987. *Origins* 18:35 (February 9, 1989): 561, 563-595.

John Paul II, Pope. *Code of Canon Law*. Latin-English Edition. Translation prepared under the auspices of the Canon Law Society of America. Washington, D.C.: Canon Law Society of America, 1983.

John Paul II, Pope. "Instruction on Certain Questions Regarding Collaboration of the Non-Ordained Faithful in the Sacred Ministry of Priest." Written by a committee consisting of representatives of the Congregation for the Clergy, the Pontifical Council for the Laity, the Congregation for the Doctrine of the Faith, the Congregation for Divine Worship and the Discipline of the Sacraments, the Congregation for Bishops, the Congregation for the Evangelization of Peoples, the Congregation for Institutes of Consecrated Life and Societies of Apostolic Life, and the Pontifical Council for the Interpretation of Legislative Texts. Approved "in forma specifica" by Pope John Paul II. Promulgated on August 15, 1997. Posted on the Internet at the Catholic Information Network web site, November 13, 1997.

John Paul II, Pope. "Novo Millennio Ineunte" (Apostolic Letter "At the Beginning of the New Millennium," January 6, 2001) Origins 30:31 (January 18, 2001): 489, 491-508.

John Paul II, Pope. "Shared Responsibility in the Church." Address of January 23, 1979 to the Permanent Council of the Italian Bishops' Conference. *Origins* 8:38 (March 8, 1979): 602-603.

Kavanagh, John P., "Yes, We Have a Council" [letter to the editor], *Commonweal* 122 (12/15/95): 4, 24.

Keating, Charles J. *The Leadership Book* (first edition, 1978). Revised Edition. New York and Ramsey: Paulist Press, 1982.

Keating, Charles J. *The Pastoral Planning Book*. New York and Mahwah: Paulist Press, 1981.

Keating, John. "Consultation in the Parish." *Origins* 14:17 (October 11, 1984): 257, 259-266.

Kenedy, P. J. and Sons. *The Official Catholic Directory: 1994*. New Providence, New Jersey: P. J. Kenedy and Sons in association with R. R. Bowker, a Reed Reference Publishing Company, 1994.

Kennedy, Robert T. "Shared Responsibility in Ecclesial Decision Making." *Studia Canonica* 14:1 (1980): 5-23.

Kim Se-Mang, Peter. *Parish Councils on Mission: Coresponsibility and Authority among Pastors and Parishioners*. Kuala Lumpur: Benih Publisher, 1991.

Kippley, John F. "Parish Councils: Democratic Process or New Absolutism?" *America* 123:4 (August 22, 1970): 94-97.

Klostermann, Ferdinand. "Decree on the Apostolate of the Laity." In Herbert Vorgrimler, editor, *Commentary on the Documents of Vatican II*. Translated by William Glen-Doepel, Hilda Graef, John Michael Jakubiak, and Simon and Erika Young. Vol. III. Freiburg in Breisgau: Herder; and Montreal: Palm Publishers, 1968.

Komonchak, Joseph. "The Church: God's Gift and Our Task." Address to the National Pastoral Planning Conference and to the Parish and Diocesan Council Network, 3/10/87. *Origins* 16:42 (4.2.87): 735-741.

Koper, Rigobert. "Die Lage der Katholischen Kirche in Holland: das holländische Pastoral-Konzil." *Theologisch-praktische Quartalschrift* 119 (1971): 220-228.

Küng, Hans. "Participation of the Laity in Church Leadership and Church Elections." Trans. by Arlene Swidler. *Journal of Ecumenical Studies* 6:4 (Fall, 1969): 511-533.

Kurtz, Arnold. "The Pastor as a Manager of Conflict in the Church." *Andrews University Seminary Studies* 20:2 (1982): 111-126.

Lambert, Norman M. "How to Motivate a Parish Council." *Today's Parish* 9 (May-June, 1977): 28.

Larsen, Earnest, C.Ss.R. *Spiritual Renewal of the American Parish*. Liguori, MO.: Liguori Publications, 1977.

Lawyer, John W. and Neil H. Katz. *Communication Skills for Ministry*. Second edition. Dubuque, IA: Kendall/Hunt Publishing Company, 1987.

Laz, Medard. *Making Parish Meetings Work*. Notre Dame: Ave Maria, 1997.

Leckey, Dolores. "Laity Councils: Developments in Lay Ministry." *Origins* 8:16 (Oct. 5, 1978): 245-248.

Leege, David, and Joseph Gremillion, Editors. *Notre Dame Study of Catholic Parish Life*. Reports 1-10. Notre Dame, Indiana: University of Notre Dame, 1984-1987. Ninth Report. "Parish Life Among the Leaders," by David C. Leege. Published in December, 1986 as one of ten independent reports. See Castelli and Gremillion.

Legrand, Francis X. "The Parish Councils: Reflections on Their Principal Purpose." *Christ to the World* 14:2 (Nov. 2, 1969):118-120.

Lynch, J. "The Parochial Ministry in the New Code of Canon Law." *The Jurist* 42 (1982): 383-421.

Lyons, Bernard. *Leaders for Parish Councils: A Handbook of Training Techniques*. Techny, IL: Divine Word Publications, 1971.

Lyons, Bernard. *Parish Councils: Renewing the Christian Community*. Foreword by Bishop John J. Wright. Techny, IL: Divine Word Publications, 1967.

Lyons, Bernard. *Programs for Parish Councils: An Action Manual*. Techny, IL: Divine Word Publications, 1969.

Lyons, Enda. *Partnership in Parish: A Vision for Parish Life, Mission, and Ministry*. Blackrock, County Dublin: Columba, 1987.

Mahony, Roger (Archbishop of Los Angeles). "Life of the Laity: A Church that Is Collaborative." *Origins* 16:29 (1.1.87): 526-530.

Maher, William. *A Question of Values*. "Introduction" by Richard H. Dement. Washington, D.C.: National Council of Catholic Laity, 1974.

Marceaux, Sidney J. "The Pastoral Council." Doctor of Canon Law dissertation. Rome: Pontifical University of Studies at St. Thomas Aquinas in the City, 1980.

Martin, George. "Basic Options for Parish Councils." *Today's Parish* (Jan., 1969): 8-9.

McAvoy, Thomas T. *A History of the Catholic Church in the United States*. Notre Dame and London: University of Notre Dame Press, 1969.

McBrien, Richard P. "The Place of Parish Councils within the Developing Theology of the Church." In Coleman (ed.), *Parish Leadership Today*.

McCadden, Joseph J. "The Specter of the Lay Trustee." *America* 117:6 (8/5/67): 133-136.

McCarthy, Edward, "Is a Laity Secretariat Needed?" *Origins* 6:24 (Dec. 2, 1976): 378.

McEniry, Robert. "Parish Councils and Group Dynamics." *Pastoral Life* 26:9 (October, 1977): 22-29.

McKinney, Mary Benet. *Sharing Wisdom: A Process for Group Decision Making*. Allen, TX: Tabor Publishing, 1987. Reprint edition: Chicago: Thomas More Press, 1998.

McManus, Frederick R. "Diocesan Pastoral Councils." *The Jurist* 34 (Winter/Spring 1974): 168-171.

McNamara, Robert F. "Trusteeism in the Atlantic States, 1785-1863." *The Catholic Historical Review* 30 (July, 1944): 135-154.

Mealey, Mark S. "The Parish Pastoral Council in the United States of America: Applications of Canon 536." Doctor of Canon Law Dissertation, St. Paul University, Ottawa, 1989.

Meredith, Owen. *The Parish Activities Handbook: A Practical Guide for Pastors, Staff, Councils, Committees, and Volunteers*. Mystic, CT: Twenty-Third Publications, 1996.

Michael, Paul. "Everyone Responsible, No One in Charge." *U.S. Catholic* 40 (April, 1975): 28-32.

Miragoli, Egidio. "Consejo Pastoral Diocesano – Lombardia." *Tesi gregoriana. Serie Diritto*

Canonico, no. 43. Roma: Pontificia Università Gregoriana, 2000.

Montgomery, Mary. "Sharing More than a Pastor." In Fischer and Raley, editors, *Four Ways*.

Morrow, Debbie. "A Parish Council of Ministries." *Church* 6:1 (Spring 1990): 42-44.

Morseth, Ellen. *Call to Leadership: Transforming the Local Church*. Kansas City: Sheed and Ward, 1993.

Murnion, Philip J., et al. *New Parish Ministers: Lay and Religious on Parish Staffs*. New York: National Pastoral Life Center, 1992.

Murnion, Philip. "The Unmet Challenges of Vatican II." *Origins* 11:10 (August 13, 1981): 145, 147-154.

Murnion, Philip J., and David DeLambo. *Parishes and Parish Ministers*. New York: National Pastoral Life Center, 1999.

Murphy, Thomas (Bishop of Great Falls - Billings, Montana). "On Parish Councils and Lay Ministry." *Origins* 11:41 (3/25/82): 648-651.

Murray, John Courtney. *We Hold These Truths: Reflections on the American Proposition* (1960). Kansas City: Sheed and Ward, 1988.

Myers, R., and Richard Schoenherr. "The Baptism of Power." *New Catholic World* 274 (1980): 217-228.

National Conference of Catholic Bishops. "A Discussion Guide on Pastoral Councils." Prepared as a background paper for the U.S. Bishops' annual meeting, April 10-13, 1972. *Origins* 1:45 (April 27, 1972): 754, 764.

National Conference of Catholic Bishops. *The Parish: A People, A Mission, A Structure*. Statement of the Committee on the Parish of the NCCB. Washington, D.C.: United States Catholic Conference, 1980.

National Conference of Catholic Bishops (Committee on Priestly Life and Ministry, Committee for African American Catholics, Committee for the Diaconate, Committee on Hispanic Affairs, Committee on Home Missions, Committee on Pastoral Practices, Committee on Vocations, and Sub-Committee on Lay Ecclesial Ministry). *The Study of the Impact of Fewer Priests on the Pastoral Ministry*. Supplementary Document "D," including research conducted for the Bishops by the Center for Applied Research in the Apostolate (CARA). Spring General Meeting in Milwaukee, WI, June 15-17, 2000. Washington, DC: NCCB, 2000 [Unpublished].

National Conference of Catholic Bishops. "The Quest for Shared Responsibility." U.S. Bishops' "Steering Committee for the Advisory Council." *Origins* 2:44 (April 26, 1973): 693, 695, 705-708.

National Conference of Catholic Bishops. Lay Ministry Subcommittee of the Committee on the Laity. "Lay Ecclesial Ministry: State of the Questions." *Origins* 29:31 (January 20, 2000): 497, 499-512.

National Council of Catholic Men. *Diocesan Pastoral Council*. Proceedings of the Bergamo Conference, 15-17 March 1970 [in Dayton, Ohio on DPCs sponsored by the National Council of Catholic Men]. Washington, D.C.: NCCM, 1970.

National Council of Catholic Men. *Parish Councils: A Report on the Principles, Purposes, Structures and Goals*. Washington, D.C.: NCCM, 1968.

Newsome, Robert R. *The Ministering Parish: Methods and Procedures for Pastoral Organization*. New York and Ramsey: Paulist Press, 1982.

Novak, Francis A. "Where Parish Councils Are Shaping Up." *Liguorian* 61:3 (March, 1973): 15-18.

O'Brien, J. Stephen, Editor. *Gathering God's People: Signs of a Successful Parish*. Huntington, Indiana: National Catholic Education Association with Our Sunday Visitor, Inc., 1982.

Ochoa, Xaverius, Editor. *Leges Ecclesiae post Codicem iuris canonici editae*. Collegit, digessit notisque ornavit Xaverius Ochoa (until 1985). Institutem Iuridicum Claretianum. 8 volumes. Vatican

City: Libreria Editrice Vaticana; and Rome: Commentarium Pro Religiosis, 1973-1998.

O'Connor, James I., Editor. *The Canon Law Digest.* Vol. VII: Officially Published Documents Affecting the Code of Canon Law 1968-1972. Chicago, IL: Chicago Province of the Society of Jesus, 2345 West 56 Street, 1975.

O'Connor, James I., Editor. *The Canon Law Digest.* Vol. VIII: Officially Published Documents Affecting the Code of Canon Law 1973-1977. Mundelein, IL: Chicago Province of the Society of Jesus, St. Mary of the Lake Seminary, 1978.

O'Dea, Thomas F. "Authority and Freedom in the Church: Tension, Balance and Contradiction." James A. Coriden, Editor, *Who Decides in the Church?*, pp. 223-249.

O'Leary, Dennis J. "Parish Pastoral Councils: Instruments of Visioning and Planning." In Arthur X. Deegan, II, Editor. *Developing a Vibrant Parish Pastoral Council.* New York and Mahwah: Paulist Press, 1995. Pp. 19-35.

Olsen, Charles M. "Parish Pastoral Councils: Giving Members Bread Not Stones." *Church* 11:2 (Summer, 1995): 33-35.

Olsen, Charles M. *Transforming Church Boards into Communities of Spiritual Leaders.* New York: The Alban Institute, 1995.

O'Meara, Thomas F. "The National Pastoral Council of a Christian Church: Ecclesiastical Accessory or Communal Voice?" In United States Catholic Conference, *A National Pastoral Council Pro and Con*, pp. 21-34.

O'Neill, David P. *The Sharing Community: Parish Councils and Their Meaning.* Dayton: Pflaum, 1968.

Pagé, Roch. *The Diocesan Pastoral Council.* Translated by Bernard A. Prince. Paramus, NJ: Newman Press, 1970. Translation of Roch Pagé, *Le conseil diocésain de pastorale.* Lieu du dialogue entre les laïcs, les religieux, les prêtres et L'évêque. Thèse présentée à la Faculté de Droit canonique de l'Université Saint-Paul en vue de l'obtention du doctorat en Droit canonique et du Ph.D. (Université d'Ottawa). Montréal: Fides, 1969.

Pagé, Roch. "The Parish Pastoral Council." *Proceedings* of the 43rd Annual Convention of the Canon Law Society of America 43 (1981): 45-61.

Parise, Michael. "Forming Your Parish Pastoral Council." *The Priest* 51:7 (July 1995): 43-47.

Paul VI, Pope. "The Council for the Lay Apostolate and the Pontifical Commission Iustitia et Pax." Issued Motu Proprio, 6 January 1967. In T. Lincoln Bouscaren and James I. O'Connor, Editors. *The Canon Law Digest.* Vol. VI. Officially Published Documents Affecting the Code of Canon Law, 1963-1967. New York: The Bruce Publishing Company, 1969. Pages 299-302. Translation of Paul VI, "Catholicam Christi Ecclesiam." Apostolic Letter issued Motu Proprio. *Acta Apostolicae Sedis* 59 (January 6, 1967): 25-28.

Paul VI, Pope. *Ecclesiam Suam* (August 6, 1964). Encyclical Letter on "The Paths of the Church." With a Commentary by Gregory Baum, OSA. Glen Rock, NJ: Paulist Press, 1964.

Paul VI, Pope. "Ecclesiae Sanctae I." Apostolic Letter, written Motu Proprio, on the Implementation of the Decrees Christus Dominus, Presbyterorum Ordinis and Perfectae Caritatis. August 6, 1966. Translated from the Latin text in *Acta Apostolica Sedis* 58 (1966): 757-787, by Austin P. Flannery. In Vatican Council II. *The Documents of Vatican II.* Austin P. Flannery, General Editor. Preface by John Cardinal Wright. New York: Pillar Books, 1975.

Paul VI, Pope. "Roman Curia Reorganized." Apostolic Constitution "Regimini Ecclesiae Universae." August 15, 1967. In Bouscaren and O'Connor, eds., *The Canon Law Digest*, vol. VI, pp. 324-357. Translated from Paul VI, Pope, "Regimini Ecclesiae Universae, Constitutio Apostolica," (August 15, 1967), in *Acta Apostolicae Sedis* 59 (1967): 885-928.

Penderghast, Thomas F. "Parish Council: Barriers to Groupthink." *Church* 6:2 (Summer, 1990): 42-44.

Pereira, Joseph A. "The Juridical Status of the Parish Council." Dissertation for the Degree of Licentiate in Canon Law. Rome: Pontifical Urban University, 1982.

Pfnausch, Edward G., Editor. *Code, Community, Ministry: Selected Studies for the Parish Minister Introducing the Code of Canon Law*. Second revised edition. Washington, D.C.: Canon Law Society of America, 1992.

Phan, Peter C. *Grace and the Human Condition*. Vol. 15 of the series "Message of the Fathers of the Church." Wilmington: Michael Glazier, 1988.

Pitchford, John. *An ABC for the PCC: A Handbook for Parochial Church Councillors*. Third Edition. London: Mowbray Parish Handbooks, 1993.

Pope, George M., III and Bernard Quinn, Editors. *Planning for Planning: Perspectives on Diocesan Research and Planning*. Washington, D.C.: Center for Applied Research in the Apostolate (CARA), 1972.

Provost, James H., ed. *Code, Community, Ministry: Selected Studies for the Parish Minister Introducing the Revised Code of Canon Law*. Washington, D.C.: Canon Law Society of America, 1983.

Provost, James H. "Structuring the Community." *Chicago Studies* 15 (1976): 269-280.

Provost, James H. "The Foundations and Structures for Shared Responsibility," chapter I of Burke and Hemrick, *Building the Local Church*, pp. 5-10.

Provost, James H. "The Working Together of Consultative Bodies—Great Expectations?" *The Jurist* 40 (1980): 257-281.

Provost, James H. "Canon Law and the Role of Consultation." *Origins* 18:47 (May 4, 1989): 793, 795-799.

Quinn, Bernard. "Theological Reflections on the Planning Process." Chapter 4 of George M. Pope, III and Bernard Quinn, Editors. *Planning for Planning: Perspectives on Diocesan Research and Planning*. Washington, D.C.: Center for Applied Research in the Apostolate (CARA), 1972.

Rademacher, William J. *Answers for Parish Councillors*. West Mystic: Twenty-Third Publications, 1973.

Rademacher, William J. *Answers for Parish Councillors*. With Three Chapters on the History, the Theology, and the Future of the Parish. Mystic: Twenty-Third Publications, 1981.

Rademacher, William J. *Lay Ministry: A Theological, Spiritual, and Pastoral Handbook*. New York: Crossroad Publishing Company, 1991.

Rademacher, William J. *New Life for Parish Councils*. West Mystic, Twenty-Third Publications, 1976.

Rademacher, William J. "The Parish Council: A Series of Relationships." *The Priest* 27:12 (January, 1972): 19-26.

Rademacher, William J. "Parish Councils—A Direction for the Future." *The Priest* 31:9 (September, 1975): 30-38.

Rademacher, William J. "Parish Councils: Consultative Vote Only?" *Today's Parish* 32:3 (March 2000): 6-9.

Rademacher, William J. *The Practical Guide for Parish Councils*. West Mystic: Twenty-Third Publications, 1979.

Rademacher, William J. *Starting a Parish Council*. West Mystic, Twenty-Third Publications, 1974.

Rademacher, William J. *Working with Parish Councils?* Canfield, Ohio: Alba, 1976.

Rademacher, William J., with Marliss Rogers. *The New Practical Guide for Parish Councils*. Foreword by Most Rev. Rembert G. Weakland, OSB. Mystic: Twenty-Third Publications, 1988.

Rahner, Karl. *Foundations of Christian Faith: An Introduction to the Idea of Christianity* (1976). Translated by William V. Dych. New York: Seabury Press (A Crossroad Book), 1978. A translation of Karl Rahner, *Grundkurs des Glaubens: Einführung in den Begriff des Christentums* (1976). Eighth edition. Freiburg im Breisgau, Basel, and Vienna: Herder, 1997.

Rausch, James (General Secretary of the NCCB/USCC). "Improving Pastoral Councils." *Origins* 3:17 (Oct. 18, 1973): 262.

Read, Denis. "Review Article: *The Once and Future Church* and *Who Decides for the Church?*" *The American Ecclesiastical Review* 166:6 (June 1972): 421-424.

Renken, John A. "Parishes without a Resident Pastor: Comments on Canon 517, §2." In Pfnausch, Editor, *Code, Community, Ministry*, pp. 100-108.

Renken, John A. "Pastoral Councils: Pastoral Planning and Dialogue among the People of God." *The Jurist* 53 (1993): 132-154.

Robert, Henry M. *Robert's Rules of Order*. Ninth, newly enlarged edition. Edited by Sarah Corbin Robert, with the Assistance of Henry M. Robert III, William J. Evans. New York: Scott, Foresman, 1990.

Rodimer, Frank. "Are Parish Councils on the Right Track?" *Origins* 6:46 (May 5, 1977): 727-730.

Rogers, Marliss. "Renewing Parish Councils: Five Rules for the Second Generation." *Church* 1:1 (Spring 1985): 34-36.

Rogers, Marliss, Editor. *Weekly Prayer Services for Parish Meetings: Lectionary-Based for Cycle C*. Mystic, CT: Twenty-Third Publications, 1994.

Ryan, Edward E. *How to Establish a Parish Council: A Step-by-Step Program for Setting Up Parish Councils*. Chicago: Claretian, 1968.

Sacred Congregation for the Clergy. "Patterns in Local Pastoral Councils" (Circular letter *Omnes Christifideles*, January 25, 1973). *Origins* 3:12 (Sept. 13, 1973): 186-190. Also published in reference to canon 423 in James I. O'Connor, editor, *The Canon Law Digest*, vol. VIII, pp. 280-288. For the Latin text, see Sacra Congregatio Pro Clericis. "Litterae circulares ad Patriarchas, Primates, Archiepiscopos, Episcopos aliosque locorum Ordinarios. De Consiliis Pastoralibus iuxta placita Congregationis Plenariae mixtae die 15 Martii 1972 habitae: Normae statuuntur novae circa compositionem, naturam, munera modumque procedendi Consilii Pastoralis in unaquaque Dioecesi." *Omnes Christifideles*, 25 Ianuarii 1973. In Ochoa, Xaverius, Editor. *Leges Ecclesiae post Codicem iuris canonici editae*. Collegit, digessit notisque ornavit Xaverius Ochoa (until 1985). Institutem Iuridicum Claretianum. 8 volumes. Vatican City: Libreria Editrice Vaticana; and Rome: Commentarium Pro Religiosis, 1973-1998. See vol. V: "Leges Annis 1973-1978 Editae" (1980), columns 6444-6449.

Sacred Congregation for Bishops. *Directory on the Pastoral Ministry of Bishops* (Ecclesiae imago, May 31, 1973). English translation prepared by the Benedictine monks of the Seminary of Christ the King in Mission, British Columbia. Ottawa: Canadian Catholic Conference, 1974. Excerpts from the translation were published as "Bishops and Shared Responsibility/Vatican Text," *Origins* 4:4 (June 20, 1974): 62-64. Original text: Sacra Congregatio Pro Episcopis, *Directorium de Pastorali Ministerio Episcoporum*. Vatican City: Typis Polyglottis Vaticanis, 1973.

Sarno, Ronald A. "Using Group Dynamics to Activate a Parish Council." *Pastoral Life* 24 (September, 1975): 37-44.

Schaefer, Gerald M., et al. "Guide for Parish Council Elections." *Today's Parish* 9 (September, 1977): 36-39.

Schaefer, Vernon. "A Different Kind of Parish Council." *Pastoral Life* 44:1 (January 1995): 2-6.

Schaupp, Klemens. *Der Pfarrgemeinderate. Eine qualitative Interview-Analyse zum Thema "Biographie und Institution."* Innsbruck Theological Studies, Volume 26. Innsbruck and Vienna: Tyrolia Verlag, 1989.

Schmitz, Robert E., "Volunteerism: Increasing Sophistication and Complexity." In Doyle et al., Editors, *Laity, Parish, and Ministry*, pp. 34-43.

Schoenherr, Richard A., and Lawrence A. Young, with the collaboration of Tsan-Yuang Cheng. *Full Pews and Empty Altars: Demographics of the Priest Shortage in United States Catholic Dioceses*. Madison, WI: University of Wisconsin Press, 1993.

Schoenherr, Richard A., and Eleanor P. Simpson. *The Political Economy of Diocesan Advisory Councils*. Comparative Religious Organization Studies Respondent Report no. 3. Madison: University of Wisconsin, 1978.

Schwartz, Robert M. *Servant Leaders of the People of God: An Ecclesial Spirituality for American Priests*. New York: Paulist, 1989.

Shaw, Russell. "The Pastoral Council that Never Was." *Catholic World Report* 6:9 (October 1996): 40-45.

Shea, Francis (Bishop of Evansville). "A Bishop Suspends His Pastoral Council." Letter dated 9 September 1976. *Origins* 6:15 (September 30, 1976): 229, 231-232.

Sheehan, Michael. "Commentary: The Vatican's Letter on Pastoral Councils." *Origins* 3:12 (Sept. 13, 1973): 190-191.

Sheehan, Michael J., and Russell Shaw. *Shared Responsibility at Work: The Catholic Bishops' Advisory Council, 1969-1974*. Washington, D.C.: United States Catholic Conference, 1975.

Sofield, Loughlan; Rosine Hammett and Carroll Juliano. *Building Community: Christian, Caring, Vital*. Notre Dame, IN: Ave Maria, 1998.

Sofield, Loughlan; and Brenda Hermann. *Developing the Parish as a Community of Service*. New York: Le Jacq Publishing, 1984. Copyright now owned by the Jesuit Educational Center for Human Development in Hartford, Connecticut.

Sofield, Loughlan; and Carroll Juliano. *Collaborative Ministry: Skills and Guidelines*. Notre Dame, IN: Ave Maria Press, 1987.

Sofield, Loughlan; and Carroll Juliano. "Developing a Pastoral Council." *Today's Parish* 19:4 (April/May,1977): 17-19.

Stritch, Alfred G. "Trusteeism in the Old Northwest, 1800-1850." *The Catholic Historical Review* 30 (July 1944): 155-164.

Suenens, Léon Joseph. *Co-responsibilité dans l'église d'aujourd'hui*. Bruges: Descleé De Brouwer, 1968. Translation: *Coresponsibility in the Church*. Translated by Francis Martin. New York: Herder and Herder, 1968.

Sweetser, Thomas P. "Parish Accountability: Where the People Are At." *Chicago Studies* 12 (Summer, 1973): 115-128.

Sweetser, Thomas. *Successful Parishes: How They Meet the Challenge of Change*. San Francisco: Winston Press, 1983.

Sweetser, Thomas, and Carol Wisniewski Holden. *Leadership in a Successful Parish*. San Francisco: Harper and Row, 1987.

Sweetser, Thomas P., and Mary Benet McKinney. *Changing Pastors: A Resource for Pastoral Transitions*. Kansas City: Sheed and Ward, 1998.

Synod of Bishops (1971). "The Ministerial Priesthood" (*Ultimis temporibus*, November 30, 1971). Published in reference to canon 329 in James I. O'Connor, editor, *The Canon Law Digest*, vol. VII, pp. 342-366. Original text: Synodo Episcoporum, "De Sacerdotio Ministeriali." *Acta Apostolicae Sedis* 63 (1971): 897-922.

Synod of Bishops (1987). "Synod 1987: The Synod Propositions." *Origins* 17:29 (December 31, 1987): 499-509.

Synod of Bishops (1987), Vatican General Secretariat. "Vocation and Mission of the Laity: Working Paper for the 1987 Synod of Bishops." *Origins* 17:1 (May 21, 1987): 1, 3-20.

Tewey, Thomas J. *Recycling the Parish*. Washington, D.C.: National Council of Catholic Laity, 1972.

[Thero, Cynthia S., owner and president of The Source International.] The Source, a Division of Triptych, Inc. *New Exodus: A Training Experience on Specific Skills Vital to All Catholic Lay Leaders*. Denver: The Source, 1988.

Tighe, Marie Kevin. "Council Spirituality: Foundation for Mission." In Deegan, *Developing a Vibrant Parish Pastoral Council*, pp. 88-99.

Turley, Kathleen. "The Parish Pastoral Council and Prayer." In Deegan, *Developing a Vibrant Parish Pastoral Council*, pp. 100-106.

United States Catholic Conference, USCC Advisory Council, Steering Committee to study the feasibility of an NPC. *A National Pastoral Council Pro and Con: Proceedings of an Interdisciplinary Consultation August 28-30, 1970, in Chicago, Illinois.* J. Paul O'Connor, Chairman of the Steering Committee. Washington, D.C.: USCC, 1971.

United States Catholic Conference, USCC Advisory Council, Steering Committee [to study the feasibility of an NPC]. *A National Pastoral Council: Yes, No, and Maybe.* With an "Introduction" by J. Paul O'Connor. Washington, D.C.: USCC, 1971.

United States Catholic Conference. *A Survey of Diocesan Pastoral Councils in the U.S.A.* Prepared by the Steering Committee of the USCC Advisory Council. Washington, D.C.: USCC, 1972.

Vatican Council II. "Declaration on Religious Liberty." *Dignitatis humanae*, 7 December 1965. Translated by Laurence Ryan. In Vatican Council II. *The Documents of Vatican II.* Austin P. Flannery, General Editor. Preface by John Cardinal Wright. New York: Pillar Books, 1975. Translation of "Decretum: De libertate religiosa." In Vaticani II, Cura et Studio Archivi Concilii Oecumenici. *Acta Synodalia Sacrosancti Concilii Oecumenici Vaticani.* Volumen IV. Periodus Quarta. Pars VII: Congregationes Generalis CLXV – CLXVIII. Sessiones Publicae IX-X. Vatican City: Typis Polyglottis Vaticanis, 1978. Pages 663-673.

Vatican Council II. "Decree on the Apostolate of Lay People." *Apostolicam actuositatem*, November 18, 1965. Translated by Father Finnian, OCSO. In Vatican Council II, *The Documents of Vatican II.* Austin P. Flannery, General Editor. Preface by John Cardinal Wright. New York: Pillar Books, 1975. Translation of "Decretum: De Apostolatu Laicorum." In Vaticani II, Cura et Studio Archivi Concilii Oecumenici. *Acta Synodalia Sacrosancti Concilii Oecumenici Vaticani.* Volumen IV. Periodus Quarta. Pars VI: Congregationes Generalis CLVI – CLXIV. Session Publica VIII. Vatican City: Typis Polyglottis Vaticanis, 1978. Pages 609-632.

Vatican Council II. "Decree on the Church's Missionary Activity." *Ad Gentes Divinitus*, December 7, 1965. Translated by Redmond Fitzmaurice. In Vatican Council II, *The Documents of Vatican II.* Austin P. Flannery, General Editor. Preface by John Cardinal Wright. New York: Pillar Books, 1975. Translation of "Decretum: De Activitate Missionali Ecclesiae." In Vaticani II, Cura et Studio Archivi Concilii Oecumenici. *Acta Synodalia Sacrosancti Concilii Oecumenici Vaticani.* Volumen IV. Periodus Quarta. Pars VII: Congregationes Generalis CLXV – CLXVIII. Sessiones Publicae IX-X. Vatican City: Typis Polyglottis Vaticanis, 1978. Pages 673-704.

Vatican Council II. "Decree on the Ministry and Life of Priests." *Presbyterorum Ordinis*, 7 Dec. 1965. Translated by Archbishop Joseph Cunnane, of Tuam, and revised by Michael Mooney and Enda Lyons of St. Jarlath's College, Tuam, County Galway. In Vatican Council II. *The Documents of Vatican II.* Austin P. Flannery, General Editor. New York: Pillar Books, 1975. Translation of "Decretum: De Presbyterorum ministerio et vita." In Vaticani II, Cura et Studio Archivi Concilii Oecumenici. *Acta Synodalia Sacrosancti Concilii Oecumenici Vaticani.* Volumen IV. Periodus Quarta. Pars VII: Congregationes Generalis CLXV – CLXVIII. Sessiones Publicae IX-X. Vatican City: Typis Polyglottis Vaticanis, 1978. Pages 704-732.

Vatican Council II. "Decree on the Pastoral Office of Bishops in the Church." *Christus Dominus*, October 28, 1965. Translation by Matthew Dillon, Edward O'Leary and Austin P. Flannery. In Vatican Council II, *The Documents of Vatican II.* Austin P. Flannery, General Editor. Preface by John Cardinal Wright. New York: Pillar Books, 1975. Translation of "Decretum: De Pastorali Episcoporum Munere in Ecclesia." In Vaticani II, Cura et Studio Archivi Concilii Oecumenici. *Acta Synodalia Sacrosancti Concilii Oecumenici Vaticani.* Volumen IV. Periodus Quarta. Pars V: Congregationes Generalis CLI – CLV. Session Publica VII. Vatican City: Typis Polyglottis Vaticanis, 1978. Pages 564-584.

Vatican Council II. *The Documents of Vatican II.* In a New and Definitive Translation, with

Commentaries and Notes by Catholic, Protestant, and Orthodox Authorities. Introduction by Lawrence Cardinal Shehan. Walter M. Abbott, General Editor. Translations directed by Joseph Gallagher. New York: Herder and Herder; and Association Press, 1966.

Vatican Council II. "Dogmatic Constitution on the Church." *Lumen Gentium,* Nov. 21, 1964. Translated by Father Colman O'Neill, O.P. In Vatican Council II, *The Documents of Vatican II.* Austin P. Flannery, General Editor. New York: Pillar Books, 1975. Translation of "Constitutio Dogmatica: De Ecclesia." In Vaticani II, Cura et Studio Archivi Concilii Oecumenici. *Acta Synodalia Sacrosancti Concilii Oecumenici Vaticani.* Volumen III. Periodus Tertia. Pars VIII: Congregationes Generalis CXXIII – CXXVII. Session Publica V. Vatican City: Typis Polyglottis Vaticanis, 1976. Pages 784-836.

Vaticani II. Cura et Studio Archivi Concilii Oecumenici Vaticani II. *Acta Synodalia Sacrosancti Concilii Oecumenici Vaticani.* 24 Volumes. Volumen I: Periodus prima, Pars I-IV; Volumen II: Periodus secunda, Pars I-VI; Volumen III: Periodus tertia, Pars I-VIII; Volumen IV: Periodus quarta, Pars I-VI. Vatican City: Typis Polyglottis Vaticanis, 1970-1978.

Vaughn, David L. "Implementing Spirituality in Catholic Parish Councils." Thesis submitted in partial fulfillment of the requirements for certification in the National Association of Church Business Administration at the University of St. Thomas. St. Paul, MN: University of St. Thomas, June, 1994. 79 pp.

Vroom, Victor H. and Philip W. Yetten. *Leadership and Decision-Making.* Pittsburgh: University of Pittsburgh Press, 1973.

Wall, David F. "Parish Councils in the Catholic Church: Participation and Satisfaction of Members." Unpublished Ph.D. [sociology] Dissertation. Washington, D.C.: Catholic University of America, 1978.

Walsh, James F. *Advisory Council Plan: Commentary.* "Designed for Use by the Pastor, Officers, and Parliamentarian of the Parish Council." Mimeograph, 27 pp. Memphis: St. Michael Catholic Church, 1967.

Walsh, James F. *Advisory Council Plan: Constitution, By-Laws and Agenda for Parish Council.* Mimeograph, 40 pp. Memphis: St. Michael Catholic Church, 1967.

Walsh, Jr., James F. "Empowering the Laity: A Proposal to Implement Section 26 of the Decree on the Laity." Unpublished paper. March 7, 1992.

Walsh, James F. (Director, Office of Lay Affairs). *Suggested Guidelines for Regional Councils.* Nashville: Diocese of Nashville, 1975.

Weber, Francis J. "Episcopal Appointments in the U.S.A." *American Ecclesiastical Review* 155:3 (Sept., 1966): 178-191.

Weber, Thomas J. (Executive Secretary, Councils Office, Diocese of Evansville). "Establishing a Council." *Proceedings* of the Center for Applied Research in the Apostolate Symposium on Diocesan Councils, May 28, 1971. *Origins* 1:4 (June 14, 1971): 76-77, 85-86.

Weldon, Christopher (Bishop of Springfield). "Era of the Parish Council." *Origins* 2:2 (June 1, 1972): 19, 21, 26.

Welsh, Thomas (Bishop of Arlington). "A Parish in Conflict." *Origins* 4:26 (December 19, 1974): 411-413.

Whelan, T. "Thoughts on Setting Up a Council of Parishioners." *Clergy Review* 52 (July 1967): 546-555.

Whetton, David A., and Kim S. Cameron. *Developing Management Skills.* Glenview, IL: Scott, Foresman and Company, 1984.

Whitehead, James D., and Evelyn Eaton Whitehead. *The Emerging Laity: Returning Leadership to the Community of Faith.* New York: Doubleday, 1986.

Wilson, George B. "Some Versions of 'Pastoral,'" *Church Personnel Issues,* National Association of Church Personnel Administrators (February 1987): 4-6.

Wilson, Marlene. *How to Mobilize Church Volunteers.* Minneapolis: Augsburg Publishing, 1983.

Wister, Robert J., Editor. *Priests: Identity and Ministry.* Wilmington: Michael Glazier, 1990.

Work, Martin H. "Commentary" on the Laity Decree. In Vincent A. Yzermans, Editor, *American Participation*, 1967.

Work, Martin H. "Diocesan Pastoral Councils and Substructures." In National Council of Catholic Men, *Diocesan Pastoral Council*, p. 41.

Wright, John J. "Foreword." In Bernard Lyons, *Parish Councils*, 1967.

Wuerl, Donald W. "Pastoral Councils." *Homiletic and Pastoral Review* 73:11-12 (August-September, 1973): 21-25, 93-94.

Youngstown, Diocese of. "Relating Pastoral Councils and Senates of Priests." Position paper of the Senate of Priests and the Diocesan Pastoral Council. *Origins* 2:10 (August 25, 1972): 164-165.

Yzermans, Vincent A., Editor. *American Participation in the Second Vatican Council.* New York: Sheed and Ward, 1967.

A Partial Bibliography of Pastoral Council Guidelines
(Guidelines Published by Dioceses in the United States)

Region 1

Boston

Parish Pastoral Councils. Created during the Eighth Synod. Published by the Archdiocese of Boston, 1989. 16 pages. This guideline was surveyed in Fischer, "Parish Pastoral Councils," 1990. See also "Parish Council/Element of Team Ministry." [Parish Council Guidelines]. *Origins* 3:3 (June 14, 1973): 35-37. This guideline is examined in Chapter Eleven.

Fall River

Diocesan Statutes for Parish Pastoral Councils. Prepared by the Presbyteral Council. Published by the Office of the Bishop, 1990. 4 pages.

Hartford

Parish Council Guidelines 1988. Prepared by the Archdiocesan Pastoral Council, with a letter by Archbishop John F. Whealon. Hartford: Archdiocese of Hartford, 1988. 13 pages. This guideline is examined in Chapter Three.

Norwich

Parish Pastoral Council Guidelines. Prepared by the Presbyteral Council. Published by the Office of the Bishop, 1989. 7 pages.

Portland, Maine

The Parish Council. Prepared and published by the Office of Pastoral Planning (no date). 42 pages.

Springfield, MA

Parish Pastoral Council and Finance Council Guidelines. With a letter from Most Rev. John A. Marshall, the late Bishop of Springfield, and from Most Rev. Thomas L. Dupré, Diocesan Administrator. Prepared and Revised by a 12-member committee, including Rev. David J. Joyce and Rev. James K. Joyce, co-chairs, and ten deanery representatives. Springfield: Office of the Auxiliary Bishop, 1994. 24 pages.

"Era of the Parish Council." *Origins* 2:2 (June 1, 1972): 19, 21, 26. This includes a pastoral letter, first published in the 5/5/72 issue of the "Catholic Observer," along with council "norms" under the heading "Areas of Competence." This guideline is examined in Chapter Eleven.

Worcester   "Basic Bylaws for Parish Council." *The Jurist* 28:3 (1968): 352-361.

Region 2

Albany   *Parish Councils: From Vision to Reality.* No author listed.
                            Published by the Pastoral Planning Office, 1984. 16 pages.

Buffalo   "The Buffalo Parish Council Guidelines." *Origins* 3:17 (October
                            18, 1973): 260-261. This guideline is examined in Chapter
                            Eleven.

New York   *Handbook for Parish Councils.* By Sr. Rosalie Kaley, SC. Published
                            by the Office for Parish Councils, 1992. 76 pages. See also
                            Guidelines for Parish Councils. Produced by the Office of Parish
                            Councils, Rev. Henry J. Mansell, Director. Published by the
                            archdiocese, 1969. 23 pages. This guideline was surveyed in
                            Fischer, "Parish Pastoral Councils," 1990.

Ogdensburg   *Diocesan Guidelines for Parish Councils and Trustees.* With a letter
                            by Bishop Stanislaus J. Brzana. Issued by the bishop "after
                            extensive consultation with the Council of Priests and the
                            Diocesan Pastoral Council." Ogdensburg: Office of the Bishop,
                            1991. 1 page letter, 17 pages of guidelines, 4 pages of appen-
                            dices. This guideline is examined in Chapter Three.

Rochester   *Parish Pastoral Council Guidelines.* Approved by Bishop Matthew
                            H. Clark. Rochester: Diocese of Rochester, June 26, 2000.
                            http://www.dor.org/Planning/parish_pastoral_councils.htm. 5 pages.
                            See also *Parish Pastoral Councils.* Written by the staff of the Office
                            of Parish Services. Rochester, Diocese of Rochester, 1990. 5 pages.

Rockville Centre   *Guidelines for Pastoral Councils.* No author listed. Published by
                            the Office of Research and Planning, 1987. 16 pages.

Syracuse   *We Are the Church.* Prepared by Most Rev. Frank Harrison and
                            Committee. Published by the Office of Worship and Parish Life,
                            1981. 14 pages.

Region 3

Altoona - Johnstown   *Pastoral Letter to the Diocese.* By Most Rev. Joseph V. Adamec.
                            Published by the Office of the Bishop, 1989. 9 pages.

Camden   *Guidelines for Parish Pastoral Councils.* Prepared by the Synod
                            Implementation Committee. Published by the Diocesan Synod
                            Office, 1994. 25 pages.

Greensburg   *New Wine, New Wineskins: Revisioning the Parish Through the
                            Ministry of the Parish Pastoral Council.* Produced by the Office of
                            Parish Life and Ministry; Mary Ann Gubish, Director. Published
                            by the Diocese, 1996. 59 pages.

Harrisburg   *Called to Serve: Parish Council Policy and Guidelines.* Second
                            Edition. Prepared by the Office of Parish Leadership Services,
                            Kathleen O'Connor, Director. Published by the Office of Parish
                            Leadership Services, 1985. 52 pages. This guideline was sur-
                            veyed in Fischer, "Parish Pastoral Councils," 1990.

Metuchen   *Basic Guidelines for Parish Pastoral Councils.* By Rev. Msgr. John B.
                            Szymanski and Eileen Tabert. Published by the Office of Parish
                            Leadership Services, 1993. 20 pages.

Newark

Growing in Shared Responsibility: Guidelines for Parish Pastoral Councils. Third Edition. Prepared and Published by the Department of Shared Responsibility, 1996. 60 pages. See also *Manual for Parish Pastoral Councils.* By Sr. Mary McGuinness, OP, and Sr. Regina Suplick, SC. Published by the Department of Shared Responsibility, 1986. 106 pages. See also *Parish Council Guidelines, Archdiocese of Newark.* With a letter from Archbishop Peter L. Gerety. Prepared by the Office for Pastoral Renewal (also published as "The Parish Council at Work," *Origins* 6:17 (October 14, 1976): 272-276). The editorial introduction in *Origins* quotes the 1976 guidelines as saying, "Planning is the major task of the parish council," but this part of the guidelines (about planning) is not in the *Origins* excerpt. This guideline is examined in Chapter Eleven.

Philadelphia

Rationale, Principles and Guidelines for Parish Pastoral Councils. With a letter by Anthony Cardinal Bevilacqua. Philadelphia: Office of the Cardinal, 1992. 7 pages. This guideline is examined in Chapter Three.

Pittsburgh

Parish Council: Diocesan Guidelines. No author listed. Expresses in terms of statutes and regulations the basics necessary for the establishment of the parish council. Published by the Office for Parish Councils, 1972. 32 pages. *Parish Council: Spiritual Renewal Through Structural Reform.* Supplement to the Diocesan Guidelines. Describes the role of the council, its responsibilities, and its relation to the rest of the parish in the context of shared responsibility. By Rev. B. Michael Harcarik. Published by the Office for Parish Councils, 1972. 35 pages.

Scranton

Guidelines for Parish Pastoral Councils. Prepared and published by the Office of Parish Life and Worship, 1988. 5 pages.

Trenton

Parish Pastoral Council Models for the Diocese of Trenton. Recommendations of the Diocesan Pastoral Council (Charles Lapadula, Chairman), based on Inputs from the Priests and Laity of the Diocese. Presented to Bishop John C. Reiss. Published by the Chancery, June 5, 1993.

Region 4

Arlington

Pastoral Letter on Consultation in the Parish. By Most Rev. John R. Keating, Bishop of Arlington. Published by the Office of the Bishop, 1984. 22 pages.

Atlanta

Christ Calls Us Together. Prepared by the Diocese of Cleveland, 1990. 60 pages.

Baltimore

Building One Body in Christ: The Ministry of the Parish Pastoral Council. With a letter from William Cardinal Keeler, Archbishop of Baltimore. First published, 1995. Second Printing. Baltimore: Archdiocese of Baltimore, 1997. 31 pages, plus 14 pages of appendices. See also *The Ministry of Shared Responsibility: Serving as Parish Council in the Archdiocese of Baltimore.* Revised Edition. Produced by the Division of Collegial Services. With a letter by Archbishop William D. Borders. Baltimore: Office of the Archbishop, 1988. 47 pages. This guideline is examined in Chapter Three.

Charleston	*Recommendations for Parish Pastoral Councils*. Prepared by a Committee of the Presbyteral Council and the Diocesan Pastoral Council. Published by the Office of Continuing Education of Priests, 1993. 6 pages.
Charlotte	*Parish Pastoral Council and Commissions Manual* By Sr. Jean Linder, OSF, and a Committee of the Diocesan Synod Committee. Published by the Office of Planning, 1987. 50 pages.
Miami	*Pastoral Outline: Synod Decrees of the Archdiocese of Miami*. Results of the First Synod, 1985-1988. Issued by Most Rev. Edward A. McCarthy, Archbishop of Miami. Published by the Office of the Synod, 1988. 19 pages. The synod decrees pertaining to parish pastoral councils are outlined on pages 11-16.
Orlando	*Parish Pastoral Council Guidelines*. Prepared by Robert Shearer. Published by the Office of Development, 1990. 50 pages.
Raleigh	*Parish Pastoral Council Norms*. By John P. Riedy, Diocesan Chancellor. Published by the Office of the Chancery, 1994. 4 pages. See also *Pastoral Council Norms*, approved by the Senate of Priests, published by the diocese, 1985, 4 pages. This guideline was surveyed in Fischer, "Parish Pastoral Councils," 1990.
Richmond	*Called to Serve*. Second Edition. Prepared by the Diocesan Pastoral Council. Published by the Office of the Auxiliary Bishop, 1986. 26 pages. On finance councils, see *Norms for Parish Finance Councils*, 1991.
St. Augustine	*Ten Guiding Principles of Parish Councils*. By Rev. Msgr. Joseph Champlin in consultation with the Presbyteral Council. Published by the Office of the Chancery, 1985. 9 pages.
Wilmington	*One Lord, One Faith, One Baptism, One Call to Serve*. Prepared by a Task Force called for in the Diocesan Plan, "A Church Called to Serve." Published by the Episcopal Vicar for Administration, 1992.

Region 5

Alexandria	Contained in the *Handbook of Faculties and Policies*. Prepared by an Episcopal Committee. Published by the Office of the Chancery, 1993. 2 pages.
Covington	*Norms and Guidelines for Parish Pastoral Councils*. Prepared by a Consultant for Parish Services. Published by the Office of Pastoral Planning and Research, 1993. 50 pages. *Parish Pastoral Council Manual*. Revised Edition. Prepared by Sr. Margaret Collins, CSJ. Published by the Department of Evangelization, 1990. 24 pages.
Lexington	*Handbook for Parish Pastoral Councils*. Prepared by a Committee staffed by the Director of Pastoral Services, Sr. Helen Maher Garvey, BVM. Published by the Office of Pastoral Services, 1991. 31 pages.
Louisville	*Your Parish Council: Guidelines*. Prepared by the Office of Councils, Sr. Elizabeth Wendeln, SCN, Director. Published by the Office of Parish Leadership Development, 1984. 72 pages. This guideline was surveyed in Fischer, "Parish Pastoral Councils," 1990. See also Thomas McDonough (Archbishop of

	Louisville). "The Parish Council's Role: Appeals Structures/Consensus Decisions." *Origins* 5:36 (February 26, 1976): 571-579. This guideline is examined in Chapter Eleven.
Memphis	James F. Walsh. *Advisory Council Plan: Constitution, By-Laws and Agenda for Parish Council.* Mimeograph, 40 pages. Memphis: St. Michael Catholic Church, 1967. See also Walsh, *Advisory Council Plan: Commentary.* "Designed for Use by the Pastor, Officers, and Parliamentarian of the Parish Council." Mimeograph, 27 pages. Memphis: St. Michael Catholic Church, 1967.
Nashville	*Handbook: Parish Pastoral Councils.* Produced by the Ministry Formation Services Team, Sr. Adrian Mulloy, RSM, Director. With a letter by Bishop James D. Niedergeses. Nashville: Ministry Formation Services, 1989. 75 pages. This guideline is examined in Chapter Three.
New Orleans	*Guidelines for Parish Pastoral Councils.* Prepared by the Archdiocesan Pastoral Council. Published by the Office of the Archbishop, 1995. 8 pages. *Parish Pastoral Council Resource Manual.* New Orleans: Office of Archbishop Francis B. Schulte, 1995. 26 pages.
Owensboro	*Guidelines and Policies for Parish Pastoral Councils.* Prepared by a Diocesan Committee. Published by the Office of Lay Ministry and the Office of the Vicar General, 1988. 50 pages.
Shreveport	*Policy and Guidelines for Parish Pastoral Councils.* Prepared by the Diocesan Chancellor, Sr. Margaret Daues, CSJ, and Committee. Published by the Office of the Chancery, 1994. 32 pages.

Region 6

Cincinnati	*Called to Be Church: A Guide for Parish Pastoral Councils.* Office of Pastoral Planning, 1998. *Parish Council Guidelines.* Prepared by the Archdiocesan Council of the Laity Committee. Published by the Archdiocesan Councils Office, 1972. 26 pages.
Cleveland	*Christ Calls Us Together: Parish Pastoral Council Policy.* Prepared and published by the Diocesan Pastoral Planning Office, 1990. 60 pages. See also *Parish Council Guidelines,* prepared by the Diocesan Pastoral Planning Office, 1979, 51 pages. This guideline was surveyed in Fischer, "Parish Pastoral Councils," 1990. On finance councils, see *Parish Finance Council Policy,* 1991.
Columbus	"Parish Council Rationale: New Level of Ministry." Excerpts from the Parish Council Guidelines. *Origins* 7:16 (October 6, 1977): 241, 243-246. This guideline is examined in Chapter Eleven.
Detroit	*Parish Pastoral Council Guidelines and Handbook.* A revision of the 1979 Directives and Guidelines by the 13-member Parish Pastoral Council Guidelines Committee, James Kiefer, chairman. Detroit: Office of the Archbishop, 1991. Guidelines: 37 pages; Handbook: 62 pages; plus a 10-page Glossary and Acknowledgments. This guideline is examined in Chapter Three. See also "Directives and Guidelines for Parish Councils." First published in 1972. Revised in 1974 and 1979. Archdiocese of Detroit: Ministry to Councils Office, 1979.

Gaylord	*Parish Pastoral Council Guidelines.* No author listed. Prepared and published by the Office of the Bishop, 1985. 8 pages.
Kalamazoo	*Resource Manual for Parish Pastoral Councils and Parish Finance Councils.* Prepared by a Task Force under the Council Ministry Director, Sr. Mary Sullivan, OP. Published by the Council Ministry Office, 1994. 75 pages.
Lansing	*Parish Pastoral Councils and Parish Finance Councils.* Second edition. Prepared by Sr. Rita Wenzlick OP, and Ronald Henderson. Published by the Pastoral Council Office, 1994. 20 pages.
Saginaw	*The Parish Council — Renewed in the Lord.* Prepared by Barbara Walkley. Published by the Diocesan Planning Office, 1984. 58 pages.
Steubenville	*Handbook for Parish Council Ministry.* Prepared and published by the Office of Christian Formation, 1991. 52 pages.
Youngstown	*A Guide for Parish Pastoral Councils: People of Mission and Vision.* With a "Letter of Greeting" from Bishop Thomas J. Tobin. Produced by the Diocesan Parish Pastoral Council Policy Review Committee, Eileen W. Novotny, Chairperson. Youngstown: Office of Bishop Thomas J. Tobin, 1999. 12 pages.
	Policies and Guidelines for Parish Councils. Prepared by the Diocesan Pastoral Council, chaired by Sr. Elizabeth Apel, CDP. Published by the Pastoral Development Office, 1990. 46 pages.

Region 7

Evansville	*Parish Pastoral Council Policies and Guidelines.* Prepared by the Parish Pastoral Council Guidelines Committee. Published by the Office of the Chancellor, Sr. Louise Bond, SNJM, 1994. 50 pages.
Gary	*Pastoral Council Manual.* Written by Anne Verbeke, Director of Parish Pastoral Councils. Gary: Diocese of Gary, 1997. 7 chapters (92 pages) plus appendix (23 pages).
Green Bay	*That All May Be One: Norms for Parish Pastoral Councils.* With a letter from Bishop Adam J. Maida. Prepared by Rev. Larry Canavera and Sr. Luanne Smits, SSND. 10 pages of "Norms," together with a 33-page "Commentary and Resources" by Rev. Larry Canavera and Sr. Luanne Smits, SSND; and 51 pages of "Appendices." Published by the Office of Parish Services, 1986. This guideline is examined in Chapter Three.
Indianapolis	*Parish Council Guidelines.* By Sr. Marie Kevin Tighe and Sr. Catherine Schneider, OSF. Published by the Office for Pastoral Councils, 1986. 40 pages.
Joliet	*Parish Pastoral Council: Vision and Goals.* Revised edition. By Jean Bohr and a task force of consultants. Published by the Office of Ministry Formation, 1990. 51 pages.
La Crosse	*On Consultation in the Parish and Deanery.* By Most Rev. John Paul, Bishop of La Crosse. Office of the Bishop, 1985. 36 pages.
Milwaukee	*Living the Spirit: A Parish Council Manual.* Fourth Edition. Denise Pheifer, Principal Editor. Published by the Office of Parish Stewardship and Lay Leadership Development, 1991. 106 pages. See also *Living the Spirit: A Parish Council Manual.* Revised Second Edition. Rev. Mike Hammer and Marliss Rogers,

Editors. 1987. This guideline was surveyed in Fischer, "Parish Pastoral Councils," 1990. On parish finance councils, see also *Parish Committee Ministry,* 1991.

Springfield in Illinois   *Parish Pastoral Councils: A Reflection.* By Most Rev. Daniel L. Ryan. Published by the Office of the Bishop, 1991. 5 pages.

Region 8

Bismarck   *Parish Pastoral Councils: The Call and the Ministry.* Produced by the Ad Hoc Committee on PPC Guidelines of the Diocesan Pastoral Council. With a letter from Bishop John F. Kinney. Bismarck: Diocese of Bismarck, 1989 [?]), 55 pages. This guideline is examined in Chapter Three.

Fargo   *Handbook for Parish Councils in the Diocese of Fargo.* Author unknown. Published by the Diocese of Fargo, 1983. 44 pages. This guideline was surveyed in Fischer, "Parish Pastoral Councils," 1990.

New Ulm   "Statutes of Parish Pastoral Councils." *Handbook of Diocesan Policies.* By Most Rev. Raymond A. Lucker and Rev. Jerome E. Paulson. Published by the Office of the Chancery, 1990. 14 pages.

St. Cloud   *Parish Pastoral Councils: Principles, Guidelines, Recommendations.* Signed by Most Rev. Jerome Hanus, Bishop of St. Cloud. Developed by Rev. Msgr. Daniel J. Taufen, STL, Vicar General. St. Cloud: Chancery Office, 1991. 7 pages.

St. Paul – Minneapolis   *Guidelines for Parish Pastoral Councils.* Revised Edition. Published by the Office of Pastoral Planning, 1995. 7 pages. See also "Sharing Responsibility: Parish Councils." Archdiocesan Parish Council Guidelines. *Origins* 5:41 (April 1, 1976): 645, 647-651. This guideline is examined in Chapter Eleven.

Winona   *Parish Pastoral Councils and Parish Finance Councils.* By the Vicar General in consultation with the Pastoral Council, Presbyteral Council, and Curia. Published by the Office of the Vicar General, 1991. 26 pages.

Region 9

Des Moines   *Pastoral Council Manual.* By Bishop Maurice Dingman and members of the chancery administrative staff. Published by the Office of the Bishop, 1986. 88 pages.

Dubuque   *Parish Council Guidelines of the Archdiocese of Dubuque.* Promulgated, January 1, 1985, Archbishop Daniel W. Kucera, O.S.B. 12 pages text plus "Appendix A: Guidelines for Parish Council Committees," 5 pages; and "Appendix B: The Deanery Council," 2 pages. See also *Pastoral Council of the Archdiocese of Dubuque: Constitution and Bylaws.* Adopted September 15, 1984; revised in 1992, 1994, 1997, and in May, 2000. 6 pages plus "Appendix: The Deanery Council," 1 page.

Jefferson City   *Parish Council Guidelines and Directives.* Written and published by the Office of Leadership Services, 1981. 57 pages.

Kansas City - St. Joseph   *Call to Leadership: Transforming the Local Church.* By Ellen Morseth, BVM. Kansas City: Sheed and Ward, Publishers, 1993. 96 pages.

Omaha

Parish Pastoral Council Handbook. Written and published by the Office of Pastoral Development, Sr. Rita Parks, RSM, Director, 1994. 86 pages. See also *Guidelines and Directives for Parish Councils,* revised edition of 1986, 19 pages. This guideline was surveyed in Fischer, "Parish Pastoral Councils," 1990.

Salina

Guidelines for Parish Pastoral Councils and Guidelines for Parish Finance Councils. Unsigned but written by Rev. Kenneth Lohrmeyer and approved by Bishop George K. Fitzsimons. Published by the Office of the Bishop, 1993. 14 pages. This guideline is examined in Chapter Three.

Springfield -
Cape Girardeau

Guidelines for Parish Councils. Produced by the Diocesan Pastoral Council. Published by the Office of the Bishop, 1988. 26 pages.

St. Louis

Guidelines for the Ministry of Parish Councils. Revised Edition. Produced and published by the Council of the Laity, 1985. 106 pages.

Region 10

Amarillo

Constitutional Bylaws of Parish Pastoral Councils. By Rev. Msgr. James Gurzynski, V.G. Published by the Diocesan Pastoral Center (date and length unknown).

Austin

"Pastoral and Finance Council Norms." Submitted by Erwin A. Sladek, Jr., Carol Graves, Louise Hajovsky, Charles Hoelscher, Rev. Elmer Holtman, Rev. Al Palermo, and Ed Radl. In *Documents of the Second Synod, Diocese of Austin.* Developed by the People of God Living in the Austin Diocese, the Catholic Church of Central Texas, During the Process of the Second Synod, Beginning on Easter Sunday, 1988, and Concluding March 27, 1992. With a letter by Most Rev. John McCarthy, Bishop of Austin. Austin: Office of Synod Implementation, 1992. Pages 55-62 (Pastoral Council Norms) and 63-66 (Finance Council Norms).
See also *A Pastoral Council Resource Guide.* Third Revision, March 1995. This document includes the "Pastoral Council Norms" (as published in the 1992 synod document), plus "A Suggested Model for Operational Guidelines for Pastoral Councils," pp. 2-6, and a number of supplementary materials, pp. 7-28. [Austin: Office of Synod Implementation, Patricia E. Stankus, Director, 1995].

Brownsville

Directives and Guidelines for the Ministry of Parish Pastoral Councils. Produced by the Diocesan Pastoral Council. Published by the Pastoral Planning Office, 1987. 52 pages. This guideline was surveyed in Fischer, "Parish Pastoral Councils," 1990.

Dallas

Guidelines for Parish Pastoral Councils. Produced and published by the Pastoral Planning Office, Mary Edlund, Associate Director, 1993. 11 pages.

Fort Worth

Handbook for Consultative Bodies. Produced by the Office of Parish Planning Stewardship, Mary Raley, Director. Fort Worth: Office of Parish Planning and Stewardship, 1995. 11 pages of "Guidelines" and 48 pages of "Practical Suggestions." This guideline is examined in Chapter Three.

Galveston – Houston	*Diocesan Norms for Parish Pastoral Councils.* Most Rev. Joseph A. Fiorenza. Published by the Bishop's Office, 1987. 8 pages.
Little Rock	*Norms and Implementation Guide — Parish Pastoral and Finance Councils.* Produced and published by the Office of Lay Ministry, 1988. 36 pages.
San Antonio	*Guidelines for Parish Pastoral Councils.* Produced by a Commitee of the Office of Pastoral Leadership, Sr. Carol Kottewitz, R.C., Director. Published by the Office of the Chancery, 1990. 19 pages.

Region 11

Honolulu	*Parish Pastoral Councils.* Produced by the Diocesan Renewal Committee. Published by the Office of the Bishop, 1990. 31 pages.
Los Angeles	*Communion and Consultation: Pastoral Council Guidelines.* Pastoral Council Guidelines Revision Committee, Mark F. Fischer, Chairman. Los Angeles: Archdiocesan Pastoral Council Office, Maria Elena Uribe, Coordinator, March, 1999. Published in a dual-language format (English and Spanish), *Comunión y Consulta: Normas para Consejos Pastorales,* Spanish translation by Maria Elena Uribe, revision by Rev. Francis Boronat, Sch.P. See also *Together in Mission: Parish Pastoral Council Guidelines.* Produced and published by a committee of the Pastoral Councils Office, Sr. Clare Reinert, SSND, Director, 1991. 35 pages.
Oakland	*Guidelines for Parish Pastoral Councils.* Produced by a Joint Committee of the Diocesan Pastoral Council and the Senate of Priests. Published by the Office of the Chancery, 1990. 16 pages.
Sacramento	*Consultation in the Parish: Guidelines for Parish Councils.* With a letter from Bishop Francis A. Quinn. Sacramento: The Chancery, 1985. 2-page letter, 6 pages of "Guidelines," 1 page of "Acknowledgments," and a 2-page "Appendix on Parish Finance Councils." This guideline is examined in Chapter Three.
San Bernardino	*Parish Council Guidelines.* Produced by the Diocesan Pastoral Council. Published by the Diocesan Pastoral Center, 1984. 100 pages. This guideline was surveyed in Fischer, "Parish Pastoral Councils," 1990.
San Diego	"San Diego Guidelines for Parish Councils." *Origins* 7:3 (June 9, 1977): 36-39. This guideline is examined in Chapter Eleven.
San Francisco	*Guidelines for Parish Pastoral Councils,* by Rev. David M. Pettingill, Director of the Office of Parish Life. San Francisco: Office of Parish Life [May, 1999].

Region 12

Boise	*Diocesan Guidelines for Parish, Deanery, and Diocesan Pastoral Councils.* Produced by a Subcommittee of the Presbyteral Council. Published by the Office of the Bishop, 1992-94. 2-3 pages. each.
Helena	*Acts of the Synod of the Diocese of Helena* (August 8-11, 1988).

	Most Rev. Elden F. Curtiss, Bishop of Helena. Published by the Catholic Diocese of Helena, 1989. Pages. 53-55 pertain to parish pastoral councils.
Juneau	*Cathedral Pastoral Council.* The constitution of the pastoral council of the Cathedral of the Nativity, 416 Fifth Street, Juneau, AK 99801. No date. 3 pages.
Portland in Oregon	*Parish Pastoral Councils: Policies and Commentary.* Produced by the Archdiocese of Portland. 2 pages. Memo from Archbishop Power plus 17 pages (including one page of "Policies"). Published by the Office of the Archbishop, 1983. 19 pages. This guideline was surveyed in Fischer, "Parish Pastoral Councils," 1990.
Seattle	*Policy and Guidelines for Parish Consultative Structures.* Produced and published by the Planning and Research Department, 1990. Fourth printing, December, 1993. 45 pages. *Guidelines for Parish Consultative Structures.* Prepared by the Planning and Research Office, Dennis O'Leary, Director. Seattle: Archdiocese of Seattle, 1988. 58 pages. This guideline is examined in Chapter Three.
Spokane	*Norms for Councils in Parishes.* Approved by Bishop William S. Skylstad in April, 1992, following consultation with the Presbyteral Council. Spokane: Parish Services Office, 1992. 4 pages plus a 3-page "Sample Constitution for Parish Pastoral Councils." See also *Diocesan Pastoral Council Constitution.* Spokane: Diocese of Spokane, May 1983, 5 pages.
Yakima	*Guidelines for Pastoral Councils.* By Robert Fontana and Bishop George. Published by the Office of Evangelization, 1994. 4 pages.

Region 13

Cheyenne	*Recommendations for Parish Councils: Report to the Pastoral Council.* Produced and published by the Ministry of the Laity, CoCo Soper, Director [no date]. 25 pages. This guideline was surveyed in Fischer, "Parish Pastoral Councils," 1990.
Colorado Springs	*Parish Pastoral Council Handbook.* Produced by Bannon and Associates. Published by the Office of the Vicar General, 1991. 113 pages.
Denver	*Parish Pastoral Council and Parish Finance Council Norms.* Prepared by a committee of the Presbyteral Council chaired by Rev. Leonard Alimena. With a letter by Archbishop J. Francis Stafford. Denver: Archdiocese of Denver, 1988. 2-page letter and 11 pages of "Norms." This guideline is examined in Chapter Three.
Las Cruces	*Directives and Guidelines for Parish Pastoral Councils,* Written by the Ministries Office. Published by the Ministries Office, 1992. 18 pages, plus 4 pages of appendixes.
Phoenix	*Guidelines for Parish Councils.* With a letter from Most Rev. Thomas J. O'Brien, Bishop of Phoenix. Produced by a Subcommittee of the Diocesan Pastoral Council. Published by the Office of the Bishop, 1993. 14 pages.
Pueblo	*Norms and Procedures for Parish Pastoral Councils.* Produced by

the Diocesan Ministry Formation Team. Published by the Office of the Chancery, 1992. 25 pages.

Salt Lake City

Guidelines for Parish Pastoral Councils. Produced by the Presbyteral Council. Published by the Office of the Bishop, 1988. 3 pages.

Index

I Like Being in Parish Ministry: Pastoral Council
Mark F. Fischer

The author extends a straightforward invitation for parish council members and those thinking of being part of the parish council. With practical suggestions and clear definitions, he opens the window on the imortant workings of the spiritual as well as the action dimensions of parish councils.

1-56595-176-5, 48 pp, $4.95 (X-09)

The New Practical Guide for Parish Councils
William J. Rademacher
with Marliss Rogers
Foreword by Most Rev. Rembert G. Weakland, OSB

Includes information on forming a good parish council, selecting members, pastoral planning guidelines, organizing more satisfying meetings, and ways for councils to grow in holiness.   0-89622-371-X, 264 pp, $12.95 (W-81)

A User-Friendly Parish
Becoming a More Welcoming Community
Judith Ann Kollar

The author points out some of the day-to-day elements in parish life that affect the way a parish functions and the way it is perceived by parishioners, visitors, and inquirers.   0-89622-937-8, 80 pp, $7.95 (C-10)

Parish Pastoral Councils
The Role of the Council Today: Consultative Only?
William Rademacher, Kathie Fuller, William Bausch, Mark Fischer,
Paul Boudreau, Judith Ann Kollar, and Kevin McKenna

What kind of authority does a pastoral council have? What is the best relationship between a pastor and a council? What happens when they disagree? These questions are answered honestly, practically, and from several points of view in this convenient reprint from *Today's Parish* magazine.

32 pp, $1.95, (BT4)